THE DOCUMENTARY FORM-HISTORY OF RABBINIC LITERATURE

VI. The Halakhic Sector
The Talmud of the Land of Israel
A. Tractates Berakhot and Shabbat through Taanit

by

Jacob Neusner

Scholars Press
Atlanta, Georgia

THE DOCUMENTARY FORM-HISTORY OF RABBINIC LITERATURE
VI. *The Halakhic Sector*
The Talmud of the Land of Israel
A. Tractates Berakhot and Shabbat through Megillah

by
Jacob Neusner

©1998
University of South Florida

Publication of this book was made possible by a grant from the Tisch Family Foundation, New York City. The University of South Florida acknowledges with thanks this important support for its scholarly projects.

Library of Congress Cataloging in Publication Data
Neusner, Jacob, 1932–
        The documentary form-history of rabbinic literature / by Jacob
    Neusner.
              p.   cm. — (South Florida studies in the history of Judaism ;
        no. 167)
        Includes bibliographical references.
        Contents: 1. The documentary forms of the Mishnah.
        ISBN 0-7885-0455-X (alk. paper)
        ISBN 0-7885-0467-3 (alk. paper) vol. VI. A
        1. Rabbinical literature—History and criticism—Theory, etc.
    I. Title. II. Series.
    BM496.5.N47929   1998
    296.1—dc21   98-15589

Printed in the United States of America
on acid-free paper

THE DOCUMENTARY FORM-HISTORY OF RABBINIC LITERATURE

SOUTH FLORIDA STUDIES IN THE HISTORY OF JUDAISM

Edited by
Jacob Neusner
Bruce D. Chilton, Darrell J. Fasching, William Scott Green,
Sara Mandell, James F. Strange

Number 175
The Documentary Form-History of
Rabbinic Literature
VI. The Halakhic Sector
The Talmud of the Land of Israel
A. Tractates Berakhot and Shabbat through Taanit

by
Jacob Neusner

TABLE OF CONTENTS

Preface

The history of the forms of the Rabbinic literature of late antiquity emerges from the comparison and contrast of the forms that govern in the various documents, read sequentially in the order in which, the prevailing consensus presently maintains, they reached closure. That is what I set forth in the present project.

Having completed the work on the Mishnah and the Aggadic compilations, here we turn to the catalogues and analyses of the forms of the canonical Halakhic compilations of late antiquity, specifically the two Talmuds. I investigate the rules of writing — in particular, the fixed forms of the writings of the originally-oral Torah and their rhetorical program. These guided the ancient sages who produced the writings of the Oral Torah on how they should formulate whatever they wished to say. The form-history — the account of the conventional patterns as these unfolded from the earliest to the latest periods in the writing down of the oral Torah — emerges in a sequential reading of the canonical writings of that Judaism, beginning with the Mishnah, ending with the Talmud of Babylonia.

In this work I answer the question, How did our sages of blessed memory write, meaning, what protocols of expression guided their work? When did they write however they wished, and when did they write in accord with fixed conventions? The documents as a whole come to us out of a process of sages' writing anonymously, collectively, in a process governed by consensus and the explicit identification of schism. To produce most of the composites and compositions that comprise the canonical writings, sages adhered to well-defined conventional patterns of formulating thoughts within fixed forms. These governed the syntax and structure of expression. The forms, chosen from a repertoire of considerable proportions, for any given document were remarkably few. The selected forms paramount in a given document responded to and realized the intentions of framers of that document.

After five volumes on the Aggadic sector, the main results have come to the fore. What I have now proved up to this stage of the present project is that the character of the documents — that is, large-scale completed and cogent statements conforming to a predetermined program involving logic of coherent discourse, rhetoric, and topic ("books" in our terms) — dictates the configuration of the forms that define the rules of writing that govern those documents. This result is in two parts. First, forms have no autonomous existence, but are given definition by the framers of the respective documents. Second, the principal components of those documents, the definitive elements, conform to the requirements of a very limited repertoire of forms or patterns.

Most writing that reaches us from our sages of blessed memory who flourished in ancient times conforms to the rules of writing that the documents reveal; in the formation of the distinctive markers of a composition — the opening lines, which set the character and signal the classification of the whole — very little is free-hand, less still, idiosyncratic and personal. If among our sages of blessed memory free-hand writing was carried on, as we must assume it was, relative to the formidable dimensions of the documents, very little of it has made its way through the editorial processes that produced the large-scale compilations, the documents, that we do have. Working from the document downward to the components thereof, we find that nearly the entire corpus of compositions and composites of which a document is comprised conforms to the formal program characteristic of the document as a whole; very little turns out to stand formally independent of the document, and by the criterion of the document's formal preferences overall, we find only a negligible proportion of a document made up of free-standing or extra-documentary compositions or composites. But each document dealt with in this study imposes its particular qualifications upon the generalizations just now stated, and secondary development and expansion and amplification of the highly-formalized opening section of a given composition or composite do not exhibit equivalent formalization at all.

In this project I complete my form-analytical work, the project begun nearly three decades ago of describing the formal traits of the canonical writings of Rabbinic Judaism. The present, and I expect, final part of the on-going literary analysis takes shape is in several steps. First, in Volume I, I turned to the initial document of the Rabbinic canon to reach closure, the Mishnah, which, along with Sifra, is the most formalized of all Rabbinic writings. I have now identified the paradigms that define that document's literary protocol. To the best of my knowledge, not a single line of a scholarly book has called into question the form-analytical results I have now set forth for the entire Mishnah (inclusive of the Tosefta read in the context of the Mishnah). In Volume II and in the subsequent parts of the work through Volume V I proceed to the successor-documents of the canon and show, how, from the Mishnah forward, the forms of the later documents relate to those of the earlier ones, thus tracing the documentary form-history of the Rabbinic canon. Now in Volumes VI and VII we consider the forms of the Yerushalmi and the Bavli. Presently we shall have catalogues, worked out in accord with the conventional sequence in which the documents are ordered, for the forms of the canonical writings.

This form-history history shows how in the unfolding of successive documents early forms persisted or were dropped, and, further, how — and to serve what task — new forms took shape and came to define the literary character of the later documents. My working hypothesis suggests that [1] formalization of prose characterizes writing for documents; [2] writing that is not formalized, such as narratives of various kinds, tends also to take a position outside of the main frame of the documents in which it occurs; [3] peripatetic compositions and composites — writing that travels freely from one document to another but identifies itself with no documentary forms where it surfaces — unsurprisingly lack indicative traits of documentary formalization (accounting for their remarkable capacity to move hither and yon). Of these, the second bears the most interesting implications, the first I have now demonstrated beyond all doubt, and the third is reasonable but not very important.

Form-analysis and form-history have told me what I wished to find out in my larger quest for the definition of Rabbinic Judaism, and, as I explain in the Introduction, the logical next step in that quest with the end of this inquiry will become possible. But first, the two Talmuds and their special problems of form-analysis require attention.

The organization of this form-history requires explanation, divided as it is into the Aggadic and the Halakhic sectors, respectively. The canon conventionally divides into two, aggadic and halakhic, lore and law, theological and behavioral norms, and while that classification of the documents promises a more orderly division between lore and law than actually characterizes the several canonical books, it serves. Roughly characterized, the aggadic sector deals with Scripture, the halakhic, with the Mishnah. But that characterization is indeed rough, for Sifra and the two Sifrés, called "halakhic Midrashim," cover aggadic as much as halakhic matters.[1]

"Aggadah" and "halakhah" define native categories of the Rabbinic canon; they work well for the present inquiry too, since the two sectors go their separate ways in choosing useful forms, while at the same time continuities of forms tend to mark the unfolding of each sector. By "the aggadic sector," I mean those compilations that deal with theological, moral, or exegetical problems, by contrast to "the halakhic sector," referring to those documents that take up legal norms. The halakhic sector flows from the Mishnah via the Tosefta to the Talmud of the Land of Israel and the Talmud of Babylonia. The last three items all organize their discussions around the Mishnah and take up the exegesis, amplification, and extension of the Mishnah's rules. I bypass the Tosefta, because the form-analytical work I have already done in my *History of the Mishnaic Law* shows that the Tosefta formally is difficult to differentiate from the Mishnah. For the moment I ask co-workers to stipulate that the results of form-analysis of the Tosefta would replicate those already set forth in the Mishnah; future work will refine that judgment and, arguably, set it aside.

---

[1] I postpone to a later volume Mekhilta deR. Ishmael, because that document exhibits blatant formal differences from Sifra and the two Sifrés, with which is is commonly identified.

If the halakhic sector organizes itself around the Mishnah, the aggadic sector utilizes Scripture for the same purpose, or, more accurately, certain privileged Scriptural books. These are the works of Scripture selected for special prominence by synagogue liturgy, specifically, Genesis, Exodus, Leviticus, Numbers, and Deuteronomy and four of the five scrolls associated with principal holidays, Ruth, Lamentations, Song of Songs, and Esther. The canonical compilations that correspond are Genesis Rabbah, Mekhilta Attributed to R. Ishmael, Sifra (to Leviticus) and Leviticus Rabbah, Sifré to Numbers, Sifré to Deuteronomy, and the Rabbah-compilations, Ruth Rabbah, Lamentations Rabbati, Song of Songs Rabbah, and Esther Rabbah I.

In the category of aggadah fall, also, Pesiqta deRab Kahana, organized around the synagogue lections, and the Fathers According to Rabbi Nathan, organized around tractate Abot.   So, seen all together, the canon in the main organizes itself around the Mishnah, for law, and Scripture, for theology and lore. But that division, quite serviceable as it is for form-analysis, implies a separation of types of compositions that, in fact, the documents do not exhibit. Some aggadic documents contain halakhic materials — Sifra and the two Sifrés for instance — and all of the halakhic ones present rich repertoires of aggadah as well. Not only so, but form-analysis has already produced its own subdivisions within the canon, distinguishing the earlier Midrash-compilations, Sifra and the two Sifrés, from the Rabbah-compilations, for instance. If the division is rough, however, it will serve to organize matters for this study.

The principle of organization I have chosen, well justified on formal grounds, means that we follow the chronological order of the documents only within their respective sectors. I do not think that the work of following the historical sequence is vastly complicated by the fact that our results run in parallel lines, each sector, aggadic, then halakhic, laid out in its own terms and corresponding in its results to the other. A simple correlation at the end will suffice. In accord with the present consensus of matters, the accepted order is as follows, by roughly contemporary groups: [1] the Mishnah, tractate Abot (the Fathers), Tosefta (ca. 200-300 C.E.), [2] Sifra, Sifré to Numbers, Sifré to Deuteronomy, and possibly Mekhilta Attributed to R. Ishmael (ca. 300-400); [3] Talmud of the Land of Israel (ca. 400); [4] Genesis Rabbah, Leviticus Rabbah, Pesiqta deRab Kahana (ca. 400-500); [5] Lamentations Rabbati, Song of Songs Rabbah, Ruth Rabbah, Esther Rabbah I (ca. 500-600); [6] Talmud of Babylonia and Fathers According to Rabbi Nathan (ca. 600). But, as is clear, because of the connections among some sets of documents but not others — Abot to Abot deRabbi Nathan, for one example, Mishnah, Tosefta, the two Talmuds, for another — it makes more sense to follow the forms of one sector, then of the other.

The result, for literary history, proves uniform. It yields the documentary history of forms, that is, a history that follows from one document to the next the utilization of forms and changes that are made in forms and their patterns. As I explain in the Introduction, these literary traits lead us deep into the theological foundations of Rabbinic Judaism. Writing in formalized prose, adhering to specified paradigms of expression — these represent in literary style a profoundly theological conviction, spelled out in the Introduction.

No work of mine can omit reference to the exceptionally favorable circumstances in which I conduct my research. I wrote this book at the University of South Florida, which has afforded me an ideal situation in which to conduct a scholarly life. I express my thanks for not only the advantage of a Distinguished Research Professorship, which must be the best job in the world for a scholar, but also of a substantial research expense fund, ample research time, and some stimulating and cordial colleagues. In the prior chapter of my career, I did not know a university that prized professors' scholarship and publication and treated with respect those professors who actively and methodically pursued research, only those that did not. The University of South Florida, and all ten universities that comprise the Florida State University System as a whole, exemplify the high standards of professionalism that prevail in publicly-sponsored higher education in the USA and provide the model that privately-sponsored universities would do well to emulate. Here there are rules, achievement counts, and presidents, provosts, and deans honor and respect the University's principal mission: scholarship, scholarship alone — both in the classroom and in publication. Here at last I find integrity, governing in the lives of people true to their vocation and their mission.

My second academic affiliation also deserves mention, Bard College. My thanks go also to the President of Bard College, Leon Botstein, and Dean of the Faculty, Stuart Levine, as well as to my colleague, the chairman of the Department of Religion and co-worker in many projects, Bruce D. Chilton. Their encouragement and practical support of my research work mean a great deal to me. No administration evinces greater appreciation for research-scholarship than that of that small liberal arts college, which consequently boasts a faculty of remarkable accomplishment.

I am proud to be identified with these centers of academic learning — teaching and scholarship alike — so different in all things but the one that counts: thorough-going professionalism in the work of students, administration, and faculty alike.

JACOB NEUSNER

DISTINGUISHED RESEARCH PROFESSOR OF RELIGIOUS STUDIES
UNIVERSITY OF SOUTH FLORIDA, TAMPA
AND
VISITING PROFESSOR OF RELIGION
BARD COLLEGE
ANNANDALE-ON-HUDSON, NEW YORK

Introduction

I. THE CONTEXT AND PURPOSE OF THIS STUDY

Here I take up in historical-temporal sequence the formal preferences of the canonical writings of Rabbinic Judaism — hence the title: the documentary form-history of Rabbinic literature. I propose to examine the traits of the canon that is comprised by all the documents seen all together and all at once. As explained in the concluding two units of this introduction, my intent from here is to move from the comprehensive view of the canon afforded by systematic form-analysis and comparison to an equally comprehensive view of the canon seen as a coherent whole: its theological perspective.[1] My hypothesis is that for a religion that identifies canonical writing as its principal medium of expression, the qualities and characteristics of that canon define the points of structure and order of the normative — legal and theological — propositions set forth by the canon. If, therefore, we seek to know how the whole holds together, we ask the canonical writings — their formal signals as much as their substantive statements — to tell us. But then description of historical theology must stand aside, formulation of a theory in description of the literary history takes priority.

---

[1] The relationship of form-analysis to theological analysis is explained in the concluding section of this Introduction. For the theological project, my first model, as in the past, is Rudolph Bultmann, who moved from form-criticism to theology and saw close and constant connections between them. My second and equally valued model is Brevard S. Childs, who pioneered in the frontier territories beyond form-criticism and asked how, now that we know the parts, we conceive the whole to hold together. His canonical theological studies set the standard for the rest of us. My problem is a different one from theirs, but their insistence upon the theological dimensions of literary analysis strikes me as validated by their own respective *oeuvre*. Essentially, the task defined through form-analysis is, first, to find the key to authentic category-formation, and, second, to decipher the principles of association (comparison and contrast) that govern so as to erect a stable and coherent structure of thought. To state the whole in advance: the literature divides into law and exegesis, and theology unites the divided parts into a single cogent statement. But defining the halakhah that is explained in aggadah, and identifying the aggadah that is realized in halakhah — these form the twin-tasks of all future theological studies of Rabbinic Judaism in its formative age. Any other approach to theological study of this literature defines the task as one of mere collecting and arranging sayings and stories, and, in my view, we have moved far beyond that primitive stage.

In preparation for this historical reading of the forms that dictate the character of the canonical documents, I have conducted form-analytical studies of nearly all the documents of the late antique canon,[2] one by one. Now I propose to see the whole all together and all at once. The rest of the preparatory work has been carried out in the completed form-analytical studies of the composition of the Rabbinic literature. These are, first, in my *Academic Commentaries* to the two Talmuds, which mark out the building blocks of sustained discourse, explain the formation of large composites into a single coherent statement, and differentiate primary from secondary and tertiary discourse, second, in the outlines of the two Talmuds, which pay attention to the logic of coherent discourse and to forms as well, and, third, in the comparison of those outlines of tractates treated by both Talmuds. The counterpart for the Midrash-compilations, second, is comprised by the twelve volumes, in thirty parts, of the *The Components of the Rabbinic Documents: From the Whole to the Parts.* There I mark off primary from secondary discourse, show what is intruded from what is critical, and outline (in a way appropriate to the documents) the entirety of each of the Midrash-compilations, so showing what is essential and what is peripheral, and also what is extra-documentary

---

[2] "Nearly all" means to exclude the synagogue liturgies collected in the Siddur and Mahzor, which Rabbinic literature encompasses but does not treat as distinctive to the realm of the sages of that literature. Sages make rulings about the synagogue liturgy, but the received liturgy, as attested to antiquity by the Rabbinic documents, exhibits none of the formal traits and few of the indicative doctrinal traits of the Rabbinic system(s); any one indicative trait, whether formal or doctrinal — the dispute, the doctrine of the dual Torah — we name is lacking in those writings. The liturgical compilations, Siddur and Mahzor, form a distinct problem in the description of formative Rabbinic Judaism. For the study of the theology of Rabbinic Judaism, however, they certainly take a central position. I also bypass some of the documents listed as belonging to the period in question by M. D. Herr in his article, "Midrash," (*Encyclopaedia Judaica,* s.v.). That is for diverse reasons. In some instances dating these documents to late antiquity is not firm; in others, assigning them to the authorship of our sages of blessed memory in particular is far from assured; and in still other instances, the documents are accessible only in truncated form or in dubious manuscript representation. But so far as I know, no one questions that to Rabbinic Judaism in late antiquity and to that Judaism alone belongs the score of documents on which I do work, from the Mishnah through Tosefta to the Talmuds, from Scripture through Sifra and the two Sifrés to the Rabbah-Midrash-compilations. These serve to define the indicative traits of all (other) documents that may claim a position within the formative canon of that Judaism. We work from the known to the unknown.,

in each.[3]   So I have now defined the formal traits of the documents one by one, according to their classifications.[4]

This form-historical[5] reading of Rabbinic literature rests upon a now-established fact. It is that the principal compilations of Rabbinic Judaism in its formative age from the Mishnah, ca. 200 C.E., through the Talmud of Babylonia, ca. 600 C.E., and from the earliest to the latest compilations of Midrash-exegeses of Scripture as well, are written down[6] in highly formalized prose. These repetitive, stereotyped formal paradigms, or simply "forms," find definition in traits extrinsic to the sense or meaning of what is said. Rules for the formalization of thought into stereotype prose dictate how the authors or framers of statements might express

---

[3] *The Talmud of Babylonia. An Academic Commentary.* Atlanta, 1994-6: Scholars Press for *USF Academic Commentary Series*; *The Talmud of Babylonia. A Complete Outline.* Atlanta, 1995-6: Scholars Press for *USF Academic Commentary Series; The Talmud of the Land of Israel. An Academic Commentary to the Second, Third, and Fourth Divisions.* Atlanta, 1997-8: Scholars Press for *USF Academic Commentary Series; The Talmud of The Land of Israel.. An Outline of the Second, Third, and Fourth Divisions.* Atlanta, 1995-6: Scholars Press for South Florida Studies in the History of Judaism; *The Two Talmuds Compared.* Atlanta, 1995-6: Scholars Press for South Florida Studies in the History of Judaism; *The Components of the Rabbinic Documents: From the Whole to the Parts.* Atlanta, 1996-8: Scholars Press for South Florida Studies in the History of Judaism.

[4] It goes without saying that others who wish to take up the issues set forth here will want to do exactly the same systematic, analytical work, either confirming my results or producing better ones. Arguments in the abstract cannot carry weight against ample evidence in concrete and fully detailed form. The time for episodic cases, arguments resting on three examples, and other shoddy work is over. In my systematic critique of Edward P. Sanders's awry picture of "Judaism," I have already pointed out the perils of arguments from examples and propositions that comprise little more than impressions, see my *Judaic Law from Jesus to the Mishnah. A Systematic Reply to Professor E. P. Sanders.* Atlanta, 1993: Scholars Press for South Florida Studies in the History of Judaism.

[5] Twenty-five years ago I concluded that the method that New Testament scholarship calls form-history (Formen-geschichte) or form-criticism cannot apply to Rabbinic literature, since no history of forms is made possible by the character of our documents. To deal with that view, I invented the term "form-analysis," which is what I have done. But, as is clear, I do think one kind of form-history is possible, the one yielded by the documents in their historical sequence through the now-completed form-analysis. The basic method of documentary history of ideas, and now, forms, is spelled out in *Rabbinic Judaism. The Documentary History of the Formative Age.* Bethesda, 1994: CDL Press. That method, for form-history, consists in the comparison and contrast of the forms that govern in successive documents. For the documentary history of ideas, it involves the comparison and contrast of the presentation of various important ideas in the successive documents, read one by one in sequence.

[6] I think the Mishnah is originally composed for oral formulation and oral transmission, and that is manifest mnemonic traits serve that purpose. For "written down" we may substitute simply, "orally formulated," and it comes to the same thing. But the rest of the Rabbinic

their ideas and impose upon the whole a pervasive formal cogency.[7] Now that we know these rules for the several documents, we address the result.

The stylistic coherence of the whole canon, start to finish, does not obscure the variety of the forms that govern components of the parts. While some forms move from one document to the next, others take up a prominent position here and scarcely occur there. So the various documents individually exhibit distinctive formal preferences as well.[8] From the recurrent patterns of syntax and structure that characterize much of the writing in a specific document, we may define the formalization of expression that the framers of that document found critical for presenting the ideas they wished to set forth. We also distinguish one document from another by criteria of formal preference ("rhetoric") as much as by topic and logic of coherent discourse.

The formalization of the literature comes to expression not only in the traits of large-scale compilations but also, and especially, in those of the mid- and even small-scale presentation of the building blocks of documents, complete compositions whole in themselves. In the various compilations, respectively, a few formal patterns dictate how statements are made, so that two or more compositions will yield generalizations of a subtle character: the syntax of expression of suitable thought, counterpart to the substance of that same thought. Nearly all free-standing compositions, whether a few lines or many, follow rules of formalization of coherent thought that nearly everywhere exclude individual traits of style but invariably impose uniform ones.

Not only so, but compositions may well join together to make a point by repeating, in a number of different ways, the same thing time and again. That is, compositions quite commonly are formed into large-scale composites, which yield generalizations, on the one side, or systematic, topical presentations of cogent facts,

---

literature, lacking the powerful mnemonics characteristic of the Mishnah, emerges from a more complex literary history, only the final stages of which we are able to follow, and the language, "written down," serves for what we now have.

[7] It must follow that any canonical account of that Judaism — an account of the whole — must to begin with discover the sources of cogency and accept the documents' own dictates as to what holds together and what does not and, all together, what takes primary and what takes subordinate positions. In other words, any descriptive theology will take its first steps by exploring the bases of canonical cogency of the whole, and the formalization of prose throughout will then point to the first of those bases.

[8] It is also possible to differentiate on form-analytical grounds among the components of individual documents. Whether or not difference in forms signals difference in origin, so that we may trace the pre-documentary history of the compositions and even composites that now comprise our documents, remains to be demonstrated. I take up that problem in the work on extra-documentary forms and have already done a systematic probe in *Where the Talmud Comes From: A Talmudic Phenomenology. Identifying the Free-Standing Building Blocks of Talmudic Discourse.* Atlanta, 1995: Scholars Press for South Florida Studies in the History of Judaism; *The Initial Phases of the Talmud's Judaism.* Atlanta,

on the other. These composites[9] ordinarily assemble formally-uniform compositions. One fundamental trait of composites — their formal cogency — underscores the highly stereotyped characteristic of writing in the Rabbinic literature. As a matter of fact, we now have in hand a complete repertoire of the formal traits of the compositions, composites, and the several complete documents of the Rabbinic literature. We may readily define the indicative formal traits of each of those documents.[10] So much for work complete at this time but for the Mishnah and tractate Abot.

These few, simple sentences, which summarize the results of my better than twenty-five years of form-analysis of the Rabbinic literature, from the Mishnah, beginning in 1971-2, through the Yerushalmi and the Bavli, completed in 1995-6, covering the Midrash-compilations of late antiquity along the way, point to the task of this project. That is to follow the unfolding of the formal repertoire of Rabbinic Judaism as documents in sequence join the canon, from the beginning, with the Mishnah, through the end, with the Bavli. From one document to the next, the formal repertoire changes. But what about formal continuities and how do we trace the unfolding of formal differences? Over time, measured by the order in which documents came to closure, do the forms found critical in earlier compilations persist or change in later ones, and do new forms come into service, signaling new tasks not earlier addressed?

These historical questions of a literary character concerning continuity and change, development and innovation, at determinate points in the unfolding of a sequential canon, now demand attention. Until now I have not assembled the episodic results of my form-analysis of the various documents and so examined the ways in which the diverse documents' preferences for one form or another, or

---

1995: Scholars Press for South Florida Studies in the History of Judaism. I. *Exegesis of Scripture; The Initial Phases of the Talmud's Judaism.* Atlanta, 1995: Scholars Press for South Florida Studies in the History of Judaism. II. *Exemplary Virtue; The Initial Phases of the Talmud's Judaism.* Atlanta, 1995: Scholars Press for South Florida Studies in the History of Judaism. III. *Social Ethics;* and *The Initial Phases of the Talmud's Judaism.* Atlanta, 1995: Scholars Press for South Florida Studies in the History of Judaism. IV. *Theology.* I regard the work on the pre-documentary phase in the formation of the Rabbinic tradition as uncritical and vulgar, intellectually primitive and, at present, not well-founded in a solid theory of matters. My own contribution has been only to isolate those components of the documents that stand outside of the framework of the formation of the documents in which they occur.

[9] I first worked out the distinction between composition and composite and explained why it matters in *The Rules of Composition of the Talmud of Babylonia. The Cogency of the Bavli's Composite.* Atlanta, 1991: Scholars Press for South Florida Studies in the History of Judaism.

[10] These are summarized in my *Introduction to Rabbinic Literature.* N.Y., 1994: Doubleday. I have revised for the purpose of the present work the presentations of the various documents set forth in that introduction.

their invention of new forms for their own purposes, shift over time. By "shift over time," I refer in particular to the use of forms not earlier utilized in the compilation of documents that had already reached closure, or the desuetude of forms used earlier but not in evidence later on. This account of the documents' formal characteristics, start to finish, gives us the history yielded by the order of the documents and their distinctive formal traits.[11]

It also sets the stage for the companion study of the forms that do occur in various compilations but do not form part of the indicative definition of the stylistic or rhetorical program of the framers of those compilations. That is to say, when we identify forms, we forthwith differentiate those that clearly serve a particular document's compilers from those that play no documentary role in a particular document but that do occur in a number of documents. When we compare and contrast the formal traits paramount in one document with those characteristic of another, we may readily distinguish not only one compilation from another but also documentary from extra-documentary forms.[12] On that basis, I catalogue the forms that characterize the protocol of a given document as "documentary forms" and proceed, in a companion-study, to the extra-documentary ones.[13]

---

[11] I need hardly add that a documentary history in no way claims that the forms under discussion here appear uniquely in Rabbinic Judaic writings and in no other writings, e.g., those produced by another Judaism or a kindred religious system such as Christianity. Working on one canon does not necessarily yield generalizations that stand the test of data from the other canons of the other Judaisms. But as a matter of fact, the most characteristic forms that operate in the Rabbinic literature, e.g., named sages + attributive (X says) and the dispute, do not occur in any other Judaism's canonical writings. The attributive, X says, is difficult to locate outside of the Rabbinic literature, as much as the Gospels' "I say to you"-form is absent in the Rabbinic literature, and both forms lack precedents in prior Israelite writings, e.g., Scripture. The Mishnah is formally unique among all writings of all Judaisms of antiquity, and, examined with a measure of discernment, the Midrash-compilations also exhibit gross, formal traits without counterpart even in the exegetical writings of other Judaisms. Nonetheless, I am not concerned here with the comparison of forms of the several Judaisms, though the uniqueness of those of the Rabbinic writings does constitute a powerful indication of the autonomous and free-standing character of Rabbinic Judaism, which certainly drew upon data coming from other, earlier Judaisms — beginning with selected parts of Scripture itself, after all — but which utilized what it borrowed or inherited in ways particular to its own systemic purpose. But interesting dissertations on the comparison of the forms of the canonical writings of various Judaisms certainly await their authors.

[12] That is within the qualification that some documents fall into stylistic groups, e.g., the two Sifrés or the Mishnah and the Tosefta or the two Talmuds, which share certain traits of formalization. But set either Talmud side by side with any other Rabbinic compilation and the differences in formalization of speech prove blatant.

[13] A systematic catalogue of the compositions in the Rabbinic writings lacking all clear formal definition would prove remarkably slight in comparison to the catalogue of the formalized compositions and composites now fully set forth in my earlier studies and in this

II. DEFINING THE PRINCIPAL TERMS

To explain these terms: the Rabbinic literature is made up of about a score free-standing compilations, which I call "documents." We could as well call them simply "books," or "finished writings," but because of the uncertainty about how the compilations were put together and published — orally, in writing, or in a mixture of the two media — I prefer a less determinate term than "book." "Document" preserves that sense of determinacy and definition imparted by wholly intrinsic, indicative traits of rhetoric, topic, and logic of coherent discourse that I think pertains to nearly all of the compilations. For the compilations upon examination prove purposeful and planned, each with its own formal, logical, and topical or propositional traits, readily distinguished from the rest of the canon that, together, the writings comprise.[14] What is compiled is law and the exegesis of law, in the Mishnah, Tosefta, and two Talmuds; and the exegesis of Scripture, its law and theology in the Midrash-compilations from Sifra and the two Sifrés through Song of Songs Rabbah and the other late Rabbah-compilations.

Using the language of "compilation" is meant to signal that the framers of documents not only worked out in accord with their distinctive plan a large part of the writing of their compilations but also drew upon — compiled materials from — already-finished writing that does not adhere to the distinctive and indicative

---

one. As I pursued the form-analytical work, I did mark out those items lacking formal definition in the terms that govern here, and readers can judge for themselves whether or not these constitute a significant portion of the whole. In my view they do not merit much attention, except for one purpose. They do indicate that other-than-formalized writing did go on in Rabbinical circles and the results of that writing did find a place in the compilations of the day. That is all the more reason to find remarkable the enormous portion of the whole that is comprised by writing that conforms to the handful of governing paradigms I have identified. But in this volume we see some truly remarkable writing that falls outside of the framework of formalization altogether.

[14] For an account of contrary views together with my reply to critics of this view of the Rabbinic literature, those who see the various compilations as mere collections of this and that, rather than as purposeful and formed documents, see *The Documentary Foundation of Rabbinic Culture. Mopping Up after Debates with Gerald L. Bruns, S. J. D. Cohen, Arnold Maria Goldberg, Susan Handelman, Christine Hayes, James Kugel, Peter Schaefer, Eliezer Segal, E. P. Sanders, and Lawrence H. Schiffman.* Atlanta, 1995: Scholars Press for South Florida Studies in the History of Judaism. See also *Formative Judaism. New Series. Current Issues and Arguments.* Volume One. Atlanta, 1996: Scholars Press for South Florida Studies in the History of Judaism. The debate goes forward, with diminishing vigor and conviction behind the presentations of the contrary position, now mainly in dissertations of dubious value conducted under the auspices of critics of mine coming out of an earlier generation. Obviously, this formidable undertaking of mine rests upon deep foundations in prior work. I know no other way to accomplish any substantive goals in the study of Rabbinic Judaism, whether historical or theological, than doing the work completely, beginning to end. It is timely to express a simple expectation. I should expect that those who take positions different from mine will do the same, their arguments from random examples carrying no compelling

traits of the particular documents that preserve it.[15] In this sense, forms characteristic of some of the compositions and even composites must be classed as [1] "documentary," in that they conform to the definitive traits that characterize the writing in which they occur, and others, [2] "extra-documentary," in that they do not. In the companion study we identify the extra-documentary writing that is found in the successive documents.

These documents thus collect, arrange, and organize (ordinarily for a larger, encompassing purpose) small, whole units of thought, which, seen individually, make a point on their own. These I call "compositions."[16] In contemporary writing

---

force whatsoever. Exegesis of isolated phrases, out of all phase with their literary and documentary contexts, has been carried on for a lifetime of work and has persuaded few and attracted no imitators in academic learning. Simply repeating the now-disproved propositions of a prior generation of scholarship concerning the history and literature of the Rabbinic canon accomplishes nothing. Industriously collecting and arranging examples of a phenomenon the importance of which no one knows wastes time. Only systematic work makes a difference. And that work must be not only systematic and orderly, but complete and encompassing. The study of Talmudic literature in the aggregate finds itself surfeited with bright ideas and intriguing possibilities. Outside of my own corpus, I look in vain for even the simplest proposals on the definition of the literature and its traits — definition as distinct from generalization on the basis of three instances of we know not what. So much for the academic sector of Rabbinic learning. As to the yeshiva-sector, other goals than those of careful and accurate description, analysis, and interpretation govern. The results of meeting those goals bear no intellectual consequence for the world beyond the yeshivas and make no impact upon it. Nor should they — since (seen from the outside) the yeshiva-world constructs for itself a realm of utter chaos and no system at all. So on all sides the truth is the same. Arguing from cases and episodes in a massive literature that has not been systematically examined yields mere guess-work about how things might look if we examined the whole. Here we examine the whole.

[15] *Making the Classics in Judaism: The Three Stages of Literary Formation.* Atlanta, 1990: Scholars Press for Brown Judaic Studies, spells out the analytical conceptions briefly summarized here. But as my work has progressed, I am more than ever persuaded that most — though by no means all — writing was done for the purpose of contributing to documents in progress: the plan of the whole governed the preparation of the parts. That seems to me the most economical explanation for the remarkable uniformity of the parts in matters of rhetoric and logic of coherent discourse. Most, though not all, documents exhibit such traits of formal coherence, and, moreover, we are readily able to distinguish one document from another, or one group of documents from all others. These present powerful arguments against the notion that people wrote up their ideas in whatever way they liked, and only later on somebody compiled collections of these free-floating writings.

[16] On the distinction between composition and composite and the larger theoretical questions adumbrated here, see the full account in my *The Rules of Composition of the Talmud of Babylonia. The Cogency of the Bavli's Composite.* Atlanta, 1991: Scholars Press for South Florida Studies in the History of Judaism.

they may form the counterpart to self-contained sentences or, more likely, entire paragraphs in formal essay-prose, or even to small chapters. In the Rabbinic literature, then, most such compositions, complete statements bearing the propositions, facts, and (often implicit) arguments required to make a point, are formulated in accord with a limited repertoire of syntactic and morphological rules. It is rare in any document for compositions to exhibit traits of random and unpatterned language but very common for them to exhibit recurrent traits of word-order, no matter the subject of choice or the task of exposition. That fact is what imparts to the various compilations the traits of formal coherence and distinctiveness that permit us, on the basis of internal evidence alone, to differentiate one document from another and, further, to define the indicative and definitive traits of the respective documents.[17]

Language protocols and forms reveal rules not of grammar yielding meaning but of convention bearing no articulated meanings, if profound implicit messages. For formal patterning of language without regard to what is said then conveys signals of another sort altogether. Such formalization (in the present context) governs how people are permitted properly to formulate any and all of their ideas for circulation as authoritative, in documents that are received as canonical.

Let me now spell out in greater detail what I mean by "forms," whether particularly documentary or otherwise. By a "form" I mean the patterning of language in accord with rules that are extrinsic to the meaning that the language conveys and that obliterate all idiosyncratic preferences and traits of style characteristic of individuals, imposing collective and public uniformity throughout. Formalization of writing, all the more so of a whole a document, denies individuals cited in that document any characteristics of personality or individuality, making all parties speak in the same way to deliver their diverse messages and opinions. The same trait of writing insists that all topics be treated within the same paradigms, so that distinctions among subjects make no difference in how what is said is set forth.

The rules of formalization of speech may govern syntax, morphology, word-order, even word-choice, and the like. The number of syllables allotted to a given sentence in a unit of two or more completed thoughts, the matching of words in balanced sentences, the imposition of rhythm upon sentences, the number of times a given syntactic pattern is repeated and where and when it undergoes revision,

---

[17] My stress on the uniform formal traits of a given document takes account of the occasional textual diversity among representations of said documents, e.g., various manuscripts may assign to a given document quite diverse contents; in stressing what is uniform, I then regard as documentary only those uniform traits that, as a matter of fact, will impose themselves upon whatever a given textual tradition gives us as that document. I have dealt with this at some length in my *The Documentary Foundation of Rabbinic Culture. Mapping Up after Debates...*; note especially the discussion of the critique of Peter Schaefer.

however delicate — all of these considerations determining how matters are worded respond to the formal convention that applies. A form then dictates the recurrent paradigms of speech and specifies how whatever one wishes to say properly must be shaped for public reception. Acute formalization of discourse by definition marks writing that means to find acceptance: writing that by its very nature signals its authority. Adherence to form then lends to what is said the indicative trait that assures the listener or reader of the reliability of what is said.

A composition or composite that conforms to the indicative formal traits of a document is to be assigned to the authors or compilers who by defining the governing traits in fact made that document. For writing that responds to a document's formal preferences on the face of matters originated among sages intending to create the document to the formal traits of which that writing conforms. That tautologous statement shows what is at stake in form-analysis and points toward the possibilities opened up by the documentary form-history undertaken here.

Close analysis of the formal traits of patterned documents not only points to a critical element in any explanation of how that document works — the way in which, aesthetically as much as intellectually, its framers proposed to deliver their message. It also opens the way for us to recover the public history of the ideas that a highly formalized collection of writings sets forth.[18] For when we can identify and describe the forms of a given document, we also may identify what the authors of the document's distinctive compositions and the document's compilers of

---

[18] By "public history" I mean, the history of ideas as they reached official expression in documents sponsored by the authorities of Rabbinic Judaism — thus "public history" is equivalent to "the (official) history of (this particular) Judaism." We do not know the history of ideas that do not reach the official status conferred by inclusion in the books we have in hand. We do not know who, at some indeterminate time and place, thought a given thought; we do not know the state of public opinion either. What we cannot show we do not know. All we know is that, in the evidence we now have, here is the point at which such and such a notion first surfaces in that context — that alone. It is possible to show that a given idea surfaced earlier, in another canonical setting besides that of Rabbinic Judaism, for instance, in a work of Apocrypha, or in the writings of Philo, or in a book in the library at Qumran. That evidence tells us that an idea was held earlier, in another group. If we dealt with a single, unitary, incremental Judaism, then the history of an idea would transcend the limits of the documents that contain it, so that we might maintain that a given idea surfaced much earlier, and, in the context of that single, unitary, linear Judaism, continued to play its part, even though we have no clue as to what part it played. But to formulate an account of a single, unitary, incremental Judaism, we have to show that the diverse and contradictory evidence all speaks in behalf of a single "Jewish tradition," one that encompasses everything and its opposite. So far, demonstrations of that proposition have won remarkably slight credence, for obvious reasons. The opposite view and its results are spelled out in my *Rabbinic Judaism. The Documentary History of the Formative Age.* Bethesda, 1994: CDL Press.

compositions into large-scale composites and ultimately into the entire compilation in our hands made up for the purpose of producing the book before us. The document provides a terminus a quo: the point from which the ideas in the formalized compositions and composites that make up the document circulated as a statement of canonical standing (however long prior to that point those same ideas may have been held here and there, outside of the canonical setting of the nascent religious system).[19]

But every document in the canon before us contains compositions and even composites that do not conform to the indicative patterns that define the document as a whole. It follows that form-analysis also makes it possible to identify, also, the results of writing that was carried on outside of the framework of the compilation of documents. That latter category of writing, by the same criterion just now given, stands outside of the formal program of that document, and, it can be shown, any other document of the canon at hand. Compositions that fall outside the boundaries of documentary forms originate beyond the circles of those who wrote and framed the compilations so carefully defined through patterned language of a highly specific character. Frequently enough we may identify traits of formalization of language, but these traits never conform to those that characterize the formal repertoire of a document.

Those non-documentary, extra-documentary compositions can have circulated, and frequently did circulate from one document to another. When they do, they may be given superficial markings of a given document's indicative repertoire, but the substance of the compositions rarely is affected. They represent a type of writing of a different order from the patterned kind that defines the documents overall. And they derive from a different set of literary circumstances from those that produced the formalized writings collected in the canonical documents, respectively. Whether non-documentary compositions and composites belong to a period prior to, or merely a circle different from, that which is marked by the documentary ones remains an open question. But the distinction among the two types of writing on its own terms — structural, phenomenological ones — allows for considerable analytical work to go forward into the large-scale formation of ideas and the structures that hold them together.

III. AFTER FORM-HISTORY, WHAT?

Since without a clear purpose in mind I do not collect and classify data, let me now explain how I define what is at stake in the present project. That is easily explained, for over the decades my inquiry has unfolded within a certain logic, and readers who follow the results in sequence will not find surprising that, while I proceed on one project, I am thinking through its logical successor(s). The dialogue between what is underway and what is contemplated defines the dialectic that affects both components of my on-going thought. Why, then, do I think form-history a critical step — and in what direction?

---

[19] My remarks in the preceding footnote spell out what is implied here.

In my view what is at stake in form-history is nothing less than the key to the structure and cogency of the theology of Rabbinic Judaism in its formative canon. The forms, as I shall explain, signal what matters most and what least, what rationality governs the linking of one thing with something else and the exclusion of something is out of place altogether. I expect that, when the documents have been fully analyzed in their formal traits and then compared with one another, we shall have a clear picture of how our sages of blessed memory marked their main points and concerns, on the basis of which we may formulate our account of what we think those points and concerns were — and how the whole was supposed to hold together and make a single, coherent statement. The forms, after all, impart coherence to the several documents, further distinguishing one document from another; the forms define for us the purpose of each document — this, not that — and allow us to see the document not as a scrapbook of bits and pieces but as a fully-cogent and well-considered whole.

That formulation might leave the impression that at stake is the history of Rabbinic ideas, investigated in their documentary unfolding. But that is not so. Though producing results of consequence for the history of ideas held by Rabbinic canonical writings, my goal is not historical. That is to say, my principal purpose does not aim at finding out which sources are likely to represent actual events that took place or ideas that were maintained at a given place and determinate time. Nor do I conceive that we shall ever know which idea viewed in the abstract and out of some specific context of data came before some other, or in what context a given idea attained urgency and came to definitive expression: a history of ideas,[20] like a biography of a sage,[21] lies quite outside the capacities of the evidence in our

---

[20] Other than the documentary history, already done in vast detail by me and then summarized in the items cited in the next footnote.

[21] Since I reached the conclusion that rabbinic biography is not possible on the basis of the evidence we now have, I note that no further biographical studies have appeared in English. That is a conclusion announced in my *Development of a Legend. Studies on the Traditions Concerning Yohanan ben Zakkai.* Leiden, 1970: Brill; *The Rabbinic Traditions about the Pharisees before 70.* Leiden, 1971: Brill. I-III. I. *The Rabbinic Traditions about the Pharisees before 70. The Masters.* II. *The Rabbinic Traditions about the Pharisees before 70. The Houses.* III. *The Rabbinic Traditions about the Pharisees before 70. Conclusions. Eliezer ben Hyrcanus. The Tradition and the Man.* Leiden, 1973: Brill. I. *Eliezer ben Hyrcanus. The Tradition and the Man. The Tradition.* II. *Eliezer ben Hyrcanus. The Tradition and the Man. The Man,* and the dissertations of my doctoral students of the late 1960s and early 1970s. In any event I have seen nothing in German, French, Italian, or Spanish. As to Israeli work, beyond Gilat's *Eliezer ben Hyrcanus,* so far as I know, no major book-length biography has appeared in Hebrew either, though *Sidra* and *Tarbiz* continues to print some remarkably silly biographical notes and even *articles au fond.* The pseudo-scholars of the Yeshiva world print even sillier biographical pieces, printed only rarely in *Tarbis* and *Sion* but very commonly in *Sinai* and (the still more egregious) *Sidra* and other non-academic journals in Hebrew, as though, in yeshiva-learning, biography made any difference to what

hands. The reason is that I do not conceive that very much, if anything, we have in the entire corpus of Rabbinic writing meets the ordinary criteria of historicity within the conventional definition of history.[22] That is, so far as history claims to tell us about the world beyond the sources, to give us more than paraphrase of, and chitchat about, the sources, little important work goes forward. Much that we have, apart from the entirely uncritical and gullible history of a prior generation, moreover represents little more than a dull-witted paraphrase of the sources, yielding results of stupefying banality. From the sages' writings we find out what the writers of documents wished to say about the world, but on the foundation of those writings alone we can discover the world beyond the documents only with enormous difficulty, if at all.

True, on the basis of form-history, a particular kind intellectual history may be constructed: what various authorships over time found urgent to put into a well-crafted piece of writing. I have set forth the first such study in the paired works, *Rabbinic Judaism. The Documentary History of the Formative Age* and *Rabbinic Judaism. Structure and System.*[23] These moreover rest on a sizable number of topical monographs that trace the documentary history of ideas and that relate phases in that intellectual history to the political condition of Israel both in the land of Israel and in Babylonia. Not only so, but younger scholars now take up the challenge of documentary history of ideas and produce interesting results.

But for me other matters gain greater attention, for, as I just said, I simply do not regard form-analysis as an end in itself (or even as a new approach to Mishnah- and Tosefta-exegesis),[24] and I also find historical questions of limited

---

counts in scholarship. The upshot is, rabbinic biography, a very popular mode of scholarship to the earliest 1970s, has simply ceased to attract practitioners. That fact indicates the actual — as distinct from the putative — state of the scholarly consensus, which in studies of Talmudic history, literature, and religion now accords with my views here as elsewhere. Alas, I cannot point to any intellectually-ambitious work in history and religion, and much that we have in literature is repetitive and arid (or, once more, just silly). Israeli scholarship in this area has fallen silent. Some good text-editing goes on, both in the State of Israel and in Germany, but nothing of a constructive character and weighty consequence emerges.

[22] I give a full hearing to other views, besides my own, in *Judaism in Late Antiquity.* Volume Three. *Where We Stand: Issues and Debates.* In the series, *Handbuch der Orientalistik. Judaistik.* Leiden, 1997: E. J. Brill.

[23] *Rabbinic Judaism. The Documentary History of the Formative Age.* Bethesda, 1994: CDL Press, and *Rabbinic Judaism. Structure and System.* Minneapolis, 1996: Fortress Press.

[24] Form-analysis yields interesting challenges in exegetical work, as my detailed exegesis of the Mishnah and Tosefta shows. I did the work fully spelled out for the Sixth, Fifth, and Second divisions, and for the Fourth and Third,through a set of signals easily decipherable by those who understood those divisions as I present them. It seemed to me wasteful to spell out in detail what was obvious within the established methodological principles, and I wanted to move on to new problems, those of the Yerushalmi. But I was wrong to think that

interest.[25] Specifically, the literary question that I answer here shades over into the kind of theology resting on canonical collections that Judaism in its formative age, still lacks, even after George F. Moore's *Judaism: The Age of the Tannaim* and its many competing pictures. I refer to the need for canonical theology, theology that responds to the evidence of the documents, that forms its categories out of those documents and that assigns to those categories importance, indeed, even centrality, based on the position accorded to them in the documents themselves. Canonical theology will show how all of the documents hold together within the framework that the collectors and framers of the document themselves defined.

For now, we have theologies of Rabbinic Judaism that claim to set forth the standing of the whole, but that assign to categories of contemporary design the sayings and stories compiled in the Rabbinic documents. In other words, the writings are treated as random compilations of this and that, available for us to use any way we like, rather than as crafted and carefully constructed, as I have shown that they really are. What we learn from the contemporary theological studies of the Rabbinic writings therefore is not the shape and structure of canonical theology — I cannot overstate, how the whole holds together, the absolutely critical problem in the study of a theological structure and system — but only random opinions on this, that, and the other thing. And those opinions respond to the questions not of the builders of the canon — *therefore the designers of its system* — but of the contemporary scholars who bring to the writings their own contemporary concerns. These have naturally found definition in apologetics, whether for much-maligned Judaism or for a defensive Christianity.

---

anyone would take the trouble to study the much-too-detailed presentation of the Sixth and Fifth Divisions and so address the exegetical method I had devised in that work and apply it through the very brief language I invented for the divisions I took up later, the Second through the Fourth. My students' systematic work on the tractates of the first division likewise would have required astute reading to grasp the method embodied in the results that were printed. Commentators using my commentary to the Second through Fourth Divisions — let alone my students' dissertations on the tractate of the First — therefore do not realize how I do the work there, or why I say what I say or do not say what I do not say. I expected too much in thinking that my signals would do the work.

[25] Clearly, much is at stake for historical study. In a variety of works I have taken up some of the issues concerning form-analysis and the pre-history of writing now collected in documents but clearly outside of the framework of those documents. The present project rests on the foundations, in historical study, of those prior monographs. My argument, over all, is that we may peel back the layers of a document, from the final layer, defined by the framer of the document, to prior layers, shaped without reference to the indicative formal traits of said document. When we identify the extra-documentary forms of Rabbinic literature, we are able to point to those statements that have been made outside of the framework of documentary compilation and composition. Compositions and composites that realize the

Recognizing the documentary and extra-documentary components of the various documents, assessing the proportions and balance of the writings that my systematic outlines have shown, and forming careful theses on what counts and what is peripheral in the various writing, we gain perspective not only on the whole but on the balance of the parts. And that perspective produces important results for the descriptive, historical theology of Rabbinic Judaism. Specifically, guided by the sense of proportion, coherence, and balance effected through formalization of speech, we may begin to ask a set of questions pertinent to theology, that is, an account of how the whole holds together. The forms and the results of patterning of compositions and composites will guide us into how large-scale structures not only took shape ("historically") but held together theologically: what ideas took shape in one way, what in another; which ones as primary to a document, which ones as peripheral, for example.

Certainly accounts of the theology of Rabbinic Judaism to this time have not only imposed categories not native to the documents but have also imparted to those categories a disproportionately great importance when the character of the documents, the rules of composition and composite-making, are taken into account.

---

documentary program speak for the document's compilers and authors. These compositions and composites tell us about ideas important at a determinate time and place, namely, the occasion and situation in which the compilers and authors of the documentary compositions and composites did their work: what they deemed urgent to say to their time and times to come. Those that ignore the document's conventions and indicative traits speak for a time and place that are indeterminate. They may represent views held prior to the time of the formation of the documents in our hands, but they do speak for people who worked outside of the documentary restraints that governed elsewhere. I argue that non-documentary, extra-documentary writing takes temporal priority over documentary writing, and for the Talmud of Babylonia, I have collected all of the principal instances of that kind of writing and classified the results. See *The Initial Phases of the Talmud's Judaism.* Atlanta, 1995: Scholars Press for South Florida Studies in the History of Judaism. I. *Exegesis of Scripture; The Initial Phases of the Talmud's Judaism.* Atlanta, 1995: Scholars Press for South Florida Studies in the History of Judaism. II. *Exemplary Virtue; The Initial Phases of the Talmud's Judaism.* Atlanta, 1995: Scholars Press for South Florida Studies in the History of Judaism. III. *Social Ethics; The Initial Phases of the Talmud's Judaism.* Atlanta, 1995: Scholars Press for South Florida Studies in the History of Judaism. IV. *Theology.* In *Making the Classics in Judaism: The Three Stages of Literary Formation.* Atlanta, 1990: Scholars Press for Brown Judaic Studies., in broader terms, I argue the proposition that the non-documentary type of writing ought to speak out of an age before documentary writing came to predominate, or for groups engaged in a kind of writing other than for documentary locations. But, as I now explain, my interest is in finding ways to grasp the whole of the canon and to learn how to assess the proportion and balance of each of the parts. The pre-history of the documents, meaning, the portions of documents written outside of the documentary disciplines, seems to me accessible, though at this time I do not choose to investigate it to a greater extent than I already have.

In the American tradition of matters, which is the dominant one, beginning with George F. Moore's *Judaism. The Age of the Tannaim,* continuing with E. E. Urbach's *The Sages,* and running on to E. P. Sanders's *Judaism,* a Protestant theological structure — dogmatic theology, if not systematic theology — is superimposed on the writings of our sages of blessed memory. In Sanders's case, the blatant apologetics involved in describing Judaism as a religion of covenantal nomism certainly finds ample support in the sources, even though the principle of covenantal nomism lies inert at the foundations of an elaborate system concerned with other matters altogether.

The French, German, and British counterparts to Moore's and Sanders's theologies of Rabbinic Judaism need not detain us, being just so many dull collections and arrangements of sayings about this and that — and not so competent at the sources as Moore and Urbach. When intellect fails, scholarship resorts to paraphrase. The one important work produced in the State of Israel and in Hebrew, E. E. Urbach's *Sages,* follows suit, but with an important qualification. Urbach has the merit of paying a bit of attention to the halakhic writings and understands that within them active and influential theological ideas operate. But he permitted the influence of Moore and counterpart Protestant and Catholic theologies of Rabbinic Judaism to govern the larger part of his categorical structure, and he furthermore sets forth an ample portion of pseudo-history. So he can be said marginally to improve upon his predecessors — at best. Not only so, but he resisted the entire critical-historical program of the modern humanities and insisted that we believe everything the sources allege, unless we have solid reason to disbelieve. That self-serving, subjective judgment masked not so much fundamentalism as intellectual sloth; his results emerge as dull, derivative apologetics for his version of Orthodoxy. He would have done better to trust his instincts and sidestep questions of critical-historical character, allowing the sources to guide him to their interests and concerns, rather than asking them to tell him exactly what happened that morning or what Rabbi X really said to Rabbi Y.

All in all, the descriptive theologies that we do have prove tangential and disproportionate, not so much for overemphasizing what was unimportant (though that takes place) as for understating what for our sages of blessed memory constituted the heart and soul of matters. So the real goal of form-analysis, inclusive of the documentary form-history laid out here, is theological: to see what matters, and how the framers of the documents themselves signal to us what matters. That is surely the starting point of any descriptive theology of nascent Rabbinic Judaism that, in time to come, may take shape.

My primary interests lead to the history of Judaism within the study of the history of religions, and in my view, the study of the history of any religion encompasses a picture of how that religion holds together and makes a cogent statement subject to sustained inquiry: the study of the theology of a religion. In my view all accounts of the theology of Rabbinic Judaism in its formative age have failed, always for the same reason: the category-formation that has served as the medium for description (selection and classification of pertinent data) violates the integrity of the canon that alone sets forth that religion. Historians of theology have botched the descriptive work and turned themselves into constructive theologians of a religion that, in the case of Judaism, most of them simply do not hold. But no constructive theology can come forth as a matter of abstract theory. No one has properly undertaken the description, analysis, and interpretation of historical theology — the theology that encompasses the canon and that at each point animates it. That is because the traits of the writings that all together make the theological statement of that Judaism have not been properly weighed in the formulation of the category-formation that will dictate the character of the theological description, analysis, and interpretation. I intend in the work that the present project makes possible to ask the documents themselves, speaking in chorus if not in unison, to dictate their category-formation, its components and proportions, its cogency and inner logic: the canonical theology of formative Judaism.[26]

IV. THE THEOLOGICAL USES OF FORMALIZED WRITING

These remarks point to the hypothesis I presently entertain, which is that, for the Rabbinic canon, the medium bears an important part of the message. Let me explain.

Why do I deem so urgent a clear understanding of exactly how the Rabbinic literature works? Because, as I shall now explain, only when we know how each canonical document makes its points and how all of them together form a coherent whole shall we find possible an authentic account of the theology that animates each writing and states the rationality of all of them all together.[27]

---

[26] I should be disingenuous if I did not admit that, even now, I have some clear ideas on these matters, but they are still wholly in mind, and it would be premature to articulate them.

[27] In my earliest reflections on seeing the documents one by one and then all together, I formulated the relationships among documents as tripartite: autonomy, connection, continuity. See for example *Canon and Connection: Intertextuality in Judaism.* Lanham, 1986: University Press of America. *Studies in Judaism* Series, and *Midrash as Literature: The Primacy of Documentary Discourse.* Lanham, 1987: University Press of America *Studies in Judaism* series. That is to say, each document stands by itself (except for the Tosefta). Second, each document, including the Tosefta, is relates to some other(s) in program and even in form. Third, all of the documents by definition constitute a coherent and consistent statement, that is, Judaism. In the various documentary monographs, I promised that at some point I would move from the reading of a document as autonomous and as connected to some other(s) to the examination of all documents in their canonical context, as a statement, whole and (to that point) complete, of the Torah of Sinai. That is how subsequent generations received this corpus of authoritative writings, and since for many centuries everyone has known that everything fits with everything else, I should like to know, if that is the case, then what is the set of statements that the documents read as an internally consistent and coherent corpus proposes to make? That defines the theological problem at hand, which I deem accessible through the correct understanding of how the documents speak and, themselves, signal their points of order and structure, emphasis and significance.

Therein lies the mystery I wish to penetrate: how the canon holds together and makes a single coherent statement. For it is an odd canon indeed, both in its parts and seen as a whole. Take for example the simple fact that each document collects sayings of many authorities. How are we supposed to know what we are to think and to do? Contrast the writings of other Judaisms, the traits of their respective canonical collections. Writings of Judaisms prior to Rabbinic Judaism rarely cite conflicting views of named authorities and usually speak for a given figure and in the language and idiom of that singular author, e.g., Moses or a prophet, a particular writer such as Ben Sira, for the teacher of righteousness, for the community of Elephantine, or, in apocalyptic books, in the names of supernatural figures. If it is common for writings to speak for particular authors, not anonymously, it also is uncommon for those writings to cite two or more conflicting authorities on any given subject. Moses and Korach are not cited side by side in the book of Numbers, for instance, or Jeremiah and Hananiah, or Elijah and the prophets of Baal in the narratives of Kings.[28]

Both of these traits — presentation of a single view, utilization of language distinctive to a single author or voice — strikingly contrast with those characteristic of the Rabbinic literature. For Rabbinic documents speak anonymously and collectively, in a uniform pattern of speech, but they constantly cite named authorities, paying special attention to the conflict of opinion between a named authority and "sages" or another named authority.[29] So no prior Judaism produced a writing so engaged by identified, conflicting opinion, set forth in the framework of an objective and neutral, impersonal language, making a stylistically uniform statement in behalf of the entire collegium of sages.

That intense engagement with identified sages and their differences of opinion makes all the more paradoxical the anonymous quality of the formalized prose that characterizes the books deemed authoritative by that same Judaism. No named sage wrote a book under his own name. It is rare for a named sage to speak in a singular idiom of his own, but common for all sages to formulate their opinions in undifferentiated ways and in impersonal language. Rabbinic Judaism in late antiquity produced a sizable canon of public, collective writing. Its canon preserved occasional snippets of idiosyncratic prose but no corpus of private, individual writing

---

[28] The writer of Qohelet may indeed assemble several voices to conduct an internal argument, but if so, the cited authorities are not given autonomous standing.

[29] See my *Jerusalem and Athens: The Congruity of Talmudic and Classical Philosophy.* Leiden, 1997: E. J. Brill. *Supplements to the Journal for the Study of Judaism,* and *The Philosophy of Religious Argument: The Intellectual Foundations of Christian and Jewish Discourse.* London, 1997: Routledge. [With Bruce D. Chilton.]

whatsoever.[30] In the entire canon of Rabbinic Judaism we do not possess a single entire work signed by a named sage and composed in language personal to him alone.[31] Not only so, but where individuals do play a role, their sayings are given episodically, here and there, never as a coherent formulation of an individual and autonomous viewpoint, never within the context of a documentary program of propositions and arguments particular to the named individual.

When a complete canon, formed over six hundred years, conforms to a single policy of speaking in an anonymous and collective voice but citing opinions of individuals within that same uniform voice, we must wonder why. How come all individual initiative is subsumed within the consensus of sages, and no individual imparts his taste and judgment to the character of a document accepted for canonical preservation? Given the character of the writing — its insistence that what is written down forms part of the Torah at Sinai, its emphasis upon the divine origin of what is set forth and standing of the authorities of the writings, we may reasonably turn first of all to a theological explanation.

Indeed, given its theological purposes, Rabbinic Judaism could have done no other than put forth writing of exactly the collective and impersonal kind that we have in hand. When we realize the alternatives and contemplate what was achieved through the acute formalization of all speech, we shall understand why that aesthetics was inevitable and necessary. We may go a step further and claim that theological conviction explains why in Rabbinic Judaism we have no counterpart to Paul's personal letters, to signed Gospels, to the other large-scale personal writings such as Christianity knows in abundance. This formalization of writing represents the realization in aesthetics of fundamental theological convictions.

Let us dwell on the powerful emphasis upon consensus, extending to the suppression of most evidence of individual traits of speech or writing. The great sages said many things, but none wrote a book in his own behalf. Still further, groups of sages assembled here and there, but no assembly of sages produced its own compilations of either law or doctrine. Sayings of "the sages of Pumbedita"

---

[30] Within various documents, we do find compositions, rarely composites, that are assigned to named sages, e.g., letters dictated by Gamaliel, compilations of sayings attributed to Abbayye or Raba or Rabbah, chapters of the Mishnah that focus upon the opinions of a single authority, such as Mishnah-tractate Kelim Chapter Twenty-Four. These snippets prove that individuals could stand behind sustained writing. But compositions that bear idiosyncratic traits of style and ignore the rules of formalization of prose prove few and far between, while, as we know, those that impose on everything that is said a single set of paradigms of speech vastly predominate.

[31] Attribution of various documents to specified authorities, e.g., the Mishnah to Judah the Patriarch, Mekhilta to Ishmael, Sifra to Judah bar Ilai, and the like, rests on no foundations subject to verification, and the internal evidence of documents rarely, if ever, sustains, or even bears upon, those allegations of specified authors behind various documents.

assemble a few hundred words at most, a composite of odds and ends. But rare and episodic materials aside, nearly everything reaches us in a single, homogenized state, document by document. Rules of formulation obliterate traits of individuality throughout. Individuals conflict on principles — their names may even stand for positions taken consistently in diverse cases in accord with a single principle. But the conflict always finds its way into writing as a detail of a vast and coherent statement of unanimity on basic matters.

Not only so, but where in the context of anonymous documents individuals are given sayings, these ordinarily conform to the style of the documents in which they occur overall, rather than to the preferences that would appeal to one but not to another sage.[32] Individuals, cited in virtually every line of the canonical writings, not a single one of which lacks massive numbers of attributed sayings, play no recognized role in the formulation or sponsorship of any writing. Because all documents are impersonal and anonymous, the very character of the writings of Rabbinic Judaism exercises a centripetal force in behalf of that Judaism, concentrating, consolidating, unifying, integrating the parts into a coherent whole.[33]

We should not regard as a given that impetus toward consensus. When we recall that, out of earliest Christianity, numerous documents, written by named authorities and bearing an idiosyncratic message (accepted as canonical to be sure), came forth, the anonymity and stylistic uniformity of the whole Rabbinic-Judaic canon prove still more striking. Compare the standing of the letters of Paul or the Gospels attributed to named figures, Mark, Luke, John, or Matthew, with that of the Mishnah or Tosefta or Sifra, for instance. The latter assemble and state

---

[32] In the Mishnah, we have compilations of opinions associated with a named authority, e.g., lists of opinions of a given sage. But these compilations conform to the formal rules that govern in the Mishnah throughout. In the Talmud of Babylonia, by contrast, we do have collections of sayings that clearly ignore the paradigms governing the formalization of language in that document, e.g., sets of statements attributed to Abbayye or Rabbah or Raba that in no way respond to the rules of stylistic formalization that generally pertain. These collections rarely amount to much, and when authoritative statements of law or theology are set forth, by contrast, whether bearing names or given anonymously, the statements can be shown to adhere to the formal requirements of the Talmud overall. The documents that reached closure between the Mishnah and the Talmud of Babylonia rarely preserve idiosyncratic sayings, that is, sayings that ignore the documentary rules that otherwise govern.

[33] That is why the description of the theology of Rabbinic Judaism set forth in its canonical documents must begin with documentary wholes, not with topics fabricated for the occasion. We may find ample evidence in sayings and stories that our sages of blessed memory held, or would have accepted, diverse propositions, but until we have formulated the propositions that their collective authority sponsored through the media of expression chosen by them — anonymous documents, each of them crafted in a distinctive way — we cannot claim to describe their theology in its terms and context, that is, historically and not, in the end, anachronistically.

coherently a variety of views, the former give the particular position of the specified authority behind the writing. In more general terms: the canonical books of Rabbinic Judaism take over and present in a coherent statement whatever individual views were found authoritative, so that, as a matter of fact, labeling an opinion by the name of a specific sage ordinarily[34] signals the schismatic character of what is said.

The character of a considerable portion of the counterpart writings of earliest Christianity shows the opposite quality. If the one exerts centripetal, the other exercises a centrifugal force. A large part of the canonical writings of earliest Christianity sets forth distinct and individual accounts of matters — whether Paul's or the Evangelists' or the great and massive corpus of writing by Church Fathers in Greek, Latin, and Syriac. The authoritative writings, speaking for individuals, each in his own name and manner, do exercise a centrifugal force in Christianity, starting with four distinctive, disharmonious pictures of Jesus, which would require centuries of work on harmonization, not to mention the free-standing letters of Paul, the autonomous system set forth by the letter to the Hebrews, and numerous other distinct writings to be drawn together. Not only so, but for Church fathers it was routine to write as individuals, to speak to the Church and to shape its consensus. Whether Aphrahat in Syriac, Origin in Greek, or Augustine in Latin, the traits of individual style of intellect and also aesthetics govern. A paragraph by Augustine or Aphrahat will exhibit the distinctive trait of the style of those remarkable writers. But if we assembled two dozen statements attributed to Aqiba or Meir or Judah by the Mishnah, on the basis of style we should know only that the statements originated in the Mishnah (or the Tosefta).

Working our way through complete documents of Rabbinic origin, we recognize the coherent viewpoint, the cogent propositions, that pervade the whole. Even while our sages strive to identify contradiction and harmonize conflict, we identify the integuments of a massive consensus everywhere operating in detail. That constitutes the intellectual counterpart to the acute formalization of language. In fact, the remarkable theological cohesion of the Rabbinic writings derives from the very way in which the writings are put together: it was coherence that was imparted to begin with, in the process of compiling a document, rather than, as in the case of Christianity, at the end. A book (or, as I prefer, a document) stood for the consensus of sages and made a definitive statement upon its subject.

---

[34] That is particularly the case when we have an anonymous opinion followed by, "Rabbi X says...," or "Rabbi X says," followed by, "and sages say...." In disputes formulated in that way, the assignment of a position to a named authority serves to stigmatize that position as schismatic, and that is said in so many words. Where we have the statement of a problem followed by X says.., Y says..., there two equally possible positions are set forth. Hence I stress, "ordinarily."

For the Christian theologians, by contrast, theological coherence would come not at the outset with the formulation of an authoritative document but only at the end of a massive process conducted by the Church order. So in Christianity individuals wrote down what they thought ,and then councils or other Church authorities sorted out the true from the heretical positions and further formed of diverse truths those cogent and coherent statements — whether of theology or of law — that would govern the Church in time to come. Thus the work of selection and harmonization carried on by Councils and later theologians alike would after the fact select what was authoritative and hold the whole together. So the doctrinal point at which, for antiquity, Christianity ended up — with conciliar creeds, for instance — corresponds to the doctrinal point at which Rabbinic Judaism commenced. That is to say, the Mishnah and the Talmuds set forth to begin with the harmonious pattern of the Torah's truth. Only through a long process of theological debate was Christianity able to set forth the pattern of Christian truth. Both religious systems found it possible to make authoritative and coherent statements, but for the Judaic sages those collective and uniform statements defined the task of composing documents. Then it was the document that formed the medium of theological discourse, coming at the end of a process of forming a cohesive and proportionate position on the topic covered by said document.

The upshot is that for Rabbinic Judaism book-making took as its task a very different assignment from that which Christianity would set forth. On the basis of its generative myth, in particular, each religion defined for itself what should constitute the task of formulating documents (e.g., writing books). Just as the Founder of Christianity spoke in the language of "I say to you," so his followers would set forth their personal and individual statements for the edification of the Church. But Rabbinic Judaism presented itself as the Torah revealed by God to Moses at Sinai and its sages as links in the chain of tradition: "Moses received Torah at Sinai and handed it on to Joshua, Joshua to elders, and elders to prophets. And prophets handed it on to the men of the great assembly" (Abot 1:1) — and onward to Hillel and Shammai and the sages who stemmed from them. The task of the sage then was to confirm the tradition, not to invent new truth:

A. (1) A summer garment which has colored and white checks-
(2) they spread from one [white] to another [white square].
B. They asked R. Eliezer, "And lo, it is a distinctive check?"
C. He said to them, "I have not heard."
D. Said to him R. Judah b. Beterah, "May I teach concerning it?"
E. He said to him, "If to confirm the words of sages, yes."
F. He said to him, "Perhaps it will remain on it for two weeks, and that which stands on garments for two weeks is unclean."
G. He said to him, "You are a great sage, for you have confirmed the words of sages."

MISHNAH-TRACTATE NEGAIM 11:7

The mark of great sagacity came not from personal originality but from the collectivity of sages and their shared mastery of the Torah: traditionality. For "our sages of blessed memory" the task of formulating a document was to set down the conclusions and spell out the whole and coherent truth, once for all time, on the topic of said document. Anonymity and uniformity of speech defined the formal media for accomplishing that goal. The one signed names and preserved the traits of individuality and personality. The other set forth collective and anonymous statements, citing alternative opinions but never imparting to a document the distinctive traits of an individual, named voice. The following makes this point in so many words:

I.43 A. *Our rabbis have taught on Tannaite authority:*

B. What is the order of Mishnah teaching? Moses learned it from the mouth of the All-Powerful. Aaron came in, and Moses repeated his chapter to him and Aaron went forth and sat at the left hand of Moses. His sons came in and Moses repeated their chapter to them, and his sons went forth. Eleazar sat at the right of Moses, and Itamar at the left of Aaron.

C. R. Judah says, "At all times Aaron was at the right hand of Moses."

D. Then the elders entered, and Moses repeated for them their Mishnah chapter. The elders went out. Then the whole people came in, and Moses repeated for them their Mishnah chapter. So it came about that Aaron repeated the lesson four times, his sons three times, the elders two times, and all the people once.

E. Then Moses went out, and Aaron repeated his chapter for them. Aaron went out. His sons repeated their chapter. His sons went out. The elders repeated their chapter. So it turned out that everybody repeated the same chapter four times.

F. On this basis said R. Eliezer, "A person is liable to repeat the lesson for his disciple four times. And it is an argument a fortiori: If Aaron, who studied from Moses himself, and Moses from the Almighty —so in the case of a common person who is studying with a common person, all the more so!"

G. R. Aqiba says, "How on the basis of Scripture do we know that a person is obligated to repeat a lesson for his disciple until he learns it [however many times that takes]? As it is said, 'And you teach it to the children of Israel' (Deut. 31:19). And how do we know that that is until it will be well ordered in their mouth? 'Put it in their mouths' (Deut. 31:19). And

> how on the basis of Scripture do we know that he is liable to
> explain the various aspects of the matter? 'Now these are
> the ordinances which you shall put before them' (Ex. 31:1)."
>
> BAVLI ERUBIN 54B

We see that the task of the sage is to memorize and transmit the Torah, not to
change or vary the wording in any detail. In such a setting we should hardly
expect sages to go off and write books under their own names or even to invest
great efforts in preserving their own individual traits of style.

That is why the canonical books of that Judaism set forth not diverse
opinions in the inimitable style of individuals but rather the clear and authoritative
position of the Torah on any topic — whether the reading of a book of Scripture or
the definition of a principle of theology or the specification of a rule governing a
given transaction. They further encompassed diverse, conflicting opinions as well
as schismatic opinion, so that a full range of viewpoints accompany the systematic
and orderly exposition of the accepted norm of theology or law. So the Mishnah
states in so many words:

> 1:5 A. And why do they record the opinion of an individual along
> with that of the majority, since the law follows the opinion
> of the majority?
>
> B. So that, if a court should prefer the opinion of the individual,
> it may decide to rely upon it.
>
> C. For a court has not got the power to nullify the opinion of
> another court unless it is greater than it in wisdom and in
> numbers.
>
> D. [If] it was greater than the other in wisdom but not in
> numbers,
>
> E. in numbers but not in wisdom,
>
> F. it has not got the power to nullify its opinion —
>
> G. unless it is greater than it in both wisdom and numbers.
>
> > 1:6 A. Said R. Judah, "If so, why do they record the
> > opinion of an individual against that of a
> > majority to no purpose?
> >
> > B. "So that if a person should say, 'Thus have I received the
> > tradition,' one may say to him, 'You have heard the tradition
> > in accord with the opinion of Mr. So-and-so [against that of
> > the majority].'"
>
> MISHNAH TRACTATE EDUYYOT 1:5-6

The law then was formulated to begin with both to signal the right ruling and also
to mark as schismatic other opinions. But individuals on their own were not free
to collect and preserve their own rulings, in their own words. For these same goals
— clear, authoritative, orderly statements of how things are to be believed and to
be done — Christian theologians, working with conflicting and diverse writings

labor for many centuries. And, indeed, while Rabbinic Judaism retained remarkable coherence, legal and theological cohesion, from the beginning to the present, Christianity for its part exhibited perpetually fissiparous tendencies, from then to now.

To accomplish their goal of providing authoritative, uniform, integrated, and coherent statements on various topics, our sages of blessed memory chose to write in highly formalized, stereotype paradigms, imposed upon all topics, on the one side, and upon the opinions of all authorities, on the other. The formalization of their writings corresponded to the theological tasks accomplished therein: to speak in one voice about many things, to say the same thing about many things — all in order to turn language itself into a medium for the centripetal and against the centrifugal forces of religious intellect. So, as I said, the medium embodies the message. But to unpack that rather ordinary observation will take much work, and a fair amount of heavy lifting too.

To state matters in a simple way: once we know the rules that govern the patterning of language, we here find our way into the laws of rationality — right thinking. And when we know the media of expression and thought, we ought to find reliable guidance into the canonical message, in its proportion and with its emphasis, balance, order, and structure: Judaism. So my goal — that of the history of theology — leads from collecting and arranging sayings on topics of theological interest to an inquiry into the cogency and coherence, the structure and the system, that sustains the whole and holds the parts together. No one has done that yet, it is the Everest of the study of formative Judaism. And, viewing the entire range of issues and problems, each presenting its own challenges, we see, from the farthest distance and up close as well, it is the height to scale. So the issue is simple: how do we know we are right when we allege, "the rabbis say...," or "Judaism [in its normative statement] teaches..."?

I

An Initial Probe

The formalization of discourse into recurrent patterns that govern not what is said but how the message is set forth defines the data subject to form-analysis. The questions that pertain are these: To what degree, at what point, is a document formalized at all? What forms persist, and how do they affect the writing? These are the only questions that form-analysis answers — by definition. The answers for the Talmud of the Land of Israel are, [1] the opening statement of a composition will nearly always yield the tell-tale marks of formalization, e.g., repeating a patterning of language that is common to many such compositions; the secondary expansion of compositions rarely exhibits the marks of formalization. And [2] the writing of a composition will respond to the requirement of a form by framing whatever the author wishes to say within the limited repertoire of formulating and ordering sentences that the form affords.

The category-formation that governs the classification of the data — Chapters Two through Six of the present and companion volumes — shows that a remarkably economical repertoire serves the whole of this Talmud. In the case of the Rabbinic writings the tasks of a document — a commentary to a work of Scripture or to a tractate of the Mishnah — dictate the formal repertoire that governs the writing of compositions and the formation of composites for use in that document. Forms, we now know, do not circulate intact from one compilation to the next but can be shown to take shape and find meaning in the context of the authorship that uses them to accomplish its goals. That simple statement summarizes the results of Volumes I-V. The comparison and contrast of the formal choices made by the authorships of the several documents then yields the history of the forms of the Rabbinic literature as that history unfolds from documents that reached closure earlier to those that concluded only later on.

Our category-formation — exactly what forms shall we anticipate finding? — now requires reconsideration through a probe of a sample of the document. The reason is that here the intellectual program of a different type of writing from that paramount in the Aggadic documents comes to the fore. Do the forms of the principal Halakhic documents, the two Talmuds, correspond to those in the Aggadic ones we have now considered? The latter govern statements of three classes: hermeneutical, exegetical, and syllogistic. In general, as we shall see, the same structure serves here, but with a difference. While forms in the Aggadic sector do not respond to the contents of what is said, in the Halakhic sector they do. That is to say, the formalization or patterning of language encompasses messages of substance that the patterned language is meant to convey. And that is because the Halakhic sector of the canon differs in its fundamental, intellectual character from the Aggadic. Before we can proceed, therefore, we take note of those differences, spelling out the reasons to persist in the pattern established in Volumes I-V.

How, formally, do the two sectors compare? The Aggadic literature identifies and spells out the revealed patterns of truth that Scripture set forth and takes as its task the exposition of the given. Writing for Aggadic compilations carried out no analytical tasks, only synthetic and expository ones. We find not a single dialectical argument in all of the middle and later Midrash-compilations, nor can I point to sustained, analytical inquires of any consequence. The category-formation that served to classify the dominant formal structures therefore paid no attention to the substance of what was said, only to its function within the larger document, e.g., [1] hermeneutical (the intersecting-verse/base-verse form), [2] exegetical (the commentary-form), or [3] syllogistic (the propositional form) — the three effective forms of Aggadic compilations.[1] The upshot is that while in the Aggadic sector the forms tell us the kind of exposition we confront in a given piece of writing, they do not guide us in the actualities of reading — making sense — of that composition. That is because in the Aggadic sector the forms have no bearing on the substance of that exposition. The literature seen whole constitutes a massive exercise of show-and-tell, systematic re-presentation of established and incontestable truth. The formal signals always tell us where we are in this labor of exposition of norms of theology, inclusive of scriptural exegesis of a theological character.

Now matters change, though the formalization of prose characterizes the Halakhic as much as the Aggadic sector, and in much the same ways. But we have to notice differences as well. We begin with the task of this sector of the canon: the Halakhic sector expounds the Mishnah. What is required is not only or mainly a labor of recapitulation in a systematic framework, exposition in a disciplined

---

[1] Readers will recall that parables do not qualify as forms, rather as subdivisions of the category, narrative, which itself exhibits no recurrent, formal traits I can discern. Other classifications of narrative clearly conform to rules of writing that pertained and that we can identify, but these do not introduce fixed forms or patterns into the narrative, so far as I can see. I had no difficulty classifying narratives by various indicative traits, but these do not constitute formal characteristics. As to large-scale topical miscellanies, I found no evidence of the formalization of the prose. So when it comes to form-analysis and form-history, only the three types listed here qualify.

program, or demonstration of a set of propositions. The Mishnah itself is a highly systematic document. Its own forms constitute a powerful medium of exegesis, so that, if we understand the Mishnah's forms and how they work, we can ordinarily make excellent sense of what they Mishnah is saying. And as we saw in Volume I, the Mishnah's forms amply succeed in setting forth the propositions that its authorship wishes to express. In sum, that document is organized by topic and is set forth in such a way as systematically to state the norms of conduct. The work of show-and-tell being accomplished in the base-document, the consequent Halakhic-exegetical literature, for its part, undertakes a different task from the one that occupied the writers of the Aggadic-exegetical and propositional literature.

Presentation and recapitulation not being required of the Mishnah as it is of Scripture, the Mishnah's heirs undertook an analytical, argumentative task, one of explaining and analyzing the law of the Mishnah. They brought to the document a formidable hermeneutical program, which governed their concrete exegeses of sentences of the law. They aimed, for example, at demonstrating the encompassing proposition that the Mishnah and its law conform to the highest standards of perfect rationality: proportion, harmony, coherence, integrity. To accomplish their analytical goals the writers of the Halakhic documents had to do more than assert their propositions as in the Aggadic sector; even in the very context of Mishnah exegesis they had to assemble evidence and construct arguments in their behalf; and, above all, they bore responsibility to test and disprove contrary propositions.

All well-composed demonstrations in the Talmuds therefore take up not only the hypothesis but the null-hypothesis, commonly in the form of the dialectical argument, the best suited medium for setting up and testing a null-hypothesis. That is to say, sages took as their task testing and proving not only the truth of what is alleged but the falsity of the contrary allegation. Presenting not merely assertion but argument, not merely allegation but demonstration through probative, well-crafted evidence, the writing iterates not merely propositions but vivid arguments pro and con. By contrast, the Aggadic documents allege truth, present assertion, lay out propositions lacking argument of a sustained character. In the secondary expansion of exegetical propositions, moreover, the Talmuds following a systematic program set forth sufficient data to permit the recapitulation of the thought-processes that come before and sustain the propositional, analytical arguments. The authorships wish to open the entry into the intellectual exchange of rational inquiry and criticism that comes before the expression of proposition and counter-proposition, argument and counter-argument.

But does form-analysis of the Talmuds require attention to the signals as to substance, not only to form — considerations that we have not kept in mind in identifying and classifying the patterning of language in the Aggadic sector? Must we differentiate within commentary-form, in a way in which, in the Aggadic sector, we did not? In principle we should not. For by definition form-analysis identifies the indicative traits of the patterning of language without regard to the substance of what is said; it is the external manifestation of the grammar of the language of the document with which we deal in our quest within the repetition of constructions of a given sort for the basic rules of writing that governed the formation of the documents and the materials included in them. And for that purpose, whether the citation and gloss of a passage of Scripture or of the Mishnah yields a statement of one kind or of another makes very little difference. The rule of writing is the same, the simple form persists. True, we may identify different sorts of indicative traits for the work of Mishnah-exegesis. But if we want to know the rules of writing that governed in the (re)presentation of that exegesis, the classification by type of argument or of analysis plays no role that I can discern.

At issue in these somewhat abstract remarks is whether or not form-analysis requires the cataloguing and classifications of fixed particles that signal meaning, as much as fixed grammatical patterns or arrangements of clauses. They function to indicate the character as to type of argument and the context as to our situation in the unfolding of the analysis in the writing that is to come, not merely the classification of that writing. To understand what is at issue, we have to recall that, formally, the work of writing commentaries to clauses or sentences of Scripture and the Mishnah followed the same rule. That is the case even though the type of comment that was expected differed from one document to the other. The analytical, argumentative task of the two Talmuds was defined by their relationship to the Mishnah, as much as the Aggadic documents' work was defined by their relationship to synagogually-privileged Scripture. For the purpose of conducting argument and making possible the recapitulation of the thought behind the argument, forms have to convey only the classification of writing. But the Talmuds utilize within the commentary-form fixed particles, which signal the type of analysis that is to take place. A subset of the form, the particle that signals the classification of the exposition that is to follow, makes no impact upon the basic structure of the writing itself. The particles inserted in the form ("we have learned there," "We have learned in the Mishnah," "it has been taught on Tannaite authority," "Rabbi So-and-so objected," to name four) bear a quite distinctive task.

Let me spell this matter out with some care, since the persistence of the category-formation used in Volumes III through V in the present and the final part of the project requires explanation. The important forms for patterning language that govern in the Aggadic sector of the formative canon of Rabbinic Judaism — intersecting-verse/base-verse-, commentary-, and propositional-form[2] — do not bear substantive meaning. They are forms in the purest sense: formalities that govern syntactic patterns and relationships but bear no meaning in themselves. They tell us whether a composition serves hermeneutical, exegetical, or syllogistic discourse. That is to say, when we identify a given pattern or formulation, we do

---

[2] In general, the dispute-form takes a subordinated role in the formal structures of the Aggadic sector, much as it does in the Mishnah.

not on that account gain a signal on the sense of a composition, only its order and procedure and intent; forms define the problem, but play no role in the substantive exegesis, of a passage. They do tell us what to expect and guide us in the reading of the passage, but when it comes to detailed exegesis of the specific message, forms offer no guidelines. Thus, through the forms that govern the formulation of critical components of the Aggadic writings, we know what kind of passage confronts us. But the form on its own bears no implication as to the meaning of the composition as a whole or the function of its parts.

Take for example the single most influential form in the later and latest Midrash-compilations of late antiquity. Merely knowing that the author frames his thought — the proposition he wishes to set forth — in intersecting-verse/base-verse-form, for instance, tells us nothing about the issues or propositions he has in mind, only the way in which we are to interpret the writing that conveys his message — as an exercise of hermeneutics, yielding implications for the exegesis of verses to follow. And that is so whether or not a fixed particle, e.g., *Rabbi X opened,* marks the presence of the form. Other fixed particles serve equally well, e.g., "that is in line with the following verse of Scripture," lacking all reference to *Rabbi X opened.* So, in general, in the Aggadic sector of the canon, form-analysis bears little consequence for exegesis.[3] It follows that, when we undertake form-analysis and then, through a process of comparison and contrast, documentary form-history of the Aggadic compilations, the work rests wholly on extrinsic traits of writing. We know, then, what we want to know; our question defines itself.

When we come to the great corpus of Halakhah — the two vast commentaries to the Mishnah, the Talmud of the Land of Israel and the Talmud of Babylonia — that description serves to tell us how forms work and therefore are to be classified. That is so, even though within the articulation of the base-form (in the present instance, commentary-form) diverse further conventions will govern. If, therefore, we identify a recurrent syntactic pattern or, more to the point, a repeated formalization of thought in a fixed and conventional set of words, in the Halakhic sector that form or pattern, encompassing its fixed particle, tells us in a very specific way how to make sense of the very words in hand, far in excess of what to expect in the passage to follow.[4] While the Talmuds' writing contains many more signals through the patterning of language than we find in the Aggadic sector, these signals

---

[3] But, as I have suggested in the Introduction, form-analysis provides important guidance in the consideration of hermeneutics of the respective documents.

[4] I commented a number of times in Volumes I-V that the classification of the divisions of "commentary-form" would require attention. But I did not find it necessary to distinguish the species of the genus "commentary-form," since I could not find formal indicators that would correspond to the substantive (e.g., hermeneutical) points of differentiation I was noticing. The fact that fixed particles define formal patterns in the Halakhic compositions of the two Talmuds is what makes the difference.

convey information on what is being said, intrinsic information on the sense of a patterned composition, not only extrinsic data on the general classification into which a patterned composition is to be assigned. That explains why, to form-analysis and the consequent comparison and contrast of the forms of the Halakhic sector of the Rabbinic writings, that intrinsic information makes no contribution.

The recurrent patterning of language, involving reiterated formal phrases that function as formal particles, bears blatant signals that dictate the exegesis of a passage. In the Talmuds the formal particles always dictate not the patterning or formalization of language to follow, but the classification of the argument to be set forth within said form.[5] But upon the basic formal structure of the passage, the appearance of the fixed particle has no affect at all. To give a simple example, the particle "what is the source of this statement?" (*mina hani mili*) always bears in its wake, "as it is said...," (*shene'emar*). This pattern — the particle, triggering a single continuation, a citation of Scripture, often then bearing in its wake a secondary amplification — recurs throughout. When sages wished to write a composition on the scriptural foundations of a law in the Mishnah, they would utilize this pattern and no other: the one consisting of the cited particle and the conventional citation of a verse of Scripture, sometimes then adding further explanation. And the fixed forms and conventional patterning of language always instruct us on what, substantively, to expect: how to read the passage at hand. But the commentary-form, which commonly cites a clause of the Mishnah and glosses that clause, defines the setting for that particle and all others, and if we differentiate among all of the particles within the commentary-form, we do not know more about the form itself than if we refrain from cataloguing the particles in distinct lists.[6] Now to the formation of a hypothetical repertoire of forms.

II. FRAMING A THEORY OF THE YERUSHALMI'S FORMS

To formulate a hypothesis on the formal repertoire of the Yerushalmi, we turn to a specific chapter and examine the character of the patterning of its language: types of forms, extent of the use of forms, effects of the reduction of thought to

---

[5] Note the contrast to the parables in the Aggadic compilations. The particle, *Mashal, lemah haddabar domeh,* sometimes abbreviated to simply, *le...,* which indicates the unstated presence of, "the matter may be compared" then to, does not then carry in its wake instructions on the syntax of the sentences to follow, as my analysis constantly pointed out. Sometimes the particle signalled the use of a metaphor stated in narrative form, other times we would have a fully-spelled out tale. But never could I discern the resort to a recurrent syntactic pattern, extrinsic to the meaning of the passage, that the introduction of the indicative particle would precipitate.

[6] But just as I pointed out how interesting would be a classification of the types of scriptural exegesis, all of them served by the commentary-form, so I should underscore that a systematic study of the types of Mishnah-exegesis and the particles and fixed formulas that indicate the presence of one type as against another would produce most interesting results on how the Talmud works. But strict form-analysis would not be advanced by such a study, so far as I can tell.

formal patterns. This permits us to identify recurrent patterning of language, now with close attention, for reasons elaborately set forth, to the substance of that patterning of language. As is my way, I start with one of my favor chapters of the Mishnah, Tosefta, and two Talmuds, which is the opening chapter of Moed Qatan, with its remarkable generative problem: how do the work-restrictions involved in intermediate days of the festival compare with the festival days themselves, on the one side, and with the Seventh Year, on the other.

To explain the procedures implicit in the forms of my translation (which is as literal as I can make it), some of the signals that I consistently give have to be explained. As is my way, I print the Mishnah and Tosefta citations in bold face type, to underscore the character, as commentary, of the discussion of the Talmud. I further distinguish between Hebrew and Aramaic, with the latter given in italics. By reproducing my academic commentary, with its successive indentations to mark turnings in the composition and building blocks of the composite, I am able to show two definitive traits of discourse. The first is how a given composition or composite is put together, the components and their relationships. Second is what is primary and what is subordinate in a given composition or composite. That is important, because, as we have already noted in the Aggadic sector of the canon, the point of formalization of prose will come very early in a composition or composite, and later, secondary materials rarely exhibit the same use of stereotype language. Accordingly, it goes without saying, by this point in the project, I deal with the forms that govern the writing of large-scale compositions and composites, not with free-floating sentences or brief sets of sentences. The rules of writing that formalization of language reveals affected sizable aggregates of composition, not stray sentences here and there.[7] Hence form-analysis both makes possible the academic commentary and also constitutes its principal outcome.

---

[7] Colleagues whose exegetical work rests on the interpretation out of context of singleton sentences and sayings have the task of framing their theory of how the literature holds together and why we have it in the condition in which we now know it. Those colleagues fall into the class of both historians and exegetes. The former utilize sayings or stories as evidence of things really said and done by the participants; they then propose to tell us why one detail is "historical" and another not. But they give us no theory of literary history to account for the formulation, formation, and preservation of the stories over the centuries from the event or saying itself to the closure of the document that records the event or saying. That failure to do their literary-critical and literary-historical homework leaves their historical account simply groundless. Exegetes who treat each sentence as free-standing have also to tell us how they think the sentence circulated in its autonomous existence and further how the same sentence entered into its present setting as part of a composition (or composite), and, finally, how the whole made its way into the setting in which we now have it. I look in vain for theories of the literature, its construction and history, in the writings of both historians and exegetes working with the Rabbinic literature. Arguments from contents, resting on alleged plausibility, count for nothing but fill the journals (in this area of learning, few write books and sustain ambitious arguments of any kind).

Once we have taken a close look at the character of my form-analysis on a particular site, we have to address the way in which I have already translated the results of the form-analysis into useful data. That is through my outline of the Yerushalmi. Since in the shank of this book, my classification of the forms of the Yerushalmi is worked out on the basis of my outline of the tractates of the second, third, and fourth divisions, in the third section of this chapter we then turn to see how the classification of forms that the outline yields compares with the classification of forms produced by our detailed reading of the chapter. In this way I hope to show that my classification as signalled in the outline on the basis of which we work is reliable and comprehensive: very closely tied to the actualities of the text as literally translated.[8]

YERUSHALMI MOED QATAN

CHAPTER ONE

1:1

[A] [80a] **They water an irrigated field on the intermediate days of a festival and in the Seventh Year,**

[B] **whether from a spring that first flows at that time, or from a spring that does not first flow at that time.**

[C] **But they do not water [an irrigated field] with collected rain water, or water from a swape well.**

[D] **And they do not dig channels around vines.**

[I:1 A] *There is no difficulty understanding why* one may utilize a spring that does not first flow at that time. But in the case of a spring that first flows at that time, is this not a considerable amount of work [for the intermediate days of the festival]?

[B] *The law accords with the view of R. Meir. For* **R. Meir has said, "From a spring that first flows on the intermediate days of a festival they irrigate [even] a field that depends upon the rain [and does not need this water]"** [T. Moed 1:1 A].

[C] Said R. Yosé, "In the opinion of all parties, if the spring had a single flow and it divided into two, or if the water was spare and became abundant[, they may make use of such a spring on the festival]. [It does not fall into the category of a spring that first flows at that time.]"

---

[8] It seems to me beyond any reasonable doubt that, with a text as literally translated as this one has been, we can pursue form-analysis in translation as easily as in the original language. I claim that working in Hebrew and Aramaic, rather than in American English, would yield identical results. That claim can be tested by translating the American English back into Mishnaic Hebrew and Talmudic Aramaic; the exceedingly tight fit between the translation and the original will then emerge, so that someone working in the original languages ought to produce results exactly in conformity with those set forth here.

[D] *And so it has been taught:*

[E] "[From] a spring that first flows [on the intermediate days of a festival], they irrigate a field that depends upon the rain," the words of R. Meir.

[F] And sages say, "They irrigate from it only a field that depends upon irrigation, [the spring of which] has gone dry" [T. Moed 1:1 A-B].

[G] *In the view of R. Meir* they may draw water from it for a crop that will not perish [if not watered on the intermediate days of the festival], and they may draw water from it even if it is much work.

[H] *In the view of rabbis,* they may draw water from it only for a crop that otherwise will perish, and that is on condition that it is not much work.

[I] In the case of a crop that will perish, but in which much labor is involved for drawing water, *what is the law in the view of rabbis?*

[J] *Let us derive the answer from the following:*

[K] Any field that progressively dries up — this falls into the category of an irrigated field [which may be watered on the intermediate days of a festival].

[L] If the field stopped deteriorating, this field is in the category of a field that depends upon the rain, subject to the dispute of R. Meir and sages. [So the principal consideration, in answer to I, is the loss of the crop in the field rather than the amount of labor involved.]

[M] How long does the deterioration of the field go on for it to be considered an irrigated field? For two [or] three days prior to the festival.

[N] *Let us consider the following case:*

[O] *A field belonging to associates deteriorated for lack of water for three days before the festival, and the water flow came back on the festival. The case came before R. Huna [for a decision on whether it was permitted to water the field on the festival]. He ruled, "For those fields that had deteriorated, they may draw water. For those fields that had not deteriorated, they may not draw water."*

[P] *R. Jonah and R. Yosé gave a decision in the case of a shaded field, planted in barley, that they might have the crop cut so that it would not sprout and go to ruin.*

The obvious classification of I:1 is Mishnah-commentary, since the composite presupposes knowledge of the Mishnah-paragraph and undertakes an analysis. Can we identify patterned language or stereotype formulations? The answer is clear at underlined language of the opening entry:

There is no difficulty understanding why one may utilize a spring that does not first flow at that time. But in the case of a spring that first flows at that time, is this not a considerable amount of work [for the intermediate days of the festival]?

This way of introducing the problem that the exegete wishes to explore — granted this, but what about that... — then presents itself as a candidate for inclusion in a list of fixed forms, patterning of language to express in one particular way a thought that can come to expression in a great many ways. The stereotype language exhibits the virtue of economy, allowing us to reconstruct for ourselves the stages of thought and recapitulate the steps in the argument that are all together implicit in the language at hand. That is what I meant in referring to the classification of forms by appeal to both extrinsic and intrinsic traits. If we find an ample representation of resort to this language, we have ourselves a form.

The secondary expansion of the composition, that is, the expansion of B raised at C, carries forward the analytical process, but within my theory that the formalization of the document affects the principal, but not the subordinate and secondary, parts, we concern ourselves only with the stereotype language that signals the character of the entire discourse to follow: Mishnah-commentary of a particular type. That everything beyond B forms a secondary articulation of the primary statement is show in my paragraphing, which identifies the points of amplification and extension.[9]

[II:1 A] [...whether from a spring that first flows at that time, or from a spring that does not first flow at that time. But they do not water [an irrigated field] with collected rain water, or water from a swape well.:] It is not difficult to understand why they may not water the irrigated field with water from a swape well [since it is laborious to get it]. But why not use collected rain water [M. 1:1C]?

---

[9] The role of Aramaic in bearing the main beams of discourse is self-evident. It seems to me clear that the language-choice in both Talmuds defines part of the formal repertoire that sustained the work of the authorships, as I have argued in *Language as Taxonomy. The Rules for Using Hebrew and Aramaic in the Babylonian Talmud.* Atlanta, 1990: Scholars Press for South Florida Studies in the History of Judaism, and, with reference to the Yerushalmi, in *Are the Talmuds Interchangeable? Christine Hayes's Blunder.* Atlanta, 1996: Scholars Press for South Florida Studies on the History of Judaism. But for form-analysis, the language-preferences of one form or another will be treated here as both definitive and not requiring further comment, being signalled in the context of the academic commentary. Further work will differentiate forms defined by the use of Aramaic from those defined by the use of Hebrew and will signal yet another stage in form-analysis, but the purpose of the present form-history does not require discussion of that subject.

[B] Said R. Yohanan, "They issued a decree concerning rain water because it is in the category of water of a swape well."

[C] R. Bisna in the name of R. La: "They have referred specifically to the intermediate days of a festival. Lo, with regard to the Sabbatical Year it is permitted [to use such water]."

[D] What is the difference between the Sabbatical Year and the intermediate days of a festival?

[E] In the case of the Sabbatical Year, since it is permitted to work, sages have permitted labor, whether it is burdensome or not burdensome. But as to the intermediate days of a festival, since it is not permitted to work, sages have permitted only labor in connection with what will perish, and that is on condition that it is not burdensome labor.

[F] *There is he who proposes to derive* the difference on the basis of the following consideration:

[G] In the Sabbatical Year, since it goes on for a long time, they have permitted the matter. In the intermediate days of a festival, since it is for only a brief time, they have forbidden [heavy labor].

[H] *As to those last seven days of the Sabbatical Year, is it not reasonable to treat them* as equivalent to the seven days of a festival and to forbid [onerous labor on them] (cf. M. 1:3)?

In this entry, it suffices to underline what I conceive to define the formal element in the formulation of the whole. The form sustains secondary development of a variety of types; in this case we have two solutions to the problem, but they do not constitute a dispute. Then we have a secondary expansion of the second opinion. The rest of the composite develops that same principle.

[II:2 A] *R. Jeremiah asked*, "As to water of rain-drippings [80b] which has not ceased to flow from the hills, into what category does it fall?"

[B] *Let us derive the answer from the following:*

[C] **And what are rain-drippings? So long as the rains fall and the mountains trickle with water, lo, they are like the water of a spring. If they ceased to trickle, lo, they are like the water of pools [T. Miq. 1:13H-L].** [Y. continues:] **If they ceased to trickle, lo, they are like water in pools.** [So long as the flow continues, therefore, the water is not in the category of that in a swape well and may be used on the intermediate days of the festival.]

[D] To what extent [do we maintain that the rain has not ceased]?

[E] Hiyya bar Bun in the name of R. Yohanan, "Until the groves bloom [and are covered with vegetation]"

[F] R. Eleazar b. R. Yosé in the name of R. Tanhum b. R. Hiyya: "Until [the rain drops splash] like duck feet."

[G] *R. Jeremiah asked,* "If the groves bloom and the rain has not ceased, is the flow of water treated as a spring retroactively or henceforward?"

[H] *For what purpose would such a ruling be required?*

[I] In the case of immersing needles and hooks [in such water, in line with the passage of the Tosefta cited above]. If you rule that the water retroactively is in the category of spring water, then the needles and hooks are clean. If you rule that it is so only henceforward, then they have not been made clean.

[II:3 A] *R. Eleazar b. R. Yosé asked,* "As to cascades of water, how do you treat them?

[B] "Are they in the status of swape-well water or not? [No answer is given.]

[C] "As to a pool that was filled with spring water, the flow of which then ceased, what is the law as to watering a field from [such a pool]?"

[D] *Let us derive the answer from the following:* **But they do not water [an irrigated field] with collected rainwater or water from a swape well [M. 1:1 C].**

[E] *Now how shall we interpret that rule?* If we deal with a time in which the rain is falling, then [why should there be such a prohibition]? Is it not like irrigating the Great Sea? *But we must interpret the passage to speak* of the time in which the rain has ceased.

[F] If, then, it is a time that the rain has ceased, then is it not tantamount to a pool that has been filled by a spring, which has stopped flowing? And you rule that they do not irrigate a field from such water. That then indicates that in the case of a pool that had been filled from a spring, which had ceased to flow, they likewise do not water a field from such a pool.

[G] A pool that had been filled by water from a swape well, and into which a spring began to flow — what is the law concerning watering a field from such a pool [on the intermediate days of a festival]? *Let us derive the answer from the following:* An irrigated field into which trickled water from another irrigated field — they irrigate [yet another field] from it.

[H] Said R. Jeremiah, "But that is the case when water is yet trickling into it."

[I] And is it because of the trickling water that it may be irrigated? Is it not on its own account, that it is filled with water? And yet you say that they may irrigate another field with its water.

> [J] *That then indicates that* a field that had been filled by water from a swape well, and a spring began to flow into it — they irrigate with its water.
>
> [K] *So did Samuel teach:* "The water channels and the pool that one filled prior to the festival — one may not irrigate with water from them on the festival [lest the water run out and cause much work]. But if there was a water ditch passing among them, one may irrigate with their water and need not refrain from doing so."

Here again, we have a type of Mishnah-commentary; now the issue is how to classifying interstitial classes of data, secondary matters that the Mishnah does not settle; the patterning recurs in pairs, once more signalled by a key-word, this time, *asked*.... The response concludes the exchange, and everything else is secondary. I do not classify as constitutive of the composite the utilization of the dispute form at II:2D-F. We note, moreover, that the same stereotype language, here, *asked*, bearing in its wake rules as to the proper formulation of a response, recurs in the tertiary exegesis of the amplification of the primary component of the composite. II:3 conforms to the same pattern, but II:3B-C elaborate the question. The secondary amplification and extension, from G onward, is comprised by a series of dialectical exercises; we can stop at any point, prior to the following indentation, without a loss of clarity for what has gone before; the extension is required by the inner logic of argument made up of challenge and response, not the exposition of the initial question and its answer.

[III:1 A] And they [do not] dig channels around trees [M. 1:1D].

[B] **What are the channels dug around a tree?**

[C] **These are the ditches dug around the roots of trees [T. Moed 1:2B-C].**

> [D] *This is in line with that which we have learned there:* **The shaft of a spade is four handbreadths [M. Kel. 29:7].**

The Mishnah-commentary-form — citation and gloss of Mishnah-clause — defines the formulation at hand, which is supplied by the Tosefta and then copied by the Yerushalmi's framer.[10] A catalogue of the Yerushalmi's forms will encompass materials taken by the Yerushalmi's framers from the prior compilation.

---

[10] That seems to me the simplest way of describing the phenomenon before us. One can argue that an independent formulation of the Mishnah with its gloss is preserved by the compilers of the Yerushalmi, on the one side, and by those of the Tosefta, on the other. It comes down to the same thing, and I do not find the present project an appropriate setting for investigating the phenomenon of materials shared by the Tosefta and the Yerushalmi as we now have them. The reason is that the result of such an investigation has no bearing on form-analysis.

The sole secondary expansion is the introduction of a confirming case. But the question must arise, what, exactly are the rules of language-patterning at hand? The answer is, a question selecting a phrase out of the base-text introduced with what are...answered by the formulation, these are. (The Hebrew counterparts are readily identified.) And that way of framing matters — should it recur, and it does! — certainly qualifies as formalized language.

1:2

[A]   R. Eleazar b. Azariah says, "They do not make a new water channel on the intermediate days of a festival or in the Seventh Year "

[B]   And sages say, "They make a new water channel in the Seventh Year,

[C]   "and they repair damaged ones on the intermediate days of a festival."

[D]   They repair damaged waterways in the public domain and dig them out.

[E]   They repair roads, streets, and water pools.

[F]   And they do all public needs, mark off graves, and go forth [to give warning] against Diverse Kinds [= M. Sheq. 1:1].

[I:1   A]   *There we have learned:* [One may pile up all his dung together. R. Meir forbids, unless it is heaped in a special place, three handbreadths above or below ground level. If he had only a little, he may go ahead and pile it on the field.] R. Eleazar b. Azariah forbids, unless it is heaped in a special place three handbreadths above or below ground level [so that it not appear to be manuring the field], or it is laid on rocky ground [M. Sheb. 3:3].

[B]   *One may interpret this matter in two ways:*

[C]   In one, it is a case in which the farmer had a small amount of manure stored at home on the eve of the Seventh Year. He wants to take it out into his field in the Seventh Year. Lo, he may continue adding to this manure once those who carry on ordinary labor have ceased [so that he cannot be thought to be cultivating his field during the Seventh Year].

[D]   R.Eleazar b. Azariah declares it forbidden.

[E]   *What is the reason for the view of R. Eleazar b. Azariah?*

[F]   Perhaps he will not find sufficient manure [to make piles of appropriate size, which indicates that the manure is stored, not used for fertilizing the field], and he will turn out to be merely manuring that spot [on which he is storing the manure]. [Accordingly, Eleazar requires the manure to be stored in such a way that it cannot possibly fertilize the spot on which it is located.]

[G] *The view of R. Eleazar b. Azariah accords with the opinion of R. Yosé.* Just as R. Yosé has said, "Manure is not readily available," so R. Eleazar b. Azariah has said, "Manure is not readily available."

[H] *There is yet a second possible explanation for the cited passage.*

[I] It is a case in which he had a small amount of manure stored at home on the eve of the Seventh Year, and he wants to take it out into his field during the Seventh Year. Lo, he may continue adding to this manure, once those who perform labor in the fields have ceased to do so.

[J] R. Eleazar b. Azariah prohibits.

[K] *What is the reason of R. Eleazar b. Azariah?*

[L] Perhaps he will not find sufficient manure [as above], so that he will turn out to be manuring that spot.

[M] But is that spot not going to be manured in the time prior to the beginning of the Seventh Year?

[N] R. Jeremiah, R. Bun bar Hiyya in the name of R. Ba bar Mamel: "It is for appearance' sake. [He will look as if he is manuring the field] unless he brings out ten baskets of manure at one time."

[O] *Do not rabbis invoke the principle of appearance' sake?*

[P] Said R. Iddi of Hutra, "The farmer's basket and pitchfork testify that he is making a manure heap [and not manuring the field, and that is why sages have no compunction in the matter]."

[Q] *R. Yosé b. R. Bun said, "These traditions here [at Y. Sheb. 3:2] run along the lines of those that we have learned there:*

[R] R. Eleazar b. Azariah says, "They do not make a new water channel on the intermediate days of a festival or in the Seventh Year [M. 1:2A]."

[S] Said R. Jeremiah, "It is because he prepares the sides of the water channel for sowing."

[T] R. Jeremiah, R. Bun bar Hiyya in the name of R. Ba bar Mamel: "It is for appearance' sake."

[U] *They proposed to rule as follows:* He who has said there [at M. M.Q. 1:2] that the reason is because of appearance' sake will maintain here [at Y. Sheb. 3:2] that the reason is for appearance' sake. *He who has said there that* the reason is because he prepares the sides of the channel for sowing — *what do you have to say in the present case [of the prohibition pertaining to the Seventh Year]?*

[V] *You can only reply for the present case,* "He may not find sufficient manure to add to the heap [to bring it to a level at which it is meant for the storage of manure], and the man will turn out to be manuring that place on which he is storing his manure."

[W] *What is the practical difference between these two reasons?*

[X] If one dug out a ditch, making a water channel with built-up sides [formed of twigs and stones].

[Y] *This is what they proposed to say:* "He who holds there that the operative reason is on account of appearance' sake will prohibit doing so here because of appearance' sake. *He who has said there that* the prohibition is because he prepares the sides of the channel for sowing — lo, in this case he does not prepare the sides of the channel for sowing."

[Z] **All concur that if he had available stones, pebbles, mortar, or gypsum, it is permitted [to build the water channel in the Seventh Year]. [No one will suppose the digging is in order to engage in agriculture.]**

The entire composition falls into the category of Mishnah-commentary, specifically, in the class of commenting upon the intersection of two discrete passages of Mishnah-law. This is signified with the formal particle, <u>there we have learned</u>. The reason for the intersection is obvious: Eleazar b. Azariah's rulings on the Seventh Year, which treat the rules governing the intermediate days of a festival as tantamount to those governing the Seventh Year. What is implicit in the introduction of the intersecting passage is that there is a point of conflict that requires attention. But the only point of formalization affecting the composite as a whole is the opening particle. That signals the basic intellectual program of all that follows. The run-on quality of the whole underscores the limitations of formalization of language.

[II:1 A] And they repair damaged ones on the intermediate days of a festival [M. 1:2C].

[B] That is the case for one that is necessary for the festival.

[C] But in the case of one that is not necessary for use on the festival, it is prohibited to do so.

[D] That is the case in the instance of a channel belonging to an individual. But in the case of a channel available for public use, even in the instance of one that is not for use on the festival, it is permitted.

[E] *This is in line with the following: The bathhouse of Sakkota fell down on the intermediate days of the festival, and R. Abbahu permitted them to rebuild it on the festival.*

[F] *Now this was a considerable labor, and they had intended [to postpone the matter, so it would fall down on the festival, and they would rebuild it at that time].*

[G] *Do they not concur with the statement:* **So long as one had not had the intention to do work on it on the intermediate days of the festival [M. 1:1 OF]?**

[H] *They replied, "If it was not rebuilt in this way, it would not be rebuilt again."*

[I] *The water duct of Sepphoris was damaged during the intermediate days of the festival.*

[J] *Associates reasoned that it should be permitted to repair it, on the basis of this statement:* **And they repair damaged ones on the intermediate days of a festival [M. 1:2C].**

[K] Said R. Phineas, "R. Jeremiah prohibited [doing so in a case such as this] solely because of the law of the hammer [at M. M.S. 5:15]."

[L] *The mausoleum belonging to Bar Miqtayya was damaged on the intermediate day of a festival.*

[M] *R. Huna considered ruling that it was permitted to repair it, on the basis of the following:* **And they do all public needs [M. 1:2F].**

[N] *Said to him R. Mana, "And did not Samuel teach that* it is permitted only to fill up cracks [but not to rebuild]?"

The underlined words signal that we shall deal with a comment on the Mishnah and also convey the character of the comment: a discussion of the extent to which the law of the Mishnah pertains. Once more, it is clear, the secondary expansion of the composite follows its own rules, e.g., the dialectic challenge, "do they not concur...," "they replied..", so too the introduction of a test-case for analysis, followed by a sequence of practical rulings. The ordering of types of entries in the encompassing composite clearly follows its own rules, and an analysis of the rules of the framing of such a composite will take account of that ordering. But the rules of constructing the sugya have no bearing upon the work of form-analysis. What we want to know is, when someone sat down to write (or — less likely — make up for oral transmission) a composition of Mishnah-commentary, what patterns governed the way in which he would formulate his ideas, and what aspects of his writing were left to his own preferences. It is clear that the forms for the Talmud's Mishnah-commentary involved a number of subdivisions; it is equally clear that all of the species do form a single genus.

[III:1 A]   **They dig them out [M. 1:2D]**. They dig them out, *in line with that which we have learned there:* He who cleans out a spout removing pebbles that have collected therein.

Here the required form, which is underlined, signals the introduction of a complementary ruling.

[IV:1 A]   **And they do all public needs [M. 1:2F]:**

[B]   What are public needs?

[C]   They judge capital cases, property cases, and cases involving fines [cf. M. M.Q. 3:3].

[D]   And they burn a red cow.

[E]   And they break the neck of a heifer [in the case of a derelict corpse].

[F]   And they pierce the ear of a Hebrew slave [who wishes to remain with his master].

[G]   And they effect redemption for pledges of personal valuation, for things declared *herem,* for things declared consecrated, and for second tithe [through coins to be taken up to Jerusalem].

[H]   And they untie a shoe from the last,

[I]   so long as one does not put it back [T. Moed 2:11/I-O].

Tosefta's formulation certainly falls into the class of Mishnah-commentary, and its formulary language is obvious; equally obvious is the use of the list as integral to the form.

[V:1 A]   **They mark off graves [M. I:2F]:** Were they not marked off in Adar?

[B]   Interpret the passage [to speak] of a case in which there were heavy rains, which washed away the marking.

Once more the language that is underlined defines the character of the writing, and its formulary character is obvious.

[VI:1 A]   **And they go forth to give warning against Diverse Kinds [M. 1:2F]:**

[B]   And was this not done in Adar?

[C]   Interpret the law [to speak] of a case in which it was such a year in which even the sprouts [in Adar] were not discerned.

The same language-pattern recurs.

[VI:2 A]   And how do we know that graves must be marked off?

[B]   R. Berekhiah, R. Jacob, son of the daughter of Jacob, in the name of R. Honaiah of Beth Hauran, R. Yosé said in the name of R. Jacob bar Aha in the name of R. Honaiah of Beth Hauran, R. Hezekiah, R. Uzziel son of R. Honaiah of Beth Hauran: "'The leper . . . shall cry, 'Unclean, unclean' (Lev. 13:45). That is so uncleanness [80c] will cry out with its own mouth and say, 'Keep away.'"

[C]   R. La in the name of R. Samuel bar Nahman: "'And when these pass through the land and any one sees a man's bone, then he shall set up a sign by it' (Ezek. 39:15). It is on the strength of that verse that people mark off places in which bones of a human being are found.

[D]   "['A man's bone'] — on this basis we prove that they mark off a place in which the backbone or skull are found.

[E]   "'And he shall set' — on this basis we learn that they mark off such a place on bedrock.

[F]   "If you say that it is located on a rock, which is turned over, then it may wash away and impart uncleanness to some other place.

[G]   "'By it' — in a place of cleanness. [That is, the marker is not set upright at the corpse-matter, but beside it.]

[H]   "'A sign' — On this basis that they set up a sign."

[I]   If one found a rock that was marked off (even though they do not do things that way [since the uncleanness is marked off at its side, not on top of the bone itself], he who overshadows it is unclean.

[J]   I say, the corpse was buried sitting up, and it is located underneath it.

[K]   If there were two markers, he who overshadows the markers is clean, but he who overshadows the ground between them is unclean.

[L]   But if the ground between them was ploughed up, lo, they are treated as individual markers. He who overshadows the ground between them is clean. He who overshadows the ground round about them is unclean.

[M]   *It has been taught:* They do not place a marker at a spot at which flesh was found, for the flesh may putrefy.

[N]   *R. Yusta bar Shunam asked before R. Mana,* "Will it not retroactively turn out to impart uncleanness to foods kept in a state of cleanness?"

[O] He said to him, "It is better that people be put in disarray by it for a short time and not be put in disarray by it for all time."

The critical formalization occurs in the opening clause, how do we know that...? Presupposed is the rule of the Mishnah, and the intent of the Mishnah-commentary is to identify the scriptural foundations of the Mishnah's rule. Here again, among the many ways in which a discussion of that question may be introduced, one way is utilized time and again, and that allows us to single out the cited language as formal — the presupposition that the Mishnah is at hand, the introduction of a question that explicitly signals that presupposition, the use of stereotype language — and to class the entire composite as a formalized presentation of Mishnah-commentary.

1:3

[A]   **R. Eliezer b. Jacob says, "They lead water from one tree to another,**

[B]   **"on condition that one not water the entire field.**

[C]   **"Seeds that have not been watered before the festival one should not water on the intermediate days of the festival."**

[D]   **And sages permit in this case and in that.**

[I:1 A]   R. Mana stated the following without specifying an authority, while R. Abin in the name of Samuel [said], "[As to **M. Sheb. 2:10: 'They may water the while soil (= ground between trees) (= ground not planted with trees),'** the words of R. Simeon. R. Eliezer b. Jacob prohibits,] the dispute [at M. 1:3A-B] pertains to an average situation [in which the trees are not planted very closely together or very far apart].

[B]   *"For how [otherwise] may be interpret* the dispute about leading water from one tree to another, either in the Seventh Year or in the intermediate days of the festival?

[C]   "If we deal with a field in which the trees are far apart, then in the view of all parties it will be prohibited. If we deal with a field in which the trees are close together, all parties will concur that it will be permitted.

[D]   *"Accordingly, we must deal with* an average situation, in which trees are planted at the rate of ten per *seah's* space of ground. R. Eliezer b. Jacob treats such a case as if the trees were far apart, *and rabbis treat such a case* as if the trees were planted close together."

[E]   Lo, rabbis rule that when they are far apart, it is forbidden to water the entire field. What then is the rule as to channeling the water from tree to tree?

[F] *Let us derive the position of rabbis from the view of R. Eliezer b. Jacob.*

[G] Just as R. Eliezer b. Jacob has said, "When the trees are far apart, it is forbidden to water the field but permitted to lead water from one tree to another" [M. 1:3A], *so rabbis maintain that* when the trees are far apart, it is forbidden to water the field but permitted to lead water from one tree to another.

[H] *But have we not reasoned that* in the case in which the trees are far apart, all parties concur that it is forbidden? And since we deal with white soil [on which there are no trees], is this not a case in which the trees are far apart?

[I] But a better answer is to make a distinction between the rule prevailing in the case of the Sabbatical Year [in which case the work will be permitted], and that prevailing in the case of the intermediate days of the festival [in which case it will be forbidden].

[J] What is the difference between the Sabbatical Year and the intermediate days of a festival?

[K] In the case of the Sabbatical Year, since it is permitted to work, sages have permitted labor, whether it is burdensome or it is not burdensome. But as to the intermediate days of a festival, since it is not permitted to work, sages have permitted only labor in connection with what will perish, and that is on condition that it is not burdensome labor.

[L] *There is he who proposed to derive the difference on the basis of the following consideration:*

[M] In the Sabbatical Year, since it goes on for a long time, they have permitted the matter. In the intermediate days of a festival, since it is for only a brief time, they have forbidden [heavy labor].

[N] As to those last seven days of the Sabbatical Year, is it not reasonable to treat them as equivalent to the seven days of a festival and to forbid [onerous labor on them]?

[O] *There is the following teaching [in support of the distinction proposed above]:* They water white soil in the Seventh Year but not in the intermediate days of the festival.

The form — the underlined words — signals an inquiry into the specific point of difference in a dispute, a recurrent problem in Mishnah-exegesis. What the form further requires is the citation of a pertinent passage of the Mishnah, which is subjected to the distinctive type of analysis at hand.

[II:1   A]   And sages permit in this case and in that [M. 1:3D]:

    [B]   <u>What is the meaning of</u> "in this case and in that"?

    [C]   [Could the meaning be,] whether they were watered before the festival and whether they were not watered before the festival? [Surely not! There will be no loss if there was no watering before the festival. The seeds cannot require water on the festival if the process of growth has not been initiated by a watering prior to the festival.]

    [D]   <u>But here we deal with</u> a tree [in which case it is permitted to water, so as to prevent loss], <u>while there we deal with</u> seeds [in which case there will not be much of a loss if there is no watering, unless the seeds have been constantly irrigated up to now].

The Mishnah-commentary now requires the form, "what is the meaning of...," meaning, the identification of a clause of the Mishnah and the inquiry into its sense.

1:4

    [A]   They hunt moles and mice in a tree-planted field and in a field of grain,

    [B]   [not] in the usual manner,

    [C]   on the intermediate days of a festival and in the Seventh Year.

    [D]   And R. Judah says, "They do so in a tree-planted field in the normal manner,

    [E]   "and in a grain field not in the normal manner."

    [F]   They block up a breach in the intermediate days of a festival.

    [G]   And in the seventh year, one builds it in the normal way.

[I:1   A]   [The unstated question: what is a mole?] "A mole" is a weasel. <u>Even though there is no proof for that proposition, there is at least a hint about it, in the following verse of Scripture:</u>

    [B]   "Let them be like the snail that dissolves into slime, like the untimely birth that never sees the sun" (Ps. 58:8).

    [C] There is no difficulty understanding why it should be permitted in a tree-planted field [M. 1:4A] [since there will be substantial loss], but why should it be permitted in a field of grain?

    [D] It is near a tree-planted field [cf. T. Moed 1:4C- D].

The form here is constituted by an implicit question: what is the meaning of such and so? That then provokes the formulation of an answer, it is thus and so, with the secondary proof-text appended. So the rule of writing that functions is: [1] cite an odd word or phrase and [2] define it, sometimes with [3] a proof-text or pretext, as Scripture permits.

[II:1   A]   In the usual manner [M. 1:4B]:

    [B]   This is hunting with a trap.

    [C]   **Not in the usual manner?**

    [D]   He drives a stake [into the spot] or strikes it with a pick and flattens out the soil underneath [T. Moed 1:4B].

[II:2 A]   *It has been taught:* **They destroy ants' holes on the intermediate days of a festival.**

[B]   How do they execute the destruction?

[C]   Rabban Simeon b. Gamaliel says, "One takes dirt from one hole and puts it into another, and they strangle one another" [T. Moed 1:5].

   [D] And that is so when there is a channel of water flowing between them.

Here at II:1 is Mishnah-commentary form in its simplest statement: a citation of a clause of the Mishnah followed by a few words of explanation. The form requires the selection and arrangement of words from appropriate sources, first, the Mishnah, then, any other source, whether redacted or otherwise. The citation of the Tosefta at II:2 complements the Mishnah's rule, but apart from the citation-formula, *it has been taught,* I do not see any formalization of language.

[III:1 A]   **They block up a breach in the intermediate days of a festival [M. 1:4F]:** Stone on stone, pebble on pebble.

   Here is another example of standard Mishnah-commentary.

[IV:1 A]   **And in the seventh year one builds it in the normal way [M. 1:4G]:** stone on pebble and pebble on stone.

[B]   [Where it is permitted to build up a wall in the normal way in the Seventh Year,] that is the case of a breach [in a wall] which does not support the ground [behind it from seeping through]. But in the case of a breach [in a wall] which does keep the earth behind it from falling through, it is forbidden to repair such a breach in the Seventh Year. [It will appear that the repair is for maintaining the soil, and that may not be done in the Sabbatical Year.]

[C]   *And so too has it been taught:* In the case of any breach in which the wall holds up the dirt behind it from coming through, it is forbidden to repair such a breach in the Seventh Year. And in the case of one that does not hold up the dirt from falling through, it is permitted to repair such a breach in the Seventh Year.

   [D] [It is forbidden to repair such a breach] if it does not endanger the public. But if it endangers the public, even though it holds back dirt from coming through, it is permitted to repair such a breach in the Seventh Year.

      [E] That is in line with the following:

      [F] [In the case of a wall in a courtyard,] if one's wall was crumbling, one may tear it down and rebuild it.

      [G] But why should he not simply tear it down and not rebuild it [until after the festival]?

[H] R. Hananiah in the name of R. Yohanan: "They permitted completing the work because of the need to begin it. For if you say to him that he may not rebuild it, he will not even tear it down, and it will turn out that people will be at risk."

The formalized unit repeats the form of III:1. I do not see how IV:1.B and following adheres to a well-defined form. The secondary exposition also is governed by rules of presentation — this type of item before that — but I do not see any formalized language.

1:5

[A] R. Meir says, "They examine negas [the skin ailments described at Lev. 13-14] [to begin with] to provide a lenient ruling, but not to provide a strict ruling."

[B] And sages say, "Neither to provide a lenient ruling nor to provide a strict ruling "

[C] And further did R. Meir say, "A man may go out and gather the bones of his father and his mother,

[D] "because it is a time of rejoicing for him."

[E] R. Yosé says, "It is a time of mourning for him."

[F] A person may not call for mourning for his deceased,

[G] or make a lamentation for him thirty days before a festival.

[I:1 A] *There we have learned:* A bright spot the size of a split bean —

[B] and it spread to the extent of a split bean —

[C] and there appeared in the spreading quick flesh or white hair —

[D] but the primary sign disappeared —

[E] R. Aqiba declares unclean.

[F] And sages say, "Let it be inspected anew" [M. Neg. 4:10]. [A bright spot of requisite size has spread to the extent of a split bean. The spreading then develops quick flesh or white hair. But the primary sign has disappeared. Aqiba declares the man unclean because he regards the two signs as joined together. The spreading takes the place of the original sign. We have, therefore, sufficient evidence of uncleanness. The sages' position is that we have a new sign, for the first spot has disappeared.]

[G] Lo, R. Aqiba declares [the man] unclean and certifies his uncleanness, while rabbis says, "Let it be inspected anew"; they too [are prepared to] certify [that he is unclean, if the inspection warrants it when the inspection takes place a week later].

[H] *What is the difference, then, between the two positions just now outlined?*

[I] R. Yohanan said, "[An inspection] on the eve of a festival is what is at issue between them.

[J] "R. Aqiba says, 'This [situation, in which the primary sign has disappeared] is tantamount to the original diseased spot, and you are not required to examine him, either to make a lenient ruling or to make a stringent ruling' [= sages, M. 1:5B].

[K] "Sages say that this [spot] is another, new one, and you thereby declare him exempt from uncleanness on the count of the original spot.

[L] "And as to the position not to provide a strict ruling, you are not obligated to examine the second spot either to present a lenient or to give a strict ruling. [The sage does not examine this second spot, prior to the festival, so as to avoid having to give a strict ruling, which would ruin the festival for the man. Hence the matter is postponed (= M. 1:5A).]"

[M] [We now line up the authorities of M. 1:5 against those of M. Neg. 4:10. Sages before us want neither a strict nor a lenient ruling, just as Aqiba has said, while Meir permits a lenient, but not a strict, ruling, in line with sages of M. Neg. 4:10. We must therefore determine the decided law, by finding out the true position of sages.] *R. Yosé in the name of R. Aha: "Does the view of the individual here [at M. Neg. 4:10] accord with the anonymous [therefore authoritative] position there [at M. 1:5], and does the opinion of a named individual here accord with the anonymous position here?* For the individual opinion here accords with the anonymous view there, in that R. Aqiba says, 'It is the original sign, and one is not obligated to make a ruling on it, either to provide a lenient ruling or to provide a strict ruling.' *And the individual opinion there accords with the anonymous opinion here, in that rabbis say,* 'It is a new spot, and you may declare him exempt from the contaminating effects of the original sign.' *And we have here:* **R. Meir says, 'They examine negas to begin with to provide a lenient ruling [= "It is a new spot"] but not to provide a strict ruling'"** [M. 1:5A].

[N] [At issue is a different matter, not Aha's at all.] *R. Yosé b. R. Bun in the name of R. Aha, "Both the individual here and the rabbis here concur [at M. Neg. 4:10] with rabbis there that* one gives neither a lenient ruling nor a strict one. [One does not inspect *negas* on the intermediate days of a festival under any circumstances.] There we deal with a case in which the primary sign has disappeared, while here we deal with a case in which the signs of uncleanness have disappeared while primary sign remains. [In this latter case all parties concur that no inspection is carried out.]"

[I:2   A]   Said Rabbi, "The opinion of R. Meir [M. 1:5A] makes more sense in the case of one who is [merely] shut up for inspection [the second time], and the opinion of R. Yosé [= sages, M. 1:5B] makes more sense to me in the case of one certified [as unclean]" [T. Hag. 1:8]. [Rabbi sees no disadvantage for the one who may, after all, be declared clean. But there is nothing to warrant pronouncing the decision for the one who is subject to certification. Even if he is declared clean, he has to count seven days and cannot have intercourse in that period.]

[I:3   A]   [Reverting to the problem of unit I:1] R. Zeira said, "They dispute a case involving the intermediate days of a festival [in the case of one who is subject to a second inspection]. R. Aqiba says, 'It is the original sign, [and if the man is declared clean] he may not enter the Temple courtyard as wholly clean. Sages say it is a new sign, and he may enter the Temple courtyard [since we must wait a week to see whether or not he is clean]."

[B]   Lo, R. Aqiba declares the man unclean and certifies him so, and rabbis say "Let it be inspected as at the outset," and they too certify him.

[C]   What then is at issue between [Yohanan and Zeira]??

[D]   Samuel said, "[As to entering the courtyard, all parties concur that he is unclean and may not do so. At issue] is blossoming forth. [If the man turns completely white, and has been certified unclean, he then is regarded.as clean. If he had been deemed clean, he then is regarded as unclean; see M. Meg. 8:1.] R. Aqiba says, 'It is the original mark. Hence we deal with a case in which the blossoming forth is from an unclean person, so he is clean.' Sages say, 'It is a new mark of uncleanness. Hence it is a blossoming forth from a clean person, and he is unclean.'"

[E]   And there are those who say in Samuel's name: "A case of blossoming forth and a dripping boil is at issue between them [see M. Meg. 10:5]. R. Aqiba says, 'It is the original mark. Hence we deal with a case in which the blossoming forth is from an unclean person, so he is clean.' Sages say, 'It is a new mark of uncleanness. Hence it is a blossoming forth from a clean person, and he is unclean.'"

[F] *Since it is a new mark of uncleanness, he is unclean. Lo, if it had not been so, he would have been clean. Then this accords with the view of R. Simeon b. Laqish.*

[G] *For there was the following dispute:* If it blossomed forth in the case of one who had a dripping boil,

[H] R. Yohanan said, "He is clean [having been unclean]."

[I] R. Simeon b. Laqish said, "He is unclean [having been clean], since the boil is not a mark of uncleanness (= F)]."

The Mishnah-commentary here bears an explicit signal that we are going to compare our Mishnah-passage with another pertinent one, in the language, There we have learned. The secondary development, noted in indentation follows its own rules of exposition, beginning with the obvious question, what is the difference? While conventions of exposition clearly dictate the order and type of issues to be raised, the formalization of language is limited to the introductory component of the composition. It is not necessary, in the framework of form-analysis, to spell out the obvious rules for the organization and presentation of secondary and subordinate discourse.

[II:1 A] **And further did R. Meir say, "A man may go out and gather the bones of his father and his mother, because it is a time of rejoicing for him" [M. I:5C-D].**

[B] At first they would collect the bones and bury them in mounds. When the flesh Ωhad putrefied, they would collect the bones and bury them in cedar chests.

[C] On that day the mourner would engage in the rite of mourning. The next day he would rejoice, saying [80d] that his ancestors would free him from the rigors of judgment.

This composition simply glosses the Mishnah's statement whether further information. So far as rules of writing govern, the author has to follow the syntax and diction of the Mishnah.

[II:2 A] *It was taught:* He who moves a bier from place to place is not subject to [the rite of mourning required when] one gathers bones [of an ancestor for secondary burial]. [Merely moving the bier is not part of the reburial process. So new fresh rites of mourning are not required, e.g., for that day only.]

[B] *Said R. Aha, "That statement which you have laid down* applies to a bier made of marble. But as to one made of wood [in which case there will have been putrefaction of the bier itself], the person is subject to [carry out rites of mourning involved when] one gathers bones [of an ancestor for secondary burial]."

[C]   Said R. Yosé, "<u>Even in the case of</u> a bier made of wood, [there is no consideration of the rite of mourning required when one] gathers bones [of an ancestor for secondary burial]."

[D]   What constitutes the act of gathering bones [for secondary burial]?

[E]   They carry the skeleton, wrapped in sheets, from one place to another.

[F]   *And so it has been taught:* Gathering up the bones means that one collects the bones once the flesh has putrefied.

[G]   Haggai in the name of R. Zeira: "Secondary collection and burial of the bones of an ancestor do involve the rites of mourning applicable on the day on which one hears of the death."

[H]   *It was taught:* Merely hearing about the secondary collection and burial of the bones of an ancestor do not impose [upon a relative] the obligation of mourning on that day.

[I]   Said R. Haggai, "That is so if one heard a day later. But if one heard on the same day that the bones were collected, then merely hearing about the collection of the bones of an ancestor does impose the obligation to carry out the rites of mourning on that day."

[J]   Is there a lower limit to the number of bones? *Nichomachi taught before R. Zeira,* "There is no lower limit [to the number of bones that must be collected in a case of] the gathering of bones [for secondary burial, so that even if only a few bones have been collected, the rites of mourning are invoked]."

[K]   *That is in line with the following:* R. Mani instructed R. Hillel of Kapra to make a tear in his garments and to go into mourning, in line with the view of R. Aha [above, B],

[L]   but not to undergo cultic uncleanness [if he was a priest, that is, he is not to become unclean to collect his father's bones], in accord with the view of R. Yosé [above, C].

[M]   *It was taught:* **As to a case of gathering of the bones, one does not say in that connection lamentations** of obsequies, nor does one state the blessing due to mourners, nor does one express the consolation due to mourners.

[N] What is the blessing due to mourners?

[O] It is that said in the synagogue.

[P] What is the consolation due to mourners?

[Q] It is that which is said when passing in line before the mourners.

[R] *It was taught:* A mourner says something to them.

[S] What does one say?

[T] Rabbis of Caesarea say, "One expresses praises [of the deceased]."

II:2.A glosses the Mishnah by introducing a comment that extends its rule. That in turn bears its own gloss at B-C, a dispute. Then we have a clarification of the implicit rite of secondary burial, plus a topical composite, Gff. The pattern, start to finish, involves citation of a rule in the model of the Mishnah's and then gloss of that rule. But for the purpose of classifying the composite, we concentrate on the opening formulation, which relies simply on *It was taught,* with the expectation that we shall select the appropriate passage of the Mishnah to which the cited Tannaite ruling pertains. Everything else proceeds from there.

[III:1 A] **A person may not call for mourning for his deceased [M. 1:5F]:**

[B] What is a call for mourning for the deceased?

[C] He speaks of him among the deceased [in general, but not speaking of him in particular].

The form of the Mishnah-commentary is familiar: citation of a clause of the Mishnah, followed by a few words of explanation.

[IV:1 A] **Nor make a lamentation for him [M. 1:5G]: What is a lamentation?**

[B]   When one speaks of the deceased in particular [and not merely mentions his name among the deceased in general].

[C]   *That which you have said* applies to a death some time ago, but in the case of a recent death, it is permitted.

    [D] What is the definition of one that is recent, and one that is some time ago?

    [E] A recent death is one that has taken place in the past thirty days. One that has taken place some time ago is one prior to the span of thirty days [cf. M. 1:5G].

    [F] *It has been taught:* A woman should not arouse herself to mourning on an intermediate day of the festival.

    [G] R. Nahman in the name of R. Mana said, "This 'arousing of oneself' is in line with that which you say in the following verse of Scripture: 'Let those curse it who curse the day, who are skilled to rouse up Leviathan'" (Job 3:8).

        [H] *It has been taught:* A man should not marry a wife who has children, even if they are already in the grave.

        [I] Said R. Yosé, "That is because of an actual case."

    The form presupposes the cited Mishnah-clause and then adds a few words of clarification, in this case, explaining how the rule applies. There is, then, secondary gloss of the gloss, and so on to the end.

1:6

[A]   They do not hew out a tomb-niche or tombs on the intermediate days of a festival.

[B]   But they refashion tomb-niches on the intermediate days of a festival.

[C]   They dig a grave on the intermediate days of a festival,

[D]   and make a coffin,

[E]   while the corpse is in the same courtyard.

[F]   R. Judah prohibits, unless there were boards [already sawn and made ready in advance].

[I:1 A] What is the meaning of refashioning a grave [M. 1:6B]?

    [B] R. Yosé bar Nehorai said, "One plasters it with plaster."

    [C] R. Hisda said, "If it was too long, one may shorten it."

    [D] R. Joshua b. Levi said, "One may lengthen it on one side and broaden it on the other."

        [E] *R. Hiyya taught [in T.'s version]:* **What is the meaning of "refashioning tomb-niches" [M. 1:6B].**

        [F] One makes it broader or longer.

        [G] This applies to a grave and a burial niche [M. 1:6C] [T. Moed 1:9].

Here the form is that of a Mishnah-comment, joined with a dispute; the components of the dispute are not carefully matched or balanced.

[II:1 A]   **One may dig a grave on the intermediate days of a festival [M. 1:6C]:**

[B]   This is breaking through the ground in any measure at all.

[C] A place for sitting is called such a resting place.

The gloss follows the familiar form: implicit reference to the Mishnah, then a gloss thereof.

[III:1 A]   **And make a coffin while the corpse is in the same courtyard [M. 1:6D-E]:**

[B]   That which you have said applies to a deceased person who was not well known. But in the case of a deceased person who was well known, one may make a coffin even in the marketplace.

[C] *When R. Hananiah, associate of the rabbis, died, they made him a coffin in the marketplace.*

[D] All parties concur that one should not cut down cedars for that purpose and, *along these same lines,* that one should not hew out stones.

[E] If they were already hewn out, *we come to the dispute of R. Judah and rabbis [at M. 1:6F].*

The Mishnah-comment now employs a particle that conveys the problem at hand: the application of the law to case A but not to case B; the program then requires an illustration (C), and a further gloss, D-E.

1:7

[A]   **They do not take wives on the intermediate days of a festival,**

[B]   **whether virgins or widows.**

[C]   **Nor do they enter into levirate marriage,**

[D]   **for it is an occasion of rejoicing.**

[E]   **But one may remarry his divorced wife.**

[F]   **And a woman may prepare her wedding adornments on the intermediate days of a festival.**

[G]   **R. Judah says, "She could not use lime, since this makes her ugly."**

[I:1 A]   [With reference to M. 1:7A-D:] Simeon bar Abba in the name of R. Yohanan, "It is because [people will hold up weddings until the festival, and so have one meal for the two events, the festival and the wedding]. [Consequently, they will postpone marriages and so] nullify the act of procreation [for the interval]."

[B] *They asked before R. Yosé,* "As to a slave, what is the law about his marrying a woman on the festival['s intermediate days]?"

[C] *He said to him, "Let us derive the answer from the following:* **Shall he refrain? But was not the world made only for**

procreation [M. Git. 4:5E-F]? [Consequently, he too must not postpone his wedding until the intermediate days of a festival.]"

[D] And Simeon bar Abba said in the name of R. Yohanan, "[Anyone who is subject to] the religious duty of procreation [is prohibited from marrying a wife on the intermediate days of a festival]."

[E] That is to say that a slave is subject to the religious duty of procreation, and whoever is subject to the religious duty of procreation is prohibited from marrying on the intermediate days of a festival.

[F] R. Ila, R. Eleazar in the name of R. Hananiah: "It is because people must not confuse one cause of rejoicing with some other."

[G] R. La derived that lesson from the following verse of Scripture: "[And on the eighth day they held a solemn assembly;] for they had kept the dedication of the altar seven days and the feast seven days" (2 Chron. 7:9).

[H] R. Jacob bar Aha derived the rule from the following: "Complete the week of this one, and we will give you the other also in return for serving me another seven years" (Gen. 29:27).

[I] R. Abbahu in the name of R. Eleazar: "The prohibition is on account of the excessive work [involved in preparing for the wedding]."

[J] *It has been taught:* But one may decide to get married on the eve of the festival.

[K] *That lenient ruling, moreover, does not stand at variance with the view of R. Eleazar, R. Yohanan, or even R. Haninah.*

[L] *Said R. Ba, "When the bride enters [the marriage canopy], the work is gone and done."*

The Mishnah-form here calls upon an implicit citation of the Mishnah-clause and then a stated reason. My indentation underscores that a dispute is contained in A, F, I, and, as before, the dispute is subordinated to the requirement of Mishnah-commentary. I see no formalization of language, but there is a clear program of citation and gloss that frames the expression of the comment. The secondary question is introduced for its own reason; it is part of a systematic glossing of the clauses of the dispute, as the indentation clearly indicates.

[II:1 A]   But one may remarry his divorced wife [M. 1:7E]:

[B]   It is because it is no particular joy for him.

[C] *That which you have said* applies to remarrying a woman whom one has divorced out of a fully consummated marriage. But as to remarrying one whom he has divorced at the stage of betrothal, that is forbidden.

The gloss, as underlined, preserves the form established at I:1.

[III:1 A] **And a woman may prepare her wedding adornments on the intermediate days of a festival [M. 1:7F]:**

[B] What are these adornments? Fixing her hair, parting her hair, cutting her hair and fingernails, and rubbing her face with a clay utensil [to heighten her skin color].

[C] *Said R. Yudan, father of R. Mattenaiah, "The Tannaite teaching just now cited speaks in euphemisms."*

We have a particle introducing the exegetical problem, and the list completes the gloss.

[IV:1 A] **R. Judah says, "She should not use lime, since this makes her ugly" [M. 1:7G],** [and this prohibition applies on the festival itself even though later on the woman will be beautified,] for it is disfiguring. [So, on the occasion of the festival we do not take account of later advantage.]

[B] *Two Amoraic authorities, R. Haninah and R. Mana — one said,* "Concerning lime that the woman removes on the festival itself do the sages dispute, but concerning lime that she removes after the festival [there is no dispute], for it is forbidden [on the festival to make use of lime which imparts its benefit only afterward]."

[C] *The other said,* "Concerning lime that the woman removes after the festival itself do the sages dispute, but concerning lime that she removes on the festival [there is no dispute], for it is permitted."

[D] *Now we do not know which one said this, and which one said that.*

[E] *Now [let us infer the position of each] from that which R. Haninah, R. Yosé in the name of R. Yohanan said, "R. Judah is consistent with his established position, as* R. Judah has said in that case, 'Disfiguring for a moment is disfiguring [and is prohibited], *so did he say in the present case that* what is painful for a moment is painful [at the moment, even though he will be happy about it later, thus M. A.Z. 1:1 E-F]."

[F] [In the light of R. Haninah's observation about the position of R. Judah, then, we may infer] that it is he who said, "Concerning lime that the woman removes on the festival itself do the sages dispute, but concerning lime that she removes after the festival [there is no dispute], for it is forbidden." [For Judah will prohibit the lime removed during the festival, since it is disfiguring at *that* time, and this is without regard to the fact that later on — even on the festival itself — the woman will be glad she had put the lime on her skin.]

The gloss, supplying a reason for the ruling, recapitulates the simple Mishnah-commentary form — citation, gloss. The secondary development then glosses the gloss, and so on on down.

1:8

[A]   An unskilled person sews in the usual way.

[B]   But an expert craftsman sews with irregular stitches.

[C]   They weave the ropes for beds.

[D]   R. Yosé says, "They [only] tighten them."

[I:1 A]   The House of Yannai said, "Sewing in the normal way means drawing a needleful [of stitches in one sweep]. Sewing with irregular stitches means doing it one by one."

[B]   R. Yohanan said, "Doing so in the usual way means doing it one by one. Irregular stitching means skipping."

[C]   *The following Tannaite teaching supports the view of R. Yohanan:* Leather workers on the intermediate days of a festival sew with irregular stitches.

[D]   *If you say that* they do so one at a time, that is the normal procedure of their craft.

[E]   *But we must interpret the matter to mean that* they skip a stitch.

The dispute-form falls here within the category of Mishnah-commentary, the Mishnah-statement being presupposed.

[I:2 A]   What is the definition of an unskilled person, and what is the definition of an expert craftsman?

[B]   Said R. Yosé b. Haninah, "Any who [cannot] sew an even hem [on his garment] — such a one is unskilled."

[C]   *Said R. Yosé, "The Mishnah speaks of a case of* one who sews pockets [of a garment]. [This is not work for an expert.]"

Here we have commentary-form, the Mishnah-language being cited and glossed. The formal particle is underlined.

[II:1 A]   They weave the ropes for beds [M. 1:8C]:

[B]   *R. Yosé said, "There is a dispute on this matter between Hezekiah and R. Yohanan.*

[C]   *"Hezekiah said, 'Weaving means one weaves warp and woof. Tightening means either the warp or the woof.'*

[D]   *"R. Yohanan said, 'Weaving means either the warp or the woof. Tightening means that it was loose and one tightens it.'"*

[E]   Said R. Hiyya bar Ba, "All concur with regard to weaving that it involves warp and woof. Concerning what do they differ? It is with regard to tightening the rope bed.

[F]   "Hezekiah said, 'It is either warp or woof.'

[G]   "R. Yohanan said, 'If it was loose, one tightens it.'"

[H] R. Yosé instructed Samuel bar Haninah, "Weaving is warp and woof."

[I] *But we do not know whether he referred to the statement of Hezekiah or to that of R. Hiyya bar Ba in the name of all parties.*

[J] *Said R. Bun bar Hiyya before R. Zeira, "The Mishnah has indicated that* weaving involves warp and woof.

[K] *"For we have learned there:* **As to the rope, at what point is it deemed connected to the bed? It is when one will have woven three stitches with it [M. Kel. 19:1].**

[L] *Can you then say* we deal with the warp and not the woof, or the woof and not the warp? [Surely not!] What would be the result of making the woof and weaving? [Null. Hence we must refer to both warp and woof.]

The dispute-form is adopted for the purpose of Mishnah-commentary. I have underlined the principal elements of the dispute and then subordinated the secondary (but necessary) exposition. The secondary amplification, H-I, is integral to the whole — a beautifully worked out composition, start to finish.

1:9

[A] **They set up an oven or double stove or a hand-mill on the intermediate days of a festival.**

[B] **R. Judah says, "They do not rough the millstones for the first time."**

[I:1 A] *R. Halapta bar Saul taught,* "But [M. 1:9A's] rule is on the stipulation that one not set up an oven [81a] to begin with."

[B] *It has been taught:* As to a new oven or double stove, they do not grease them, rub them with a rag, or seal them with cold water so that they will be sealed. But if it is to pour out a pot on them, it is permitted.

[C] *And so has it been taught:* A new oven or double stove — lo, they are in the category of all other utensils that are carried about in a courtyard.

[D] R. Yudan b. R. Ishmael gave instructions that if it is absolutely necessary, it is permitted to bring a new oven from the craftsman's workshop to set a spit for a pot on the oven to begin with on the festival day [if the householder had no other way of cooking].

The Mishnah-commentary form is followed, with the expansion of the composition following a logical and conventional program: further data, confirmation thereof, then a practical ruling.

1:10

[A]   They make a parapet for a roof or a porch in an unskilled manner,

[B]   but not in the manner of a skilled craftsman.

[C]   They plaster cracks and smooth them down with a roller, by hand, or by foot, but not with a trowel.

[D]   A hinge, socket, roof beam, lock, or key [any of] which broke

[E]   do they repair on the intermediate days of the festival,

[F]   so long as one had not had the intention to do work on it on the intermediate days of the festival.

[G]   And all pickled foods that a man can eat during the intermediate days of a festival he also may pickle.

[I:1 A]   A parapet for a roof may be made up to three handbreadths high, and one for a porch [more commonly used] may be built up to ten handbreadths high on the festival.

Here we have the Mishnah implicitly cited plus a gloss, Mishnah-commentary form pure and simple.

[II:1 A]   **They plaster cracks [M. 1:10C]:** *R. Hiyya taught:* He who plasters does so by foot, and he who smooths down does so by hand.

[B]   *The Mishnah speaks of a small roller, and R. Hiyya's teaching speaks of a large roller.*

Once more, the simple requirement of the form is met.

[III:1 A]   **A hinge, socket, roof beam, lock, or key, which broke, do they repair on the intermediate days of the festival, so long as one had not had the intention to do the work on it on the intermediate days of the festival [postponing the work from some earlier time] [M. 1:10D-F].**

[B]   *This is in line with the following: The trundle of a ladder belonging to R. Mana broke. He asked R. Jonah, his father, who permitted him to repair it.*

[C]   *And even so, he said to him, "Go see how a certain elder behaves, and rely upon his decision." He went out and found R. Bun bar Kahana, and asked him, and he permitted him to repair lt.*

The Mishnah is cited and ther glossed. But the gloss consists of a free-standing story, which is introduced with the underlined particle; that then serves as both joining language and indication of the character of the Mishnah-comment.

[IV:1 A]   **And all pickled foods that a man can eat during the intermediate days of a festival he also may pickle [M. 1:10G].**

[B]   Lo, as to pickled foods that he cannot eat on the festival, he may not [pickle] them.

[C]   *Said R. Ba, "That which you have said* applies to things that are not perishable. But as to things that are perishable, it is permitted [to pickle them]."

[D] *It has been taught:* One should not go out and collect herbs and sell them in the market, for it is not usual to eat them on the festival.

[E] Said R. Hoshaiah, "If you say [otherwise], you will turn out to permit one's carrying out his ordinary craft on the festival."

[F] *Did not R. Ba say, "That which you have said* applies to things that are not perishable. But as to things that are perishable, it is permitted to pickle them"?

[G] *The Tannaite [passage above, D,]* speaks of a case in which one collected them on the festival, while what R. Ba has said applies to a case in which one has collected them on the eve of the festival.

[IV:2 A]   R. Hoshaiah had wheat. Nonetheless on the intermediate days of the festival he ground wheat.

[B]   R. Zeira said to R. Jonah, "Go, buy us black wheat for grinding [on the festival]."

[C]   He said to him, "We have a portion adequate for the festival."

[D]   And he was angry with him [since that is no consideration].

At IV:1 the Mishnah is cited and then glossed, the case covered by the Mishnah being complemented by the one that is omitted. A little analytical composition then extends the discussion, C, itself expanded by D-G. The story, IV:2, makes the point that even though one has food of a given category, on the intermediate days of the festival he may prepare more food of the same category, and that principle is articulated. That story illustrates the principle that underlies the Mishnah's case-ruling, but it has to be classified, in form, as a free-standing story (used, to be sure, for Mishnah-commentary, but in no way adhering to the forms of Mishnah-commentary).

III. FROM OUTLINE TO FORM-ANALYSIS

Now how are we to proceed, short of reproducing the entire preliminary translation of the Yerushalmi and commenting on the formal traits of each of the compositions and composites that comprise those tractates? The answer, obviously, is to make use of the outline that I have already prepared, since the outline is constructed out of the key words of each of the compositions and reproduces the result of the academic commentary. Hence on the basis of the outline we should find it possible to classify the formal traits of the principal components of the Talmud. To test that surmise, we now review the outline of the same chapter of the Yerushalmi that we have just now analyzed and ask, on the basis of the outline should we have attained the same result as to form-analysis that our reading of the entire unit of discourse has produced? What is required is a cross-check, to make certain that the outline serves adequately the purpose for which we now propose to utilize it. At each point, then, I gloss the outline-entry with a cross-reference to the foregoing form-analysis.

I. Yerushalmi Moed Qatan 1:1

[A] They water an irrigated field on the intermediate days of a festival
and in the Seventh Year

1. I:1: There is no difficulty understanding why one may utilize a
    spring that does not first flow at that time. But in the case of a
    spring that first flows at that time, is this not a considerable
    amount of work [for the intermediate days of the festival]? The
    law accords with the view of R. Meir. For R. Meir has said,
    "From a spring that first flows on the intermediate days of a
    festival they irrigate [even] a field that depends upon the rain
    [and does not need this water]" [T. Moed 1:1 A].

The outline clearly signals that the composition falls into the category of
Mishnah-commentary and tells us the classification of Mishnah-commentary at
hand.

[B] whether from a spring that first flows at that time, or from a
spring that does not first flow at that time. But they do not
water [an irrigated field] with collected rain water, or water
from a swape well.

1. II:1: It is not difficult to understand why they may not water the
    irrigated field with water from a swape well [since it is laborious
    to get it]. But why not use collected rain water [M. 1:1C]? Said
    R. Yohanan, "They issued a decree concerning rain water because
    it is in the category of water of a swape well."
2. II:2: R. Jeremiah asked, "As to water of rain-drippings which
    has not ceased to flow from the hills, into what category does it
    fall?"
3. II:3: Eleazar b. R. Yosé asked, "As to cascades of water, how do
    you treat them? "Are they in the status of swape-well water or
    not? [No answer is given.] "As to a pool that was filled with
    spring water, the flow of which then ceased, what is the law as
    to watering a field from [such a pool]?" Let us derive the answer
    from the following: But they do not water [an irrigated field]
    with collected rainwater or water from a swape well [M. 1:1 C].
    Now how shall we interpret that rule? If we deal with a time in
    which the rain is falling, then [why should there be such a
    prohibition]? Is it not like irrigating the Great Sea? But we must
    interpret the passage to speak of the time in which the rain has
    ceased. If, then, it is a time that the rain has ceased, then is it not
    tantamount to a pool that has been filled by a spring, which has
    stopped flowing? And you rule that they do not irrigate a field
    from such water. That then indicates that in the case of a pool
    that had been filled from a spring, which had ceased to flow,
    they likewise do not water a field from such a pool.

The classification of II:1 is properly signaled here. The slight variation in my translation leaves no confusion on the matter. The outline certainly shows the presence of the Mishnah-commentary, indicated by the use of *asked* in the context of the cited clause of the Mishnah. In our examination of the passage we noted that the same form can serve other than the purpose of Mishnah-commentary. But if we classify II:2, 3 as Mishnah-commentary, we are on very firm ground, and if we further allege that they conform to a particular formal pattern of stating a comment on the Mishnah, the evidence before us suffices to sustain that allegation.

[C] AND THEY DO NOT DIG CHANNELS AROUND VINES.

1. III:1: And they dig channels around trees [M. 1:1 D]. What are the channels dug around a tree? These are the ditches dug around the roots of trees [T. Moed 1:2B-C].

That we have a statement in the form of a Mishnah-commentary is certainly indicated by this citation.

II. YERUSHALMI MOED QATAN 1:2

[A] R. ELEAZAR B. AZARIAH SAYS, "THEY DO NOT MAKE A NEW WATER CHANNEL ON THE INTERMEDIATE DAYS OF A FESTIVAL OR IN THE SEVENTH YEAR " AND SAGES SAY, "THEY MAKE A NEW WATER CHANNEL IN THE SEVENTH YEAR, "AND THEY REPAIR DAMAGED ONES ON THE INTERMEDIATE DAYS OF A FESTIVAL."

1. I:1: There we have learned: [One may pile up all his dung together. R. Meir forbids, unless it is heaped in a special place, three handbreadths above or below ground level. If he had only a little, he may go ahead and pile it on the field.] R. Eleazar b. Azariah forbids, unless it is heaped in a special place three handbreadths above or below ground level [so that it not appear to be manuring the field], or it is laid on rocky ground [M. Sheb. 3:3]. One may interpret this matter in two ways: In one, it is a case in which the farmer had a small amount of manure stored at home on the eve of the Seventh Year. He wants to take it out into his field in the Seventh Year. Lo, he may continue adding to this manure once those who carry on ordinary labor have ceased [so that he cannot be thought to be cultivating his field during the Seventh Year]. R.Eleazar b. Azariah declares it forbidden. What is the reason for the view of R. Eleazar b. Azariah? Perhaps he will not find sufficient manure [to make piles of appropriate size, which indicates that the manure is stored, not used for fertilizing the field], and he will turn out to be merely manuring that spot [on which he is storing the manure]. [Accordingly, Eleazar requires the manure to be stored in such a way that it cannot possibly fertilize the spot on which it is located.]

The particle at the outset conveys the information that allows us to make sense of all that follows and to classify the entire composite as an exercise in Mishnah-commentary, in this case, the comparison and contrast of teachings of the same authority in two or more Mishnah-passages.

[B] THEY REPAIR DAMAGED WATERWAYS IN THE PUBLIC DOMAIN:

1. II:1: <u>That is the case</u> for one that is necessary for the festival. <u>But in the case of</u> one that is not necessary for use on the festival, it is prohibited to do so. <u>That is the case in</u> the instance of a channel belonging to an individual. <u>But in the case of</u> a channel available for public use, even in the instance of one that is not for use on the festival, it is permitted.

The outline presents the formalized language, and enough of it to show the presence of a governing pattern.

[C] AND DIG THEM OUT. THEY REPAIR ROADS, STREETS, AND WATER POOLS.

1. III:1: They dig them out [M. 1:2D]. They dig them out, <u>in line with that which we have learned there:</u> He who cleans out a spout removing pebbles that have collected therein.

The particle that signals the citation of counterpart rulings serves as the form to tell us we deal with Mishnah-commentary.

[D] AND THEY DO ALL PUBLIC NEEDS:

1. IV:1: <u>What are</u> public needs? They judge capital cases, property cases, and cases involving fines [cf. M. M.Q. 3:3]. And they burn a red cow (cf. Num. chap. 19). And they break the neck of a heifer [in the case of a derelict corpse]. And they pierce the ear of a Hebrew slave [who wishes to remain with his master]. And they effect redemption for pledges of personal valuation, for things declared *herem,* for things declared consecrated, and for second tithe [through coins to be taken up to Jerusalem]. And they untie a shoe from the last, so long as one does not put it back [T. Moed 2:11 /I-O].

The classification of the composition, Mishnah-commentary, in the subdivision of the list of items that instantiate the Mishnah's general rule, is indicated by the material given in the outline.

[E] MARK OFF GRAVES:

1. V:1: <u>Interpret the passage [to speak] of a case in which</u> there were heavy rains, which washed away the marking.

[F] AND GO FORTH [TO GIVE WARNING] AGAINST DIVERSE KINDS.

1. VI:1: <u>And was this not</u> done in Adar? <u>Interpret the law [to speak] of a case in which</u> it was such a year in which even the sprouts [in Adar] were not discerned.

2. VI:2: <u>And how do we know that</u> graves must be marked off? R. Berekhiah, R. Jacob, son of the daughter of Jacob, in the name

of R. Honaiah of Beth Hauran, R. Yosé said in the name of R. Jacob bar Aha in the name of R. Honaiah of Beth Hauran, R. Hezekiah, R. Uzziel son of R. Honaiah of Beth Hauran: "'The leper . . . shall cry, 'Unclean, unclean' (Lev. 13:45). That is so uncleanness [80 c] will cry out with its own mouth and say, 'Keep away.'" R. La in the name of R. Samuel bar Nahman: "'And when these pass through the land and any one sees a man's bone, then he shall set up a sign by it' (Ezek. 39:15). It is on the strength of that verse that people mark off places in which bones of a human being are found. "['A man's bone'] — on this basis we prove that they mark off a place in which the backbone or skull are found. "'And he shall set' — on this basis we learn that they mark off such a place on bedrock. "If you say that it is located on a rock, which is turned over, then it may wash away and impart uncleanness to some other place. "'By it' — in a place of cleanness. [That is, the marker is not set upright at the corpse-matter, but beside it.] "'A sign' — On this basis that they set up a sign."

The formalization at V:1, VI:1 is made accessible in the outline. VI:2's points of formalization — the presupposition of a clause of the Mishnah, the framing of a question, the use of a fixed particle — all emerge in the outline.

III.   YERUSHALMI MOED QATAN 1:3

[A] R. ELIEZER B. JACOB SAYS, "THEY LEAD WATER FROM ONE TREE TO ANOTHER, "ON CONDITION THAT ONE NOT WATER THE ENTIRE FIELD. "SEEDS THAT HAVE NOT BEEN WATERED BEFORE THE FESTIVAL ONE SHOULD NOT WATER ON THE INTERMEDIATE DAYS OF THE FESTIVAL."

1. I:1: Mana stated the following without specifying an authority, while R. Abin in the name of Samuel [said], "[As to M. Sheb. 2:10: 'They may water the while soil (= ground between trees) (= ground not planted with trees),' the words of R. Simeon. R. Eliezer b. Jacob prohibits,] the dispute [at M. 1:3A-B] pertains to an average situation [in which the trees are not planted very closely together or very far apart]. "For how [otherwise] may be interpret the dispute about leading water from one tree to another, either in the Seventh Year or in the intermediate days of the festival? "If we deal with a field in which the trees are far apart, then in the view of all parties it will be prohibited. If we deal with a field in which the trees are close together, all parties will concur that it will be permitted. "Accordingly, we must deal with an average situation, in which trees are planted at the rate of ten per *seah's* space of ground. R. Eliezer b. Jacob treats such a case as if the trees were far apart, and rabbis treat such a case as if the trees were planted close together."

The key language of the form, as well as the type of material that the form implicitly requires to do its work, are clearly conveyed through the outline.

[B] AND SAGES PERMIT IN THIS CASE AND IN THAT.

1.   II:1: <u>What is the meaning of</u> "in this case and in that"? [Could the meaning be,] whether they were watered before the festival and whether they were not watered before the festival? [Surely not! There will be no loss if there was no watering before the festival. The seeds cannot require water on the festival if the process of growth has not been initiated by a watering prior to the festival.] But here we deal with a tree [in which case it is permitted to water, so as to prevent loss], while there we deal with seeds [in which case there will not be much of a loss if there is no watering, unless the seeds have been constantly irrigated up to now].

The formula demands the exegesis of the language of the Mishnah, and we have no difficulty classifying the form before us.

IV.   YERUSHALMI MOED QATAN 1:4

[A] THEY HUNT MOLES AND MICE IN A TREE-PLANTED FIELD AND IN A FIELD OF GRAIN:

1.   I:1: "A mole" is a weasel. Even though there is no proof for that proposition, there is at least a hint about it, in the following verse of Scripture: Let them be like the snail that dissolves into slime, like the untimely birth that never sees the sun" (Ps. 58:8).

Here the "form" consists of a question that is not asked, then the answer that is given: what is a mole? A mole is…. Then comes the proof-text.

[B] IN THE USUAL MANNER, ON THE INTERMEDIATE DAYS OF A FESTIVAL AND IN THE SEVENTH YEAR. AND R. JUDAH SAYS, "THEY DO SO IN A TREE-PLANTED FIELD IN THE NORMAL MANNER, "AND IN A GRAIN FIELD NOT IN THE NORMAL MANNER."

1.   II:1: In the usual manner [M. 1:4B]: This is hunting with a trap. Not in the usual manner? He drives a stake [into the spot] or strikes it with a pick and flattens out the soil underneath [T. Moed 1:4B].

2.   II:2: It has been taught: They destroy ants' holes on the intermediate days of a festival. How do they execute the destruction? Rabban Simeon b. Gamaliel says, "One takes dirt from one hole and puts it into another, and they strangle one another" [T. Moed 1:5].

Here the Mishnah-commentary form requires the citation of a clause of the Mishnah followed by the provision of a few words of explanation, identical in the pattern to the Aggadic sector's "commentary-form." I cannot underscore any element of the cited language, even though the composition clearly adheres to a powerful rule of organizing and expressing Mishnah-commentary. I do not regard

II:2 as formalized in any linguistic sense; its opening particle does not signal anything about how the words that follow are going to be patterned, or whether a pattern of any sort, formal or logical, will govern. In my catalogue of the forms of the Yerushalmi I do not include these items at all.

[C] THEY BLOCK UP A BREACH IN THE INTERMEDIATE DAYS OF A FESTIVAL.

1. III:1: Stone on stone, pebble on pebble.

Here is Mishnah-commentary: implicit citation followed by explicit amplification.

[D] AND IN THE SEVENTH YEAR, ONE BUILDS IT IN THE NORMAL WAY.

1. IV:1: stone on pebble and pebble on stone.

The formulary pattern is as above.

V. YERUSHALMI MOED QATAN 1:5

[A] R. MEIR SAYS, "THEY EXAMINE NEGAS [TO BEGIN WITH] TO PROVIDE A LENIENT RULING, BUT NOT TO PROVIDE A STRICT RULING." AND SAGES SAY, "NEITHER TO PROVIDE A LENIENT RULING NOR TO PROVIDE A STRICT RULING "

1. I:1: <u>There we have learned:</u> A bright spot the size of a split bean — and it spread to the extent of a split bean — and there appeared in the spreading quick flesh or white hair — but the primary sign disappeared — R. Aqiba declares unclean. And sages say, "Let it be inspected anew" [M. Neg. 4:10]. [A bright spot of requisite size has spread to the extent of a split bean. The spreading then develops quick flesh or white hair. But the primary sign has disappeared. Aqiba declares the man unclean because he regards the two signs as joined together. The spreading takes the place of the original sign. We have, therefore, sufficient evidence of uncleanness. The sages' position is that we have a new sign, for the first spot has disappeared.]

2. I:2: Said Rabbi, "The opinion of R. Meir [M. 1:5A] makes more sense in the case of one who is [merely] shut up for inspection [the second time], and the opinion of R. Yosé [= sages, M. 1:5B] makes more sense to me in the case of one certified [as unclean]" [T. Hag. 1:8]. [Rabbi sees no disadvantage for the one who may, after all, be declared clean. But there is nothing to warrant pronouncing the decision for the one who is subject to certification. Even if he is declared clean, he has to count seven days and cannot have intercourse in that period.]

3. I:3: [Reverting to the problem of I:1] R. Zeira said, "They dispute a case involving the intermediate days of a festival [in the case of one who is subject to a second inspection]. R. Aqiba says, 'It is the original sign, [and if the man is declared clean] he may not enter the Temple courtyard as wholly clean. Sages say it is a new sign, and he may enter the Temple courtyard [since we must

wait a week to see whether or not he is clean]." Lo, R. Aqiba declares the man unclean and certifies him so, and rabbis say "Let it be inspected as at the outset," and they too certify him. What then is at issue between them?

The outline amply signals that we deal with a form, the contrast of two Mishnah-statements, the exegesis of their relationship and demonstration of their harmony. The outline further encompasses the secondary developments, first a gloss, then an alternative thesis.

[B] AND FURTHER DID R. MEIR SAY, "A MAN MAY GO OUT AND GATHER THE BONES OF HIS FATHER AND HIS MOTHER, "BECAUSE IT IS A TIME OF REJOICING FOR HIM." R. YOSÉ SAYS, "IT IS A TIME OF MOURNING FOR HIM."

1. II:1: At first they would collect the bones and bury them in mounds. When the flesh had putrefied, they would collect the bones and bury them in cedar chests. On that day the mourner would engage in the rite of mourning. The next day he would rejoice, saying that his ancestors would free him from the rigors of judgment.

2. II:2: It was taught: He who moves a bier from place to place is not subject to [the rite of mourning required when] one gathers bones [of an ancestor for secondary burial]. [Merely moving the bier is not part of the reburial process. So new fresh rites of mourning are not required, e.g., for that day only.] Said R. Aha, "That statement which you have laid down applies to a bier made of marble. But as to one made of wood [in which case there will have been putrefaction of the bier itself], the person is subject to [carry out rites of mourning involved when] one gathers bones [of an ancestor for secondary burial]." Said R. Yosé, "Even in the case of a bier made of wood, [there is no consideration of the rite of mourning required when one] gathers bones [of an ancestor for secondary burial]."

II:1, so far as it is to be classed as Mishnah-commentary, is simply a complement to the Mishnah's rule with further information. II:2 adds a rule that receives its own exegesis. The outline serves quite nicely to indicate the character of the Talmud's Mishnah-commentary here.

[C] A PERSON MAY NOT CALL FOR MOURNING FOR HIS DECEASED:

1. III:1: What is a call for mourning for the deceased? He speaks of him among the deceased [in general, but not speaking of him in particular].

The form is familiar and the outline gives ample evidence on its character.

[D] OR MAKE A LAMENTATION FOR HIM THIRTY DAYS BEFORE A FESTIVAL.

1. IV:1: When one speaks of the deceased in particular [and not merely mentions his name among the deceased in general]. That

which you have said applies to a death some time ago, but in the case of a recent death, it is permitted.

The Mishnah-clause is glossed.

VI.   YERUSHALMI MOED QATAN 1:6

[A] THEY DO NOT HEW OUT A TOMB-NICHE OR TOMBS ON THE INTERMEDIATE DAYS OF A FESTIVAL. BUT THEY REFASHION TOMB-NICHES ON THE INTERMEDIATE DAYS OF A FESTIVAL.

1.   I:1: What is the meaning of refashioning a grave [M. 1:6B]? R. Yosé bar Nehorai said, "One plasters it with plaster." R. Hisda said, "If it was too long, one may shorten it." R. Joshua b. Levi said, "One may lengthen it on one side and broaden it on the other."

The dispute is introduced by Mishnah-commentary form. The outline conveys the formal traits of the passage.

[B] THEY DIG A GRAVE ON THE INTERMEDIATE DAYS OF A FESTIVAL,

1.   II:1: This is breaking through the ground in any measure at all.

The gloss of the Mishnah adheres to the standard form.

[C] AND MAKE A COFFIN, WHILE THE CORPSE IS IN THE SAME COURTYARD. R. JUDAH PROHIBITS, UNLESS THERE WERE BOARDS [ALREADY SAWN AND MADE READY IN ADVANCE].

1.   III:1: That which you have said applies to a deceased person who was not well known. But in the case of a deceased person who was well known, one may make a coffin even in the marketplace.

The Mishnah-gloss, based on the stereotype language, is clearly exposed by the outline.

VII. YERUSHALMI MOED QATAN 1:7

[A] THEY DO NOT TAKE WIVES ON THE INTERMEDIATE DAYS OF A FESTIVAL, WHETHER VIRGINS OR WIDOWS. NOR DO THEY ENTER INTO LEVIRATE MARRIAGE, FOR IT IS AN OCCASION OF REJOICING.

1.   I:1: [With reference to M. 1:7A-D:] Simeon bar Abba in the name of R. Yohanan, "It is because [people will hold up weddings until the festival, and so have one meal for the two events, the festival and the wedding]. [Consequently, they will postpone marriages and so] nullify the act of procreation [for the interval]." R. Ila, R. Eleazar in the name of R. Hananiah: "It is because people must not confuse one cause of rejoicing with some other." R. Abbahu in the name of R. Eleazar: "The prohibition is on account of the excessive work [involved in preparing for the wedding]."

The outline captures the form, the implicit citation of a clause of the Mishnah plus a few words of clarification.

[B] BUT ONE MAY REMARRY HIS DIVORCED WIFE.

    1.   II:1: It is because it is no particular joy for him.

The form follows the preceding, and the outline exposes that fact.

[C] AND A WOMAN MAY PREPARE HER WEDDING ADORNMENTS ON THE INTERMEDIATE DAYS OF A FESTIVAL.

    1.   III:1: What are these adornments? Fixing her hair, parting her hair, cutting her hair and fingernails, and rubbing her face with a clay utensil [to heighten her skin color].

The form requires a gloss of the language of the Mishnah, and the outline serves to show it.

[D] R. JUDAH SAYS, "SHE COULD NOT USE LIME, SINCE THIS MAKES HER UGLY."

    1.   IV:1: [and this prohibition applies on the festival itself even though later on the woman will be beautified,] for it is disfiguring. [So, on the occasion of the festival we do not take account of later advantage.]

The same form recurs, and the outline leaves no ambiguity.

VIII.   YERUSHALMI MOED QATAN 1:8

[A] AN UNSKILLED PERSON SEWS IN THE USUAL WAY. BUT AN EXPERT CRAFTSMAN SEWS WITH IRREGULAR STITCHES.

    1.   I:1: The House of Yannai said, "Sewing in the normal way means drawing a needleful [of stitches in one sweep]. Sewing with irregular stitches means doing it one by one." R. Yohanan said, "Doing so in the usual way means doing it one by one. Irregular stitching means skipping."

    2.   I:2: What is the definition of an unskilled person, and what is the definition of an expert craftsman?

I:1 takes the dispute-form, and No. 2 is a simple Mishnah-gloss, the outline leaving no problems in either instance. The outline-entry at I:2 leaves no doubt as to the formal traits of the composition.

[B] THEY WEAVE THE ROPES FOR BEDS. R. YOSÉ SAYS, "THEY [ONLY] TIGHTEN THEM."

    1.   II:1: Yosé said, "There is a dispute on this matter between Hezekiah and R. Yohanan. "Hezekiah said, 'Weaving means one weaves warp and woof. Tightening means either the warp or the woof.' R. Yohanan said, 'Weaving means either the warp or the woof. Tightening means that it was loose and one tightens it.'"

The dispute-form once more is adopted to serve the purpose of the Mishnah-commentary, and enough of the source is given to indicate that fact. But the exact elements of the dispute are not signalled, since omitted is the second half of the dispute, which is as follows and which should have been included in the outline:

> [E]   Said R. Hiyya bar Ba, "All concur with regard to weaving that it involves warp and woof. Concerning what do they differ? It is with regard to tightening the rope bed.
>
> [F]   "Hezekiah said, 'It is either warp or woof.'
>
> [G]   "R. Yohanan said, 'If it was loose, one tightens it.'"

Here is one point at which the outline would have lacked important information, even though the outline's indication to classify the entry as a dispute remains valid.

IX.   YERUSHALMI MOED QATAN 1:9

> [A] THEY SET UP AN OVEN OR DOUBLE STOVE OR A HAND-MILL ON THE INTERMEDIATE DAYS OF A FESTIVAL. R. JUDAH SAYS, "THEY DO NOT ROUGH THE MILLSTONES FOR THE FIRST TIME."
>
> 1.   I:1: Halapta bar Saul taught, "But [M. 1:9A's] rule is on the stipulation that one not set up an oven to begin with." It has been taught: As to a new oven or double stove, they do not grease them, rub them with a rag, or seal them with cold water so that they will be sealed. But if it is to pour out a pot on them, it is permitted. And so has it been taught: A new oven or double stove — lo, they are in the category of all other utensils that are carried about in a courtyard.

The indicative trait of the Mishnah-commentary-form is present and clearly shown by the outline.

X.   YERUSHALMI MOED QATAN 1:10

> [A] THEY MAKE A PARAPET FOR A ROOF OR A PORCH IN AN UNSKILLED MANNER, BUT NOT IN THE MANNER OF A SKILLED CRAFTSMAN.
>
> 1.   I:1: A parapet for a roof may be made up to three handbreadths high, and one for a porch [more commonly used] may be built up to ten handbreadths high on the festival.
>
> [B] THEY PLASTER CRACKS AND SMOOTH THEM DOWN WITH A ROLLER, BY HAND, OR BY FOOT, BUT NOT WITH A TROWEL.
>
> 1.   II:1: They plaster cracks [M. 1:10C]: R. Hiyya taught: He who plasters does so by foot, and he who smooths down does so by hand.
>
> [C] A HINGE, SOCKET, ROOF BEAM, LOCK, OR KEY [ANY OF] WHICH BROKE DO THEY REPAIR ON THE INTERMEDIATE DAYS OF THE FESTIVAL, SO LONG AS ONE HAD NOT HAD THE INTENTION TO DO WORK ON IT ON THE INTERMEDIATE DAYS OF THE FESTIVAL.
>
> 1.   III:1: This is in line with the following: The trundle of a ladder belonging to R. Mana broke. He asked R. Jonah, his father, who permitted him to repair it. And even so, he said to him, "Go see how a certain elder behaves, and rely upon his decision." He went out and found R. Bun bar Kahana, and asked him, and he permitted him to repair it.

All three entries follow the same form: citation of the Mishnah, then a gloss; the outline supplies the required data.

[D] AND ALL PICKLED FOODS THAT A MAN CAN EAT DURING THE INTERMEDIATE DAYS OF A FESTIVAL HE ALSO MAY PICKLE.

1. IV:1: Lo, as to pickled foods that he cannot eat on the festival, he may not [pickle] them. Said R. Ba, "That which you have said applies to things that are not perishable. But as to things that are perishable, it is permitted [to pickle them]."

2. IV:2: Hoshaiah had wheat. Nonetheless on the intermediate days of the festival he ground wheat. R. Zeira said to R. Jonah, "Go, buy us black wheat for grinding [on the festival]." He said to him, "We have a portion adequate for the festival." And he was angry with him [since that is no consideration].

IV:1 is standard Mishnah-commentary. IV:2 provides a free-standing story; the outline does not convey the information that explains why the story is included, but for form-analytical purposes, the data of the outline suffice.

On the strength of the outline, we may proceed to classify the forms of the Yerushalmi, secure that the outline provides sufficient data accurately to assess the indicative traits of each composition. The outline does not allow us to deal with the secondary and subordinated expansions of the various compositions, only the definitive form of the opening statements. But as we see, these are the sole points of operative formalization.

iv. The Result of the Initial Probe

For the Talmud of the Land of Israel our probe of tractate Moed Qatan Chapter One has yielded only two forms, [1] Mishnah commentary, and [2] the free-standing story. Within the form, Mishnah-commentary, we discern a number of subdivisions.[11] As we proceed through the several tractates, we shall identify further forms and add them to our catalogue.

We have now once again to ask whether form-analysis requires differentiation among the data of the formal category, Mishnah-commentary. We recall that in the Halakhic sector, we find a simple signal, given by a particle, which precipitates the selection of evidence of a certain type to make possible analysis of a given sort. In the chapter before us, for example, a verbal signal *such as X poses no problem but what about Y,* will lead us into an analysis of the issue of the more complex case contained in Y and the way in which important authorities resolve the anomaly. So too the language, *we have learned there,* will introduce

---

[11] All of them presuppose the text of the Mishnah; in the printed version, that hardly surprises, since the printers cite the pertinent clause of the Mishnah at the head of a given composition or composite. But in the MSS we may or may not find such a citation, so we take due cognizance of the fact that the Talmud's text on its own presupposes the presence of a clause or sentence of the Mishnah.

the citation of a passage of the Mishnah that intersects with the one at hand and that contains an anomaly that requires attention. We now see clearly that these and other formulations cannot be treated as forms in the way in which the Aggadic sector's forms are defined; what is patterned here, treated as a matter of convention, is the type of problem that will be set forth, inclusive of the kind of evidence that will be cited (or formulated) to spell out the problem and sustain its solution. The fixed particles therefore signal a kind of analysis and dictate the character of the particular passage that will be cited and of the problem that requires attention. That represents a patterning of language only as part of a larger patterning of thought. A fixed repertoire of analytical initiatives governs the Talmud's Mishnah-exegesis, conventions of inquiry dictate the character of the writing, and these correspond to the forms of the Aggadic sector in the way in which they define the rules of writing. But for this sector of the canon, those rules play off the substance and not the forms of the writing.

I maintain that, since, as with commentary-form in the Aggadic documents, the fundamental formal traits of the various compositions of Mishnah-commentary-form are uniform, we do not. The indicative traits of differentiation affect not the syntax or arrangement of words but signal the particular type of exegesis. Since all types of Mishnah-exegesis follow the same basic form — citation of the Mishnah (explicitly or implicitly) and then a few words of gloss, followed by secondary expansion, all types fall into the same classification for the purpose of form-analysis.

While form-analysis in the Aggadic compilations focuses upon extrinsic indicative traits, form-analysis in the Halakhic setting focuses our attention, in the very classification of indicative traits, upon indicators of the character of thought, not only the form in which thought is expressed. That is because subsets of the principal form, Mishnah-exegesis, — citation (sometimes implicit) of a clause of the Mishnah followed by a gloss — are differentiated from one another by the use of fixed particles, which bear important signals as to the character of analysis to follow. Recognizing that fact, we have to determine whether such particles require us to differentiate within the single paramount pattern.

We recall that, for the Aggadic sector, we treated as part of a single classification all compositions consisting of a citation of a verse of Scripture followed by a gloss thereof. What raises the question of whether such differentiation within the commentary-form is required? It is that certain fixed marks — particles — are affixed to instances of the commentary-form, and these demand consideration. But, as I argued in the opening section of this chapter, pure form-analysis accomplishes its goals without differentiation of conventional particles and their diverse signals as to meaning: the type of argument, the sort of analysis, at hand.

II

Mishnah-Commentary Form

The commentary-form requires a clause of the Mishnah, stated or implied, and then a simple declarative sentence, with or without the attributive. That form encompasses a broad variety of arrangements and word-choices, and it takes account of distinctive particles that convey further signals of meaning. But the form is a clear and simple one, and it differs from all the other patterns we shall consider here. The only close counterpart is Scripture-commentary-form. I give a few words to signal, for each entry, the particularity of the commentary-form, with the proviso that formulaic particles that signal the citation of another corpus of writing, e.g., Tosefta or the baraita-corpus or another passage of the Mishnah, are not accompanied by a further sample of the formulation; it suffices to note that when people wished to comment upon the Mishnah, they would cite pertinent documents with fixed particles; what is cited, then, conforms to the rules of writing that govern those other documents (for the Mishnah and the Tosefta) or bodies of disciplined statements (baraitot).

I. BERAKHOT

YERUSHALMI BERAKHOT 1:1

I:1:   We learn as the Tannaite rule:
I:2+3:   It was taught:
I:4:   We may find an indication concerning this
I:5:   The [stars] about which we speak
5. I:6-7: It was taught
I:9-10
I:11:   It was taught
II:1:   R. Yosa in the name of R. Yohanan, "The law follows the sages."
II:2-3:   It was taught
III:1:   Rabban Gamaliel's [ruling] agrees with [that of] R. Simeon. For it was taught in the name of R. Simeon
IV:1:   And Rabban Gamaliel disputed the [view of the] sages [who said one may recite, Until midnight [M. 1:1 E]]. And did he [then go ahead to defy their ruling and] act in accord with his own view?

V:1:   [In some versions of M.] we have the phrase, "And the eating of Paschal sacrifices." Other versions omit the phrase.

VI:1:   All which must be eaten within one day — [this refers to offerings classified as] the lesser holy things. And [what is the explanation of

YERUSHALMI BERAKHOT 1:2

I:1:   Interpret the Mishnah [B] in this way

I:2:   [Concerning the requirement to recite the Shema' in the morning:] Truly they said,

II:1:   [When is sunrise?]

III:1: R. Idi and R. Hamnuna and R. Ada bar Aha in the name of Rab, "The law follows

III:2: There it was taught

YERUSHALMI BERAKHOT 1:3-4

I:1:   The House of Hillel [M. 1:3 F] derives its [rules] from two Scriptural passages

I:2:   And it was taught: M'SH:

I:3:   Said. R. Tarfon, "I was coming by the road and I reclined to recite the Shema' in accordance with the words of the House of Shammai.

I:4:   Regarding this [principle that one who follows the Shammaite view endangers himself]

YERUSHALMI BERAKHOT 1:5

I:1-2: R. Simon in the name of R. Samuel bar Nahman, "[They recite these blessings before and after the Shema'] based on [the verse],

I:3:   It was taught in the Mishnah

I:4:   Samuel said,

I:5:   It was taught

I:6:   These are the blessings [whose formulae] they may lengthen

I:7-8: These are the blessings for which they bow

I:9:   It was taught

I:10:   These are the blessings which begin

I:11:   [A rule regarding the recitation of blessings:] [The efficaciousness of] a blessing is determined by [the correct recitation of the blessing at] its conclusion.

YERUSHALMI BERAKHOT 1:6

I:1:   Why does it say concerning

I:2:   They say there [in Babylonia],

I:3:   We learned

1:4R.   Simon in the name of R. Joshua b. Levi said, "If one did not

YERUSHALMI BERAKHOT 2:1

I:1:   Said R. Ba, "That is to say [we deduce from M.'s rule at 2:1 A] that

I:2:   R. Huna, R. Uri, R. Joseph, R. Judah in the name of Samuel, "One must accept

I:3: It was taught

II:1: R. Mana said in the name of R. Judah who said in the name of R. Yosé the Galilean, "If one

II:2: It was taught

II:3: Secondary supplement to the foregoing.

II:4: And at the breaks [between the paragraphs of the Shema']

YERUSHALMI BERAKHOT 2:2

I:1: Said R. Levi, "The scriptural basis

YERUSHALMI BERAKHOT 2:4

I:1: Rab said, "In both [disputes A-B and C-E] we follow the lenient ruling,"

I:2: We learned

I:3: The following [phrases in the Shema'] require special care

II:1: R. Jonah said, "R. Nahman bar Ada taught [the following]." And R. Yosé said, "Nahman Saba taught [the following]." "[Scripture says,

II:2: R. Aha in the name of R. Joshua b. Levi, "Also

II:3: Gloss of a detail of the foregoing.

II:4: Said R. Tanhuma, "Why did they

II:4: Said R. Tanhuma, "Why did they

III:1: One who recited and erred

YERUSHALMI BERAKHOT 2:5

I:1: We must emend the Mishnah as follows

I:2: It was taught

I:3: It was taught

I:4: R. Samuel bar R. Isaac in the name of R. Huna, "A person may not

I:5: Said R. Hanina, "Even one

YERUSHALMI BERAKHOT 2:6

I:1: R. Eleazar b. Antigonos in the name of R. Eliezer of the house of R. Yannai, "This means

I:2: Gloss of a secondary detail of the foregoing

YERUSHALMI BERAKHOT 2:7

I:1: Who taught

I:2: Said R. Yosé of the House of R. Abun, "Whoever permits

I:3: It was taught

YERUSHALMI BERAKHOT 2:8

I:1: [B says that one does not accept condolences for slaves in general. It does not specify that they must be one's own slaves. This seems to imply that] one may accept

I:2: When R. Hiyya bar Adda, the nephew of Bar Qappara, died Resh Laqish accepted [condolences] on his account because

YERUSHALMI BERAKHOT 2:9

I:1: It was taught

I:2: Said R. Zeira

YERUSHALMI BERAKHOT 3:1
I:1:   It was taught
I:2:   Said R. Bun, "It is written,
I:3:   When do they turn over the beds [making it lower to the floor in a house of mourning, as a sign of mourning]?
I:5:   It was taught
I:9:   R. Jonah, R. Yosé the Galilean, in the name of R. Yasa bar R. Hanina, "They do not
YERUSHALMI BERAKHOT 3:2
I:1:   It was taught
I:2:   It was taught
I:3:   Said R. Samuel bar Abedoma
I:4:   It was taught
YERUSHALMI BERAKHOT 3:3
I:1:   Whence [do we learn] that
I:2:   It was taught elsewhere in the Mishnah
I:3:   It was taught
I:4:   R. Yosé and R. Judah b. Pazzi were sitting [and discussing the obligations of reciting blessings]. They said
I:5:   It was taught
YERUSHALMI BERAKHOT 3:4
I:1:   What [words] does he meditate?
I:2:   R. Jacob bar Aha, R. Yosa in the name of R. Joshua b. Levi, "The discharge of semen [which renders one unclean, referred to in Mishnah]
I:3:   Said R. Jacob bar Abun, "They only ordained
I:4:   It was taught
XVIII. YERUSHALMI BERAKHOT 3:5
I:1:   The Mishnah [A-D refers to
II:1:   The Mishnah refers
II:2:   It was taught
II:3:   It was taught
II:4:   It was taught
II:5:   One must place
II:6:   It was taught
YERUSHALMI BERAKHOT 3:6
I:1:   Thus far [from M. we understand that]
YERUSHALMI BERAKHOT 4:1
I:1:   It is written
I:2:   One might think that
I:4:   Whence did they derive the [obligation
I:5:   From words in Scripture R. Judah [M. 4:1B] derived [his rule
I:6:   What is the basis for the rule of the rabbis

I:7:   R. Hiyya in the name of R. Yohanan

II:1:   And when is mid-afternoon?

II:3:   Whence [do we derive the obligation to recite] the Closing Service

II:4:   R. Isaac bar Nahman in the name of R. Joshua b. Levi

II:5:   What passage do they read

II:6:   Rabbi instructed his spokesman Abdan to announce to the congregation, "Whoever wishes to recite the [Saturday] Evening Prayer may do so, even while it is still daytime [after mid-afternoon]." R. Hiyya bar Abba [Wawa] instructed his spokesman to announce to the congregation, "Whoever wishes to recite the [Saturday] Evening Prayer may do so, even while it is still daytime."

II:7:   Said R. Jacob bar Aha, "It was taught there

YERUSHALMI BERAKHOT 4:2

I:1:   When he enters [the study hall] what does he say?

I:2:   R. Pedat in the name of R. Jacob bar Idi, "R. Eleazar used to recite

II:1:   And when I exit I give thanks for my portion [M. 4:2].

YERUSHALMI BERAKHOT 4:3

I:1:   And why [do they recite]

I:2:   Whence [is the source

I:3:   Whence [is the source

I:4:   Whence [is the source

I:5:   R. Zeira in the name of R. Jeremiah

II:1:   What is the meaning of

YERUSHALMI BERAKHOT 4:4

I:1:   R. Abbahu in the name of R. Eleazar, "[R. Eliezer means]

I:2:   R. Yosé of Tyre in the name of R. Yohanan

II:1:   R. Simeon bar Abba in the name of R. Haninah

III:1: Aha in the name of R. Asa, "[In all their crises (prst h'ybwr) (M. 4:4C)

III:2: There is a Tannaite authority who taught And there is a Tannaite authority who taught

III:3: R. Abba, R. Hiyya in the name of R. Yohanan

III:4: R. Yasa, R. Helbo, R. Berekhiah, R. Helbo of Tobah, in the name of R. Abedoma from Haifa, "A person must

YERUSHALMI BERAKHOT 4:5-6

I:1:   It was taught

I:2:   Said R. Jacob bar Aha, "It was taught there

I:3:   It was taught

I:4:   Said R. Joshua b. Levi, "[We find the following phrase in a verse referring to the Temple,]

II:1:   To which chamber

III:1: The term ... which means the same as the term...

YERUSHALMI BERAKHOT 4:7
I:1:   R. Bibi in the name of R. Hannah said, "The law follows
I:2:   Rab said, "[One who
I:3:   R. Shila in the name of Rab, "One who
I:4:   It was taught there
YERUSHALMI BERAKHOT 5:1
I:1:   R. Jeremiah in the name of R. Abba, "One who
I:2:   It was taught
I:3:   R. Jeremiah said, "One should
I:4:   Hezekiah, R. Jacob bar Aha, R. Yasa in the name of R. Yohanan,
I:5:   One may stand to recite the Prayer only with a solemn frame of mind [M.
         5:1]. R. Joshua b. Levi said, "[Scripture says,]
I:6:   Said R. Joshua b. Levi, "One who is
I:8:   Huna said, "One who
I:9:   Jonah in the name of R. Tanhum b. R. Hiyya, "One who has
II:1:   Even if a king extends to him a greeting, he should not respond [M. 5:1].
         Said R. Aha, "This applies only\
II:3:   R. Simeon b. Yohai taught
II:4:   Resh Laqish was accustomed
III:1:   R. Huna in the name of R. Yosé, "This only applies to
YERUSHALMI BERAKHOT 5:2
I:1:   [Why do they
I:2:   R. Zeira in the name of R. Haninah, "If one was
I:3: .   Zeira in the name of R. Haninah, "If one was
I:4:   Once in Nineveh they had to declare a fast day after Passover [and to pray
         for rain]. They went and asked Rabbi [what to do regarding the Prayer].
         Rabbi told them, "Go and do so [declare a fast day] but do not change the
         structure of the Prayer [by adding a special mention of rain]."
II:1:   Simeon bar Abba posed this question to R. Yohanan
III:1:   R. Eliezer says, "[One inserts
IV:1:   R. Jacob b. Aha in the name of Samuel says, "[They say it
IV:2:   Eleazar b. R. Hoshaiah
IV:3:   R. Eleazar b. Antigonos in the name of R. Eleazar b. R. Yannai
IV:4:   R. Zeira, R. Eleazar bar Antigonos [L: his son] in the name of R. Yannai,
         in the name of R. Judah his son, "If one did not
IV:5:   R. Zeira in the name of R. Judah, R. Abba in the name of Abba bar
         Jeremiah, "Even
IV:6:   R. Jeremiah, R. Zeira in the name of R. Hiyya bar Ashi, "One must
YERUSHALMI BERAKHOT 5:3
I:1:   R. Pinhas in the name of R. Simon, "[One who
II:1:   Said R. Samuel bar R. Isaac, "'For the mouth of liars will be stopped' [Ps.
         63:11]. This applies

III:1:   R. Yosé b. Haninah in the name of R. Haninah b. Gamaliel, "If he erred

III:2:   R. Aha and R. Judah b. Pazzi were sitting in a certain synagogue. A person got up before the ark [to lead the Prayer of Eighteen] and he skipped a blessing. They went and asked R. Simon [what to do about this case]. R. Simon said to them in the name of R. Joshua b. Levi, "If a leader of the Prayer [of Eighteen] skipped two or three blessings, they do not make him repeat [the Prayer of Eighteen]."

III:3:   R. Jacob bar Aha, R. Simeon bar Abba in the name of R. Eleazar, "If there was

III:4:   Abba son of R. Hiyya bar Abba, R. Hiyya in the name of R. Yohanan, "If while one was

III:5:   Said R. Joshua of the Sout

III:6:   Batyty [was leading the Prayer of Eighteen] and he was struck dumb

YERUSHALMI BERAKHOT 5:4

I:1:   It was taught

I:2:   Said R. Hanina

I:3:   R. Judah b. Pazzi in the name of R. Eleazar,

YERUSHALMI BERAKHOT 5:5

1.I:1:   R. Aha bar Jacob said, "[It is only a bad sign if one errs in the first blessing,] 'The Patriarchs.'"

I:3:   Said R. Samuel bar Nahmani, "If you

YERUSHALMI BERAKHOT 6:1

I:1:   It is written

I:2:   R. Haggai and R. Jeremiah went to a [grocery] store [to inspect its scales for accuracy]. R. Haggai eagerly recited a blessing …Said to him R. Jeremiah, "You have acted very well. For blessings must be [recited] for the performance of all the commandments."

I:3:   Yohanan ate olives and recited blessings before and after. And R. Hiyya bar Abba [Wawa] stared at him.

I:4:   "Over wine when it is in its natural state [thick, undiluted] they recite

I:5:   R. Jacob bar Zabedi in the name of R. Abbahu, "Over olive oil one recites

I:6:   R. Abba said, "Rab and Samuel both say

I:7:   R. Hiyya bar Abba [Wawa] in the name of R. Yohanan, "Over a pickled olive one recites

I:8:   Jacob bar Aha said, "R. Nahman disputed with the sages

I:9:   According to the view of R. Nehemiah [over wine] one recites

I:11:   What is the minimum quantity

I:12:   R. Abba in the name of Rab, "It is forbidden

I:13:   R. Huna said, "[After reciting the blessing over the bread, but before partaking of it,] he who says [aloud to others some command related to the meal such as], 'Take [this food] and recite the blessing,' 'Take [that food] and recite the blessing,' — this is not a [significant] interruption between the recitation of the blessing [and partaking of the food.

I:14:   He who chews grains of wheat, recites
           I:15: Gloss of the foregoing
I:16:   R. Jacob bar Idi in the name of R. Hanina, "Over all foods
I:17:   Why does one conclude
I:18:   It was taught
I:19:   R. Jacob bar Aha in the name of Samuel, "One recites
YERUSHALMI BERAKHOT 6:2
I:1:   R. Hezekiah in the name of R. Jacob bar Aha, "This [rule, M. 6:2A,]
           accords with the view of R. Judah
I:2:   It was taught
YERUSHALMI BERAKHOT 6:3
I:1:   If one's wine turned to vinegar he says
YERUSHALMI BERAKHOT 6:4
I:1:   R. Joshua b. Levi said, "Concerning what case do R. Judah and sages
           dispute?
I:2:   Concerning the dessert tray [of assorted nuts and fruits] — R. Jeremiah in
           the name of R. Ammi, "One recites
I:3:   If one had before him several foods of the seven kinds, over which does
           he recite the blessing? [What is the order of priority among the foods of
           the seven kinds?]
YERUSHALMI BERAKHOT 6:5
I:1:   Said R. Hisda, "Mishnah teaches [specifically],
I:2:   R. Helbo, R. Huna, Rab in the name of R. Hiyya the Elder, "Over a des-
           sert cake [which one eats] after the meal one is required to recite
I:3:   Said Marinus of the House of R. Joshua, "Where one ate from a dessert
           tray [of nuts and fruits], and ate porridge [made from flour], even if he
           recites
YERUSHALMI BERAKHOT 6:6
I:1:   R. Joshua b. Levi said, "The Mishnah refers to
I:2:   It was taught
I:3:   They asked Ben Zoma
II:1:   [M. implies that
II:2:   Geniba said
YERUSHALMI BERAKHOT 6:7
I:1:   R. Samuel bar Nahman in the name of R. Jonathan, "The Mishnah refers
           to
YERUSHALMI BERAKHOT 6:8
I:1:   R. Simon, R. Tadai in the name of R. Joshua, "If one ate
II:1:   Said R. Jonah, "[He recites the blessing over
YERUSHALMI BERAKHOT 7:1
I:1:   There [M. 7:4] it says: [Three who ate together] are not permitted to sepa-
           rate. [This implies that if they finished eating at the same time, they must

recite the blessings together.] And here [M. 7:1A] it says, [Three who ate together] are obligated to invite. [This implies that once they start eating together, they must recite the blessings together, even if they do not finish together. Is this not contradictory?]

I:2: R. Abba in the name of R. Huna, and R. Zeira in the name of Abba bar Jeremiah, "It is compulsory for

I:3: R. Huna said, "Three who

I:4: If three ate together and one wanted to leave

I:5: It is written in the Torah [i.e. one may find a basis in Scripture concerning the obligation to recite] a blessing before it [i.e. studying Torah]. But it is not written in the Torah [i.e. one can find no basis in Scripture for the obligation to recite] a blessing after it [i.e. studying Torah].

II:1: In accord with this they have said:

YERUSHALMI BERAKHOT 7:2

I:1: R. Simon in the name of R. Joshua b. Levi, R. Yosé b. Saul in the name of Rabbi, "They may count

I:2: Samuel bar Shilat posed this question to Rab

I:3: R. Jeremiah posed the question

YERUSHALMI BERAKHOT 7:3

I:1: Once [four rabbis] R. Zeira, and R. Jacob bar Aha, and R. Hiyya bar Abba, and R. Hanina, the associates of the sages, were sitting and eating. R. Jacob bar Aha took the cup and recited [the invitation to recite the blessings of the meal]. And he said, "Let us recite the blessings." He did not say, "Recite the blessings" [as M. 7:3B says one should say with four persons present]. R. Hiyya bar Abba said to him, "Why did you not say, 'Recite the blessings'?" He said to him, "Was it not taught: One is not strict regarding the matter [T. reads: a minor]. Whether one said, 'Let us recite the blessings,' or 'Recite the blessings,' they do not take him to task for it. But the over-scrupulous take him to task for it [T. 5:18]."

I:2: Samuel said

I:3: R. Abba bar Zimna used to serve Zeira

II:1: For one hundred he says, ["Let us recite the blessings to our God."] [M. 7:3E]. Said R. Yohanan, "This is [in accord with]

II:2: Whence [is the Scriptural basis] that ten comprise a congregation?

II:3: How do sages deal with R. Yosé the Galilean's Scriptural proof

III:1: Hiyya bar Ashi came up to read from the Torah. He said

III:2: It is written

YERUSHALMI BERAKHOT 7:4

I:1: It was taught

I:2: It was taught

YERUSHALMI BERAKHOT 7:5

I:1: [The ruling at M. 7:5A is obvious. Why does M. teach it?] R. Jonah and R. Abba bar Zimna in the name of R. Zeira

II:1:   Zeriqa in the name of R. Yosé b. Hanina, "The sages will agree with

II:2:   Jeremiah in the name of R. Yohanan, "The ancient [sages] used to ask

II:3:   Said R. Tanhum bar Yudan

II:4:   R. Zeriqan, the brother-in-law of R. Zeriqan, mentioned

II:5:   R. Ba, son of R. Hiyya bar Abba, "One who

YERUSHALMI BERAKHOT 8:1

I:1:   What is the basis of the House of Shammai's view?

I:2:   Said R. Yosé, "[We may deduce that] both [Houses] agree

I:3:   Said R. Zeira, "[We may deduce that] both R. Yosé and R. Mana agree

I:4:   And a question was raised regarding the view of the House of Shammai

I:5:   A festival day which fell on the day after the Sabbath

YERUSHALMI BERAKHOT 8:2

I:1:   What is the basis for the [ruling of] the House of Shammai?

I:2:   R. Yosé in the name of R. Shabbetai and R. Hiyya in the name of R.
          Simeon b. Laqish...R. Abbahu in the name of R. Yosé b. R. Haninah,
          "This applies to

I:3:   It was taught

YERUSHALMI BERAKHOT 8:3

I:1:   The Mishnah speaks of

I:2:   What is the basis for the House of Shammai's view?

I:3:   It was taught there

YERUSHALMI BERAKHOT 8:4

I:1:   What is the basis for the House of Shammai's view?

YERUSHALMI BERAKHOT 8:5

I:1:   It was taught: Said R. Judah, "The House of Shammai and the House of
          Hillel did not dispute

I:2:   The House of Shammai say

II:1:   [One might argue that] according to the view of the House of Shammai

II:2:   Fire and mules

II:3:   Fire [T. 5:31

YERUSHALMI BERAKHOT 8:6

I:1:   R. Jacob taught before R. Jeremiah

I:2:   Over a lantern, even if it was not extinguished [i.e., it burned throughout
          the Sabbath], they may recite

I:4:   It was taught

I:5:   R. Abbahu in the name of R. Yohanan, "They may recite

II:1:   R. Hezekiah and R. Jacob bar Aha in the name of R. Yosé b. R. Hanina,
          "Those to which we refer

III:1:   Are those not the same as those

IV:1:   R. Zeira son of R. Abbahu expounded

IV:2:   Said R. Berekhiah, "Two great men, R. Yohanan and R. Simeon b. Laqish,
          expounded accordingly,

V:1:   Rab says, "[The correct spelling of...And Samuel says, "[The correct spelling is]

V:2:   R. Judah in the name of Samuel, "[How much

YERUSHALMI BERAKHOT 8:7

I:1:   Yusta bar Shunam said, "Two Amoraim [interpreted this Mishnah]. One explained the House of Shammai's view and the other explained the House of Hillel's view

II:1:   R. Hiyya in the name of Samuel, "Until

YERUSHALMI BERAKHOT 8:8

I:1:   Said R. Ba, "[The House of Shammai reasons as follows:]

I:2:   But did we not learn

I:3:   Taught R. Oshaia

YERUSHALMI BERAKHOT 9:1

I:1:   The Mishnah speaks of

I:2:   One who sees

I:3:   Zeira and R. Judah in the name of Rab, "Any blessing which does not

I:4:   R. Yohanan and R. Jonathan went to help bring peace to the villages of the South. They came to one place and found the leader reciting [in the first blessing of the Prayer of Eighteen Blessings], "God, the great, mighty, awesome, powerful ['byr] and valiant ['mys]" [adding these last two terms]. And they silenced him. They said to him, "You do not have the right to add to the [standard] formula which the sages established for the blessings."

I:5:   It was taught

I:10:   Zeira, son of R. Abbahu, and R. Abbahu in the name of R. Eleazar

I:11:   Said R. Simeon b. Laqish

II:1:   The Mishnah [speaks of a time when

II:2:   It was taught

II:3:   Said R. Aha

II:4:   One who passes before

II:5:   One who sees

II:6:   One who sees

II:7:   When one hears

II:8:   One who sees

YERUSHALMI BERAKHOT 9:2

I:1:   Taught Bar Qappara, "They sound

I:2:   Samuel said, "The world would be destroyed if a comet passed through the constellation of Orion."

II:1:   R. Jeremiah and R. Zeira in the name of R. Hasdai, "It is sufficient

II:2:   If one was sitting

III:1:   The Mishnah speaks of

III:2:   Said R. Joshua b. Hananiah, "When

III:3:   [He only recites this blessing] when
III:4:   Simeon Qamatraya asked R. Hiyya bar Ba
III:6:   One who sees
III:7:   In the Prayer [of the Additional Service for the new moon] R. Yosé bar
          Nehorai said
III:8:   One who passe
III:9:   One who sees
III:10:   Hezekiah in the name of R. Jeremiah
IV:1:   Why did they see fit to juxtapose [in Mishnah 9:2D-E the rule
IV:2:   R. Judah bar Ezekiel said, "My father used to recite
IV:3:   Said R. Zeira, "If one sees prices decline

YERUSHALMI BERAKHOT 9:3

I:1:   Said R. Hiyya bar Ba, "[This rule that he recites a blessing applies]
I:2:   [One recites a blessing over the performance of all the commandments.]
          One who makes for himself a sukkah recites
I:3:   When does one recite
II:1:   The House of Yannai say, "Our Mishnah refers to a situation
II:2:   What may one who was coming home off the road say

YERUSHALMI BERAKHOT 9:4

I:1:   One who
I:2:   One who enters
I:3:   One who enters

YERUSHALMI BERAKHOT 9:5

I:1:   R. Berekhiah in the name of R. Levi, "[One must
II:1:   It was taught
III:1:   It was taught
IV:1:   It was taught
VI:1:   Said R. Yosé bar Bun,
VII:1:   It is the time for the Lord to act, for thy law has been broken" (Ps. 119:126).
          R. Nathan transposed the verse.
VII:2:   Hillel the Elder used to say
VII:3:   It was taught: R. Meir used to say

II. SHABBAT

YERUSHALMI SHABBAT 1:1

I:1:   Transportation of objects from one domain to the other on the Sabbath is
          of two sort
I:2:   Yosé in the name of R. Yohanan: "If one brought
I:3:   R. Yosé in the name of R. Yohanan: "He who takes an object
I:4:   Said R. Yannai, "If one swallowed
I:5:   Said R. Yohanan, "he who takes an object
I:6:   R. Huna in the name of Rab: "All concur in the case of one who
I:7:   R. Yohanan raised the following question

I:8:   Said R. Yohanan, "If one was standing

I:9:   If one was standing inside private domain

II:1:   R. Judah in the name of Samuel: "And that rule applies

II:2:   R. Hisda in the name of Ashi: "In the case of a reed

II:3:   How do we know that

III:1:   R. Jacob bar Aha in the name of Hezekiah, rabbis in the name of R. Yohanan: "[They are exempt] because

YERUSHALMI SHABBAT 1:2

I:1:   We have learned [for the formulation of M. 1:2A]

II:1:   What is the point at which we regard a haircut as having begun?

II:2:   What is the point at which the bath begins [and subsequently cannot be interrupted]? II:3: Exegetical gloss

III:1:   Now look here. One is supposed to keep distant from someone who smells bad, [and yet you teach M. 1:2E, they need not break off]

IV:1:   What is the beginning of the eating of a meal [at which point, the meal cannot be interrupted for the Prayer?]?

V:1:   Jeremiah and R. Joseph:One said, "Once they have gone into session in court [they do not interrupt]." The other said, "Once the judges have heard the claims of the contending parties [they do not interrupt]." If they began, they do not interrupt.

VI:1:   Said R. Aha, "The recitation of the Shema derives from the authority of the Torah, while the recitation of the Prayer does not derive from the authority of the Torah [This is why one may interrupt to say the Shema but not to say the Prayer.]." Said R. Ba, "As to the recitation of the Shema, the time for saying it is fixed, while the time for saying the Prayer is not fixed." Said R. Yosé, "Recitation of the Shema need not be accompanied by appropriate concentration, while saying the Prayer must be accompanied by appropriate concentration."

YERUSHALMI SHABBAT 1:3

I:1:   [In T.'s version:] A tailor should not go out carrying his needle near nightfall, lest he forget

II:1:   This is forbidden [in the public domain] even on other days of the week

II:2:   R. Hiyya taught, "[With reference to M. 1:3D,

III:1:   Samuel said, "This rule has been taught only

IV:1:   Said R. Eleazar, "In any case in which we have learned, 'nonetheless,' we deal with a law revealed to Moses at Sinai."

IV:2:   It has been taught

V:1:   It has been taught

V:2:   It has been taught

V:3:   On this basis, R. Phineas b. Yair says

YERUSHALMI SHABBAT 1:4

I:1:   And that day was as harsh for Israel as the day on which

I:2:   These are the matters on which they issued decrees

I:3:   Their bread [cf. M. A.Z. 2:8B(2)

I:4:   [Stewed and pickled vegetables into which it is customary to put wine and vinegar…these are prohibited (M. A.Z. 2:8D(4)):]

I:5:   Their cheese: Said R. Jeremiah, "Milk produced by a gentile's cow] — why is it forbidden? Because of the mixture

I:6:   [Their oil (M. A.Z. 2:8B(3):]

I:7:   Their daughters

I:8:   R. Joshua Onayya taught

I:9:   Their semen [is unclean, by decree of the Houses]

I:10:   As to one who has suffered a nocturnal emission

I:11:   And concerning the laws about territory of the gentiles

I:12:   Samuel said, "[As to the statement that a court may not annul the ruling of another court unless it is superior to it,] that statement applies

YERUSHALMI SHABBAT 1:5

I:1:   What is the scriptural basis for the view

I:2:   The House of Shammai stated one argument to the House of Hillel, and they could not answer them.

YERUSHALMI SHABBAT 1:6

I:1:   [In allowing time to steam the flax while it is still day,] what do the House of Shammai profit? [After all, the bleaching will not be completed in any event during the Sabbath.]

I:2:   [As to M. 1:6B-C,] R. Judah in the name of Samuel: "And [the House of Hillel permit]

YERUSHALMI SHABBAT 1:7

I:1:   [= Y. Besah 3:2, treating M. Besah 3:2A, which states that "Nets for wild beasts, fowl, or fish made before the holiday, one should not take from them on the holiday, unless he knows that [the catch] was caught by the eve of the holiday. [The question now must be asked

I:2:   [With reference to M. Bes. 3:2A-C:] R. Hiyya in the name of Rab declared that that rule is indeed the law.

I:3:   [As to M. Bes. 3:2D, Gamaliel's view that fish caught by a gentile are permitted, but he would not accept them: R. Zeira in the name of Rab]: "They considered ruling that

YERUSHALMI SHABBAT 1:8

I:1:   What is the definition of "a nearby place"?

I:2:   [With reference to the meaning of M. 1:8C,] there is he who wishes to say

I:3:   They do not hand over to a gentile [food] on the stipulation that he will take it out.

I:4:   It has been taught

I:5:   They do not send letters with a gentile either on Friday or on Thursday. The House of Shammai prohibit doing so even on Wednesday. And the House of Hillel permit.

YERUSHALMI SHABBAT 1:9

I:1:   [In the view of the House of Shammai,] what constitutes sufficient time [M. 1:9C]?

I:2:   If one handed over his garments to a gentile laundryman, and came and found him working on it on the Sabbath, it is forbidden [to derive benefit from his labor].

II:1:   [B] They referred only to white ones. Lo, as to colored ones, that is not the case. Accordingly, we infer that white ones are harder to do than colored ones [T. Shab. 1:22F-G].

III:1: Both R. Samuel and R. Yosé b. Haninah say

YERUSHALMI SHABBAT 1:10

I:1:   R. Bun bar Kahana in the name of rabbis: "A dish that had sufficiently cooked may remain

II:1:   R. Jacob bar Aha in the name of R. Assi: "Women are more prompt with regard to bread than to a cooked dish. [That explains the lenient ruling of M. 1:10D.]"

III:1: R. Eliezer [M. 1:10E] concurs in the case of showbread [that the rule of M. 1:10D applies]

YERUSHALMI SHABBAT 1:11

I:1:   There we have learned: After nightfall they went out and roasted their Passover offerings [but not on the Sabbath itself] [M. Pes. 5:10], and you say this

I:2:   [As to a Passover offering which one took off the fire while it was still day and found it was not sufficiently cooked,] if the Passover offering is whole, one may put it back into the oven [for further cooking, on its own, on the Sabbath]. But if it was cut into pieces

II:1:   R. Zeira, R. Judah in the name of Rab: "Four sorts of fires [may be kindled

YERUSHALMI SHABBAT 2:1

I:1:   R. Hiyya bar Ba said, "It is the wooly substance of cedar twigs." R. Aha in the name of R. Hiyya: "Cedar wood."

II:1:   R. Hinena in the name of R. Phineas: "It is linen that has not been hatcheled."

III:1: The cissaros blossom

IV:1:   [This is] ornita.

V:1:   This is meant literally [a grass that grows in the desert].

VI:1:   It is similar to flax.

VII:1: Up to this point we have dealt with wicks. From this point onward we deal with fuel for the lamp.[The reason for the various rulings is now supplied.]

VIII:1: R. Yosé in the name of R. Hiyya: "It is oil of ivy seeds."

IX:1:   Said R. Hisda, "That is to say that it is prohibited

IX:2:   R. Yosé taught before R. Yohanan, "How do we know from Scripture that

IX:3:   All those who are liable to immerse do so under ordinary circumstances by day

IX:4:   An Israelite girl who came to kindle a lamp from a priest girl['s light]

X:1:   R. Barona said, "In the case of tallow, one may drip into it any amount of oil and kindle such a lamp for the Sabbath."

X:2:   R. Hananiah, R. Baronah in the name of Rab: "Tallow which one has chopped up, and the innards of fish — they kindle a lamp with them."

X:3:   There is a Tannaite authority who teaches: They may kindle the lamp with naphtha. There is a Tannaite authority who teaches: They may not kindle the lamp with naphtha.

YERUSHALMI SHABBAT 2:2

I:1:   With reference to M. 2:2A,] lo, [the exclusion only of the listed item means that] all of the other items listed above are permitted for use in the lamp for the festival day.

II:1:   What is the difference between tar [which is prohibited] and the innards of fish [which are permitted]?

III:1:   R. Yohanan b. Nuri got up on his feet and said, "What will the people in Babylonia do

III:2:   It has been taught:

YERUSHALMI SHABBAT 2:3

I:1:   [As to M. 2:3A,] said R. Simeon bar R. Isaac, "It is written

I:2:   It has been taught

I:3:   Said R. Eleazar

II:1:   R. Eleazar asked, "What is the law as to

II:2:   There we have learned

II:3:   [As to Aqiba's view at M. 2:3E,] it is not the end of the matter that

YERUSHALMI SHABBAT 2:4

I:1:   Why may one not do what is prohibited at M. 2:4A?]

II:1:   It is different in this case, for the whole constitutes one utensil.

III:1:   Judah is consistent with rulings stated elsewhere

YERUSHALMI SHABBAT 2:5

I:1:   Said R. Samuel bar R. Isaac, "[When we say,] because of…gentiles, it is specifically to gentiles who pose a danger, and likewise, thugs

II:1:   [With reference to the language, to spare the lamp, oil, wick, M. 2:5D:] What is the difference between

III:1:   [With regard to M. 2:5F-G,] said R. Yohanan

III:2:   There we have learned

III:3:   If one made a fire and blew it out with a single breath, one is liable on both counts

III:4:   He who stirs up coals on the Sabbath is liable for a sin offering

III:5:   [If a person] kindled a fire and cooked [on it] — There is a Tannaite authority who teaches, "He is liable on two counts." There is a Tannaite authority who teaches, "He is liable on only one count."

III:6:   A non-priest who served in the Temple on the Sabbath, or a blemished priest who served at the altar while in a state of uncleanness — R. Hiyya the Elder said, "Such a one is liable on two counts."Bar Qappara said, "He is liable on one count [not being a priest, or being a blemished priest, respectively]."

YERUSHALMI SHABBAT 2:6

I:1:   There is a Tannaite authority who [at M. 2:6A] repeats the formulation as, "die young." There is a Tannaite authority who repeats it as, "die in childbirth."

II:1:   [Menstrual separation:] The first man was the lifeblood of the world.

III:1:   The first man was the clean dough offering for the world, for it is written, [reading Gen. 2:6 here and not in B:] "But a flow would well up from the ground and water the whole f

IV:1:   The first man was the light of the world, since it is written,

YERUSHALMI SHABBAT 2:7

I:1:   [A continuation of the baraita cited immediately above, at M. 2:6:] It has been taught

I:2:   [Following the more logical order of the stringency of the requirement for these several actions,] would it not have been more appropriate to follow the following order?

II:1:   The following story concerns R. Eliezer, who was dying on the eve of the Sabbath at dusk. Hyrcanus, his son, came in to remove his phylacteries.

III:1:   The Mishnah speaks of large utensils. But as to small ones, one may practice cunning and immerse them.

IV:1:   [In explaining the meaning of the word for doubtfully tithed produce, "demai," said] R. Yosé in the name of R. Abbahu, R. Hezekiah in the name of R. Judah b. Pazzi

V:1:   Said R. Hiyya bar Ashi, "That which you say concerns

YERUSHALMI SHABBAT 3:1

I:1:   The meaning of the Mishnah [at M. 3:1B, putting cooked food on] is that they may keep cooked food on the stove. The formulation of the Mishnah's rule accords with the principle of R. Judah. I:2: Secondary expansion of the foregoing.

II:1:   Daniel, son of R. Qattina, in the name of R. Assi: "The spines of palm branches are in the category of peat and wood [M. 3:1C]."

II:2:   He who sweeps out the ashes — must he do so until he sweeps out all that is necessary?

II:3:   For it has been taught

II:4:   It has been taught

II:5:   "He who plants seed on the Sabbath, if he did so inadvertently, may preserve

III:1:   [As to M. 3:1G-H, from the Hillelite viewpoint:] If one removed the pot

YERUSHALMI SHABBAT 3:2

I:1:   Bar Qappara taught, "It is forbidden even to put anything near it [M. 3:2A]."

I:2:   Said R. Yosé, "As to laws of the Sabbath

YERUSHALMI SHABBAT 3:3

I:1:   There we have learned:

I:2:   It has been taught

I:3:   An unripe fig which one stored in straw,

II:1:   [With reference to M. 3:3B,] there they say,

III:1:   At first they would stop up the stoppers to the bath on the eve of the Sabbath [leaving hot water in the bath], and people would come in and wash on the Sabbath.

IV:2:   A certain philosopher asked Bar Qappara, [and so too] Ablat asked Levi Sarisa, "Why should it be permitted to drink the water but forbidden to wash in it [in line with M. 3:3/I]?"

V:1:   Lo, if it is not clear of ashes, one may not do so.

VI:1:   R. Hananiah, R. Yosé, R. Aha Abba in the name of R. Yohanan: "It is because it [the water] will be heated up by its sides [which are hot]."

YERUSHALMI SHABBAT 3:4

I:1:   R. Ba the son of R. Hiyya bar Ba, R. Hiyya in the name of R. Yohanan: "They have taught only

I:2:   It has been taught

I:3:   "A man may go down and immerse in cold water and come up and heat himself by the fire," the words of R. Meir. And sages prohibit doing so.

I:4:   All concur with regard to

YERUSHALMI SHABBAT 3:5

I:1:   What is the law as to

I:2:   What is the law as to

II:1:   In the view of R. Judah, anything salted falls into the category of fish brine, and wine falls into the category of vinegar.

YERUSHALMI SHABBAT 3:6

I:1:   R. Haggai asked, "If the flame, kindled prior to sunset, went out while it was still daylight on Friday, but the householder found out about it only after it had gotten dark, [is the oil in the lamp in the status of that which has not been designated for use on the Sabbath and hence inaccessible on that day]?"

I:2:   Said R. Yohanan, "You have nothing that is in fact available [to the householder] and not regarded as ready and designated for use on the Sabbath except for one thing alone.

YERUSHALMI SHABBAT 3:7

I:1:   Hiyya bar Aha objected

I:2:   R. Simeon b. Laqish gave a decision in Tripolis: "A small candlestick may be carried about. [It has no fixed place and may be moved around.]"

I:3:   It has been taught

II:1:   [R. Simeon says, "All sorts of lamps do they carry, except

II:2:   R. Ba bar Hiyya in the name of R. Yohanan: "As to a counter it is forbidden to move it about." R. Ammi gave a decision that it is permitted to do so.

II:3:   R. Aha bar Hinena, R. Yosé in the name of R. Yohanan: "As to a small candelabrum, it is permitted

YERUSHALMI SHABBAT 3:8

I:1:   Here you say: On the Sabbath they do not put a utensil under a lamp to capture the sparks, nor should one put water into it, because he thereby puts out the sparks [cf. M. 3:8], while here you say, They do put a utensil under the lamp [M. 3:8A]

II:1:   R. Samuel in the name of R. Zeira: "This represents the view of R. Yosé."

YERUSHALMI SHABBAT 4:1

I:1:   [Explaining why one may not

I:2:   There we have learned:

I:3:   [They forbade keeping food warm through covering it up on account of the possibility of leaving the food on the stove.

I:4:   It has been taught

I:5:   If [things which add heat were] mixed up [with things which do not add heat,] what is the law

II:1:   There we have learned

III:1:   Straw is like a bailee: it returns just what you give to it.

IV:1:   It is not the end of the matter that they may not

V:1:   [With reference to M. 4:1D-F's mention of wet and dry grass:] there we have learned

VI:1:   We have learned the formulation of the Mishnah using the word nesoret, while teachers of the house of rabbi read, neoret.\

YERUSHALMI SHABBAT 4:2

I:1:   R. Judah b. Pazzi in the name of R. Jonathan: "That which you say

II:1:   R. Judah and R. Yohanan: "That which you say

II:2:   R. Jeremiah in the name of Rab: "They spread out

II:3:   R. Bisna in the name of R. Yosé bar Hanina: "It is forbidden

YERUSHALMI SHABBAT 4:3

I:1:   If one removed the cover from the food while it was still day

I:2:   R. Ba in the name of R. Judah

I:3:   It has been taught

I:4:   And just as they do not cover up hot water to begin with on the Sabbath [M. 4:3A], so they do not cover up snow and ice [vs. M. 4:3C] [T. Shab. 3:23E-F].

YERUSHALMI SHABBAT 5:1

I:1:   It has been taught

II:1:   There is a Tannaite authority who gives the word as

III:1:   [Noting the repetition of the rule for the horse with its chain at M. 5:1C, all beasts which wear a chain,] R. Samuel in the name of R. Zeira: "Just as you make that point with respect to the prohibition, so the same point applies with regard to all other beasts

III:2:   And a horse with its chain [M. 5:1B]:

IV:1:   And will the chain not make some sort of a ditch [in the dirt, when it is dragged along]?

V:1:   There we have learned

YERUSHALMI SHABBAT 5:2

I:1:   [With reference to M. 5:2A,] Samuel said, "That is the case if it is tied to him in advance of the Sabbath. [But if one merely spreads the blanket, that may be done on the Sabbath itself.]"

II:1:   One puts a tanned hide against the heart [of the beast], and it protects the female

III:1:   There is a Tannaite authority who repeats the word as

III:2:   As to protective cloths

III:3:   As to tying something under [thus lowering] their tails [KBWLWT], it is so that a male will not mount them.

IV:1:   It has been taught: R. Judah b. Betera says, "Whether it is to keep them dry or to collect the milk, it is forbidden."

\YERUSHALMI SHABBAT 5:

I:1:   [The pad] is like a rock [of a plumb line] to level the crookedness [of a wall].

II:1:   Said R. Ba, "It is so that people will not

YERUSHALMI SHABBAT 5:4

I:1:   It has been taught

I:2:   R. Jeremiah asked before R. Zeira, "Whence do we learn these various rules?

II:1:   It is because it makes a ditch in the ground.

III:1:   R. Judah said, "It is a ball of wool."

IV:1:   R. Huna said, "It is a small plow." R. Hisda said, "It is a wooden board."

V:1:   The herdsman puts such a skin around her teats so that it will not give suck to its calf.

VI:1:   R. Ba, Rab and Samuel — both of them say, "In the view of sages

VI:2:   [As to the view of Eleazar b. Azariah that a cow may go out with a strap between the horns, M. 5:4J-K,] Genibah said, "It is merely a law that Eleazar came to teach [but it is not that he actually did so]."

YERUSHALMI SHABBAT 6:1

I:1:   R. Nahman bar Jacob said, "[As to M. 6:1C,] since the woman loosens [these objects],

I:2:   There we have learned

I:3:   Kahana asked Rab, "What is the law on

I:4: And we learn thus

II:1: Or with a forehead band [M. 6:1D]: R. Bun bar Hiyya: "It is a kind of

II:2: On what account are ornaments prohibited [for wear on the Sabbath]?

II:3: R. Halapta b. Saul taught

II:4: They do not look into a mirror on the Sabbath. But if it was affixed to the wall [T. Shab. 13:16] — Rabbi permits doing so. And sages prohibit.

II:5: It has been taught

III:1: R. Judah said, "For instance

III:2: There we have learned

III:3: R. Inyano bar Sisai said in the name of R. Eliezer, "In any setting in which they have said

YERUSHALMI SHABBAT 6:2

I:1: For what reason did they make a decree against

I:2: And how many nails may there be in a sandal

I:3: A sandal whose two straps were broken, or whose strappings were torn, or from which even one sole separated, is [deemed broken, and so] insusceptible to uncleanness.

II:1: Said R. Abba, "It is because

III:1: Lo, if he has a wound on his foot, he may put on his sandal. On which foot does he put his sandal?

IV:1: They leave home on Friday, near dark, wearing phylacteries, but they do not leave home wearing a nail-studded sandal on Friday at dark.

V:1: What is the definition of an amulet made by an expert?

V:2: R. Yosé b. R. Bun in the name of R. Yosé: "In the case of a wound that has healed

YERUSHALMI SHABBAT 6:

I:1: A tailor should not go out carrying his needle on the eve of the Sabbath near nightfall, lest he forget and cross a boundary [M. 1:3A-B], nor a carpenter with the beam

I:2: With reference to M. 6:3A: A ring which has a seal produces liability. Hence such a ring is not an ornament for a woman. But in general women's rings are regarded as ornaments, whether with a seal or not.] R. Aha in the name of R. Abba bar R. Nahman: "It represents the view of R. Nehemiah

YERUSHALMI SHABBAT 6:4

I:1: It is written

I:2: What is the scriptural basis for the position of R. Eliezer?

R. Hiyya in the name of R. Yohanan: "A berit is on one leg

I:4: It is written

YERUSHALMI SHABBAT 6:5

I:1: Hanan [bar Immi said before R. Judah [in the name of] Menassia bar Jeremiah, "But that [M. 6:5A] is on condition that

I:2:   [As to the word for locks,] said R. Abbahu, "Whatever rests on the hair is called a lock."

I:3:   [As to M. 6:5: wool in the ear:] R. Yannai

II:1:   [As to M. 6:5H-J,] said R. Mana, "I heard a reason for this matter

II:2:   R. Yosé and R. Ammi: One of them had a toothache, and the other gave him instructions [on what is permitted to do on the Sabbath], and the other had an earache, and the one gave him instructions [on the matter]. But we do not know who said this and who said that.

III:1:   [As to M. 6:5E, as qualified by F,] R. Yannai interpreted

YERUSHALMI SHABBAT 6:6

I:1:   They go out with a sela coin on a bunion [M. 6:6A]: [A bunion is a] sore on the sole of the foot. R. Aha in the name of R. Ba bar Mamel: "Even a piece of silver foil [may be used for that purpose]."

YERUSHALMI SHABBAT 6:7

I:1:   It has been taught

YERUSHALMI SHABBAT 6:8

I:1:   [As to the principle of M. 6:8A,] Samuel said, "They go forth in it on the count of

II:1:   What is the meaning of, An artificial arm is insusceptible to uncleanness, [and they do not go out in it] [M. 6:8F]?

YERUSHALMI SHABBAT 6:9

I:1:   Boys go out in garlands [M. 6:9A]: Garlands of leaves.

II:1:   They go out with a locust's egg: It is good for the ear.

III:1:   Samuel, R. Abbahu in the name of R. Yohanan: "Whatever serves to bring healing is not prohibited on the count of 'the ways of the Amorite' [M. 6:10D-E] .

YERUSHALMI SHABBAT 7:1

I:1:   What is the meaning of this reference to a general principle [at M. 7:1A]?

II:1:   We have learned [at M. 7:1B], Whoever forgets the basic principle of the Sabbath. But there is a Tannaite authority of the household of Rabbi who repeats the tradition as follows

III:1:   How do we know [that

III:2:   Associates say

III:4:   We have learned there

III:5:   What is the difference between a case in which there have been deliberate violations of the Sabbath and inadvertent practice of many acts of forbidden labor, and a case in which there have been inadvertent violations of the Sabbath and deliberate performance of acts of forbidden labor?

III:6:   If one inadvertently violated the Sabbath and also inadvertently performed acts of forbidden labor

III:7:   Jeremiah asked before R. Zeira, "If

YERUSHALMI SHABBAT 7:2

I:1:   How from the Torah do we know that

II:1:   For what purpose [is the figure specified]?

II:2:   If two things were specified as distinct from the general rule, what is the law as to their being divided [so that one is punishable on each count]?

II:3:   Where we have a general rule stated affirmatively, and a specific instance of the rule expressed negatively [how do we interpret the matter, and for what purpose]?

II:4:   There we have learned

III:1:   And is plowing a generative category?

III:2:   R. Hiyya in the name of R. Yohanan: "He who

III:3:   On account of any action that serves to improve the produce, one is liable on the count of sowin

IV:1:   R. Hiyya taught

V:1:   He who binds sheaves: R. Samuel bar Sisartai asked, "What are the derivatives of sheaf binding?"

V:2:   As to a woman, when she mixes wheat, she is liable on the count of winnowing.

V:3:   Hiyya in the name of R. Yohanan: [Salted] fish which one pressed out — if it was so as to eat the flesh of the fish itself, he is exempt. If it was to get at the brine, he is liable.

VI:1:   Said R. Yudan, "There is he who may

VI:2:   R. Jonah asked, "If one did so [selected food] on the Sabbath, in the view of the House of Shammai [at M. Bes. 1:10], what is the law as to his being liable?

\VI:4:   It is taught: They do not

VI:5:   R. Zeira, R. Hiyya bar Ashi in the name of Samuel: "He who strains [wine to remove the lees] is liable on the count of selection [winnowing]."

VII:1:   Grinding: One who

VIII:1: With reference to the inclusion of baking, M. 7:2, and the failure to mention cooking

VIII:2: As to all of these measures [which the rabbis have supplied, this is how they apply:]

IX:1:   He who shears wool

IX:2:   There we have learned

X:1:   He who washes [lit., "whitens"] it [M. 7:2C(13)]: He who pitches wood for vessels or ropes for a windlass.

XI:1:   He who hatchels baste, down, or papyrus is liable on the count of beating.

XII:1:   What sort of dyeing was there in the tabernacle?

XII:2:   He who launders and he who wrings out — it is a single type of forbidden labor.

XIII:1: He who makes ropes and he who makes cord are liable on the count of

XIV:1:   What sort of tying was done in the tabernacle?

XIV:2:   R. Hoshaiah taught

XIV:3:   [With relevance to M. Kil. 9:10, : He who fastens (wool and linen to-gether) with a single fastening (of thread) (i.e., with an incomplete stitch) — it (i.e., the fastening) is not considered a connector (for uncleanness), and it (i.e., the fabrics joined by the fastening) is not subject to (the laws of) diverse kinds

XIV:4:   The language of "tearing" is used with reference to garments

XV:1:   He who captures a mollusk and crushes it — there is a Tannaite authority who teaches

XVI:1:   R. Simeon b. Laqish said, "There should be no reference to 'slaughtering' here.

XVII:1: He who cures its hide [M. 7:2H(29)]: What sort of curing of hides was done in the tabernacle?

XVIII:1: What sort of scraping was in the tabernacle?

XVIII:2: He who rubs a hide on a pillar is liable. On what count is he liable?

XIX:1:   If one blotted out a single large letter, in the space of which there is suffi-cient area to write two ordinary letters, he is liable

XX:1:   What sort of building was involved in the tabernacle [with reference to M. 7:2J(34)]?

XXI:1:   He who destroys [M. 7:2J(35)]: That pertains in particular to

XXII:1: ...are liable on the count of transporting the refuse.

XXII:2: And why is the matter of stretching out [an object from one domain and the other] not taught along with the list [at M. 7:2L(39), transporting an object from one domain to another]?

YERUSHALMI SHABBAT 7:3

I:1:   [Explaining the reference to something's being not suitable for storage] R. Huna in the name of R. Eleazar: "This speaks of something which has been used

YERUSHALMI SHABBAT 7:4

I:1:   R. Jonah, R. Yosé of Galilee in the name of R. Yosé b. Haninah: "What is subject to a stricter rule

I:2:   R. Hoshaiah taught, "If one took out

II:1:   [With reference to M. 7:4B] R. Bun bar Hiyya asked, "But what i

III:1:   [As to M. 7:4H] Zeira bar Hananiah in the name of R. Hanina: "That which you have said applies to

YERUSHALMI SHABBAT 8:1

I:1:   Zeira asked R. Josiah, "What is the minimum measure

I:2:   [As to the authority behind M. 8:1A, wine enough to mix a cup,] R. Yosé b. R. Bun in the name of R. Yohanan: "This represents the view of R. Judah."

I:3:   What is the requisite measure of the cups of wine [to be drunk at the Passover seder]? R. Abin said

I:4:   It has been taught

I:5:   R. Simon in the name of R. Joshua b. Levi, "There was the case of a mule

I:6:   It has been taught

I:7:   Milk [M. 8:1A]: That which you have said speaks of

I:8:   Honey [M. 8:1A]: That which you have said speaks of the old kind.

I:9:   Oil enough to anoint a small limb [M. 8:1A]:That refers in particular to

I:10:   Water enough to rub off an eye salve [M. 8:1A]: Said R. Eleazar, "That
         which you have said applies to

I:11:   R. Ba in the name of R. Hisda: "The Mishnah speaks of

II:1:   Sages reply to R Simeon, "Surely it is not possible to speak of

III:1:   Said R. Mana, "So far as people who store them away are concerned

YERUSHALMI SHABBAT 8:2

I:1:   That which you have said [at M. 8:2A] refers to

I:2:   Reed cord enough to make a hanger for a sifter or a sieve [M. 8:2A]: That
         which you have said refers to

II:1:   But that refers to a child who knows how to lace up a sandal.

III:1:   It has been taught

IV:1:   It is taught: If there is open space sufficient to contain two letters, he is
         liable [T. Shab. 8:12A].

YERUSHALMI SHABBAT 8:3

I:1:   There is a Tannaite authority who repeats the version [at M. 8:3A]: Enough
         to put on an amulet.

II:1:   That which you have said applies to

II:2:   As to ink, if one took out

III:1:   Said R Bun bar Hiyya, "For a woman puts eye shadow on one of her eyes
         and goes out to the market."

IV:1:   R. Yosé bar Hanina said, "They have taught this rule with reference to
         these things in liquid state."

V:1:   R. Hiyya taught, "Enough to put over a crack."

YERUSHALMI SHABBAT 8:4

I:1:   What is clay?

I:2:   Samuel said, "As to dirt: enough to cover up the blood of a small bird."

I:3:   It has been taught

II:1:   [As to M. 8:4F-G:] Said Rabbi, "The opinion of R. Judah appears to me
         preferable when it is of the volume of an egg, and the opinion of R.
         Nehemiah when it is mashed" [T. Shab. 8:20F].

YERUSHALMI SHABBAT 8:5

I:1:   R. Hiyya in the name of R. Yohanan: "[With reference to M. 8:5F's pen,]
         that is to say, a pen which reaches up to the joints of the fingers."

I:2:   Said R. Yosé, "Every reference to an egg which we have learned with
         reference to Mishnah tractate Kelim [at chapter 17] refers to an actual
         egg. But in tractate Shabbat, the volume of a fig is equivalent to that of an
         egg."

YERUSHALMI SHABBAT 8:6

I:1:   What is the meaning of "a tooth" [at M. 8:6B]?

II:1:   There we have learned

III:1:   Simeon bar Ba in the name of R. Yohanan: "Sufficient in weight to throw at the back of a bird and the bird will feel it."

III:2:   It has been taught

III:3:   Hiyya taught, "A sherd of any character at all — it is forbidden to wipe oneself therewith [on grounds of danger]."

\YERUSHALMI SHABBAT 9:1

I:1:   "Abomination" is written in connection with the menstruating woman, "abomination" is written in connection with dead creeping things, and "abomination" is written

I:2:   Said R. Haninah, "That is to say that

I:3:   What is the scriptural basis of R. Aqiba['s position

I:4:   There is a version of the Mishnah tradition which states

II:1:   Now does this statement [of M. A.Z. 3:6F] not stand at variance with that which R. Yohanan

II:2:   R. Ba in the name of Rab: "One who prostrates himself to a house has forbidden it. But if he did so to a tree, he has not prohibited it."

YERUSHALMI SHABBAT 9:2

I:1:   [Rather than citing the verse of Scripture,] may one not derive the same fact [M. 9:2A] from the analogy to the sea itself?

II:1:   The smallest number of "its seeds" is two varieties. [Why should there be more than that?]

YERUSHALMI SHABBAT 9:3

I:1:   Said R. Yohanan, "It was from the procedure at Sinai that they derived the rule [at M. 9:3A

II:1:   We have learned: They bathe a child [on the third day after circumcision, even if this coincides with the Sabbath] [M. 9:3C]: A Tannaite authority of the house of Rabbi [formulates the law], "They wash the mark of circumcision." R. Abbahu in the name of R. Yohanan: "The law follows the view of him who says, 'They wash the child.'"

III:1:   At first they would tie a crimson thread onto their windows.

YERUSHALMI SHABBAT 9:4

I:1:   There is the following pertinent statement

YERUSHALMI SHABBAT 9:5

I:1:   [As to M. 9:5B, spices in general:] There is a problem. Do cinnamon and salt join together [to form the requisite volume for culpability]?

I:2: There we have learned:

II:1:   Soda is carbonate of soda; soap is sulphur; Cimolian earth is alkaline ashes. Lion's leaf — R. Yosé b. R. Bun said, "Stones of wind."

YERUSHALMI SHABBAT 9:6
I:1:   It has been taught: Also of anything that smells bad — any quantity at all."

YERUSHALMI SHABBAT 9:7
I:1: M. 9:7A's specification that there is only liability for a single sin offering hardly requires specification. So] there is this problem: If the man had taken out over and over again various things, in a single spell of inadvertence, would he not be liable only for a single sin offering?

II:1:   What is the reasoning of R. Judah b. Betera?

III:1:   It has been taught

IV:1:   That which you have said applies to a clean locust. But as to an unclean one, the appropriate minimum is enough to fill the mouth of a dog.

V:1:   Said R. Aha, "A woman having a pustulate face sucks on such a locust and is healed."

VI:1:   Lo, may we then conclude, in the case of a clean one whether it is alive or dead, the requisite measure is a fig's bulk

YERUSHALMI SHABBAT 10:1
I:1:   R. Jeremiah said R. Yosé b. R. Haninah asked, "May we say that this law of the Mishnah [at M. 10:1A-B] represents the view of R. Judah, who has said

I:2:   If one party put the substance away and another one took it out, the latter is exempt [since he did not put away this paltry volume for storage]. R. Simeon b. Eleazar declares him liable.

YERUSHALMI SHABBAT 10:2
I:1:   Hezekiah said, "The Mishnah [at M. 10:2E-H] speaks of a basket of cucumbers or gourds, in which case

I:2:   Hezekiah said, "If one removed a bundle from private domain to public domain, if before he put it down in public domain, the top of the bundle was above ten [handbreadths], since the whole of it has not come to rest in public domain, the man is exempt."

YERUSHALMI SHABBAT 10:3
I:1:   R. Yosé raised the question

YERUSHALMI SHABBAT 10:4
I:1:   There we have learned: [The Sabbath and the Day of Atonement — one performed an act of labor at twilight but is not certain in which category he performed the act of labor — R. Eliezer declares him liable to a sin offering, and R. Joshua declares him exempt (M. Ker. 4:2K-N).] R. Simeon Shezuri and R. Simeon say, "They did not dispute about something that falls into a single category, that he is liable. Concerning what did they dispute?

II:1:   Truly [did they speak] [M. 10:4C]: Said R. Eliezer, "Every place in which the language, 'Truly,' is used, represents a law revealed to Moses at Sinai."

YERUSHALMI SHABBAT 10:5

I:1:   "By doing . . ." (Lev. 4:2) — an individual who performed [a forbidden act] is liable, while two or three who performed it [together] are exempt [= M. 10:5B].

II:1:   [With reference to M. 10:5E,] said R. Samuel bar R. Isaac, "That which you have said

III:1:   [One who carries out] a living person in a bed is exempt even on account of taking out the bed [M. 10:5G]: for a living person [theoretically] bears his own weight. If he carried out a corpse in a bed, he is liable [M. 10:5/I]: This represents the view of all parties [including Simeon], for has it not been taught, "[If one carries out something that has] a bad smell, in any volume at all, [he is liable for transporting such an object]. [Simeon will concur in this ruling, since the action is purposeful.]

YERUSHALMI SHABBAT 10:6

I:1:   R. Abbahu in the name of R. Yosé b. R. Hanina: "Where do they differ?"

I:2:   She who puts on eye shadow is liable on account of writing. She who rouges her face is liable on account of dyeing.

II:1:   [As to M. 10:6F-H,] Isaac bar Orion said, "Where do they dispute?

YERUSHALMI SHABBAT 11:1

I:1:   Throwing [an object] is a derivative of transporting an object [from private to public domain].

II:1:   Despite the dispute at M. 1:1B-D,] there is no difference between the view of [Rabbi Aqiba] and the view of rabbis

II:2:   [As to the dispute at M. 11:1B-D,] Samuel said, "They have reported the tradition [as a dispute] only when the object remains below ten handbreadths [from the ground].

II:3:   R. Isaac b. R. Eleazar asked, "If one tossed

II:4:   R. Abbahu says in the name of R. Eleazar in the name of R. Yohanan: "If one was standing in public domain and tossed

II:5:   It has been taught in the name of R. Judah, "If one tossed an object four cubits in public domain, he is liable."

YERUSHALMI SHABBAT 11:2

I:1:   Rab said, "[At M. 11:2A-C,] one should read not 'exempt' but 'permitted.'" In the view of Rab, as to space above ten handbreadths, it is permitted [to transport objects therein]. In the opinion of Samuel, as to the space above ten hand breadths, it is forbidden [to transport objects therein].

I:2:   Said R. Yohanan, "[Just as is the case with the bank of the cistern and the cistern, so] a standing part and a hole [beside it] join together to form the requisite volume of four cubits [M. 11:2/I]. And that is the case when the standing part is larger in breadth than the hole."

II:2:   With what sort of case do we deal?

II:2:   [As to M. 11:2K, If they were less than the stated measurements, he is exempt:] said R. Yohanan, "One should read here not 'exempt,' but 'permitted.'" [The clause refers to the breadth and not the height.]

YERUSHALMI SHABBAT 11:3

I:1:   The Mishnah speaks of [a wall, M. 11:3A] which has no niche. But if there is a niche [in the wall], then

I:2:   R. Hisda said [with reference to M. 11:3A's wall], "We deal with a wall that

YERUSHALMI SHABBAT 11:4

I:1:   It is not the end of the matter that one throws the object only four cubits into the sea. But even if he should throw it over the entire sea, he would be exempt, for the entire sea is regarded as neutral domain.

II:1:   And [referring to M. 11:4B, E,] why have you repeated the same statement twice?

YERUSHALMI SHABBAT 11:5

I:1:   [When we speak of boats tied together, M. 11:5E,] Abba bar R. Huna said, "It is a case in which

I:2:   A boat in the sea, ten handbreadths high — they do not carry from

I:3:   A rock in the sea ten handbreadths high — they do not carry anything from

I:4:   R. Hamnuna said, "A plank which protrudes from a ship, and is less than four cubits in breadth — it is permitted to sit on it and to utilize it for one's bodily needs on the Sabbath. [This amounts to pouring slops into the sea.]"

YERUSHALMI SHABBAT 11:6

I:1:   The meaning of the Mishnah [at M. 11:6A] is that

I:2:   R. Yosé b. Haninah said, "If the man acted inadvertently, this means, in ignorance of the fact that

I:3:   It has been taught: People should not engage themselves in [the possibility of violating the law either concerning] forbidden fat or forbidden sexual connections [so as to avoid the sorts of problems of deliberate as against inadvertent action with which we deal here].

YERUSHALMI SHABBAT 12:1

I:1:   What sort of building was involved in the tabernacle? They would put the boards on top of the bases.

II:1:   He who hews out stones or pillars or millstones,

II:2:   It has been taught

II:3:   The Mishnah [at M. Pes. 6:1] does not accord with the view of R. Simeon, for it has been taught

III:1:   Now there is this problem with the view of Rabban Simeon b. Gamaliel [at M. 12:1E-F]:If one had taken [a sickle] in order to harvest grain, but did not in fact harvest any grain, does this amount to anything? [Obviously not.]

YERUSHALMI SHABBAT 12:2

I:1:   What sort of plowing was done in the sanctuary? They plowed so as to plant herbs [for dyestuffs for the hangings].

II:1:   [With reference to M. 12:2/I-M, which goes over ground treated elsewhere], why do I need, if it is to improve the field — in any measure at all; if it is for cattle to eat — in the measure of a lamb's mouthful [M. 12:2J-L]?

YERUSHALMI SHABBAT 12:3

I:1:   Who stands behind the view that merely making a mark [less than a whole word] incurs liability? It is R. Yosé [M. 12:3H].

II:1:   What is the meaning of, "In any language [alphabet]" [M. 12:3]? Even if he wrote alef as alpha [= Greek].

III:1: And [as to Yosé's opinion] should one not take account of the possibility of putting what belongs below above, and what belongs above below [since the marks on the boards had to conform to a plan]?

III:2: It has been taught: "And Gad from Gadiel."

III:3: It has been taught in the name of R. Judah, "If one wrote the same letter twice, but it forms a word, he is liable, for instance ShSh, TT, GG, RR, HH."

III:4: The opinions attributed to R. Judah are inconsistent. For it has been taught

YERUSHALMI SHABBAT 12:4

I:1:   If one wrote with ink on vegetable leaves, with liquids or fruit juice on a proper tablet, [in either case,] he is exempt — unless he writes with something which lasts on something which lasts [T. Shab. 11:8J].

I:2:   In the case of witnesses who do not know how to sign their names — R. Simeon b. Laqish said, "One makes a mark before them in ink, and they sign in red paint, or in red paint, and they sign in ink."

I:3:   Said R. Eliezer to them, "Now did not Ben Satra learn

I:4:   ". . . and he writes her [a bill of divorce and puts it in her hand and sends her out of his house . . .]" (Deut. 24:1) and not [when he] incises [the letters with a knife]."... and he writes . . ." — and not when he forms letters by dropping [in a manner by forming the letters dot by dot]. ". . . and he writes . . ." — not when he pours."... and he writes . . ." — not when he incises.

YERUSHALMI SHABBAT 12:5

I:1:   If one was supposed to write the divine name [when writing a Scroll of the Torah] and instead intended to write, "Judah [YHWDH]," but forgot and did not write the D [thus producing the divine name, but not by intention], lo, the divine name stands blotted out [since it has not been sanctified by the scribe's intention], and he then confirms it in the status of sanctification [by writing it with appropriate intention]. R. Judah says, "He passes the pen over it and confirms it." They said to him, "Then he does not do it in the best possible way."

II:1: What is the theory of R. Joshua b. Betera [at M. 12:5K- L]?

YERUSHALMI SHABBAT 12:6

I:1: Now there is this problem with the position of Rabban Gamaliel.

YERUSHALMI SHABBAT 13:1

I:1: Said R. Ulla, "The reason for the view of R. Eliezer is that

I:2: He who weaves two threads on the hem and on the border

I:3: All concur in the case of him who

YERUSHALMI SHABBAT 13:2

I:1: The Aramaic words for heddles and slay are given in place of the Hebrew of M. 13:2A.

\I:2: R. Ba, R. Jeremiah in the name of Rab:"He who

YERUSHALMI SHABBAT 13:3

I:1: They asked before R. Ba, "[As to

I:2: It has been taught

YERUSHALMI SHABBAT 13:4

I:1: There we have learned

YERUSHALMI SHABBAT 13:5

I:1: Said R. Hinena, "The Mishnah [before us, at M. Bes. 3:1] does not accord with the view of R. Judah.

I:2: The opinions assigned to R. Judah are inconsistent. For we have learned there

I:3: R. Ulla said, "They asked before R. Aha, "Shall we learn [in M. Bes. 3:1F the formulation used in M. Shab. 13:5F:]

I:4: They slaughter animals kept in enclosures, but not those kept in hunting nets or bins [which may have been caught on the festival day itself] [T. Y.T. 3:1G].

YERUSHALMI SHABBAT 13:6

I:1: ". . . in doing it . . ." (Lev. 4:2) — an individual who does [a prohibited action] is liable, and two or three people who [together] do [a single prohibited action] are exempt [thus explaining M. 13:6B].

I:2: Huna said, "If one person was strong and one weak, if the sick person locked the door as much as was required, and the healthy person did not lock the door as much as was required, the sick person is liable, and the healthy person is exempt."

YERUSHALMI SHABBAT 13:7

I:1: R. Shimi asked, "What is the law as to putting food before them

I:2: R. Shimi asked, "What is the law on turning a utensil over

I:3: R. Shimi asked, "What is the law as to tying it with a rope [since it is already trapped]?"

YERUSHALMI SHABBAT 14:1

I:1: Zeriqan in the name of [delete: R. Yohanan] Immi: "There was a dispute between R. Yohanan and R. Simeon b. Laqish.

I:2:   He who hunts [Y.: spiders] flies [Y.: locusts] and mosquitoes [so T.'s ver-
           sion] is liable.R. Judah declares him exempt [T. Shab. 12:4F-G].

II:1:   The rule has been stated only with reference to the domain of man. Lo, if
           they were not within the domain of man, one is liable.

YERUSHALMI SHABBAT 14:2

I:1:   What is the difference between pickling brine and salt water?

I:2:   They prepare honeyed wine on the Sabbath [M. 20:2].

YERUSHALMI SHABBAT 14:3

I:1:   Somebody asked R. Simeon bar Karsena, "What is the law about

I:2:   [With reference to M. 14:3A, Greek hyssop:] But does it not affect the
           area within the

II:1:   It is maidenhair.

III:1:   That is what its name implies.

IV:1:   [As to the reference to palm-tree water, M. 14:3F:]

IV:2:   Simeon bar Ba in the name of R. Haninah: "He who whispers [over a
           wound] puts oil on the head [of the injured party] and whispers, but this is
           on condition that he not put the oil on by hand or with a utensil."

IV:3:   They whisper [an incantation] for the eye and the intestines, for snakes
           and scorpions

IV:4:   They may bathe in the Great Sea and in the waters of Tiberias, even though

IV:5:   It has been taught

YERUSHALMI SHABBAT 14:4

I:1:   It is written, "Like vinegar to the teeth, and smoke to the eyes [, so is the
           sluggard to those who send him]" (Prov. 10:26), and yet you say this?
           [How can you imply that vinegar is good for the teeth?] Said R. Simeon
           bar Ba, "The Mishnah speaks of vinegar deriving from fruit, [while Scrip-
           ture speaks of wine vinegar]."

I:2:   It has been taught

I:3:   Associates in the name of R. Ba bar Zabeda: "Any [wound] which is

I:4:   Said R. Haninah, "The Tannaitic teaching said thus, 'that one may not
           attain healing through Bloodshed.'

II:1:   R. Ba bar Zabeda in the name of Rab: "The law accords with R. Simeon
           [at M. 14:4H]. For if not, who has ever given rose oil to a poor person,
           who did not anoint with it?"

YERUSHALMI SHABBAT 15:1

I:1:   What sort of tying was done in the tabernacle? They tied the hangings.

YERUSHALMI SHABBAT 15:2

I:1:   [Since a woman ordinarily may tie or untie the slit of her shift, the sort of
           knot under discussion at M. 15:2B requires specification."It is,"] said R.
           Hezekiah, "applicable to opening the hem which adheres to the shift."

I:2:   If the thongs came out of his shoe or sandal, one may take them and put
           them back, so long as he does not tie them up [T. Shab. 12:14/0-R].

II:1:   [As to M. 15:2C,] do [his colleagues] differ from R. Eliezer b. Jacob

III:1:   R. Ba says, "the Mishnah speaks of a rope drawn through a loop [not knotted]."

IV:1:   R. Samuel in the name of R. Zeira, "This is the meaning of the Mishnah: On account of any sort of knot which does not last — for it is temporary — they are not liable.

YERUSHALMI SHABBAT 15:3

I:1:   The members of the house of R. Yannai say, "Folding up clothing by two people is forbidden. [It may be done only by an individual without assistance.]"

I:2:   R. Haggai in the name of R. Samuel bar Nahman: "Sabbaths and festivals have been given only for eating and drinking. Since the mouth is weary [if it cannot be used], they also permitted people to be engaged on them [= Sabbaths and festivals] in the study of Torah as well."

I:3:   It has been taught

I:4:   R. Zeira in the name of R. Hisda, "As to a Day of Atonement which coincided with the Sabbath, they do not sound the shofar. After the Sabbath they do not say the Habdalah prayer."

YERUSHALMI SHABBAT 16:1

I:1:   What is the meaning of the phrase

I:2:   The Mishnah's rule [M. 16:1A-B] accords with R. Simeon, for R. Simeon has said, "No matter prohibited on grounds of [mere] Sabbath rest stands against the r

II:1:   [As to M. 16:1 D, even though they are written in any language,] from whose viewpoint is it necessary to make that specification?

II:2:   There is the case of Rabban Gamaliel

II:3:   Even though they have said, "They do not read in Holy Scriptures except from the afternoon offering and onward, still, they do review [orally] what they have read in them and they do expound what is in them. [And if] one has a need to check something, he takes the Holy Scripture and checks it" [T. Shab. 13:1A-C].

III:1:   [With reference to M. 16:1E-F,] If that is the case, then

III:2:   That [M. 16:1E-F, since Mishnah is studied in the study house] is to say that study of the Mishnah takes precedence over study of Scripture. That supports what R. Simeon b. Yohai has taught

III:3:   [As to scrolls containing] blessings [e.g., amulets] in which are written [T.:even though they include the letters of the Divine Name and] many citations of the Torah, they do not save them

III:4:   Said R. Joshua b. Levi, "As to an aggadic passage

III:5:   As to the books of Evangelists and the books of the *minim,*

YERUSHALMI SHABBAT 16:2

I:1:   The Mishnah [M. 16:2A-B] speaks of a case in which

II:1:   This accords with what R. Jacob bar Aha said, Hinena Qartegenah in the name of R. Hoshaiah: "A saddlebag which contains money — one puts a loaf of bread on it and carries it about."

III:1:   Lo, as to bringing the objects to an alley open on both sides, one may not do so.

YERUSHALMI SHABBAT 16:3

I:1:   R. Bun bar Hiyya in the name of R. Ba bar Mamel: "The passage before us accords with the view of R. Nehemiah, for he has said, '[Utensils] may be moved about only in a case of need' [M. 17:4]."

I:2:   The passage before us [permitting saving food on the night of the Sabbath for three meals, even though the first of the three may already have been eaten, M. 16:3D,] accords with the position of R. Hundeqes, who has said, "Under all circumstances they save food for three meals."

I:3:   What is there to say about [a fire that broke out on the night of] the Day of Atonement?

I:4:   It has been taught:

I:5:   It has been taught

I:6:   It has been taught:\

I:7:   It has been taught

YERUSHALMI SHABBAT 16:4

I:1:   The Mishnah's rule [at M. 16:4A-C] accords with the principle of R. Yosé, for he has said, "Under all circumstances they save food for three meals" [M. 16:3G]. Since the whole [of the bread, figs, or wine] forms a single entity, it is as if the whole constitutes food for one meal.

II:1:   For so it is usual to invite guests for the Sabbath.

III:1:   There we have learned

YERUSHALMI SHABBAT 16:5

I:1:   And these are they: Cloak, under-tunic, hollow belt, linen tunic, shirt, felt cap, cotton shirt, pair of trousers, pair of shoes, pair of socks, shoes, hat on his head, girdle around his loins, and scarf around his neck.

II:1:   For so it is usual to lend clothing on the Sabbath.

YERUSHALMI SHABBAT 16:6

I:1:   Ba bar Mamel in the name of Rab: "A scroll which has caught fire on one side

I:2:   What follows serves M. 3:8B-C, above 3:8/11.A-D, and has no place here:] R. Samuel in the name of R. Zeira: "[M. 3:8B-C] represents the view of R. Yosé."

YERUSHALMI SHABBAT 16:7

I:1:   In the time of R. Immi, a fire broke out in the village. R. Immi issued a proclamation in the marketplace of the Aramaeans, saying, "Whoever does [something] will not lose out!" Said R. Eleazar b. R. Yosé before R. Yosé, "[It was all right to do this, for] it was a matter of danger." If it was a matter of danger, then even R. Immi should have put the fire out.

II:1:   But has it not been taught: "If they saw [a minor] going out and collecting herbs, you are not responsible for him"?

YERUSHALMI SHABBAT 16:8

I:1:   [M. 16:8] accords with that which R. Simeon b. R. Yannai said

II:1:   But is this not food for chickens [so why can one not simply remove it for that purpose, rather than leaving it in place]?

III:1:   R. Ulla said, "He spent eighteen years there in Arab, and only these two cases came before him. He said, 'O Galilee, Galilee, you have hated the Torah. You will end up working for tax farmers.'"

YERUSHALMI SHABBAT 16:9

I:1:   What is the law if a gentile did so for himself and also for an Israelite?

II:1:   With reference to M. 16:9H:] They said to him, "Is it all right for us to disembark?" He said to them, "Since he did not make it in our behalf, we are permitted to disembark" [T. Shab. 13:14C, G].

YERUSHALMI SHABBAT 17:1

I:1:   [The reference to] the doors of the house makes its new point, and [the reference to] the doors of utensils makes its new point.

II:1:   For they are utilized only when on the ground.

II:2:   "[All utensils may be handled on the Sabbath], except for a large saw or plowshare" [M. 1 7:M-B]. Rabban Simeon b. Gamaliel says, "Also: the anchor of a boat." [T.:] R. Yosé says, "Also a large spade" [T. Shab. 14:1C-E].

II:3:   They do not move boards of a ship on the Sabbath. But if the boards were suitable to serve as a cover for a utensil or for food, lo, they are in the status of covers of utensils, and may be carried about on the Sabbath.

YERUSHALMI SHABBAT 17:2

I:1:   Lo, if it is not to split nuts [and so throughout], one may not handle such a tool.

I:2:   A utensil which serves a distinctive purpose prohibited on the Sabbath may be handled only in the case of a need [appropriate to the Sabbath], while one which serves a distinctive purpose permitted on the Sabbath may be handled both in the case of a need appropriate to the Sabbath and otherwise.

II:1:   Said R. Simon, "R. Abbahu permitted me to take eye salve off on the Sabbath with it [a needle]."

YERUSHALMI SHABBAT 17:3

I:1:   Members of the householder of R. Yannai say, "[The Mishnah at M. 17:*3A* refers to] a reed which one adapted for inspecting the status of olives. How so? If it came up covered with liquid, one may be certain that the processing in the press is finished. And if not, one may be certain that the processing in the press is not finished."

I:2:   A reed which a householder set up with which to open and shut a door [Y.
         throughout has window] — if it was tied on and suspended [from the
         door], they open and shut the door with it, and if not, they do not open and
         shut the door with it.

YERUSHALMI SHABBAT 17:4

I:1:   R. Judah in the name of Rab: "The law accords with

I:2:   R. Yohanan and rabbis from over there [in Babylonia]: One said, "'For
         need' refers to the need of using the object in itself, and 'not for need'
         refers to not needing to use the object in itself. [Then] R. Nehemiah says,
         'They are handled only when they are needed for use in themselves.'"

I:3:   It has been taught

YERUSHALMI SHABBAT 17:5

I:1:   There we have learned:...glass enough to scrape the end of a shuttle [M.
         8:6], and here you say this [that is, stating a different criterion for the
         sherds of glass]?

YERUSHALMI SHABBAT 17:6

I:1:   We have learned [at M. 21:1:] [A man takes his son, along with the stone
         in his hand, a basket] with a stone in it. It has been taught by the house-
         hold of Rabbi

YERUSHALMI SHABBAT 17:7

I:1:   [As to M. Er. 10:11A, A bolt that is dragged on the ground, thus fastened
         to the gate by a long rope and not merely suspended, is permitted in the
         Temple and forbidden in the provinces,] what is a bolt that is dragged on
         the ground? Said R. Yohanan

II:1:   Abba bar Kahana, R. Hiyya bar Ashi in the name of Rab: "The law ac-
         cords with the position of R. Yosé."

YERUSHALMI SHABBAT 18:1

I:1:   Zeira asked R. Josiah, "What is the measure of these baskets [at M.
         18:1A]?"

I:2:   [In the case of a storage room which one has not cleared out prior to the
         Sabbath,] what is the law as to clearing out the storage room [M. 18:1C]
         following this order?

I:3:   There is a Tannaite authority who teaches: "They may handle produce in
         which heave offering has accidentally been mixed." There is a Tannaite
         authority who teaches: "They may not handle

II:1:   [With reference to M. 21:1C: They handle unclean heave offering along
         with clean heave offering or with unconsecrated food,] who stands be-
         hind the view that one may handle [such unclean heave offering]?

II:2:   [With reference to M. Dem. 7:5: If a man had fully untithed figs at home
         and he was in the house of study or in the field and unable to attend to
         them, he says, "Two figs out of one hundred which I shall separate, be-
         hold, these are made heave offering, and the following ten are made first

tithe, and the following nine are made second tithe,"] R. Eleazar said, "A man may stand on the eve of the Sabbath [Friday] and say, 'Lo, this is made heave offering tomorrow,' but a man may not

II:3:   It has been taught (in Tosefta's version)

III:1:   How shall we interpret the matter?

YERUSHALMI SHABBAT 18:2

I:1:   Said R. Zeira, "This passage [at M. 18:2A-D] accords only with the view of R. Hanina

I:2:   The Mishnah stands at variance with the position of him who has said

YERUSHALMI SHABBAT 18:3

I:1:   How do they help out [T.: in the delivery of a cow on a festival]?

II:1:   That accords with the following

III:1:   Samuel said, "They make a fire for her, even in summer."

IV:1:   This accords with the following: A servant girl of Bar Qappara went and brought forth a child on the Sabbath. A woman came and asked Rabbi [whether they might tie and cut the umbilical cord]. He said to her, "Go and ask the midwife." She said to him, "There is no midwife [here]." He said to her, "Go and follow your usual practice." She said to him, "There is no established practice." He said to her, "Go and cut the umbilical cord, in line with the view of R. Yosé [at M. 18:3F]."

V:1:   With reference to the meaning of M. 18:3G,] the Mishnah means to say that all that is necessary for a woman in childbirth do they carry out on the Sabbath [and the reference to circumcision is not meant to be limiting, but rather, illustrative].

V:2:   It has been taught

YERUSHALMI SHABBAT 19:1

I:1:   Said R. Yohanan, "We originally supposed that in all matters [involving the doing of a religious commandment], R. Eliezer takes a position different [from that of sages and holds that in every instance making ready things that facilitate, but are not directly involved in, the doing of a religious duty is permissible on the Sabbath]. But since R. Eliezer found it necessary to provide an exegesis to that effect in the repeated usage of the word, 'firstfruits,' [it follows that not in all instances, but only in some, does the making ready of things only indirectly needed for carrying out a religious action override the restrictions of the Sabbath.]

I:2:   It has been taught

I:3:   R. Simon in the name of R. Joshua b. Levi: "As to a knife for use for a circumcision

I:4:   They asked Hillel the Elder [in connection with M. Pes. 6:1], "What should the people do

I:5:   There we have learned I:6: Now why should not [Hillel] have permitted them

I:7:   It has been taught

YERUSHALMI SHABBAT 19:2

I:1:   "Circumcising, he shall be circumcised" (Gen. 17:13) — The repetition of the same word represents a decree that

I:2:   Rab said, "'Circumcising, he shall be circumcised' (Gen. 17:23) — on the basis of this verse, we know that

I:3:   He whose mark of circumcision was covered over, one who was born circumcised, and one who had been circumcised prior to conversion — in all instances

II:1:   [With reference to M. 19:2E, If one did not mix wine and oil on the eve of the Sabbath, let this be put on by itself and that by itself,] R. Yohanan bar Mareh asked

YERUSHALMI SHABBAT 19:3

I:1:   We have learned: They bathe a child [on the third day after circumcision, even if this coincides with the Sabbath] [M. 9:3C = M. 19:3E].

II:1:   As to the androgyne [bearing sexual traits of both sexes], they do not violate the Sabbath on his account.

YERUSHALMI SHABBAT 19:4

I:1:   "[The formulation of M. 19:4D-G,]" said R. Yohanan, "Accords with the view of what is at issue as presented by R. Meir.

I:2:   [Following a third version of the Mishnah:] Said R. Zeira, "A statement of R. Yannai indicates that [in his view, at M. 19:4A-C,] we deal with a case in which

I:3:   [For so long as one is involved in the rite of circumcision on the Sabbath, one may go over even those shreds of flesh which do not invalidate the rite of circumcision.] But once he has ceased [to conduct the operation]

YERUSHALMI SHABBAT 19:5

I:1:   There may be an infant who is circumcised on the very day of his birth.

II:1:   [Referring to M. 19:5F] Jacob of Kefar Naborayya asked R. Haggai,

III:1: [With reference to M. 19:5I, An infant who is sick — they do not circumcise him until he gets better,] Samuel said, "[Even if] he caught a fever [for one moment], they wait on him for thirty days."

YERUSHALMI SHABBAT 19:6

I:1:   These are the shreds which render the circumcision invalid

II:1:   If he circumcised but did not trim the circumcision, it is as if he did not circumcise at all [M. 19:6E]: [The membrum must be trimmed, with shreds which invalidate the circumcision removed.] It has been taught: [If one did not trim it,] he is subject to punishment by extirpation.

II:2:   It has been taught

YERUSHALMI SHABBAT 20:1

I:1:   It has been taught

I:2:   [With reference to M. 20:1A,] said R. Hinena, "The view of R. Eliezer accords with the position of R. Judah,

I:3:   Hiyya in the name of R. Yohanan: "He who spreads out a tent

I:4:   Zeira, R. Hiyya bar Ashi in the name of Samuel: "He who strains [wine to remove the lees] is liable on the count of selection [winnowing]." Said R. Zeira, "It is surely more reasonable that it is on the count of

YERUSHALMI SHABBAT 20:2

I:1:   R. Ba in the name of R. Judah in the name of Rab: "[The rule of M. 20:2B] is on condition that one not make it like a receptacle [out of the cloths, as one does on ordinary days]." This question then wa

II:1:   [With reference to M. 20:2C:] The meaning of the Mishnah is that

III:1:   R. Yosé in the name of R. Yohanan: "Wine, honey, and pepper."

YERUSHALMI SHABBAT 20:3

I:1:   Said R. Mana, "The meaning of the Mishnah [at M. 20:3A-B] is that one places it before himself

II:1:   Said R. Mana, "The meaning of the Mishnah [at M. 20:3A-B] is that one places it before himself

III:1:   This is on the count of winnowing.

YERUSHALMI SHABBAT 20:4

I:1:   [The reason for M. 20:4A-B is:] What the fat ox leaves over, the grazing animal eats

YERUSHALMI SHABBAT 20:5

I:1:   The Mishnah [at M. 20:5A-C] speaks of a case in which

II:1:   [With reference to M. 20:5E-H,] has it not been taught

III. ERUBIN

YERUSHALMI ERUBIN 1:1

I:1:   [The following discussion serves Y. Suk. 1:1A: A sukkah which is taller than twenty cubits is invalid. R. Judah declares it valid, and also M. 1:1A-B. Judah holds that what we have is valid to serve as a doorway and so symbolically to link the dwellings within into a single domain for purposes of carrying on the Sabbath.] R. Yosé stated what follows without specifying the name of an authority; R. Aha in the name of Rab: "Rabbis [derive the requisite dimensions from the analogy of the doorway of the Temple building, and R. Judah, from the measurements of the porch *[ulam* leading to the interior of the Temple]." If the measurement derives from the doorway of the porch, then it should be sufficient if it is forty cubits high. I:2: R. Aha, R. Hinena in the name of Kahana: "The law does not accord with R. Judah."

I:4:   One should diminish [the height of the crossbeam. making it lower] [M. 1:1A]: How does one diminish the height of the crossbeam?

II:1:   And the alley entry of a breadth wider than ten cubits should one diminish, making it narrower [M. 1:1C]: How does one diminish its breadth? One sets up a beam at the gate of the alleyway and so permits [carrying in] the alleyway [cf. T. Er.1].

II:2:   [And if it has the shape of a doorway (M. 1:1D):] This statement refers to the breadth [not the height] of the doorway.

II:3:   If the alley entry was fifteen cubits wide, R. Ba and R. Huna in the name of Rab: "One sets up a board three cubits and a bit more wide

II:5:   Jeremiah in the name of R. Bun: "In the case of an alleyway in which

II:6:   An alleyway, the wall of which was broken down from the side toward the top [of the crossbeam] — the rabbis of Caesarea said R. Hiyya, R. *Yosé:*

II:7:   If there is a single crossbeam, what is the law

II:8:   Zeirah asked, "How is a courtyard rendered permissible [to transport objects therein]?"

II:9:   R. Zeira, R. Huna in the name of Rab: "An alleyway the breadth and length of which are equivalent is not permitted [for carrying] by providing [merely] a side beam and a crossbeam

III:1:   And if it has the shape of a doorway, even though it is wider than ten cubits, it is not necessary to diminish [it, making it narrower] [M. 1:1D-F]. Hananiah bar Shelamayya was in session, teaching Hiyya, son of Rab. Rab stuck his head out the window and said to him, "That is not how matters are

III:3:   R. Aha gave instruction in the case of an entry way [open to public domain] closed up only by a construction in the shape of a door, that it must be set four cubits within [the alleyway, and not at the exit point].

III:4:   [Since the space directly beneath the crossbeam is regarded as external to the alleyway, hence not an area suitable for carrying,] R. Zeira raised this question

YERUSHALMI ERUBIN 1:2

I:1:   With regard to M. 1:2D, Eliezer's statement,] what is the meaning of two side posts?

II:1:   [As to M. 1:2E-J,] it has been taught

II:2:   As to the view of sages, R: Huna in the name of Rab

YERUSHALMI ERUBIN 1:3

I:1:   Said R. Ba, "[The meaning of setting the brick lengthwise, M. 1:3C,] is

I:2:   In the case of two cross beams, each one a half handbreadth broad, how much space may there be between them [so that they may be regarded as a single crossbeam for the purpose of holding bricks]?

I:3:   If there are two cross beams, one a third and a bit more [of a handbreadth and a half, and the other a third and a bit more [of a handbreadth and a half, and between the two a space of less than a third of a handbreadth — the law governing this situation accords with that which R. Yohanan said

I:4:   As to a beam which protrudes from one wall but does not reach the other

I:5:   A crossbeam [set at an angle] so that one side lies above twenty cubits and the other below the height of twenty cubits — they so regard it that

I:6:   If there were two cross beams, one above the other — R. Yosé b. Judah
          says,

YERUSHALMI ERUBIN 1:4

I:1:   It has been taught

I:3:   For we have learned there: What is the outer area? "It is any area near the
          town," the words of R. Judah [M. Bes. 1:2E-F]. The views assigned to R.
          Judah are at variance.

YERUSHALMI ERUBIN 1:5

I:1:   From whose viewpoint is it necessary to specify [the rule of M. 1:5B]?

II:1:   Aha in the name of R. Zeira: "This represents the view of R. Judah in
          particular]."

III:1:   This too represents the position of R. Judah [in particular].

IV:1:   [As to M. 1:5D,] they derived this fact from the measurements of the
          molten sea

YERUSHALMI ERUBIN 1:6

I:1:   Where the Mishnah presents a dispute on the thickness of the side posts,
          it speaks of a case in which

I:2:   Building stones which protrude from the building — if there is not a
          space of three handbreadths between one and the other, are regarded as
          equivalent to side posts [T. Er. 1:9].

I:3:   A wall, one side of which recedes more than the other and which appears
          even from within but looks to be recessed from without, or appears even
          from without and looks to be recessed from within, is deemed equivalent
          to side posts [T. Er. 1:10].

I:4:   In the case of a wall, one side of which protrudes and one side of which is
          drawn back [so that the wall fronting on the public domain is uneven] —
          Kahana said

YERUSHALMI ERUBIN 1:7

I:1:   It has been taught

I:2:   Simeon bar Karsena in the name of R. Aha: "R. Meir, R. Yosé, and R.
          Eleazar b. Azariah — all three maintain the same view.

II:1:   [With reference to M. Git. 2:3L-M = M. 1:7G: R. Yosé the Galilean says,
          "They do not write a writ of divorce on anything that is alive or on food-
          stuffs,"] what is the scriptural basis for the ruling of R. Yosé the Galilean?

YERUSHALMI ERUBIN 1:8

I:1:   Ada in *the* name of R. Hisdai: "To whom is the rule [at M. 1:8C-D] im-
          portant?

YERUSHALMI ERUBIN 1:9

I:1:   Said R. Zeira, "They have stated this rule [cf. M. Suk. 1:10] only with
          reference to

I:2:   [As to M. 1:9A-B,] R. Simeon b. Laqish in the name of R. Judah b.
          Hananiah, "If one inserted four reeds into the four corners of a vineyard

and tied a thread above [the reeds from one to another], it affords protection

YERUSHALMI ERUBIN 1:10

I:1:   "In the case of a caravan, they may surround the camp with reeds," the words of R. Judah [M. 1:10C]. Lo, an individual [who wants to make a partition of this kind must make one formed] of warp and woof.

I:2:   A caravan is made up of no fewer than three people. A gentile may not make up the necessary number to constitute a caravan. What would be a practical case?

I:3:   R. Deripah said R. Nisa asked, "What is the law as to assigning to them three triangulated plots

I:4:   R. Aha in the name of R. Hisdai: "The view of R. Yosé b. R. Judah accords with the theory of his father and also differs from a theory of his father.

II:1:   [As to M. 1:10G-K,] how large is such a military camp?

II:2:   A military camp which goes forth for an optional war may

III:1:   R. Hiyya bar Ashi said, "That which you have said applies to

III:2:   R. Judah b. Tema says, "They make camp anywhere [even without the permission of the owner of the field], and in the spot in which they are killed, there they are to be buried" [T. Er. 2:6B-C]. That is so that you should not conclude that they should be treated as were the [gentiles] who were slain in the wars.

III:3:   Just as, when they go forth to war, they are exempt from the four matters [of M. 1:10G-K], so when they come back from war, they are exempt from [these same] four matters.

YERUSHALMI ERUBIN 2:1

I:1:   [The reason that they set up four corner-pieces] is that the breaches [in the wall surrounding the well in public domain] are more than the standing boards, and, accordingly, one has to set up corner-pieces, rather than flat boards [each of four cubits in breadth]. [Why so?

I:2:   Jeremiah in the name of Rab: "They have permitted the use of strips of wood around wells [facilitating use of the wells on the Sabbath in the way described at M. 2:1] only in the case of t

I:3:   They proposed to say, "R. Meir will concede the view of R. Judah, but R. Judah will not concede the view of R. Meir."

I:4:   If there was a single stone shaped like a cube, they examine it. If it should be divided, and there would be six handbreadths on this side and six handbreadths on that side, at the corners, it is deemed equivalent to boards [T. Er. 1:12B-C].

I:5:   If there was there [at a well] a ditch ten handbreadths deep and four broad, with six handbreadths on one side and six on the other [that is, it is an L-shaped ditch, of the stated dimensions,] then it is treated as equivalent to a corner-piece.

I:6: A wall, tree, or partition of reeds is regarded as equivalent to boards [T. 1:15A].

I:7: [If there was a courtyard open to the space enclosed by the boards, it is permitted to carry from the courtyard to the area enclosed by the boards, [Y.: but not] and from the area enclosed by the boards to the courtyard. [If] there were two there, both of them are prohibited, [but it is permitted to carry in the space enclosed by the boards] [T. Er. 1:15].

I:8: Said R. Yosé b. R. Bun, "They permitted transporting objects in the area marked off by boards around a well only for the purpose of drawing water in that area alone."

I:9: It has been taught: "[The space at issue at M. 2:1F-I] is ten cubits," the words of R. Meir. R. Judah says, "Thirteen or fourteen" [T. Er. 1:13B-C].

YERUSHALMI ERUBIN 2:2

I:1: R. Jeremiah in the name of R. Samuel bar R. Isaac: "And that measure [of a cubit of partition and a cubit of space, applicable to all other beasts,] is the same as the measure stated here [at M. 2:2B], so that

I:2: In the view of R. Meir, there may be corner-pieces or boards. In the view of R. Judah, there must be corner-pieces but not boards.

YERUSHALMI ERUBIN 2:3

I:1: [From the viewpoint of Judah, M. 2:3A,] what is the rule on

YERUSHALMI ERUBIN 2:4

I:1: Said R. Yohanan, "The two theories attributed to R. Judah are at variance with one another.

II:1: [As to M. 2:4C-D,] what is the difference between

YERUSHALMI ERUBIN 2:5

I:1: R. Samuel bar Nahman in the name of R. Jonathan: "They derived the stated dimensions from the courtyard of the tabernacle

I:2: An outer area which covers two *seahs'* space — it is permitted to carry there in only four cubits [in the case of an area not surrounded for a dwelling house, as at M. 2:5A-C].

I:3: As to an outer area which covers two *seahs* of space, said R. Abbahu, "Since such an area may be transformed into private domain through the encampment of a caravan, [it is regarded as private domain, so that] if one tossed an object from public domain into that area, he is liable."

I:4: A courtyard which is open into an outer area — they may carry an object from the courtyard to the outer area, but not from the outer area into the courtyard.

YERUSHALMI ERUBIN 2:6

I:1: The opinions assigned to R. Judah are at variance with one another, for we have learned there

YERUSHALMI ERUBIN 2:7

I:1: It has been taught

YERUSHALMI ERUBIN 2:8

I:1:   R. Abbahu in the name of R. Eliezer: "[It is not actually *a kor's* space that
           Eliezer has pronounced permitted for carrying, but rather a case in which

II:1:   "And so did I hear from him: 'The inhabitants of a courtyard, one of
           whom forgot and did not prepare an erub — as to his house, it is prohib-
           ited for him to bring in something or take it out, but for them it is permit-
           ted'" [M. 2:8B-D]:

III:1:   [As to M. 2:8F,] we considered maintaining that the reference was only to
           the matter of hart's tongue. But a teaching turned up that that statement
           [of Ilai] pertains to all three items.

YERUSHALMI ERUBIN 3:1

I:1:   Said R. Aha, "This [M. 3:1A] represents the view of R. Eliezer

I:2:   [When the Mishnah says that a meal of commingling may be prepared
           from any sort of food,] it represents the view of R. Meir

I:3:   With any sort of food do they prepare a meal of commingling for court-
           yards and alleyways, except for water and salt, both in the view of R.
           Aqiba and in the view of R. Ishmael. Now as to money in the status of
           second tithe, any sort of food may be purchased with it, in the view of R.
           Aqiba, except for water and salt. But as to the view of R. Ishmael:

I:4:   With any food do they prepare an erub and a shittuf except for water and
           salt [M. 3:1A-B]: Said R. Yosé, "It is because the body does not derive
           sustenance from them." Said R. Levi, "It is because through them a curse
           is carried out, [water with the flood, salt with Sodom]."

I:5:   Said R. Eleazar, "If one turned the two into saltwater, they may be pur-
           chased with money in the status of second tithe."

I:6:   Wine must be enough for drinking along with two meals. Oil must be
           enough to eat with food for two meals. Vinegar must be enough for dip-
           ping food for two meals [T. Er. 6:3A-C].

II:1:   He who vows to abstain from food is permitted to make use of water and
           salt [M. 3:1E]: There we have learned: He who takes a vow not to eat
           what is cooked is permitted [to eat what is] roasted or seethed [M. Ned.
           6:1A].

II:2:   If one took a vow not to eat a loaf of bread, they may use a loaf of bread
           in a meal of commingling including him. If one declared a loaf of bread
           to be sanctified, they may not make use of it for a meal of commingling
           [T. Er. 2:10C-G].

III:1:   They prepare an erub for a Nazir with wine [M. 3:1F], for someone else
           may drink it, and for an Israelite with heave-offering [M. 3:1G], for a
           priest may eat it.

IV:1:   ...and for a priest in a grave area [M. 3:1/I]. Now does the statement of
           the Mishnah accord [in specifying a grave area not a graveyard] with the
           view of the House of Shammai?

YERUSHALMI ERUBIN 3:2

I:1:   R. Jacob the Southerner raised this question: "[May we say that] the rule of the Mishnah does not accord with the position of the House of Shammai?

II:1:   [As to M. 3:2D's reference to a minor,] Samuel said, "[If one has made use, in sending his meal of commingling to the Sabbath limit,] of a child nine or ten years old, his meal of commingling is valid."

II:2:   Said R. Joshua [b Levi], "On what account do they prepare a meal of commingling of a courtyard? It is for the sake of peace."

II:3:   He who sends his erub with a deaf-mute, idiot, or minor [M. 3:2D]: [But if he said to someone else to receive it from him, lo, this is a valid erub (M 3:2G-H):] Said R. Eleazar, "But [the sender] must supervise him [anyhow]!"

YERUSHALMI ERUBIN 3:3

I:1:   Lo, this is a valid erub [M. Er. 3:3C], but it is forbidden to carry it about

II:1:   [With reference to M. 3:3C and its contrast to M. 3:3B,] do you not regard the *[erub* placed in] a deep place as equivalent to one placed in a high place? [Why is the cistern not regarded as private domain?]

III:1:   It is because the reed is uprooted and stuck into the ground. Lo, if it were not uprooted and stuck into the ground, the *erub* would not be a valid one.

III:2:   It has been taught [with reference to M. 3:3K-L]

YERUSHALMI ERUBIN 3:4

I:1:   They have stated only, And was made unclean [M. 3:4D]. If it is a matter of doubt whether it was made unclean while it was still day or after dark, [that is the rule]. But if it is a matter of doubt whether

I:2:   What is the law as to assigning the man two thousand cubits from the location of his erub-meal to his home [since he has not acquired a location for spending the Sabbath at all]?

I:3:   There we have learned

I:4:   The assumption thus far is that one who holds there that the matter of doubt is resolved in favor of cleanness there also maintains here that it is permitted, and he who rules there that the matter of doubt is resolved as unclean will maintain here that it is forbidden. But even in accord with him who said there that it is resolved as unclean here will concur that it is permitted.

I:5:   Said R. Samuel bar Sistra, "As to a meal of commingling, they have treated it as equivalent to the matter of doubt, in matters of betrothal affecting a deaf-mute.

YERUSHALMI ERUBIN 3:5

I:1:   Thus does the Mishnah teach: A man stipulates concerning his erub [that is, he has to leave two, one in one direction, one in the other]. Said R. Eleazar, "Who taught the passage in the language, 'If they came... and if they did nor come... '? It is R. Meir." I:2: R. Judah bar Shalom, R. Judah bar Pazzi in the name of R. Yohanan, "With respect to the conditional writ of betrothal they followed the theory of R. Meir of tractate Qiddushin. [The stipulation Is stated positively and negatively.]"

I:3:   If one made no stipulation, [what is the law]? Let us derive the answer from the following

II:1:   [With reference to M. 3:5C:] The meaning of the Mishnah *is,* If gentiles come from both directions... If they come from neither side... If gentiles come from the east, his *erub is* at the west [cf. M. 3:5B].

YERUSHALMI ERUBIN 3:6

I:1:   [With reference to M. 3:6A,] there is a Tannaite authority who formulates the matter "In the west."

YERUSHALMI ERUBIN 3:7

I:1:   And sages say, "He makes an erub for a single direction" [M. 3:7F]: This is the meaning of the statement in the Mishnah: Either he makes an,erub for a single direction for two days, or he does not make an erub at all.

I:2:   Eliezer concedes that they do not prepare an erub for half a day for the north and for half a day for the south. For they do not divide up a single day. And sages say, "Just as they do not divide up a single day, so they do not divide up two days" [T. Er. 4:1C-E].

I:3:   There we have learned: A flagon which is in the status of Tebul Yom [that which had been immersed on the selfsame day, and which becomes fully clean only at sunset] and which one had filled from a jar containing first tithe [wine] which was yet untithed [in respect to heave-offering of tithe] — if he said, "Lo, this will be heave-offering of tithe once it gets dark [and the flagon is clean], " lo, [his words take effect and] this is heave offering of tithe [once it gets dark].... [M. T. Y. 4:4A-D].

I:4:   R. Haggai raised this possibility: "If one was standing on Thursday and said, 'Let a place of Sabbath-rest be acquired for me for the Sabbath [at the location of the erub,]' [even though this is two days in advance], in the view of R. Eliezer, he has acquired the place of Sabbath-rest, and in the view of the rabbis he has not."

I:5:   [In T.'s version:] Said to them R. Eliezer, "Do you not concede that the one who prepares an erub with his feet for the first day has to prepare an erub with his feet for the second day? [M. 3:7K-L]. "[If] his erub was eaten before it got dark, he may not go out depending upon it on the same day" [M. 3:7N]. They said to him, "True." He said to them, "Is this not what I said: They are two days?" They said to him, "Do you not concede that they do not prepare an erub on one day [the festival] for its fellow [the Sabbath]?" He said to them, "True." They said to him, "Is this not what we said: They are one day?" [T. Er. 4:1F-L]

YERUSHALMI ERUBIN 3:8

I:1:   There is this dispute: The leftovers of a wick, fire, or oil, [of a flame] extinguished on the Sabbath — what is the law on kindling them on the

adjacent festival day? Both Rab and R. Haninah maintain that it is prohibited to do so. And R. Yohanan said that it is permitted to do so.

I:2:   In the name of four elders they have ruled, "If a person's erub is eaten up
on the first day [of a festival], lo, he is in the status of his fellow townsfolk
on the second [in which case the two days are treated as separate and
distinct from one another, and not a single, protracted holy day.

I:3:   If one has effected his act of commingling Sabbath boundaries through
the use of a loaf of bread on the first [of two holy days], he does the same
on the second, so long as it is with the same loaf of bread that he has made
the erub-meal on the second day. If he effected an act of commingling by
his feet [walking to the place at which he wishes to locate his Sabbath
limit and remaining there at sunset] on the first day, he must effect the act
of commingling by his feet [walking as above] on the second day.

YERUSHALMI ERUBIN 3:9

I:1:   R. Abin in the name of rabbis over there: "They have treated him as one
who goes to his town [and. en route, does not know which of two days
will be the festival day].

I:2:   [In the version of T.:] Lo, if there was a basket of fruit in his possession,
which had not been properly tithed, this day] he says, "If today is the
festival day, nothing that I say is so. But if not, I designate the heave-
offering and tithes which are in it[s pieces of fruit]" [M. 3:9A]. And he
leaves it. And the next day he says, "If today is the festival day, nothing
that I say is so. But if not, I designate the heave-offering and tithes which
are in its pieces of fruit]" [T. Er. 4:3A-D].

I:3:   The opinions assigned to R. Judah are at variance with one another

I:4:   Sages concur with R. Judah in the case of the two festival days of the
New Year [that they constitute a single, protracted, spell of holiness, for]
they derive from an enactment of the former prophets.

YERUSHALMI ERUBIN 3:10

I:1:   It is because he says, "If it is today or yesterday" [M. 3:10D] [that sages
did not concur with him (M. 3:10E)].

YERUSHALMI ERUBIN 4:1

I:1:   [Is not the rule at M. 4:1A-C self-evident? No, that is not so, for] if that is
not the explicit rule, then what shall we have to say?

I:2:   How do we know the limit of four cubits [which one may have as the
limit of one's private location for spending the Sabbath]?

I:3:   R. Judah b. Pazzi asked, "As to the four cubits of which they have spoken

II:1:   The text states only that they brought him back. Lo, if he went back [on
his own], he is forbidden [to move about as if he never went out].

II:2:   If a person acquired a place of Sabbath residence [e.g., in a valley], and
[on the Sabbath] gentiles came along and surrounded it with a partition
— R. Huna said

III:1:   R. Zeira, R. Huna in the name of Rab: "Since R. Joshua and R. Aqiba
           wanted to impose a strict ruling on themselves [M. 4:1 L] . that indicates
           that the law follows the view of

YERUSHALMI ERUBIN 4:2

I:1:   Rabban Gamaliel had a tube for measuring distances, through which he
           could take a visual citing of the distance on a plane.

YERUSHALMI ERUBIN 4:3

I:1:   [Is the rule of this passage not obvious? No, it is not,

II:1:   [As to the meaning of, If he was within the Sabbath line, M. 4:3D], *said*
           R. Hunah, "That is the case if

II:2:   It has been taught

YERUSHALMI ERUBIN 4:4

I:1:   Said [sages to R. Judah], "Was not the schoolhouse of R. Tarfon within
           two thousand cubits, or perhaps he had joined himself to the other resi-
           dents of his town while it was still day [on Friday]?

YERUSHALMI ERUBIN 4:5

I:1:   R. Zeira in the name of R. Hisdai: "The reason for the view of R. Yohanan
           b. Nuri [at M. 4:5B] is this

II:1:   If [within the theory of Judah, M. 4:5F, that one may select a place of
           Sabbath residence in any direction he wishes,] one has selected for him-
           self a place of Sabbath residence while it is still daylight, he may retract
           his decision while it is still daylight.

YERUSHALMI ERUBIN 4:6

I:1:   Even though R. Hananiah b. Antigonos differed from rabbis in the matter
           of cubits [at M. 4:7K], he concurs with them here in the matter of estab-
           lishing the Sabbath limit for a town.

YERUSHALMI ERUBIN 4:7

I:1:   If there were two people, one of whom knew a spot and one who did not,
           this one who knows a spot goes along [taking with him] that one who
           does not know a spot, and that one who does not know a spot goes along
           with this one who knows a spot [so that the one who can make the state-
           ment does so in behalf of the other].

YERUSHALMI ERUBIN 4:8

I:1: R. Meir maintains the view that

YERUSHALMI ERUBIN 4:9

I:1:   One may explain the statements [of M. 4:9C-D, he is permitted to go to
           the other town, but the other townsfolk of his are not,] in two ways.

YERUSHALMI ERUBIN 4:10

I:1:   Both R. Aha in *the* name of R. Hinena and R. Hisdai say, "[Eliezer] has
           specified only 'two.'

I:2:   The disciples wished to propose that the ruling of R. Eliezer applies [to a
           case in which

YERUSHALMI ERUBIN 5:1

I:1:   [If among the houses at the outskirts] one house recedes, they bring it out toward the city line. If one house projects, they draw the city line out to the house.

I:2:   Rab said, "They add a 'limb' ('BR) to a town [in connection with the Sabbath limits (M. 5:1A)]." Samuel said, "They augment from within ('BR)."

I:3:   R. Yohanan in the name of R. Hoshaiah: "They add a limb to it [in connection with establishing the Sabbath boundary of a town]."

I:4:   [As to M. 5:1A] R. Jacob bar Aha, R. Yosé in the name of R. Yohanan: "At what point do they add?

II:1:   [As to bridges or sepulchres containing a dwelling house, they extend the measure outward so as to take account of them (M.:1E-F):] Said R. Nahman

II:2:   R. Aha said, "R. Hiyya the Elder and Bar Qappara had a difference of opinion. One of them maintained that [the rule about augmenting a town, M. 5:1A] pertains to

II:3:   R. Ba, R. Judah in the name of Rab: "A town that is shaped like a bow — if the distance between the two ends of the bow is four thousand cubits less one, one measures the Sabbath limits to cover the entire encompassed area as well as two thousand cubits beyond.

II:4:   R. Ba in the name of R. Judah: "If there was a large town, with - a ditch ten handbreadths deep and four broad running through it [constituting, therefore, an autonomous domain], one regards the ditch as if

II:5:   Rab said, "In the case of a town made up entirely of tents,

III:1:   [As to M. 5:1G: They make the Sabbath limit of the area of the town as if it were shaped like a square tablet;] the sides are squared so as to correspond to the four directions of the world, the western side corresponding to the western side of the world, the southern side to the southern side of the world.

III:2:   It has been taught in the name of R. Judah: "Also its cornices and walls are measured with it" [T. Er. 4:7B].R. Hoshaiah raised the question: "The contained airspace [not roofed over] of a courtyard — what is the law as to its being measured with the town?"

III:3:   [With reference to M. 5:1G,] If one circumscribed a [circular] town by a square and formed it into the shape of a square tablet, and laid out the Sabbath limits in the shape of a square tablet (M. 5:1G), when one measures, he does not measure from the middle point [of the town]

YERUSHALMI ERUBIN 5:2

I:1:   R. Hunah in the name of Rab: "R. Meir and rabbis [at M. 5:2A-B] interpret [each in his own way] a single verse of Scripture,

II:1:   Samuel said, "That is the case when they are arranged in a line." Bar Qappara said, "That is the case when they are arranged in a triangle."

YERUSHALMI ERUBIN 5:3

I:1:   What is the measure of [the rope for measuring] the Sabbath boundary?

II:1:   [As to M. 5:4F, If one came to a mountain, he takes account only of the horizontal span,] R. Aha, R. Hinena, R. Jeremiah in the name of R. Samuel bar R. Isaac: "And that is the rule, if the measure of the mountain is at least four handbreadths, a place of which one would take account."

III:1:   Yosé, R. Abonah in the name of R. Judah, R. Yudan presented the view in the name of Rab: "As to M. 5:3/I, piercing mountains,] the man on the top holds his end on a level with his head, and the man on the bottom on a level with his feet "

III:2:   Raba in the name of R. Judah, R. Zeira in the name of Mar Uqba: "[M. 5:3A:] They measure only with a rope fifty cubits long [in order to establish the Sabbath boundaries of a town]."

III:3:   And how do we know from Scripture that they do not bury the dead in the Levites' towns?

YERUSHALMI ERUBIN 5:4

I:1:   In the case of an amateur [surveyor] who extended the limit [beyond what had been known] — they do not listen to him.

I:2:   Said R. Hoshaiah, "You have come to the point of the laws governing Sabbath limits, which is that these laws do not clearly derive from the teachings of the Torah. [Accordingly, we assign a lenient ruling.]"

YERUSHALMI ERUBIN 5:5

I:1:   As to a town belonging to an individual which was converted into a town belonging to many people,] it has been taught in the name of R. Judah

II:1:   Unless one excluded a section of it of the size of the town of Hadashah in Judah [M. 5:5E-F]: For instance,

YERUSHALMI ERUBIN 5:6

I:1:   There is a problem troubling Bar Qappara, [namely, how is it possible for his house to be further than his *erub,* M. 5:6E, if his *erub* is west of his house, and he is east of his house?

YERUSHALMI ERUBIN 5:7

I:1:   This is the sense of the Mishnah

I:2:   [As to M. 5:6H: He who placed his *erub* outside of the Sabbath limit,] with regard to the town itself, what is the law as to its being counted with the measure of two thousand cubits?

I:3:   At first the townsfolk of Tiberias would traverse the whole of Hammata. But the townsfolk of Hammata went only up to the place of the bow. Now the townsfolk of Tiberias and the townsfolk of Hammata have gone and formed a single town [for the purposes of the Sabbath limit] [T. Er. 5:2].

I:4:   R. Isaac bar Nahman in the name of R. Haninah: "Tn the case of the dispute [at M. 5:7D-G, in which one places his *erub* in another town], the two parties disagree concerning the case in which

I:6:   As to a new town, one measures from the houses. In an old one, one measures from the wall. What is a new one, and what is an old one?

I:1:   [In line with the positions of sages, M. 5:8B-E,] Jacob bar Aha in the name of R. Eliezer: "A more lenient rule applies to the case of one who

I:2:   The roof of a tower is deemed equivalent to the town; the roof of a cave is equivalent to the fields [cf. T. Er. 4:1OK-L].

II:1:   The roof of a tower is deemed equivalent to the town; the roof of a cave is equivalent to the fields [cf. T. Er. 4:1OK-L].

III:1:   [With reference to M. 5:7D-F,I said R. Isaac b. R. Eliezer, "That is to say

YERUSHALMI ERUBIN 6:1

I:1:   A courtyard inhabited by gentiles — lo, [for the purpose of carrying on the Sabbath] it is the equivalent of a cattle pen. ...[T. Er. 5:19].

I:2:   R. Yosé in the name of R. Yohanan: "The law is not in accord with R. Yohanan b. Nuri [M. 4:5]."

YERUSHALMI ERUBIN 6:2

I:1:   R. Aha, R. Hinena in the name of Kahana: "The law does not accord with R. Judah."

I:2:   Jeremiah in the name of Rab: "In the case of a courtyard with two gateways, in which an Israelite and a gentile dwell

I:3:   A resident alien, resident slave, and spiteful apostate — lo, such a one is in the status of a gentile for all purposes [having to do with the erub-meal].

I:4:   There is a Tannaite authority who teaches: A government official [quaestor] [in a courtyard] imposes a prohibition as soon as he takes up residence, and billeted troops [or travelers] after thirty days. And there is a Tannaite authority who teaches: A government official imposes a prohibition after he has been in residence for thirty days, and billeted troops [or travelers] never impose a prohibition at all [T. Er. 5:22A-B].

I:5:   R. Jacob bar Aha in the name of R. Eleazar: "[As to the dispute of Meir, who stands behind M. 6:2A-B, and Judah, M. 6:2C,] at issue between them is the possibility of

YERUSHALMI ERUBIN 6:3

I:1:   Theirs are permitted both for him and for them [M. 6:3C], for he has annulled his right of domain [and is in the status of a guest]. What is the rule as to

I:2:   It has been taught

I:3:   R. Hisdai said, "Each of ten Israelites dwelling in a single house [or courtyard] has to annul his right of domain [if he has not participated in the erub-meal, so that one of them may carry objects in the courtyard]." Said R. Yosé, "Each of ten gentiles dwelling in a single house [or courtyard] has to rent out his right of domain [to nullify his right and hence permit Israelite owners to utilize the courtyard as a common domain on the Sabbath]."

YERUSHALMI ERUBIN 6:4

I:1:   The meaning of the Mishnah is, "By what time must they nullify the right of access?" The House of Shammai say, "While it is still day." And the House of Hillel say, "Also after it got dark."

II:1:   The meaning of the Mishnah is, He who nullified his right of access and took something out.

III:1:   The meaning of the Mishnah [for the view of Meir] is, "He does not prohibit the others."

III:2:   [In T.'s version:] Three [Y: two] who were living in a courtyard, one of whom died, and the property fell as an inheritance to someone else ... [T. Er. 5:14].

III:3: What is the law as to acquiring rights of access through rental once it has gotten dark?

III:4: What is the law as to renting a right of domain from an innkeeper?

YERUSHALMI ERUBIN 6:5

I:1:   R. Ba in the name of R. Judah, "The Mishnah['s choice of words] speaks of common practice."

II:1:   since the householder will not take account of a mixture of the wine, it is not necessary to prepare an *erub*.

III:1:   since the householder will take account of a mixture of the two, it is necessary to prepare [a distinct] erub.

III:2:   R. Ba bar Kahana, R. Hiyya bar Ashi in the name of Rab: "The Mishnah speaks of a case in which the food is located in a single utensil. [But if they have two utensils, even if wine is in both, they must prepare an erub.]"

III:3:   Said R. Zeriqan, "The reason for the view of R. Simeon [at M. 6:5F] is that it is the usual way to drink an oil-and-wine-drink."

III:4:   It has been taught: R. Eleazar b. Taddai says, "One way or the other, they are prohibited unless they prepare an erub" [T. Er. 5:9G].

YERUSHALMI ERUBIN 6:6

I:1:   [If] the eating room is before them [when they are in separate rooms], then they are in a situation parallel to houses opening up onto a common courtyard [T. Er. 5:8].

I:2:   Ba in the name of R. Judah: "In the case of two houses, one inside the other, if one has

I:3:   Ba in the name of R. Judah: "In the case of two men, one of whom enjoys domain [in a courtyard] and one of whom does not

YERUSHALMI ERUBIN 6:7

I:1:   Where is the principal location of residence?

II:1:   Hiyya bar Ashi in the name of Rab: "The Mishnah speaks of a case in which

II:2:   Samuel said, "The householder, his sons, and dependents make an erub-meal through a single loaf of bread." Now does Samuel differ?

II:3:   As to the house in which they leave the erub-meal, [does that house have also to prepare an erub]?

II:4:   R. Jacob bar Aha, R. Yosé in the name of R. Yohanan: "Residents of an alleyway who placed their erub-meals in two separate places — if it was because they had no single satisfactory utensil to hold the lot, lo, this procedure is valid.

II:5:   It has been taught

YERUSHALMI ERUBIN 6:8

I:1:   ...and prohibited from doing so in the alley [M. 6:8C], for the alleyway is to courtyards as a courtyard is to houses [M. 6:8J]. The operative consideration is that

II:1:   this is the view of R. Meir [that both are needed].

II:2:   It is self-evident that people prepare an erub for courtyards and a shittuf for an alleyway. If people have prepared an erub for courtyards, [only], if they then wanted to take a share in the shittuf covering the courtyard, they may not do so.

II:3:   How many courtyards are there in an alleyway?

II:4:   Said R. Yosé, "When I was over there [in Babylonia] I heard R. Judah asking Samuel, 'If one separated his coin for the *sheqel-tax* for the Temple and then dropped dead, [what is the disposition of the designated coin]?'

III:1:   It is self-evident that people may rely on a *shittuf* for an alleyway [if they forgot to prepare an *erub* for the courtyard (M. 6:8D)]. What is the law as to relying on a *shittuf* in the case of courtyards [for which they forgot to provide an *erub*]?

III:2:   It is obvious that it is necessary to put an *erub* in a particular house in a courtyard [since the erub signifies a place of residence, which, we recall, Rab requires as the critical consideration]. But does a *shittuf* require location in a house? R. Aha in the name of Rab: "One places it either in the open air of a courtyard, or in the open air of an alleyway."

I:1:   Said R. Yosé, "This [M. 6:9A-C] represents the view of R. Aqiba

YERUSHALMI ERUBIN 6:10

I:1:   If one of the residents of the outer courtyard forgot and did not join in the erub, the outer courtyard is forbidden, for it has not been covered by an erub-meal valid for all its residents, and the inner courtyard likewise is forbidden for the people have placed their erub-meal in a location which, in any event, is forbidden [cf. T. Er. 5:27

I:2:   Hunah in the name of Rab: "The law of the courtyard's partition does not pertain to a gentile; the law of [dividing upper from lower stories by means of a] partition does not apply to a gentile."

YERUSHALMI ERUBIN 7:1

I:1:   A web of rope diminishes the dimensions of a window for purposes of the Sabbath [so separating the two courtyards, in line with M. 7:1E-F], but not for purposes of

II:1:   [As to M. 7:1B,] it is not the end of the matter that

II:2:   What is the law as to diminishing the dimensions of a window

YERUSHALMI ERUBIN 7:2

I:1:   Now why should the Mishnah specify that the wall is four handbreadths broad?

I:2:   R. Ba, R. Judah in the name of Samuel: "A wall which one surrounded by ladders on both sides — they nonetheless prepare an *erub* separately, and they do not have the option of preparing a single *erub* covering both court-yards."

I:3:   It has been taught

II:1:   [With reference to M. 7:2F:] That which you have said applies to a large wall, but in the case of a small one, the appropriate measure is the larger part of the wall. What is the definition of a large, and what is the definition of a small wall?

YERUSHALMI ERUBIN 7:3

I:1:   Lo, so far as the straw is concerned, [the Mishnah's phrasing indicates that]

I:2:   [As to the trench,] members of the house of R. Yannai said, "If one covered the trench with mats, its effect is null, [and the two courtyards are unified thereby]."

YERUSHALMI ERUBIN 7:4

I:1:   There is a Tannaite authority who [at M. 7:4D] teaches, "They prepare an erub separately, and they do not prepare an erub jointly." There is a Tannaite authority who teaches, "They prepare an erub jointly, and they do not prepare an erub separately."

YERUSHALMI ERUBIN 7:5

I:1:   Said R. Eleazar, "This is the meaning of the statement of the Mishnah [at M. 7:5D]:These fill their baskets on one side and feed the cattle, and those fill their baskets on the other side and feed their cattle."

I:2:   A heap of straw which is between two courtyards — [residents of this one] break open an entry on one side and feed their cattle, and residents of the other courtyard break open an entry on the other side and feed their cattle.

YERUSHALMI ERUBIN 7:6

I:1:   It has been taught

II:1:   [With reference to the Hebrew slave girl of M. 7:6C,] how shall we interpret the matter?

III:1:   There we have learned: He who borrowed a cow and the one who lent it sent it along with his son, slave, or messenger, or with the son, slave, or messenger of the borrower, and it died, the borrower is exempt. [If the borrower had said to him, "Send it with my son, " "... my slave, " " "... my messenger, " the borrower is liable] [M. B.M. 8:3]. Does this [latter clause] not indicate that the slave made acquisition of the object from his master in behalf of the other party?

YERUSHALMI ERUBIN 7:7

I:1: What is the meaning of "informing them"?

YERUSHALMI ERUBIN 7:9

I:1: What is the definition of "what remains later on in the erub"?

I:2: Said R. Joshua b. Levi, "On what account do they prepare an *erub* for courtyards [in addition to alleyways]?

YERUSHALMI ERUBIN 7:10

I:1: As to M. 7:10F,] R. Abbahu in the name of R. Yohanan: "That is to say that, on the authority of the law of the Torah, coins do not effect acquisition.

II:1: For they prepare an erub for a man only with his acknowledge and consent [M. 7:10H]: This statement of the Mishnah represents the view of R. Meir.

II:2: Isaac b. Haqolah in the name of R. Yudan the Patriarch: "They prepare an erub for a person against his will." And so it has been taught: Residents of an alley may impose the requirement upon one another to provide [funds to purchase] a side beam and a crossbeam [to permit carrying in the alleyway] [T. B.M. 11:1A].

YERUSHALMI ERUBIN 8:1

I:1: Now we note that [in the formula prescribed in the Mishnah,] we have not learned that

YERUSHALMI ERUBIN 8:2

II:1: [As to M. 8:2F-G,] so it has been taught: The opinions of the two in fact are close to one another.

YERUSHALMI ERUBIN 8:3

I:1: But [is not what is in the courtyard] to be assigned to the residents of the lower part [that is, of the courtyard, since, after all, the objects are located in the courtyard and not on the balcony]?

I:2: [In the case of a distinct domain between two courtyards, and each courtyard readily has access to it,] it is self-evident that if this side has an entry-way to the area, and that side likewise, both parties are forbidden to utilize the area of the house between the two courtyards so far as tossing an object or letting down an object [as the case may be].

I:3: If between two courtyards was a] ruin — R. Yohanan said, "One assigns the ruin to its owner [if he is able to utilize it conveniently]."

II:1: [With reference to M. 8:3D:] Said R. Yohanan, "The standing part of a partition and the empty spaces in it [or below it] join together to form the ten handbreadths [in height] and the four [in breadth]. And that is the case only if the standing part is greater than the empty spaces."

III:1: [As to M. 8:3/I-J,] R. Jeremiah in the name of R. Samuel bar R. Isaac: The Mishnah [speaks of a case in which

YERUSHALMI ERUBIN 8:4

I:1:   R. Judah in the name of Rab: "That which you have said [at M. 8:4A-B] applies in the case of

II:1:   Members of the household of R. Yannai say, "[With reference to M. 8:4E,] if [the householder has the right to keep in the storehouse] even a peg for hanging his sandal, [that constitutes a right of storage sufficient to provoke the rule stated by Judah]." R. Ba bar Hinena said, "Even a lid, even a tray." Rab said, "But that is on condition that it is something which may be handled on the Sabbath."

YERUSHALMI ERUBIN 8:5

I:1:   This ruling [at M. 8:5A-C] illustrates the position of R. Meir, for R. Meir says

YERUSHALMI ERUBIN 8:6

I:1:   The views of rabbis differ [with regard to M. 8:6A-D].

II:1:   The opinions assigned to R. Judah are confused. There he has said: [A woman who borrowed from her girlfriend] spice, water, or salt for her dough — lo, they are in the status of the two of them [so far as transporting these substances are concerned. R. Judah declares exempt in the case of water, for it is of no substance [M. Bes. 5:4C-E].

II:2:   Said R. Huna, "The rule [of M. 8:6A-C] applies to a case in which the partition protrudes into the open area of the cistern itself, [but the partition may not go under the surface of the water].

YERUSHALMI ERUBIN 8:7

I:1:   The Mishnah [at M. 8:7A] speaks of a water channel which is ten handbreadths deep and four broad [in which case it constitutes a domain unto itself].

I:2:   It is obvious in the case of a water channel ten handbreadths deep but not four broad [thus not constituting a distinct domain] that it is permitted to carry objects in that area, and it also is permitted to draw water from it, [since it does not constitute c distinct domain but is part of the private domain in which it is located].

YERUSHALMI ERUBIN 8:8

I:1:   R. Zeira, R. Judah in the name of Rab: "And this rule [of M. 8:8C-D] applies on condition that

II:1:   [As to M. 8:8E-H,] does it not turn out that residents of two distinct domains are utilizing a single domain in common?

II:2:   Said R. Huna, "And the rule [of M. 8:8E-H] applies only if

II:3:   It has been taught

II:4:   [As to a balcony above water, M. 8:8A,] R. Iddi said before R. Hiyya, "It is permitted to draw water but forbidden to pour out slops."

II:5:   [With reference to M. Suk. 1:10:] Said R. Yohanan, "R. Yosé has made this statement only with regard to the sukkah. But as regards the laws of the Sabbath, also R. Yosé will concur [that the partition must be within three handbreadths of the ground]."

II:6:   [Referring back to M. 8:8E-H,] R. Abbahu in the name of R. Yosé: "That which you have said applies to a case in which

YERUSHALMI ERUBIN 8:9

I:1:   They estimated that a place sufficient to absorb the amount of water used by a person in a given day is two hundred seahs, and four cubits absorb the equivalent in volume to two hundred seahs. [This explains the area specified at M. 8:9A.

I:2:   The Mishnah passage before us differs from the view of R. Yohanan

I:3:   Said R. Jeremiah, "R. Meir and R. Eliezer b. Jacob have both said the same thing. "

II:1:   [As to M. 8:9J-L:] So too it has been taught

YERUSHALMI ERUBIN 9:1

I:1:   Yosé b. R. Bun said, "There is a dispute between Rab and Samuel [relevant to the view of sages, M. 9:1C, that each roof is a domain unto itself. If that is the case, to what extent, within each domain, may one carry objects about?] "Samuel said, 'Up to two *seahs* of space [is permissible for carrying objects, no matter how large the ro

I:2:   They proposed to interpret the dispute [of M. 9:1A-C] between R. Meir and rabbis to pertain to a case in which the residents did not prepare an *erub* [joining the houses below]. But if they did prepare an *erub,* [then sages will concur with Meir's position].

II:1:   The Mishnah [M. 9:1C] speaks of a case in which the entries serving all the residents were connected to the roofs with a Tyrian or an Egyptian ladder.

II:2:   [From the viewpoint of Meir, if the roofs are flat, and from the viewpoint of sages, in the case of a single roof,] what is the law as to carrying objects about on the whole of the roof? Samuel said, "One may carry throughout the whole of it." Rab said, "People may carry only for four cubits."

II:3:   ["All the roofs of a town are a single domain [M. 9:1A]. It is prohibited to carry something up or to bring something down from the courtyard to the roofs, or from the roofs to the courtyard. But all (objects) which were kept for the Sabbath in the courtyard may be carried about in the courtyard. And those kept for the Sabbath on the roofs may be carried about on the roofs," the words of R. Meir.

II:4:   Said R. Judah, "Here is a precedent: In the time of the danger, we would

II:5:   [Reverting to the disputes at M. 9:1,] it turns out that there are three [so , rather than four] items under dispute. All roofs of a town are a single domain [M. 9:1 A].

YERUSHALMI ERUBIN 9:2

I:1:   The Mishnah speaks of that same roof. But as to a roof belonging to another party, it is forbidden.

I:2:   [Reference is made to Y. 6:8 in which Samuel rules that if a matter is permitted for part of the Sabbath, it is permitted for the whole of it.] The following passage of the Mishnah stands at variance with Samuel's position:

YERUSHALMI ERUBIN 9:3

I:1:   Zeriqa, R. Jacob bar Bun in the name of R. Haninah: "R. Eliezer's rule [imposing liability] applies only to the space in the area of the walls themselves.

YERUSHALMI ERUBIN 9:4

I:1:   Why [does the Mishnah specify that the courtyard was breached to give access to public domain] on two sides? Even if it were only at one side, [that would suffice to raise the question before us].

II:1:   [As to M. 9:4B, a house breached on two sides:] If it was breached in the middle, it remains permitted [to carry in the house, since it is roofed over]. Samuel said, "[If it is breached in the middle, even where it is roofed over], it is forbidden [to carry in the house]."

II:2:   Said R. Yohanan, "R. Eliezer [M. 9:3B] has made his statement only in regard to a courtyard and an alleyway. But as to a house, is it in the status of a bridge?"

II:3:   Rab and R. Yohanan said, "It is forbidden, both on that Sabbath and on the coming Sabbath."

II:4:   Said R. Yohanan, "Costus, a gourd, an alleyway, a proselyte, and an ordinary person are subject to a strict rule."

YERUSHALMI ERUBIN 9:5

I:1:   R. Huna said, "An area that is roofed over does not fall into the category of public domain."

I:2:   What is the law as to

YERUSHALMI ERUBIN 10:1

I:1:   He who finds tefillin brings them in one by one [pair by pair] [M. 10:1A-B], just as they are worn as clothing, one on the head, one on the arm. Rabban Gamaliel says, "Two sets at a time" [M. 10:1C], two on his head, two on his arm.

I:2:   R. Abbahu, R. Eleazar: "He who puts on *tefillin* at night violates a positive commandment, for it is said

II:1:   [As to the interpretation of M. 10:1C, two sets at a time,] said R. Yosé, "The meaning of the Mishnah is,

II:2:   It has been taught

III:1:   Under what circumstances? In the case of used ones. But in the case of new ones, he is exempt from the obligation of putting them into a protected place [M. 10:1D-F]. Why is this the case? It is because old ones have been inspected [and are certified as valid], while new ones have not.

IV:1:   But in a situation of danger, he covers them up and goes along [M. 10:1/
         I]: If it was raining, lo, this one covers himself up in a piece of leather
         [protecting the scroll], and he covers [the tefillin with his own garment]
         [cf. T. Er. 8:16D].

YERUSHALMI ERUBIN 10:2

I:1:   Both R. Eliezer and R. Abedimi in the name of R. Mana — one of them
         said, "[M. 10:2B] speaks of an infant in the time of danger."

II:1:   R. Simeon b. Laqish in the name of Levi Sokayya: "[When the Mishnah
         at M. 10:3D refers to this procedure,] the Mishnah speaks of a case in
         which

YERUSHALMI ERUBIN 10:3

I:1:   On the threshold it is permitted [to leave the scroll], but outside of the
         threshold it is forbidden [for in that case, one brings the scroll from neu-
         tral domain to private domain].

II:1:   R. Jacob bar Aha in the name of R. Yosé: "This represents the view of R.
         Judah, who has said

III:1:   Why? So that the actual writing will not be ruined.

IV:1:   The principles assigned to R. Judah are in a state of confusion. There he
         has said, "It is forbidden to make use of the airspace within ten cubits of
         the ground," and here he has said this!

YERUSHALMI ERUBIN 10:4

I:1:   [The rule of the Mishnah refers only to a] single projection, but if there
         were two [the second being below the one under discussion, and both of
         them being ten handbreadths above the ground], it is forbidden [to use
         either projection].

YERUSHALMI ERUBIN 10:5

I:1:   It is not the end of the matter that

II:1:   [With reference to M. 10:5G:] Rab said, "[Judah refers to] one's phlegm.
         [Cf. T. Er. 8:7A.]"

II:2:   It is not the end of the matter that

YERUSHALMI ERUBIN 10:6

I:1:   There is no difficulty in understanding why it should be prohibited to
         stand in private domain and drink in public domain [M. 10:6A]. But if he
         stands in public domain and drinks in private domain, is his mouth not
         above a height of ten handbreadths [and that space also is public domain?
         So why is he held to transport water from private to public domain?]

I:2:   It has been taught

I:3:   [A statement of R. Jacob bar Aha should appear here. Then:] R. Yosé b.
         R. Bun [said], "The traditions assigned to him are confused. For did not
         R. Jacob bar Aha state in the name of R. Haninah

II:1:   Said R. Hiyya, "And so is the case of a winepress [M. 10:6D]. This has to
         do with

III:1:   [As to M. 10:6E, A man scoops up water out of a gutter less than ten
           handbreadths from the ground,] R. Judah said, "This represents the view
           of R. Meir, for he has said, 'You regard the wall as leveled.'"

YERUSHALMI ERUBIN 10:7

I:1:   [Since the Mishnah specifies that the partition is ten handbreadths high, it
           would appear to exclude a case in which the cistern is in a hole ten hand-
           breadths deep. Accordingly, we must ask,] Do you not regard depth as
           equivalent to height [in the assessment of the effects of the partition]?

I:2:   Up to this point [we have dealt with such a distinct area which is suffi-
           ciently] close [so that a window is directly above it, e.g., at M. 10:7B, E,
           where it is within four cubits of the wall]. What is the rule if the cistern or
           garbage dump is more distant

I:3:   If there were two [rooms above the cistern, belonging to two different
           people,] there were two Amoraim [who differed on the space that must
           separate the two windows so that each may utilize the cistern on his own].
           One said, "A space of ten is required," and the other said, "A space of
           four."

I:4:   [As to the cistern of M. 10:7A, it is permitted to draw water from it through
           the window above,] on condition that the area of the cistern not be more
           than

YERUSHALMI ERUBIN 10:8

I:1:   R. Aha in the name of Rab: "It is forbidden to tread on the roots of a vine
           shoot on the Sabbath. The same rule applies to a tree and a cabbage." [As
           to M. 10:8D-E,]

II:1:   [As to M. 10:8F-J,] the Mishnah speaks of a case in which

YERUSHALMI ERUBIN 10:9

I:1:   R. Aha, R. Hinena in the name of Kahana: "The law is not in accord with
           the view of R. Meir."

I:2:   Abba bar Pappi asked, "To what does R. Meir compare

YERUSHALMI ERUBIN 10:10

I:1:   Said R. Yosé b. Rabbi, "In accord with the view of him who permits

II:1:   [As to M. 10:10G, a bolt that is dragged on the ground, thus fastened to
           the gate by a long rope and not merely suspended, is permitted in the
           Temple and forbidden in the provinces,] what is a bolt

YERUSHALMI ERUBIN 10:11

I:1:   [As to M. 10:11B, the reason that even in the Temple one may not put the
           upper pivot back is that], said R. Yosé b. R. Bun [or: R. Jonathan], not
           every deed prohibited by reason of Sabbath rest have they permitted in
           the sanctuary.

I:2:   It has been taught

YERUSHALMI ERUBIN 10:12

I:1:   Said R. Yosé b. R. Bun, "This represents the view of R. Simeon b. R.
           Yosé

II:1:   There we have learned: [Carrying the animal designated as a Passover-
          offering to the Temple, bringing it from outside to inside the Sabbath
          limit, and] cutting off a wen which is on it do not override the prohibi-
          tions of the Sabbath. R. Eliezer says, "They do override the prohibitions
          of the Sabbath" [M. Pes. 6:1D-E]. How then can you say this [= A]?

YERUSHALMI ERUBIN 10:13

I:1:   [With reference to M. 10:13B,] Judah b. Rabbi said, "They have taught
          [that such a procedure is permitted] only in the case of

I:2:   It has been taugh

I:3:   In the case of a courtyard on which it rained, and in which was a house of
          mourning or a house of festivities — lo, this one may take up the stone
          and pour off the water, so long as one not do it on the Sabbath in the way
          he does it on an ordinary day.

I:4:   It has been taught

II:1:   They draw water from the cistern of the Exiles and from the great cistern
          with a waterwheel on the Sabbath, and from the Haqqar Well on a festival
          day [M. 10:13E-F]: On what account do they

YERUSHALMI ERUBIN 10:14

I:1:   Said R. Yohanan b. Zeroqah to [Judah], "Do you not turn out to keep
          uncleanness in the Temple?"

I:2:   There we have learned: The leper put his head inside the Temple court,
          and the priest placed blood on the tip of his ear. He put his hand inside,
          and he placed it on the thumb of his hand. He put his foot inside, and he
          placed it on the big toe of his foot. R. Judah says, "The three of them did
          he put inside all at once" [M. Neg. 14:9A -D]

II:1:   Spelling out his argument, Judah adds,] "Furthermore, it is possible to
          leave the Temple without any real delay in keeping the uncleanness therein
          [for one may find tongs right away]."

II:2:   [If one] has removed [uncleanness] from a place in which, if a man en-
          tered while unclean deliberately, he would be liable for extirpation [and
          inadvertently, he is liable to a sin-offering,] and it fell down in a place on
          account of which [under the stated conditions], one is not liable to ex-
          tirpation, that which he was carrying already has been subjected to the
          requirement of being taken out, [and it certainly is picked up and taken
          out]. [The question is this:] If one found another [dead creeping thing]
          alongside the one which he has to take out [which had fallen down in a
          location not subject to extirpation], does one take out both of them, or
          does he take out only one of them?

II:3:   The laws of the Sabbath, festal offering, and sacrilege are like mountains
          suspended by a hair, with very little Scripture and many laws. So they do
          not have that on which to depend. [In this regard did R. Joshua say, "Tongs
          were made with tongs. Who made the first tongs? [Now is this not my

view: they were created [on the eve of the Sabbath]" [M. Abot 5:6:] Among the ten things created on the eve of the Sabbath at dusk were the tongs made with tongs [T. Er. 8:23].

IV. YOMA

YERUSHALMI YOMA 1:1

I:1:   Ba in the name of R. Yohanan derived [the proposition of M. 1:1A] from the following verse: "'As has been done today, [the Lord has commanded to be done to make atonement for you]' (Lev. 8:34).

I:2:   What is the difference between the priest who burns the red cow ant the priest who officiates on the Day of Atonement?

I:3:   Said R. Yosé bar Haninah, "The tenth *ephah* of fine flour and the priestly britches are indispensable [in the rite of consecration]. "What is the scriptural proof?

I:4:   Yosé bar Haninah asked, "As to the tenth *ephah* of fine flour [offered by the high priest on the day of his consecration], how is it offered?

I:5:   As to the rites of consecration, what is their status?

I:6:   As to the rites of consecration, what is the governing analogy [to determine the definition of a day]?

I:7:   There we have learned: These draw out the old loaves, and the others lay down the new ones. And a handbreadth of one new row lies up against a handbreadth of another, as it is said, "Before me perpetually" (Exod. 25:30). ["And you shall set the bread of the Presence on the table before me always" (Exod. 25:30)].

I:8:   [Referring to M. 1:1A, separating the high priest from his household,] Ben Beterah explained, "It is done lest he have sexual relations with his wife when she is menstruating, and then he would be put away [unclean] for seven days" [T. Yoma 1:1B].

I:9:   It has been taught: All chambers in the Temple were exempt from the requirement of having a mezuzah on their doorposts, except for the councillors' chamber, for it was the residence of the high priest seven days a year [T. Yoma 1:2A-B].

II:1:   The councillors' chamber [M. 1:1A]: Abba Saul would call it "the chamber of oil" [T. Yoma 1:3E].

II:2:   We have found that the First Temple was destroyed only because they worshiped idols, practiced fornication, and committed murder, and so in the case of the Second Temple.

III:1:   They appoint another priest as his substitute lest some cause of invalidation [of the high priest who is to officiate on the Day of Atonement] should affect him [M. 1:1B-C]. Now do they designate another priest along with him?

III:2:   Is it possible that the priest anointed for war brings the tenth of an *ephah* from his own property? Scripture says, "[The priest who is appointed from among Aaron's] sons, who is anointed to succeed him, [shall offer it to the Lord]" (Lev. 6:22).

III:3: "How do we know that just as they appoint another priest to serve as his substitute, lest some cause of invalidation should affect him, so they betroth for him another wife, on the stipulation that something may affect his wife [and if that should not be the case, the betrothal is null]? "

YERUSHALMI YOMA 1:2

I:1: And is the high priest not unclean because [purification water] has been sprinkled on him, [so how can he participate in the rite, M. 1:2A]?

II:1: For a high priest offers up a portion at the head and takes a portion at the head of the other priest [M. 1:2C]. How so? [In T.'s version:] He says, "This sin-offering is mine," "This guilt-offering is mine," "One loaf of the two Two Loaves," "Four or five loaves of the show bread [are mine]" [T. Yoma 1:5B].

II:2: [With reference to M. 1:2A,] R. Yosé b. R. Bun in the name of R. Joshua b. Levi: "Every day the high priest puts on his garments and comes and offers the continual whole-offering of the morning. If, in addition, there are animals brought in fulfillment of vows or as thank-offerings, he offers them as well, and then he goes home.

YERUSHALMI YOMA 1:3

I:1: Lest you have forgotten, or never even learned it to begin with [M. 1:3C]: Has it not been taught

II:1: Where did they set him up, inside or outside?

III:1: Why does the Mishnah not refer also to goats [since the rite of the Day of Atonement involves a goat as well]?

YERUSHALMI YOMA 1:4

I:1: It has been taught

I:2: [But why did the high priest require such guards?] Was it not one of the miracles that were done in the Temple [that the high priest never suffered an emission of semen prior to the Day of Atonement]?

YERUSHALMI YOMA 1:5

I:1: Why does he turn aside and weep [M. 1:5F]? Because it is necessary to impose an oath on him. And why do they turn aside and weep [M. 1:5F]? Because they have to impose an oath on him.

I:2: It is written, "And he shall take a censer full of coals of fire from the altar before the Lord, and two handfuls of sweet incense beaten small; and he shall bring it within the veil and put the incense on the fire before the Lord, that the cloud of the incense may cover the mercy seat which is upon the testimony, lest he die" (Lev. 16:12-13). The meaning is that he should not prepare the mixture outside and bring it inside.

YERUSHALMI YOMA 1:6

I:1: It has been taught: They read Proverbs and Psalms, because their message disturbs one's sleep.

I:2:   Kahana asked Rab, "Is it Qebutar or Qebutal?"

YERUSHALMI YOMA 1:7

I:1:   R. Huna said, "[The Mishnah means that] the finger is put into the mouth [to produce a shrill sound]."

YERUSHALMI YOMA 1:8

I:1:   Said R. Mana, "Is it not reasonable to suppose that on the Day of Atonement they do it from the end of the first watch, and on festivals from midnight, on account of thirst?

YERUSHALMI YOMA 2:1

I:1:   Mana raised the question, "And why to begin with did they not establish a lot for the taking up of the ashes from the altar?

I:3:   All concur in the case of a non-priest who laid out a pile of wood on the altar, that he is liable.

I:4:   It has been taught

I:5:   If a non-priest raised up the ashes, and the wind blew them away, there is a dispute of R. Yohanan and of R. Haninah.

I:6:   If one raised up half [of the ashes on the altar], there is a dispute of R. Yohanan and R. Joshua b. Levi.

I:7:   If one took up the ashes with his left hand, there is a dispute of R. Yohanan and R. Judah b. Rabbi.

I:8:   Said R. Mana, "I am surprised that rabbis compare the taking up of the ashes from the altar to the matter of offering up [the meal-offering]. "

I:9:   It is a religious duty to put fire on before laying on the wood

I:10:   Jacob bar Aha said, "Hilpai asked, 'The handful of meal offering which one placed on the fire by night — what is the law [governing its disposition]?'" R. Jeremiah said, "Hilpai asked, 'The limbs of the continual whole-offering of the morning which one placed on the fire by night — what is the law?'"

I:11:   As to the priestly frontlet [which effects atonement for uncleanness unintentionally imparted to the cult], what is the law as to its effecting expiation for uncleanness affecting the hands [if one washed his hands and then, accidentally, they became unclean once he had come into the courtyard]? As to the hands, what is the law on their invalidating [the rite] if one should go out [of the courtyard after washing them, and then go back in]?

I:13:   Hilpai said, "Just as the passage of the night does not invalidate in the case of the hands, so the passage of the night does not invalidate in the case of [water in the] laver."

II:1:   [With reference to M. 2:1C] Within four cubits of the altar:]

III:1:   What is the meaning of "Choose up [by raising a finger]" [M. 2:1D]? What is the meaning of "they do not count it"?

IV:1:   This is because of the possibility of deceit.

IV:2:   One does not say in the sanctuary, "From whom shall we begin the count?"
          But the supervisor would lift up the miter of one of them [T. Yoma 1:10C],
          and they would know that it was from him that the count began. And
          should we not scruple that he may select the one of some one whom he
          liked, or of a relative of his? They would stand around in the form of a
          spiral figure [T. Yoma 1:10B].

YERUSHALMI YOMA 2:2

I:1:   "[The reason that the labor of the offering was divided among thirteen
          priests,]" said R. Yohanan, "is to make the matter well known."

I:2:   On the basis of what scripture are we informed to take the ashes off the
          inner altar? R. Pedat in the name of R. Eleazar: "'[And he shall take away
          its crop with the feathers,] and cast it beside the altar on the east side, in
          the place for ashes' (Lev. 1:16).

I:3:   How do we know that the ash of the inner altar may not be used for the
          benefit [of the priests]?

I:4:   Zeirah in the name of R. Haninah: "Incense that was smothered [and
          ceased to smoke] has been spoiled, and that is the case even for large
          sherds of it. For the reference of the Scripture to 'consuming it,'

I:5:   [With reference to M. 1:2A: All seven days...he offers up incense, trims
          the lamps; M. Tam. 3:9: He who had won the right to collect the ash of the
          inner altar...he who had won the right to clean the candlestick entered
          in...; M. Tam. 5:4: He who won the right to offer the incense...followed,
          at M. Tam. 5:5A: He who won the right to take up the ashes. Accordingly,
          the implication is that trimming the lamps came before offering up the
          incense, while at M. 1:2A, the opposite order is indicated. Accordingly, it
          is asked:] Here [at M. Tam. 3:9, 5:4] you say that he trims the lamps and
          then offers incense, while there [at M. Yoma 1:2] you maintain that he
          offers the incense and then trims the lamps.

I:6:   Said R. Yohanan, "There was no lottery for the daily whole-offering at
          twilight. But they said, 'He who won the right to perform a given task in
          the morning whole-offering will retain that right for the evening one.'"

I:7:   Said R. Yohanan, "[As to bringing up two logs of wood for the fire on the
          part of two priests, M. 2:4E, below,] they did not make a decree concern-
          ing adding the two pieces of wood at dawn [but only in the evening whole-
          offering]."

II:1:   Thirteen priests acquired the right to participate in the service [M. 2:2D]:
          In this regard it has been taught

II:2:   "You shall bring it [well mixed in baked pieces like a cereal-offering, and
          offer it for a pleasing odor to the Lord]" (Lev. 6:21). It is brought prior to
          the additional offerings. And when it says, "You shall offer [it for a pleas-
          ing odor to the Lord]" (Lev. 6:21)

II:3:   [With reference to M. 2:2B,] this is how the Mishnah is to be read] [T.
          cites M. 2:2E:] Said Ben Azzai to R. Aqiba in the name of R. Joshua, "In

the way in which it walked, it was offered [M. 2:2E]: the head, the right hind-leg, the breast and throat, the two forelegs, the two flanks, the rump, the left hind-leg" [T. Yoma 1:13C].

YERUSHALMI YOMA 2:3

I:1:   Said R. Haninah, "In the entire history of the lottery no man ever won the lottery for burning the incense and then did so a second time [since only inexperienced priests participate]."

YERUSHALMI YOMA 2:4

I:1:   "And [Aaron's sons the priests] shall lay [the pieces, the head, and the fat, in order upon the wood that is on the fire upon the altar]" (Lev. 1:8). [With reference to Lev. 15:25: "(If a woman has a discharge of blood for many) days, (not at the time of her impurity, or if she has a discharge beyond the time of her impurity, all the days of the discharge she shall continue in uncleanness; as in the days of her impurity, she shall be unclean),"] is it possible to suppose that involved are a hundred [days]? Is it possible to suppose that involved are two hundred? [At issue is the number of days involved at Lev. 15:25.] Said R. Aqiba, "In any case in interpreting the law in which you have the choice of imposing either a considerable measure or a small measure, if you impose the larger criterion, you may end up holding on to nothing, while if you impose the smaller criterion [which in any case is encompassed in the larger one], you end up holding on to something. [Accordingly, one should assume the smallest possible number in interpreting a given requirement.]"

II:1:   [As to M. 2:4H: A ram was offered by eleven.] Three priests can bring it up to the altar. And why is a ram offered by eleven priests?

III:1:   [With reference to M. 2:4Q-S, we shall now prove that an ox belonging to an individual may be offered even by six priests:] Interpret the pertinent verse as follows: "And they shall lay out" refers to two priests. "Sons of Aaron" refers to two priests. "The priests" refers to two priests.

YERUSHALMI YOMA 3:1

I:1:   What is the meaning of "It is daylight"?

I:2:   Is a single witness acceptable [in the procedure described here]? This case is different

I:1:   [With reference to M. 3:1D:] Why does he ask, "To Hebron"?

YERUSHALMI YOMA 3:2

I:1:   The column of light of the moon rises straight up [like a stick], and the column of light of the sun irradiates over the entire eastern horizon.

I:2:   And R. Hanina said, "From the time of daybreak until the eastern horizon is alight, one can walk four *mils*. From when the eastern horizon is lit up until the sun rises, one can walk four *mils*.

         It has been taught: A priest who went out to speak with his fellow — if it was for some time, he has to immerse. If it was for a moment, he has to sanctify hands and feet [cf. T. Yoma 1:16A].

YERUSHALMI YOMA 3:3

I:1:   This is the way the passage of the Mishnah is to be read: A person does not enter the courtyard and the service, even if he is clean, unless he immerses [M. 3:3A]. [That is to say,] it is not the end of the matter that he comes for the service. But even if it is not for the service, [he still must immerse].

I:2:   They asked Ben Zoma, "What is the reason for this immersion?" He said to them, "If he who goes in from one holy area to an other requires immersion, he who enters from a secular area to a holy area all the more so should require immersion!"

I:3:   It has been taught [in T.'s version:] R. Judah says, "This immersion too was required only because of real dirt.

YERUSHALMI YOMA 3:4

1.I:1:   [As to M. 3:4E, he cut the windpipe and gullet,] R. Eleazar in the name of R. Hoshaiah: "He cut two or the greater part of two [of the organs of the throat, then handed the beast over to another priest]."

I:2:   It is written, "[A beautiful heifer is Egypt,] but a gadfly from the north has come upon her" (Jer. 46:20). [What is the meaning of the word "come"?]

YERUSHALMI YOMA 3:5

I:1:   With reference to the daily whole-offering, it is written, "One lamb you shall offer in the morning, and the other lamb you shall offer in the evening" (Exod. 29:39). And with reference to the wood-offering, it is written, "The priest shall burn wood on it morning by morning" (Lev. 6:12). Something concerning which morning is stated twice takes precedence over something concerning which morning is stated only one time. [That accounts for M. 3:5A, incense before the limbs, which are compared to wood.]

I:2:   They proposed to rule, Which items make possible the incense-offering? It is the coals [on the fire]. [Nothing else is required for the incense-offering.] Said R. Eleazar, "[That is not the case, for there has to be an ingredient that] makes the smoke rise.

II:1:   [With reference to M. 3:5C-D,] it has been taught: R. Judah said, "They prepared bars of iron and boiled them from the eve of the Day of Atonement, and tossed them into the cold water to relieve the chill." Does this not turn out to extinguish [the heat] on the Day of Atonement?

II:2:   R. Joshua bar Abin, R. Simon in the name of R. Iniani b. Susai:"The reason for the position of this Tannaite authority [behind the cited rule] is that someone should not say

YERUSHALMI YOMA 3:6

I:1:   [With reference to M. 3:6C, D], what is the scriptural basis for the position of R. Meir [that the priest takes off his clothes, then sanctifies his hands and feet, as against sages' reversal of the order of these actions]?

I:2:   [When Scripture says, "He shall be girded with a linen] coat" (Lev. 16:4), the implication is that they should be doubled. [Each gets two.]

I:3:   As to utensils of service, at what point do they enter the category of the sacred? Is it forthwith, or only after they have been used? If you say it is forthwith, there are no problems. If you say that it is only after they have been used, then are they sanctified simultaneously [with their first use]?

I:4:   Stones which one has hewed for the sake of a deceased person may not be used for benefit. If he hewed them both for a living person and for a deceased person, they are permitted for benefit.

I:5:   You turn out to rule: On this day he immerses himself five times and he sanctifies hands and feet ten times [M. 3:3B]: Now how do we know that there are two sanctifications of hands and feet for each immersion [that the high priest undertakes]?

I:6:   And is not a second-class garment of Pelusium linen more beautiful than a first-class garment of Indian linen?

I:7:   There was this case: Ishmael b. Phiabi's mother made for him a tunic worth a hundred manehs. And he would stand and make offerings on the altar wearing it [T. Yoma 1:21].

YERUSHALMI YOMA 3:7

I:1:   What is [the area to be defined as] the northern [side] of the altar, which is valid for slaughtering Most Holy Things?

I:2:   Said R. Yohanan, "We have not found that the slaughter of a beast in the sacrificial rite is invalid if it is done by a non-priest."

I:3:   R. Ishmael b. R. Isaac, R. Yohanan in the name of R. Simeon b. Yohai: "The bullock offered on the Day of Atonement requires [the service of] a priest."

II:1:   [With reference to M. 3:7E,] said R. Haggai, "In the first confession he says, 'O [holy] Name.' But in the second confession he pronounces the Name [of the Lord]."

II:2:   It has been taught [in T.'s version]: How does he state the confession?

II:3:   Ten times that day he expressed the Divine Name, six in regard to the bullock, three for the goat, and one for the lots [T. Yoma 2:2E].

YERUSHALMI YOMA 3:8

I:1:   What is [the area to be defined as] the northern [side] of the altar, which is valid for slaughtering Most Holy Things?

I:2:   The prefect [M. 3:8A] served for five purposes: The prefect says to him, "My Lord, high priest, raise your right hand" [M. 4:1D]. The prefect at his right hand, and the head of the father's house at the left [M. 3:8A]. The prefect waved flags. The prefect held him by the right hand and drew him up. One was not appointed high priest before he had served as prefect.

II:1:   What is boxwood?

II:2:   [As to Ben Qatin's twelve stopcocks,] why not arrange spigots one on top of the other [rather than arranging them around the laver]?

II:3:   R. Simeon bar Karsena in the name of R. Aha: "The sea was a place of immersion for priests.

II:4:   It is written, "And this was the number of them: thirty basins of gold, a thousand basins of silver, twenty-nine censers" (Ezra I:9). As to the word for basins,

III:1:   Two Amoras — one said, "It was a candelabrum." The other said, "They were snuffers."

III:2:   She also made a golden tablet, on which was written the pericope of the accused wife [M. 3:8/I]: so that when the sun rises, sparks of golden light sparkle forth from it, so people know that the sun is rising [T. Yoma 2:3C]. How was the passage written thereon?

YERUSHALMI YOMA 3:9

I:1:   The members of the household of Garmu were experts in making show bread and in removing it from the oven, and they did not want to teach others [how to make it] [M. 3:9B]. Sages sent and brought experts from Alexandria, in Egypt, who were expert in similar matters, but were not experts in removing it from the oven.

II:1:   The members of the house of Abtinas were experts in preparing the incense for producing smoke, [cf. M. 3:9C,] and they did not want to teach others how to do so. II:2: Said R. Yosé, "I came across a child of the house of Abtinas. I said to him, 'My child, from what family are you?' He said to me, 'From such-and-such a family.' "I said to him, 'My son, because your fathers wanted to augment their glory and to diminish the glory of Heaven, therefore their glory is diminished and the glory of Heaven is augmented.'"

II:4:   All of them found an excuse for their actions, except for Ben Qamsar [T. Yoma 2:8G].

II:5:   There we have learned: These are the ones who were appointed to office [in the Temple] [M. Sheq. 5:1]: R. Hezekiah said, "R. Simeon and rabbis: One said, 'The purpose is to list the suitable men of each generation.' "The other said, 'He who lived in that generation listed the suitable men in his generation.'"

II:6:   And in regard to all of them, Ben Zoma would say the following: "Yours will they give you, by your own name will they call you, in your own place will they seat you. There is no forgetfulness before the Omnipresent. No man can touch what is ready for his fellow" [T. Yoma 2:7D].

YERUSHALMI YOMA 4:1

I:1:   It is not the end of the matter [that he shakes] a box, but he may even utilize a basket.

II:1:   [With reference to M. 4:1B, writing the designation for the goats on slips,] why not bring two threads, one black, one white, and tie the threads on [the goats] and say, "This one is for the Lord, and that one is for Azazel"? Scripture states

II:2: When the lots are still in the box, if he touches them, so that they are confused [that is, after the priest has touched one of the lots, if the lots are mixed up], the disposition of the goats is not carried out in accord with its proper requirement.

II:3: Is it possible to suppose that the priest should put two lots on this goat and two lots on that goat? Scripture says, "Lots — one lot for the Lord, and the other lot for Azazel" (Lev. 16:8).

II:4: As to the priestly frontispiece, on it was written, "Holy to the Lord." "Holy" was written below, and "the Lord" was written above.

II:5: "And Aaron shall cast lots upon the two goats" (Lev. 16:8). If a non-priest did it, it is validly done. And along these same lines, if a non-priest brought up the lots, is it invalid?

II:6: "One for the Lord" (Lev. 16:8): This serves to encompass the goat that is sent away, subjecting the goat to the rule of invalidation if it is not of the proper age. [That is, the animal for the sin-offering must be of a certain age; both goats must be of that age, so that either one may serve.]

II:8: Bun bar Hiyya asked before R. Zeirah: "If one slaughtered the bullock before he cast lots for the goats, what is the law as to his being liable [for not following the proper order of the rite of the day]?

YERUSHALMI YOMA 4:2

I:1: R. Samuel bar Nahman in the name of R. Jonathan: "There are three threads. The one for the goat is to weigh a *sela;* the one for the mesora is to weigh a *sheqel;* the one for the red cow is to weigh two *selas.*" Said R. Ba bar Zabeda in the name of R. Simeon b. Halapta, "The one for the red cow is to weigh two *selas* and a half."

YERUSHALMI YOMA 4:3

I:1: So the Mishnah is to be read [at M. 4:3B]: On the fourth terrace of the courtyard [rather than the sanctuary].

I:2: It has been taught

I:3: If the priest cleared off the coals, offered up incense, then the blood of the bullock [which he had just slaughtered] poured out, let him bring another bullock and bring its blood in [and flick the blood on the altar]. If before he offered up the incense, the blood was poured out, the act of clearing the ashes is null. He has to clear away the ashes as at the outset. If it is a matter of doubt whether the blood was poured out before he had offered up the incense, or whether it was poured out after he had brought the incense — to bring another bullock and to bring in its blood is something you cannot do, for I say, Before he burned the incense the blood poured out, so that the [original] act of clearing off the ashes was null. '

YERUSHALMI YOMA 4:4

I:1:   This [M. 4:4C] is in line with that which we have learned: About a qab of cinders scattered from [the fire-pan of gold], and he swept them out into the water channel. And on the Sabbath he covered them over with a psykter [T. Tam. 5:5C-D].

II:1:   Every day it was heavy but today it was light [M. 4:4G-H]: so as not to tire him out. Every day its handle was short but today it was long [M. 4:4/I]: so as not to tire him out.

III:1:   There are seven kinds of gold: good gold, pure gold, closed gold, gold of Ufaz, refined gold, spun gold, and red gold [M. 4:4L]. "Good gold" is as its name implies: "And the gold of that land is good" (Gen. 2:12).

YERUSHALMI YOMA 4:5

I:1:   The compound of incense [was made up of] balm, onycha, galbanum, and frankincense, each in the quantity of seventy manehs; myrrh, cassia, spikenard, and saffron, each sixteen manehs by weight; costus, twelve; aromatic rind, three; cinnamon, nine manehs. You turn out to rule, They weight in all three hundred sixty- five manehs, for the days of the year.

I:2:   It has been taught

I:3:   "[Incense beaten] small" (Lev. 16:12). Why does Scripture say so?

II:1:   Said R. Jonah, "[As to M. 4:5/I:] That is except for the first act of sancti-fication [which is done in the laver]." Said R. Yosé, "Even the first act of sanctification of hands and feet [is done from the golden one]."

YERUSHALMI YOMA 4:6

I:1:   What is the scriptural basis for the position of R. Meir?

I:2:   Said R. Eleazar, "As to the limbs and parts which were not consumed in the evening in the fire, one makes them into a bonfire and burns them by themselves, and doing so overrides the prohibitions of the Sabbath."

I:3:   How do we know that, on the Day of Atonement, there is a fire [kindled for the burning of incense, rather than taking coals from the available fire for that purpose]? R. Jeremiah in the name of R. Pedat: "'[And he shall take a censer full of] coals of [fire from the altar]' (Lev. 16:12).

YERUSHALMI YOMA 5:1

I:1:   And has the Mishnah not already stated: He took the fire-pan and went up to the top of the altar [M. 4:3C]? [Why state here: They brought the ladle and fire-pan out to him (M. 5:1A)?] The meaning of the Mishnah passage here is this: the ladle and the dish [for frankincense].

I:2:   What is a ladle?

I:3:   "[And bring it to Aaron's sons the priests. And he shall take from it] a handful [of the fine flour and oil, with all of its frankincense; and the priest shall burn this as its memorial portion upon the altar, an offering by fire, a pleasing odor to the Lord]" (Lev. 2:2). Is it possible to interpret that statement to require that the priest's grasp of the meal-offering must be such that the meal comes forth on both sides?

I:4:   As to the handful [of incense under discussion at M. 5:1B], what is the law on preparing it in a utensil of service, so sanctifying [the substance itself, placing it beyond redemption and later secularization] ?

II:1:   A large one in accord with the large size of his hand [M. 5:1C]: Even in accord with that of Ben Qimhit, whose hand could hold four *qabs*. Or a small one in accord with the small size of his hand [M. 5:1C]: Even in accord with that of Ben Gamala, whose hand would hold only about two olive's bulks.

II:2:   As to a non-priest's transporting the blood, what is the law on the act's being deemed valid? Hezeqiah said, "If a non-priest transports the blood, it is valid." R. Yannai said, "If a non-priest transports the blood, it is invalid."

All concur that if he brought the objects in one by one, he has effected atonement. But he is liable on the count of entering into the inner sanctum more often than is required.

III:1:   And the space between them was a cubit [M. 5:1G]: Said R. Hila, "There is an indication of the matter in that which we have learned there: The dividing space was one cubit, and the Holy of Holies twenty cubits [M. Mid. 4:7]: "What is the meaning of "The dividing space was one cubit?" R. Jonah of Bosra said, "[It comes from a Greek word for confusion, that is,] it created confusion: What is it? Inside? Outside?"

YERUSHALMI YOMA 5:2

I:1:   It has been taught

II:1:   This was the prayer of the high priest on the Day of Atonement, when he left the holy place whole and in one piece:

YERUSHALMI YOMA 5:3

I:1:   It has been taught: Before the ark was removed, he would go in and go out by the light of the ark. Once the ark was removed, he would have to feel his way in and feel his way out.

I:2:   Said R. Yohanan, "Why was it called 'Shetiyyah'? For from it the world was founded." R. Hiyya taught, "Why was it called 'Shetiyyah'? For from it the world was given water to drink."

YERUSHALMI YOMA 5:4

I:1:   What is the meaning of like one who cracks a whip [M. 5:4E]?

I:2:   [Why does he not count to eight?] Said R. Yohanan, "It is so that he will not make a mistake."

I:3:   It is written, "Sprinkling it upon the mercy seat [and before the mercy seat]" (Lev. 16:15). Is it possible to suppose that it is sprinkled on its roof? Scripture states, "And before the mercy seat." Is it possible to suppose that it is to be on its brow? Scripture states, "Upon...and before..."

I:4:   R. Zeirah said, "[The flicked blood] has to touch [the mercy seat] ." R. Samuel bar R. Isaac said, "It does not have to touch it."

I:5:   "And he shall sprinkle it with his finger on the front of the mercy seat" (Lev. 16:14, for the blood of the bull, and Lev. 16:15, for the blood of the goat). This teaches that he puts one of the drops of blood above. "And before the mercy seat" (Lev. 16:14, 15). I do not know how many there should be. Lo, I reason as follows

I:6:   "Thus he shall make atonement [for] the holy place" (Lev. 16:16). The meaning is that he has to aim his tossings of the blood at the holy place.

I:7:   [With reference to Lev. 16:18:"Then he shall go out to the altar which is before the Lord and make atonement for it and shall take some of the blood of the bull and [some] of the blood of the goat and put it on the horns of the altar round about" (= M. 5:4CC):] said R. Nehemiah, "Since we find it stated with regard to the bullock that is brought because of violation in error of 'any of the commandments,' (Lev. 4:1ff),

I:8:   All concur in the case of the bullock of the anointed priest and of the community [mentioned at Lev. 4:1ff.] that it is not necessary that the blood actually reach [the altar].

II:1:   [With reference to M. 5:4BB:] If one poured the contents of a sanctified utensil into an unsanctified utensil, he has invalidated what he poured. Lo, if he should pour the contents of a sanctified utensil into another sanctified utensil, he has not invalidated [what he has poured].

II:2:   How do we know that one has to mix [the blood of the bullock and the goat, M. 5:4BB]? Scripture states

II:3:   If one received the blood of the bullock in three separate cups, and the blood of the goat in three separate cups, with the plan of putting blood from one of them on the projections, one on the veil, and one on the golden altar, which one is he supposed to pour into the other [for pouring on the altar in line with M. 5:4BB]?

YERUSHALMI YOMA 5:5

I:1:   Why should he not start [the purification process] at the southeastern corner of the altar [rather than at the northeastern corner]?

I:2:   It has been taught

YERUSHALMI YOMA 5:6

I:1:   And he will sprinkle...upon it..." (Lev. 16:19): [He did not sprinkle it] on the dust or on the coals, [but only on the top surface of the altar] [T. Yoma 3:2B].

I:2:   [With reference to M. Tam. 2:5: They selected from there fine pieces of fig wood with which to lay out the second altar fire, the one for the incense, toward the southwestern corner, four cubits to the north of the corner.

I:3:   "And all the remaining blood of the bullock he shall pour out at the base of the altar" (Lev. 4:7). This serves to encompass the bullock of the Day of Atonement, the blood of which is to be poured out [thus the rule at M. 5:6B].

I:4:   "And when he has made an end of atoning for the holy place [and the tent of meeting and the altar, he shall present the live goat]" (Lev. 16:20). [With reference to M. 5:7, below,] there is a Tannaite authority who teaches: If he has made an end, then he has atoned. And there is a Tannaite authority who teaches: If he has atoned, he has made an end. [Cf. T. Yoma 3:8].

I:5:   It has been taught: Said R. Ishmael, "[With reference to Lev. 4:7: 'And all the remaining blood of the bullock shall he pour out at the base of the altar,'] now if the residue of the blood of a sin-offering, which does not effect atonement, is placed at the foundation of the altar, the [two placings of blood which constitute] the beginning of the burnt-offering, which do effect atonement — is it not logical that these should be placed at the foundation of the altar?"

II:1:   [With reference to M. 5:6E,] it has been taught: "The laws of sacrilege apply to the blood," the words of R. Meir and R. Simeon. And sages say, "The laws of sacrilege do not apply to the blood," [T. Zeb. 6:9B-C] [= M. 5:6E].

YERUSHALMI YOMA 5:7

I:1:   It has been taught

I:2:   Hoshaiah in the name of R. Epes: "[When, at Y. 4:1, it is said, 'The rite of the goat is not indispensable to the rite of the bullock as to the placing of the blood between the bars projecting from the ark is concerned, but as to the placing of the blood on the veil, the rite of the goat is indispensable to the bullock,'] that refers to the placing of the blood on the projections. But as to the placing of the blood on the veil, the goat is indispensable to the bullock. [That is, one must have placed the blood of the goat on the area between the bars projecting from the ark before he puts the blood of the bullock on the veil (Y. 4:1).]"

II:1:   [As to M. 5:7G, H, under dispute is the rule governing putting the blood on the inner altar, M. 5:7D, the sanctuary, and the golden altar, M. 5:7F. Thus we have three locations on which the blood is to be tossed.

II:2:   Said R. Eleazar, "If one put on the altar part of the required placings of blood, and then the blood poured out, they bring other [blood] in their stead."

YERUSHALMI YOMA 6:1

I:1:   The smallest number of goats [Lev. 16:5: "two male goats for a sin-offering"] is two. Why then does Scripture specify "two"? To indicate that the two of them should be equivalent to one another.

I:2:   If the two goats are equivalent in the price paid for them, but in fact are not equivalent in value [one being finer than the other], the goats do not accord with the religious requirement affecting them [M. 6:1B]. If the two goats are equivalent in value, but are not equivalent in the money paid for them, the two goats do accord with the religious requirement affecting them.

II:1: This is the point of the Mishnah [M. 6:1F-H]: Let him bring the two and cast lots over them as at the outset [M. 6:1 G], and he says, "Then this one upon which the lot, 'For the Lord,' has come up is to stand in its stead" [M. 6:1H]. [As to M. 6:1/I,] which one of them is offered first? [That is, there are now two goats designated for the Lord. Which one is offered, which left to die?] Rab said, "The second of the second pair." R. Yohanan said, "The second of the first pair."

III:1: For the sin-offering of the community is not left to die. R. Judah says, "It is left to die" [M. 6:1K-L]. [Now we recall that the man has gone and gotten two more goats and cast lots over them. There is then the following] question to be addressed to R. Judah: Does someone to begin with cast lots so that [a beast who is chosen] is merely left to die?

YERUSHALMI YOMA 6:2

I:1: Bar Qappara taught, "[He did not mention, 'Your people, the house of Israel,' but only,] 'They have committed iniquity, transgressed, and sinned.' This was so as not to call to mind what was disgraceful for Israel."

I:2: "[But the goat on which the lot fell for Azazel] shall be presented alive [before the Lord to make atonement over it, that it may be sent away into the wilderness to Azazel]" (Lev. 16:10). This teaches that it is destined to die [later on].

YERUSHALMI YOMA 6:3

I:1: "[And Aaron shall lay both his hands upon the head of the live goat, and confess over him all the iniquities of the people of Israel, and all their transgressions, all their sins] and he shall put them upon the head of the goat,] and send him away into the wilderness by the hand of a man [who is in readiness]" (Lev. 16:21). This serves to validate the participation of a non-priest. "Who is in readiness" (Lev. 16:21). This means he should be destined for this task. "Who is in readiness" (Lev. 16:21). That he should be prepared. "Who is in readiness" (Lev. 16:21). Even on the Sabbath. "Who is in readiness" (Lev. 16:21). Even in a state of uncleanness.

I:2: They asked R. Eliezer, "Lo, if the goat which is to be sent fell sick, what is the law as to carrying it?" He said to them, "Can he carry others?"

YERUSHALMI YOMA 6:4

I:1: There is a Tannaite authority who teaches [that the ramp referred to at M. 6:4A refers to] a protection for the body of the goat. There is a Tannaite authority who teaches that it actually was a ramp.]

II:1: [Re. M. 6:4D-E: It is taught (in T.'s version):] "There were ten tabernacles within a distance of twelve mils," the words of R. Meir. R. Judah says, "There were nine tabernacles in a distance of ten mils."

III:1: At each booth they say to him, "Lo, here is food, here is water" [M. 6:4F]: [This was] to keep up his strength. Why so? For the evil impulse craves only what is forbidden.

YERUSHALMI YOMA 6:5

I:1:   At first they would tie a crimson thread onto their windows. In the case of some of them it turned white, and in the case of some of them it remained red. The result was that these became ashamed before those. So they went and tied it at the door of the Temple. There were years in which it turned white, and there were years in which it remained red. They went and tied it to a rock [M. 6:5C].

I:2:   It is written, "Come now, let us reason together, says the Lord: though your sins are like scarlet, they shall be as white as snow; though they are red like crimson, they shall become like wool" (Isa. 1:18). It has been taught: R. Eliezer says, "'Though your sins are like scarlet' — between heaven and earth. "'They shall be as white as snow' — more than this, they shall be as white as wool."

YERUSHALMI YOMA 6:6

I:1:   He came to the bullock, etc. [M. 6:6A]. We have learned: He came to the bullock and goat which are to be burned [M. 6:6A]. There is a Tannaite authority who [reversing the procedure, here] teaches: The high priest came to read [M. 7:1A]. [The version at M. 6:6A indicates that after the goat is sent out, forthwith the bullock and the goat which have been killed are attended to. The alternative version has the reading of Scripture take place after sending out the goat, and only then are the goat and bullock dealt with.]

I:2:   R. Zeriqan said R. Zeirah asked, "As to bullocks to be burned, and goats to be burned, which became unclean, what is the law on burning them in accord with the religious requirement for them?" [At issue is M. Zeb. 12:5

I:3:   He who burns [the carcasses becomes unclean], but not the one who kindles the fire, nor the one who lays out the wood [T. Yoma 2:17H].

YERUSHALMI YOMA 6:7

I:1:   What are sentinel posts [M. 6:7C]? Platforms.

YERUSHALMI YOMA 7:1

I:1:   How do we know that the reading of a passage of Scripture is required?

II:1:   R. Ammi in the name of R. Yohanan: "The rest of the acts of service he carries out in white garments.

III:1:   In all circumstances people go to the Torah. But here [at M. 7:1D] you say that they bring the Torah to them. But because they are important men, the Torah is exalted through them.

III:2:   [With reference to M. Sot. 7:6H,] there we have learned: They may leave out verses in the Prophets, but not in the Torah [M. Meg. 4:4]. They leave out verses in a Prophetic reading, but they do not read out verses [in skipping] from one prophet to another. But in the case of one of the Twelve Minor Prophets, it is permitted.

IV:1: And afterward he says eight blessings [M. 7:1H]. For the Torah: "...who has chosen the Torah."

YERUSHALMI YOMA 7:2

I:1: Said R. Yohanan, "This [M. 7:2D-F] represents the view of R. Eliezer and R. Aqiba, but in the view of sages all of them were offered with the daily whole-offering brought at twilight."

I:2: "Then Aaron shall come into the tent of meeting" (Lev. 16:23). Whence does he come? From reading the specified scriptural passages. And where does he go? To get the ladle and fire-pan [he had left inside] [M. 7:2/I].

II:1: R. Eleazar said, "There is yet another act of service which he carries out in white garments, and what is it? It is taking out the ladle and fire-pan [M. 7:2H-I]." Said R. Yohanan, "All parties concur with regard to taking out the ladle and fire-pan that this is done after the offering of the daily whole-offering prepared at twilight.

II:2: [As to M. 7:2H-I,] why is this done in white garments?

YERUSHALMI YOMA 7:3

I:1: On what account does the high priest serve in eight garments [M. 7:3A]? R. Hananiah, associate of the rabbis, said, "It is for the circumcision, which is eight days after birth, in line with the following verse of Scripture

I:2: R. Hiyya taught, "'He shall put them on' (Lev. 16:4). [Playing on the letters LBSM,] 'And they will rot there.' There they were put away, there they rotted, and they were not valid for a future Day of Atonement."

I:3: It has been taught: Rabbi says, "There are two separate matters under discussion, one involving the garments of the high priest, and the other involving the garments of an ordinary priest."

I:4: [With reference to the dispute between Rabbi and Eleazar b. Simeon, who had a dispute on the girdle of an ordinary priest, one saying it was made up of wool and linen in the same web, the other saying it was of fine linen,] *it has been taught*

II:1: Said R. Simon, "Just as the offerings effect atonement, so the garments effect atonement. "Tunic, underpants, head covering, and girdle [M. 7:3B]: "The tunic effected atonement for those who wore linen and wool mixtures."

II:2: Simon in the name of R. Jonathan of Bet Gubrin: "For two matters was there no atonement, but the Torah provided atonement for them, and these are they: gossiping and killing someone inadvertently.

II:3: It has been taught

III:1: As to the frontlet [M. 7:3C]: There is he who wishes to propose that it is for the sins of those who blaspheme, and there is he who wishes to propose that it is for the sins of those who are presumptuous.

IV:1:   Why are they called Urim and Thummim [M. 7:3D]? They are called
          Urim because they enlighten Israel. They are called Thummim because
          they straighten out the road before them.

IV:2:   Now two questions may not be presented at the same time. But if two
          questions have been presented [to the Urim and Thummim] at the same
          time — there is a Tannaite authority who teaches, "One receives an an-
          swer to the first question but not to the second one." And there is a Tannaite
          authority who teaches, "One receives an answer to the second question
          but does not receive an answer to the first question." And there is a Tannaite
          authority who teaches, "One does not receive an answer either to the first
          question or to the second question."

IV:3:   [In receiving answers from the Urim and Thummim,] there is a Tannaite
          authority who teaches, "He hears the voice [of God]." There is a Tannaite
          authority who teaches, "The letters [on the Urim and Thummim] stand
          out."

YERUSHALMI YOMA 8:1

I:1:   The penalty of extirpation applies to eating and drinking on the Day of
          Atonement, yet you say this, [that they are subject merely to the sort of
          prohibition affecting the other items on the list at M. 8:1A]?

I:2:   "You shall afflict yourselves" (Lev. 16:29): Is it possible to suppose that
          one should sit in the sun or in cold in order to suffer? Scripture states,
          "And you shall do no work" (Lev. 16:29). It is labor that is subject to a
          prohibition in another setting [namely, the Sabbath]

I:3:   Another matter: "You shall afflict your souls" (Lev. 16:29): This refers to
          something which afflicts the body itself. What is it?

I:4:   Bathing [M. 8:1A]: R. Zeirah bar Hama, R. Yosé b. R. Hanina in the
          name of R. Joshua b. Levi: "On the occasion of a public fast, one may
          wash his face, hands, and feet in the usual way.

I:5:   [As to putting on a sandal [M. 8:1A:] A mourner and one who had been
          excommunicated who were going from one town to another on the road
          are permitted to put on a sandal. When they come to a town, they must
          take them off.

I:6:   As to anointing [M. 8:1A]: That is in line with the following, which has
          been taught

I:7:   As to putting on a sandal [M. 8:1A]: It has been taught

I:8:   Sexual relations [M. 8:1A]: Now look here! If someone is forbidden to
          bathe, is it not an argument a fortiori that it is forbidden to have sexual
          relations?

II:1:   The king [M. 8:1B]: This is on the count of the following verse: "Your
          eyes will see the king in his beauty; they will behold a land that stretches
          afar" (Isa. 33:17). A bride [M. 8:1B]: This is on account of the possibility
          of envy.

III:1:   They supposed that to R. Eliezer is to be attributed only the concluding clause [as given above]. But a teaching turned up in which all of the preceding [also B] are to be assigned to him.

YERUSHALMI YOMA 8:2

I:1:   [Since M. 8:2A refers to the date's bulk inclusive of the pit,] said R. Yosé, "That is to say that it is necessary to crush the empty space [within the date, in measuring the amount one has eaten, dealing then only with the solid matter]. For if that is not the case, then the Mishnah should have said, 'the date's bulk of food, inclusive of its pit and the empty space within.'"

I:2:   It has been taught

YERUSHALMI YOMA 8:3

I:1:   [With reference to M. Shebu. 3:2A: "I swear that I won't eat," and he ate and drank — he is liable on only one count. Why not on two counts, one for each act?] It is because drinking is subsumed under eating, while eating is not subsumed under drinking. How do we know that drinking is subsumed under eating, [but eating is not subsumed under drinking]? R. Jonah derived the two of them from the following

I:2:   An admonition concerning not working on the Day [of Atonement]: "You shall do no work on this same day" (Lev. 23:28).

II:1:   [Illustrating M 8:3C-F:] R. Abbahu in the name of R. Yohanan: "He who eats mixed seeds in a vineyard [grain grown among vines] is flogged." R. Abbahu in the name of R. Yohanan: "[A non-priest] who chews on wheat which is in the status of heave-offering is flogged." R. Abbahu in the name of R. Yohanan, "[A non-priest] who swallows vinegar in the status of heave-offering is flogged."

III:1:   With reference to M. 8:3G-H:] As to children, they do not impose a fast on them on the Day of Atonement. R. Huna interpreted the statement of the Mishnah as follows

YERUSHALMI YOMA 8:4

I:1:   [With reference to M. 8:4A:] At the outset they roast something for her on a spit [so she can suck of it]. If she feels better, well and good. If not, they give her the actual, prohibited food [that she craves].

I:2:   If a sick person says, "I can take it," and the physician says, "He cannot take it," they listen to the physician. If the physician says, "He can take it," and the sick person says, "I cannot take it," they listen to the sick person. Where there is a problem, it is when the sick person says, "I can take it," and the physician says, "I don't know."

YERUSHALMI YOMA 8:5

I:1:   [With reference to M. 8:5A,] how do we know that they feed him figs and raisins in the status of heave-offering [even though he is a non-priest]?

I:2:   It has been taught [in T.'s version]: [He who was seized by ravenous hunger] — they feed him [that which violates the law in] the least [possible measure] [M. 8:6A]. How so?

II:1:   [With reference to M. 8:5B:] The indications of a crazy dog [are these]:

II:2:   How do we know that a matter of doubt concerning life or death overrides the prohibitions of the Sabbath?

III:1:   [As to M. 8:5G-M,] R. Zeira, R. Hiyya in the name of R. Yohanan: "In the case of an alleyway, in which only one Israelite lives along with gentiles, and which fell down in an earthquake — [on the Sabbath]

YERUSHALMI YOMA 8:6

I:1:   There we have learned: And for a deliberate act of imparting uncleanness to the sanctuary and its Holy Things, a goat [whose blood is sprinkled] inside and the Day of Atonement effect atonement. And for all other transgressions which are in the Torah — the minor or serious, deliberate or inadvertent, those done knowingly or done unknowingly, violating a positive or a negative commandment, those punishable by extirpation and those punishable by death at the hands of a court, the goat which is sen t away [Lev. 16:21] effects atonement [Y. Shebu. 1:6].

I:2:   And has not the Day of Atonement already effected atonement [so why should there be a matter of suspending punishment at all]?

YERUSHALMI YOMA 8:7

I:1:   As to violation of a positive commandment, [the Day of Atonement effects atonement] even if the person did not repent. As to violation of a negative commandment — R. Samuel in the name of R. Zeira: "[The Day of Atonement effects atonement] only if the person repented [of violating the negative commandment]."

I:2:   He who states, "The burnt-offering does not effect atonement," "The burnt-offering does not effect atonement for me," — the burnt-offering effects atonement for him.

I:3:   The burnt-offering effects atonement for the murmurings of one's heart. What is the scriptural basis for that statement? "What is in your mind shall never happen" (Ezek. 20:32).

I:4:   Rabbi says, "For all transgressions which are listed in the Torah the Day of Atonement effects atonement, except for the one who totally breaks the yoke [of Heaven] off of him, who removes the signs of the covenant, or who behaves presumptuously against the Torah. For if such a person does repent, then atonement is effected for him, but if not, it is not effected for him."

I:5:   Mattiah b. Heresh asked R. Eleazar b. Azariah, "Have you heard of the four types of atonement that R. Ishmael used to expound?" He said to him, "They ate three, besides [the requirement of] an act of repentance."

I:6: It has been taught [in T.'s version]: Matters concerning which one has said confession on the preceding Day of Atonement one does not have to include in the confession on the coming Day of Atonement, unless he did those same transgressions [in the intervening year].

I:7: The religious duty of saying the confession [applies] at the eve of the Day of Atonement at dusk.

I:8: It has been taught

I:9: It is written, "O thou hope of Israel, its savior in time of trouble, why shouldst thou be like a stranger in the land, like a wayfarer who turns aside to tarry for a night?" (Jer. 14:8). Just as the immersion pool cleans the unclean, so does the Holy One, blessed be he, clean Israel [M. 8:7/I]. And so it says, "I will sprinkle clean water upon you, and you shall be clean from all your uncleanness, and from all your idols I will cleanse you" (Ezek. 36:25).

v. PESAHIM

YERUSHALMI PESAHIM 1:1

I:1: It is written, "And you shall observe the commandment of the unleavened bread because on this very day I brought your hosts out of the land of Egypt, [you shall observe this day throughout your generations as an institution for all times]. In the first [month] on fourteenth of the month in the evening you shall eat unleavened bread," (Exod. 12:17-18A). How shall we interpret these statements?

I:2: Why [is the search to be conducted] by the light of a lamp [as specified in M. 1:1]?

I:3: Said R. Yosé, "[Even though a lamp is appropriate for searching at night,] the teaching said that searching during the day is considered a [valid] searching," for we have learned [in M. 1:3A]:

I:4: R. Jeremiah asked, "Do synagogues or study houses require searching?"

I:5: [Assuming that in general courtyards require a search:] R. Yosé asked, "Do the courtyards in Jerusalem in which [they] eat loaves of the thanksgiving offering and wafers of the Nazirites require a search?"

I:6: The upper and lower holes of the house, and the balcony, and the cellar, and the upper chamber, and the roof of a house, the roof of a tower, a straw shed, and a cattle shed, and a woodshed, and a storage shed, the wine-storage area, and the oil-storage area, and the fruit-storage area — [all] do not require searching [T. 1:3].

I:7: A wine vault requires searching.

I:8: One who goes on a journey [before Passover] prior to thirty days, does not have to search; within thirty [when the requirement to search is in effect], [the person] is required to search. [T. 1:4A].

I:9: All are reliable concerning the destruction of leaven, even women, even slaves.

I:10:   They ask concerning the laws of Passover on Passover, the laws of Pentecost on Pentecost, [and] the laws of the Festival [of Sukkot] on the Festival. In the assembly house [of study] they ask prior to thirty days [before the holiday]. Rabban Simeon b. Gamaliel says, "Two weeks" [T. Meg. 3:5].

II:1:   And in what situation did they say, [They search] two rows in the wine vault [M. 1:1C]?

II:2:   This refers to those [rows] that have spaces [in between]. But regarding those that are

YERUSHALMI PESAHIM 1:2

I:1:   Said R. Jonah, "Thus [the Mishnah] should teach:

YERUSHALMI PESAHIM 1:3

I:1:   Said R. Yohanan, "R. Judah's reason [is that

II:1:   What does he do? He covers it with a utensil

YERUSHALMI PESAHIM 1:5

I:1:   Simeon b. Laqish said in the name of R. Yannai, "[The two loaves] were fit. "

I:2:   It is taught

I:3:   Why [do they continue to eat heave-offering during the fifth hour?

YERUSHALMI PESAHIM 1:7

I:2:   There are teachers who teach, ...There are teachers who teach

YERUSHALMI PESAHIM 1:8

I:1:   [...they burn [leaven in the status of] heave-offering which is [cultically] clean with that which is [cultically] unclean on Passover:]

I:2:   [Defining Meir's referent in "their words":] Said R. Yohanan, "From the words of R. Aqiba [in M. 1:7] [and] from the words of R. Hananiah the Prefect of the Priests [M. 1:6]." R. Simeon b. Laqish said, "From the words of R. Eliezer and from the words of R. Joshua [C of the Mishnah]."

I:3:   R. Yosé [the Amora said] in the name of R. Yohanan, "All concur that on the sixteenth [of Nisan, in the midst of the festival] they

I:4:   [Supplying analogous views from M. Terumot:] There we learn:

YERUSHALMI PESAHIM 2:1

I:1:   Said R. Immi, "Who teaches, So long as it is permitted to eat [leaven], one feeds [it] to domestic cattle, to a wild beast, and to fowl, [and by implication every hour that he] is forbidden to eat, [he] is forbidden to feed? R. Meir

II:1:   Said R. Bun bar Hiyya before R. Zeira, "This [M. 2:1, in particular clause E, Once its time has passed, it is forbidden to derive benefit from it] indicates that

II:2:   [Said] R. Abbahu in the name of R. Eleazar, "Wherever it is said, 'You [sing.] shall not eat,' 'you [plur.] shall not eat,' [or] 'they shall not eat,' you should recognize a prohibition on deriving benefit [just] like a prohibition on eating, until a verse comes and specifies to you [otherwise]

III:1: If [a person] violated [this prohibition] and lit [the oven or stove, what is the law regarding what is later cooked in it]?

IV:1: It is taught

IV:2: It is taught

IV:3: Rabbi says, "[The requirement of] 'you shall remove leaven from your houses' (Exod. 12:15) [is fulfilled with] a means which would make [the leaven] impossible to be seen and to be found [requirements specified in Exod. 12:19, 13:7, and Deut. 16:4). And what is it? It is through burning" [for thus the substance can no longer be seen or found]."

YERUSHALMI PESAHIM 2:2

I:1: Lo, [the leavened bread of a gentile which has remained over Passover], is it forbidden to eat?

I:2: A gentile's roof that was adjacent to an Israelite's roof and leavened bread rolled from the gentile's roof to the Israelite's roof — lo, this one pushes it with a reed

I:3: An Israelite and a gentile who were traveling [together] on a boat, and leavened bread was in the possession of the Israelite — lo, this one sells it to the gentile

I:4: Who [is the authority] who teaches [in M. 2:2A],

I:5: There we learned:

II:1: To what extent R. Yohanan in the name of R. Simeon ben Yosedeq [said], "Up to three handbreadths." [Leaven buried more than three handbreadths below the surface of the ground is considered out of the reach of a dog.]

YERUSHALMI PESAHIM 2:3

I:1: It is taught

I:2: Bun b. R. Hiyya asked, "One who eats leaven which is in the status of heave-offering on Passover — to whom does he pay [the reparation which M. 2:3 requires, for the produce was fit for neither a priest nor a non-priest]?"

I:3: [If on Passover a non-priest acted] inadvertently in [eating] heave-offering and deliberately in [eating] leaven; or inadvertently in [eating grapes or drinking wine which were] heave-offering and deliberately in [violation of his being a] Nazi

YERUSHALMI PESAHIM 2:4

I:1: It is written [in reference to bread], "and when you eat of the bread of the land, you shall set some aside as a gift to the Lord" (Num. 15:19).

I:2: There we learn

I:3: Whence do we learn

I:4: Simon in the name of R. Joshua ben Levi, "That olive's amount with which a person fulfills his obligation on Passover must not contain any liquid [e.g., wine, oil, or honey.]"

YERUSHALMI PESAHIM 2:5

I:1:   With lettuce — lettuce; with chicory — endive; with tamkhah [pepperwort] — gingidium, another type of bitter herb; with harhavina — R. Yosé b. R. Bun said, "yasse holi [a name of another herb];" and with sonchus — a bitter vegetable with silvery appearance and possessing sap.

II:1:   Whether fresh] or withered [M. 2:5B = T. 2:21]. There are those who teach, "but not withered."

III:1: Hiyya in the name of R. Yohanan [said], "A pickled olive [which is used not for its oil but for food, though generally only after being treated] — over it one says [the blessing], '[Praised be Thou ...] who createst the fruit of the tree.'"

YERUSHALMI PESAHIM 2:6

I:1:   It is taught [regarding two terms, found, for example, in M. Hal. 1: 6]

I:2:   The Mishnah's prohibition applies] in a case in which there is fat in them

I:3:   A malagma [a bandage comprising mostly grain kneaded in water or wine] which decayed there are those who teach, "it must be removed." And there are those who teach, "It need not be removed" [T. 3:3B].

YERUSHALMI PESAHIM 2:7

I:1:   They do not put meal into haroset [the mixture of fruit, spice, and wine used for sweetening the bitter herb on Passover] or into mustard. But if one has put it in, he must eat it forthwith — as long as [one] does not tarry. R. Meir prohibits because one tarries [and the flour leavens].

I:2:   It is written, "[Do not eat any of it raw or] cooked in any way with water, [but roasted over the fire]" (Exod. 12:9). [From this verse] I only know [that] water [is prohibited for cooking the Passover offering]. From where [do I know] to include other liquids [in this ban]?

I:3:   They do not knead unleavened bread with liquids, but they form [and smooth its surfaces] with liquids [T. 3:5B].

II:1:   There are those who teach: "They pour them in the place of broken ground" [T. 3:6]. And there are those who teach: "They pour them into a sloping place."

II:2:   [If one] soaked wheat and barley in water and they leavened, lo, these are forbidden; [if they] did not leaven are permitted. R. Yosé said, "[If one] soaked barley in water, if they split, lo, these are forbidden. [If one] soaked them in vinegar, [they are] permitted because the vinegar contracts them" [T. 3: 4]..

YERUSHALMI PESAHIM 3:1

I:1:   And these [substances] are removed on Passover:

II:1:   Eliezer says, "Even women's cosmetics [M. 3:1C]." There are those who teach [that Eliezer spoke of] "cosmetics." There are those who teach (that R. Eliezer spoke of "toilet paste."

II:2: It is written, "All that is leavened you shall not eat" (Exod. 12:20) — to include Babylonian *kutah,* and Median beer, and Edomite vinegar, that they be subject to [biblical] warning [prohibiting eating them].

II:3: Jeremiah, R. Samuel b. R. Isaac in the name of Rab, "A pot in which one cooked leaven one should not cook therein from the same kind [of food] except after the Passover [for the taste of the leavened food remains in the pot]."

YERUSHALMI PESAHIM 3:2

I:1: Associates in the name of R. Yohanan, R. Simon in the name of R. Joshua b. Levi, "[The Mishnah speaks of a case] in which [the dough can be] peeled off all of it together

II:1: [First defining the referent of the rule that a person's intent (whether or not the person is bothered by the presence of a small amount of dough in a trough) affects the cleanness status of a trough:] [And so with regard to uncleanness:] if one is fastidious about it

II:2: There we say, "Thin wafers — R. Isaac instructed that on Passover making one [wafer is permitted without fear of dough rising]; two [or] three are prohibited unless the person rinses off his hands in water" [these wafers were flattened with a person's hands, to which the dough would stick — hence it became necessary to wash the hands between wafers].

II:3: Building on an assumed definition of "dumb" dough:] R. Abbahu in the name of R. Yohanan said, "Dough that cooled-' — [if] there was not another like it there which leavened [to indicate the status of the "dumb" dough], until when [after kneading does one have to wait before it becomes forbidden]?

YERUSHALMI PESAHIM 3:3

I:1: The teaching [Mishnah] deals with a case in which [the dough] became unclean after it was rolled. But if it became unclean before it was rolled,

I:2: The teaching [in the Mishnah] deals with the festival of Passover. Lo, on Pentecost or Tabernacles [where the issue of leaven is not a factor], it is permitted

II:1: How should [a person] act according to R. Eliezer [who says one can handle the dough until it is baked, when it is designated and then properly left till the evening for burning]?

II:2: Said R. Joshua to him [R. Eliezer], "Do you not end up like one who burns holy things on the holiday [in leaving the Dough offering to burn in the oven after baking the dough, which, is a distinct violation]?"

II:3: According to the opinion of R. Eliezer, let [the person] designate it [after the dough bakes] and then remove it [from the baked dough without leaving it to burn]?

II:4: There R. Jeremiah said in the name of R. Zeira, "[If] two halves of an olive's bulk [of leaven] are within a house [at different locations], the house does not join them [to make up the minimum amount]; within a utensil, the utensil joins them." But here he [the Mishnah, in particular, R. Eliezer] says

YERUSHALMI PESAHIM 3:4

I:1:   [If following Gamaliel, the women work in sequence:] It is taught

I:2:   Rabban Gamaliel says, "Three women knead [dough] at the same time and bake in one oven, one after the other." And sages say, "Three women occupy themselves with the dough: one kneads, and one rolls, and one bakes [M. 3:4]."

YERUSHALMI PESAHIM 3:5

I:1:   [Regarding Judah's opinion, in particular the need to remove the *si'ur]:* R. Huna in the name of Rab, "It is permitted to feed it to dogs. [Hence, in not prohibiting benefit beyond human consumption, it emerges as not totally inedible.]"

I:2:   Explaining why sages reject Judah's definition of *si'ur:]* Bar Qappara teaches

YERUSHALMI PESAHIM 3:6

I:1:   Meir [in M. 3: 6] is in accord with R. Eliezer [in M. 3:3] and [regarding the principle articulated] goes further than R. Eliezer

I:2:   It is taught

I:3:   R. Abbahu [said] in the name of R. Yohanan, "R. Eleazar b. R. Sadoq [in prescribing the burning of the heave-offering immediately "before the Sabbath" and unconsecrated produce at this standard hour, be it even on the thirteenth, in M. 3:6] is in accord with Rabban Gamaliel.

YERUSHALMI PESAHIM 3:7

I:1:   Said R. Yosé b. R. Bun, "Come and see how great is peace for [visiting one's in-laws which is done to establish harmony in a family] is compared to two matters over which [people] are liable for extirpation [= extirpation]: the circumcision of one's son and the slaughter of one's Passover offering!"

II:1:   What is "to establish a resting place [fora] voluntary [purpose] [M. 3:7C]?

YERUSHALMI PESAHIM 3:8

I:1:   [Defining the area within the boundary and demonstrating that this extended area is considered holy by drawing on Zechariah's picture of future pilgrims to Jerusalem:] R. Simon in the name of R. Joshua b. Levi, "It is written, 'In that day, all the shadows of ["bells on"] the horses shall be inscribed "Holy to the Lord' (Zech. 14:20) — up to the point that horses run and do not cast a shadow [being overshadowed by the shadow of the city and its walls]."

II:1:   There are those teachers who teach reversing the opinions [of R. Meir and R. Judah].

YERUSHALMI PESAHIM 4:1

I:1: Where they are accustomed to do work, [M. 4:1A]. It is written, "There shall you slaughter the Passover sacrifice, in the evening" (Deut. 16:6).

I:2: Said R. Jonah, "[Taking into account that] these daily offerings are the sacrifices of all of Israel: if all of Israel went up to Jerusalem [daily, it would not be right for] is it not written, 'three times a year all your males shall appear [before the Lord your God]' (Deut. 16:16 —

I:3: And lo, a paschal offering, behold it is a sacrifice for all of Israel, and they [the authors of M. 4:1] made it [working before noon on the day when it is offered] contingent on custom

I:4: [Regarding] all the matters [that follow] they made it contingent upon an actual custom

I:5: They sit on a Gentile's bench [on which a Gentile merchant sells wares] on the Sabbath [even though it might appear as if they were engaged in business] [T. M.Q. 2:14A].

I:6: Not only regarding Passover [e.g, not working prior to noon on the day on which the offering was brought, on the eve of Passover,] but also regarding a custom [people are to accept and maintain stringencies].

I:7: Relating to the Mishnah's concern for the impact of changing locations on a person's custom:] [If people who had taken upon themselves a prohibition] fled from place to place and wanted to retract [their prohibition, what is the law]?

II:1: Simeon b. Laqish asked R. Yohanan, "And is it not forbidden because of the ban of 'you shall not divide up into sects' (Deut. 14:1).

II:2: [Questioning this construction of the principle of *you shall not divide up into sects:*] "[In the disputes] of the House of Shammai and the House of Hillel, does not the law follow the House of Hillel

II:3: It is satisfactory [when an individual left] a place where they work [on Passover eve prior to noon] and goes to where they do not work.

YERUSHALMI PESAHIM 4:2

I:1: [The Mishnah refers to a case in which the particular produce] has ceased in Tiberias but has not ceased in Sepphoris

YERUSHALMI PESAHIM 4:3

I:1: And is it permitted to raise [small animals in the Holy Land

II:1: Why [is it forbidden]?

III:1: What is the difference between a large [animal] and a small animal?

III:2: [If] one transgressed [the local custom not to sell small animals] and sold [such an animal to a gentile], do they impose a fine on him?

IV:1: Judah permits in the case of a maimed one [M 4:3E]. R. Judah referred only to a maimed one that cannot be healed

V:1: R. Judah [ben Beterah] referred only to a male horse

V:2: [Explaining why a male horse is unreliable in battle:] Some say for it runs after a female [horse]. And some say, for it halts to urinate.

V:3:   [The above opinion represents] the words of the sages [the halakhah].
         [Supplying the rationale for Ben Beterah's anonymous disputants for pro-
         hibiting the sale of even a horse:]: R. Aha [said] in the name of R. Tanhum
         bar Hiyya, "When it [a horse] grows old

V:4:   Rabbi says, "I say that he is forbidden [to sell horses to a gentile] because
         of two matters: because of [selling] weapons and because of the laws of
         a large animal" [T. A.Z. 2:3].

YERUSHALMI PESAHIM 4:4

I:1:   Ba asked before R. Immi, "[Does the Mishnah's rule] apply even to the
         meat of a calf

I:2:   It is taught

I:3:   It is taught

I:4:   [On] the Day of Atonement that falls on the Sabbath is it permitted to
         wash pressed and steamed vegetables from [the time of] *afternoon prayer*
         onward

I:5:   Ba asked before R. Immi, "Is it permitted to wash pressed and steamed
         vegetables from afternoon prayer onward?"

YERUSHALMI PESAHIM 4:5

I:1:   R. Abun, R. Simeon b. Laqish [said] in the name of Rabban Judah Nesiah
         [grandson of R. Judah the Patriarch], "[The Mishnah] deals with a case
         in which one causes astonishment [if one refrains from working when
         others work, for example, when the individual is known in general to
         work]."

II:1:   [And is it not so that the sages never went so far as to enact idleness on
         the Ninth of Ab [but left the requirement up to local custom]?

YERUSHALMI PESAHIM 4:6

I:1:   Lo, the day is prohibited [a deduction derived from the fact that the Houses,
         in M. 4:6B, dispute only the case of the night and thus seem to accord
         with the practice in Galilee, in M. 1:6A]. R. Eleazar in the name of R.
         Hoshaiah, "[The rule at M. 1:6A receives support from the following
         verse:]

YERUSHALMI PESAHIM 4:7

I:1:   R Meir says, "Any sort of work that [a person] started before the four-
         teenth, [one] completes it on the fourteenth [M 4:7A] "

YERUSHALMI PESAHIM 4:8

I:1:   They set out hen-coops for chickens on the fourteenth [M. 4:8A] Lo, on
         the intermediate days of the festival it is forbidden [to set up the coop for
         the first time].

II:1:   And a chicken that fled — they return (it) to its place [to sit on its eggs]
         [M 4:8B] And it [the Mishnah refers to] a case such that

II:2:   Dung that is in the alleyway, they remove it to the side; [dung] that is in
         the stall and that is in the courtyard, they take it out to the dunghill [T.
         3:18].

YERUSHALMI PESAHIM 4:9

I:1:   Who teaches "they reap"? R. Meir [who, is assumed to be the anony-
        mous disputant of Judah, says that they reap with the sages' approval].
        Who teaches, "They pile"? R. Judah [who holds that they even pile and
        did not elicit sages' protest]. Said R. Jacob bar Susai before

II:1:   How would they recite the Shema' without pause?

III:1: How would they [consider] permitted fruit of trees that had been dedi-
        cated [to the Temple]?

III:2: What did rabbis believe in saying [to the men of Jericho that they [the
        ancestors] had dedicated the trunks and fruit?

III:3: Abba bar Kahana said before R. Immi, "One who rents his house to his
        fellow and [then finds] that he needs its money [which would be obtain-
        able by selling the house, what is the law]?"

IV:1:   How shall we define [this case]?

V:1:   They set aside peah [corners of their field] for vegetables [M 4:9C, the
        sixth practice]. They would give only from turnip and from porret [head
        of a leek] for they are [regularly] picked [all] at once.

YERUSHALMI PESAHIM 5:1

I:1:   The Daily Whole Offering [daily offering] is slaughtered, [M. 5:1A]. It
        is written, "Now this is what you shall offer upon the altar," ["Two year-
        ling lambs each day, regularly"] (Exod. 29:38).

I:2:   R. Joshua b. Levi said, "The [times of the required daily] prayers were
        learned from the patriarchs,'...Nevertheless they did not remove him from
        his distinction, rather they appointed him Av-Bet-Din."

II:1:   Who teaches [that the Daily Whole Offering offerings are prepared and
        slaughtered on the eve of Passover at the same time] whether [they] fall
        on a weekday or the Sabbath [M. 5:1B]? R. Ishmael

II:2:   [In response to M. 5:1B's rule that the Daily Whole Offering on Passover
        eve is sacrificed an hour early, at the eighth-and- one-half hour, and that
        the Passover offering comes an hour later, "between the evenings":] And
        let one offer the Passover sacrifice first [at the eighth-and-one-half hour]
        and the Daily Whole Offering after it [at its standard time, "between the
        evenings"]?

II:3:   It is taught:

YERUSHALMI PESAHIM 5:2

I:1:   How do we know that [a person] is required to slaughter it [the Passover
        offering] under its [proper] designation?

I:2:   [If one] slaughtered [the Passover offering] under its proper designation
        [as a Passover offering but with the intention] to toss its blood not under
        its proper designation:

I:3:   Said R. Yohanan, "Regarding this [following tradition] R. Abba bar Abba
        came [into the study session; alternatively, "up to the land of Israel"]

I:4:   [If one] slaughtered [a Passover offering] under the proper designation and [then] not under the proper designation during the rest of the days of the year [is it fit or not]? [During the rest of the year — before Passover — does intention with proper designation function to disqualify just as, on Passover, intention without proper designation does?]

YERUSHALMI PESAHIM 5:3

I:1:   How do we know that he is required to slaughter it for those who can eat it?

I:2:   How [are we to understand the case of] for those who cannot eat it [M. 5:3A]?

I:4:   [If one slaughters the Passover offering:] [both] for those who can eat an olive's amount [in bulk] and for those who cannot eat an olive's amount [in bulk] — it is fit

I:5:   [If] one slaughtered [a Passover offering with the intention] that half of his association should eat from it [with the other half excluded, but without specifying who falls into each group] — R. Jonah declares [it] invalid [although it is a case of slaughtering the animal for both those who can and those who cannot eat it, which M. 5:3A.2 declares fit

II:1:   Before the Daily Whole Offering sacrifice — it is fit [M. 5:3C]. And it was taught likewise

YERUSHALMI PESAHIM 5:4

I:1:   From where do we know that one who offers a Passover sacrifice with leaven [in one's possession] transgresses a negative commandment? the teaching says, "You shall not offer the blood of My sacrifice with anything leavened" (Exod. 34:25). I only know that one who offers [the sacrifice is liable]. From where do I know regarding one who tosses [its blood]? The teaching says, "[You shall] not [offer] blood [of .my sacrifice] with leaven" [— specifying the blood when it could have simply said, "You shall not offer My sacrifice with anything leavened"].

I:2:   [If] one burned the sacrificial portions with leaven [in one's possession]: There are those who teach — "[one] is liable"; and there are those who teach — "[one] is exempt."

I:3:   There we learn

I:5:   What is the reason for R. Judah? [The verse states,] "The blood of My offering" [read as a plural, "My offerings," which means] the blood of the Passover offering and the blood of the daily offering.

I:6:   Said R. Yohanan, "The reason of R. Simeon [is as follows]: One verse says, 'You shall not slaughter the blood of My sacrifice with anything leavened' (Exod. 34:25), and one verse says, 'You shall not offer the blood of My sacrifice with anything leavened' (Exod. 23:18)

I:7:   Said R. Yohanan, "An association [or "association" of sages or disciples, drawing on a text such as M. 9:6] would ask

YERUSHALMI PESAHIM 5:5

I:2:   It was taught

I:3:   A story [concerning:] R. Zeira and R. Jacob bar Aha and R. Abina, who were sitting [together]. Said R. Abina, "[Mishnah's procedure was] due to deceivers [who would substitute less precious for more precious basins]."

YERUSHALMI PESAHIM 5:6

I:1:   One verse says, "But the firstlings of cattle, sheep, or goats you may not redeem; they are consecrated. You shall dash their blood against the altar" (Num. 18:17), and another verse says, "and of your [other] sacrifices, the blood shall be poured out on the altar of the Lord your God" (Deut. 12:27).

YERUSHALMI PESAHIM 5:7

I:1:   There we learn [regarding the sequence of fasts for rain, when rain finally arrives:] "They went out and ate and drank and returned at twilight and read the Great Hallel" [M. Tan. 3:9]. What is the Great Hallel? R. Parnokh in the name of R. Haninah [said], "'Praise the God of Gods' (Ps. 136:7)' [T. Tan. 2:17]. Said R. Yohanan, "As long as [one starts] from [the preceding chapter] '[Give praise, you servants of the LORD] who stand in the house of our God' (Ps. 135:2)."

I:2:   It is taught, "It [the third group] was called the group of lazy ones" [T. 4:11].

YERUSHALMI PESAHIM 5:8

I:1:   Said R. Jonathan, "They did not permit every act proscribed so as to maintain the restfulness of the Sabbath in the Temple, [hence even though the washing in may have only been an act proscribed so as to maintain the restfulness of the Sabbath, sages still forbade it because technically it was not a cultic act], 'and the priests sank in blood up to their knees [T. 4:12]."

I:2:   There we learn: R. Judah makes one liable if or consuming the last blood [which oozes out at an animal's death, for it is considered forbidden blood] [M. Ker. 5:1]

YERUSHALMI PESAHIM 5:9

I:1:   R. Zeira in the name of R. Eleazar [says], "[The arrangement of] the staves [between the cakes of the show-bread on the Sabbath which does not take precedence over the Sabbath (M. Men. 11:6)] and poles [on which the Passover offering's carcass might be hung and flayed and which R. Eliezer says are not used when the Sabbath coincides with the fourteenth of Nisan] [M. Pes. 5:9] were taught before [the sages granted] permission [to move] utensils on the Sabbath" [M. Shab. 17:1].

YERUSHALMI PESAHIM 5:10

I:1:   It is written, "And [he] sprinkled some of the blood [on the altar]" —
         from all of it. [All of the animal must be intact when the dashing takes
         place.]

YERUSHALMI PESAHIM 6:1

II:1:   Said R. Yohanan, "'The Lord made everything for his honor' [usually
         rendered, "for a purpose"] (Prov. 16:4) [teaching] that [a person] should
         not appear as one taking the sacrificial parts from a disgusting offering
         [which it would be if left unscraped and uncleaned; hence such action is
         permitted on the Sabbath]."

III:1:   And burning its fat [M. 6:1B]: "And the fat of My festal offering shall
         not be left lying until morning" (Exod. 23:18)

IV:1:   We learned: Once it became dark, they went out and roasted their Pass-
         over offerings [M. 5:10C, which is assumed to refer to Saturday night, as
         if such roasting were prohibited on the Sabbath itself], but here you [M.
         Shab. 1:11] say thus

V:1:   [The Mishnah] spoke only of outside Jerusalem [where such actions are
         prohibited]. Lo, outside the [Temple] courtyard [yet within Jerusalem], it
         is permitted because [it is only a matter of the injunction to maintain]
         restfulness [on the Sabbath, which is a category] that [they] permitted in
         the Temple.

VI:1:   And cutting off a wen [...do not override (the Sabbath)] [M 6:1D] There
         [in M. Erub.] we learn: And they cut off a wart [that appeared] on a priest
         in the Temple precincts but not in the country [M. Erub. 10:13]. Here [M.
         Erub.] you say [it] overrides [the Sabbath] and here [M. Pes. 6:1] you say
         [it] does not override.

YERUSHALMI PESAHIM 6:2

I:1:   And taking it from outside [to inside] the [Sabbath] limit [M 6:1D] [which
         Eliezer at M. 6:1E claims overrides the Sabbath, can be considered, on
         the basis of Eliezer's reference in M. 6:2A, merely an act which nor-
         mally is prohibited so as to produce a "restful" Sabbath or holiday, but
         which in the special case of Passover could be overridden, and not a
         biblically prohibited labor].

I:2:   Cutting of its wart [M 6:1D] [which R. Eliezer in M. 6: IE rules does
         override the Sabbath, even] with a utensil [can it be considered, based on
         Eliezer's reference in M. 6:2A, merely a biblically prohibited labor.
         Said R. Mana, "Sprinkling [blood, in the case mentioned in M. 6:3] is a
         an injunction to rest from a "permitted" act which entails a religious duty
         and these [special cases enumerated in M. Erub. 10:15] are a an injunc-
         tion to rest from a "permitted" act which entails a religious duty Sprin-
         kling [according to R. Eliezer in M. 6:3] overrides and these [even in the
         Temple as specified in M. Erubin] do not override [the Sabbath]? Rather

[the situations must be incomparable] for this [latter set of M. Erubin cases] involves the offering and this [former case of sprinkling] involves the offerer."

Does [Eliezer in referring in M. 6:2C to "an injunction to rest from a permitted act which entails a religious duty" have in mind an act falling into the category of] an injunction to rest from a permitted act which entails a religious duty [an injunction to rest from a "permitted" act which entails a religious duty]?

YERUSHALMI PESAHIM 6:3

I:1:   For thirteen years R. Aqiba would come before R. Eliezer, who would not pay any attention to him. And this [statement regarding sprinkling the waters of purifications, presented in M. 6:3] comprised the opening of his first response before R. Eliezer. [Applying a biblical verse in appreciation of Aqiba and the astuteness of his comment:] Said R. Joshua to [Eliezer], "There is the army you sneered at; now go out and fight it" (Jud.9:38). [Proof of the ultimate ascendancy of Aqiba is the placement of his opinion before Eliezer's in the following text:] There we learned [in reference to Num. 9:10-13's rule permitting those on a "distant journey" (v. 10) or a "journey" (v. 13) to bring the Passover offering one month later:] "What is a 'distant journey'? From [the place] Modiin and outward and the equivalent distance in every direction," the words of R Aqiba R Eliezer says, "From the threshold of the courtyard and outward [hence anyone who for whatever reason is outside the Temple courtyard and, therefore, unable to bring the Passover offering may offer it one month later]" [M 9:2]

I:2:   Aqiba answered and said, "Sprinkling the water [of purification on one who has become defiled through contact with a corpse on the seventh day following one's uncleanness, should the seventh day fall on a Sabbath that coincides with the eve of Passover,] will prove [my point], for it is a religious duty" [M 6:3A] And is it a commandment to sprinkle [what commandment is fulfilled as a result of sprinkling]? You may explain [the Mishnah's terminology if the case be such] that a person's seventh day [of purification] coincided with the fourteenth of Nisan that coincided with the Sabbath; for if it were a weekday, one would sprinkle [blood] on him and afterwards he would proceed to slaughter his Passover offering and he [then would] eat it in the evening.

II:1:   And does a person say to his master, "Perhaps reverse" [your argument, the language attributed to Aqiba in M. 6:3C] ! Because R. Eliezer was in the process of teaching him the halakhah that sprinkling does not override the Sabbath, and he countered him in midst of the argument, therefore he says to him, "perhaps reverse."

II:2:   It was taught

YERUSHALMI PESAHIM 6:4

I:1:   It is taught

YERUSHALMI PESAHIM 6:5

I:1:   The teaching [Mishnah 6:5A] treats a case in which [one] knows that it is a Passover offering but [consciously] slaughtered it under the designation of an offering of well-being [thinking, however, either that such an act is not prohibited on the Sabbath, or that if prohibited it would not make one liable for a sacrifice].

I:2:   They] say, "This [response] of R. Eliezer is not a [proper] answer to R. Joshua

II:1:   Said R. Eleazar, "The opinion of R. Meir, [who exempts, applies to one who slaughtered] even a calf [under the designation of a Passover offering on the Sabbath, out of a misunderstanding of the law

II:2:   Simeon b. Laqish said, "[A matter that] entails a commandment in its performance, for example: [if] one's deceased childless brother's widow [sister-in-law whom a levir is to marry because his brother died without children] is a menstruant and [he] had intercourse with her [thus fulfilling Deut. 25:5's commandment of taking the sister-in-law, though in the process violating the laws of impurity, he is exempt].

II:3:   [As to M. Shab. 19:4: "One who had two infants, one to circumcise on the eve of the Sabbath and one to circumcise on the Sabbath, but forgot and circumcised that of Sabbath eve on the Sabbath — (all agree in declaring the person) exempt; (if) he circumcised that of after the Sabbath on the Sabbath (before the required eighth day) — R Eliezer declares (the person) liable, but R. Joshua exempts:] Said R. Yohanan, "[M. Shab. 19:4] follows R. Meir,

YERUSHALMI PESAHIM 6:6

I:1:   Said R. Eleazar, "For whom was it necessary [to teach M. 6:6B, for is not its declaration that one is liable for slaughtering a blemished animal on the Sabbath self-evident

I:2:   Lo, [the implication of M. 6:6B's mention of a defect which is *"internal"* is that one which is] external — [regarding it one is] liable.

I:3:   Said R. Yohanan, "[M. 6:8B's exemption] represents [the position even of] R. Simeon" [who makes Joshua's exemption, in M. 6:5, apply to an action that entails a religious duty, and the sages all the more so would concur]. R. Jacob bar Aha, R. Immi in the name of R. Simeon b. Laqish, "It represents [the position of even] R. Simeon."

I:4:   R. Yosé [said] in the name of R. Yohanan, "It [M. 6:6, in particular as revealed in the case of the registrants' withdrawal of their hands and in light of the Mishnah's final explanatory clause] represents [the view of] R. Judah, for we learn there [in the Mishnah:]

YERUSHALMI PESAHIM 7:1

I:1:   Why [use a spit made] of pomegranate [wood]? Said R. Hiyya bar Ba, "All trees drip moisture and that of pomegranate does not drip moisture."

I:2:   It is taught in the name of R. Judah

I:3:   There are those who teach: "[They] stick it [into the animal] from the buttocks to the mouth."

II:1:   What [is Yosé the Galilean's reason, in M. 7:1B, for placing the entrails inside the animal]?

II:2:   "Tokh bar [here assumed to mean with its insides outside]" — the words of R. Tarfon. R. Ishmael says, "Kid completely roasted [here taken as "helmeted" with all its portions inside]

II:3:   Teaches R. Yosé, "What is a gedi kid completely roasted

II:4:   It is taught

II:5:   Immi asked, "[If one] cleared out [the coals of the oven] and roasted [the Passover offering] with it [that is with the oven's residual heat preserved in its stones or sides, what is the law as to whether or not this is permitted]?"

YERUSHALMI PESAHIM 7:2

I:1:   "Roasted by fire" (Exod. 12:8) — and not roasted by a [metal] spit, not roasted by a pot, not roasted by a grill, not roasted by any [other] object.

I:2:   If [Scripture] had said, "Do not eat any of it except roasted" and had not said [the next word of the intervening phrase:] 'raw' [not cooked sufficiently to make the meat edible, and in that sense uncooked, a term which Exod. 12:9 presents after "do not eat any of it"], I would have said [that if a person] parched it and [then] roasted it — [it would be] permitted

II:1:   [If the animal] touched the earthenware of the oven — [(one) should pare away its place (of contact because it u as cooked by the heat of the earthenware and not the fire)] [M. 7:2C] — it [the portion of the meat that had touched the earthenware] is unfit in itself and is burned immediately.

YERUSHALMI PESAHIM 7:3

I:1:   [The Mishnah] stated only "[if one] basted it" [then rinsing or paring away the exterior is sufficient, depending on the situation], lo, if one seasoned it [it is] forbidden [for thereby one would nullify the taste of the Passover offering].

I:2:   Thus is the teaching [the correct rendering or reading of M. 7:3E]: They do not redeem second tithe produce in Jerusalem.

YERUSHALMI PESAHIM 7:4

I:1:   And are not all communal sacrifices offered in a state of uncleanness? [Hence the first part of M. 7:3A's apodosis is unnecessary.] [That clause] comes only in order to tell you that even though they are offered in a state of uncleanness, they are not eaten in a state of uncleanness.

I:2:   There are Tannaite authorities who teach [that] all [five] of them are
         learned from the [case of] the Passover offering; [and] there are Tannaite
         authorities who teach [that] each one is learned from its own context.

YERUSHALMI PESAHIM 7:5

I:1:   And [M. 7:5] is not in accord with R. Nathan

I:2:   The following proposition is self-evident: if the meat was made unclean,
         while the sacrificial parts remain validly available, one tosses the blood
         in behalf of the sacrificial portions. If the sacrificial portions were made
         unclean but the meat was still validly available, one tosses the blood for
         the meat. If the meat was made unclean, and the sacrificial portions were
         lost —

I:3:   Said R. Eleazar, "The teaching [M. 7:4C, which states that 'the Passover
         offering which is offered in the state of uncleanness is eaten in the state
         of uncleanness]' deals with a case in which lit] came in a state of un-
         cleanness from the first moment [= T.6:1A]]

I:4:   [In such a case with reference to the Passover offering, where M. 7:5A
         states that [one] does not toss the blood:] But according to R. Nathan
         [one] tosses the blood.

YERUSHALMI PESAHIM 7:6

I:1:   Who is the teacher [of the Mishnah who teaches that the majority must
         be of the entire Israelite people, not just that of a single tribe]?

I:2:   According to the view of R. Meir, that [Passover offering in which the
         relationship of clean to unclean registrants is] one-half to one-half [ex-
         actly], what is done with it? Is it [treated] like [a case of] a majority [of
         unclean individuals, or] like a minority?

I:3:   [If] the community was [divided into] a third one unclean with flux [Lev.
         15], a third unclean [by reason of corpse uncleanness], [and] a third clean,
         [what procedure is followed]? R. Mana in the name of Hezekiah, "The
         [combined] one unclean with flux [Lev. 15] and unclean outnumber the
         clean, and they prepare [the Passover offering] in uncleanness, but the
         one unclean with flux [Lev. 15] [themselves] prepare neither the first nor
         the second [Passover offering]."

I:4:   Members of a association, one of whom became unclean [after bringing
         the offering but before its blood was tossed on the altar], and it is not
         known which one [it was], are required to prepare a second Passover [T.
         7:15A

I:5:   Immi [said] in the name of R. Simeon b. Laqish, "Regarding erring] in-
         struction [from a court which the community follows], go after [the num-
         ber of Jews residing] in the Land of Israel. "Regarding uncleanness, go
         after the majority of those who enter the [Temple] courtyard."

YERUSHALMI PESAHIM 7:7

I:1:   The teaching [in the Mishnah] speaks of a case in which [the Passover
         offering] became unclean after [the blood] descended into the cavity of

the utensil [used to receive the blood, which completes the act of tossing of the blood and enables the frontlet to propitiate].

II:1: From where [do we derive the rule that the frontlet propitiates for] doubtful [uncleanness] of a grave of the deep [M. 7:7D]?

II:2: Concerning a community which became unclean by reason of a doubtful [uncleanness of the] deep, what is the law?

II:3: [Assuming that the Mishnah refers to the frontlet's propitiating for the uncleanness of the owners:] The officiating priest for the Passover offering, what is the law?

II:4: What is a grave "of the deep" [which would be considered unknown to people]?

II:5: [As to M. Erub. 7:3, If a trench runs between two adjacent courtyards ten handbreadths deep and four handbreadths wide, they prepare two erubs and do not prepare one jointly even if it was filled up with stubble and straw; but if it was filled up with earth or pebbles, they) prepare one Erub (jointly) and do not prepare two Erubin:] The teaching [M. Erub. 7:3 in its discounting of a straw filler for the trench] is not in accord with R. Yosé

II:6: What is a grave "of the deep"?

II:7: It is taught

II:8: There we learned

Yerushalmi Pesahim 7:8

I:1: Hama bar Uqba in the name of R. Yosé b. Haninah [says], "In order to expose him to proclaim that [the one burning the sacrifice] spoiled it."

I:2: [Explaining why they do not allow a person to burn a minor part of an unclean offering before the Temple mount with his own wood:] Said R. Jeremiah in the name of R. Hila, "To proclaim [to] the one who comes after him that [the one who is burning his unclean offering] is stingy."

I:3: [Contrasting the differing requirements for burning unclean meat with the wood pile of the altar found in M. 7:8, which specifies that the whole or most of the animal become unclean, and in M. 3:8, which treats even a small amount of unclean sacred meat: one who has gone out from Jerusalem and remembers that he has in his possession sacred meat which thereby becomes invalid" and yet which states: "if it had not gone beyond the lookout spot outside Jerusalem he returns and burns it before the Temple mount with the woodpile of the altar:]

I:4: Said R. Yohanan, "A tower stood on the Temple mount and was called birah." R. Simeon b. Laqish said, "The whole Temple mount was called birah."

Yerushalmi Pesahim 7:9

I:1: Teaches R. Hiyya: "[A case of] unfitness in itself is burned immediately. [A case of] unfitness, regarding a precondition [of the offering that does not make the animal in itself unfit, for example, when the owners died or became unclean] requires [disfigurement of] appearance [being left to spoil overnight]" [T. 6:6].

II:1:   Hama bar Uqba in the name of R. Yosé bar Haninah [said], "R. Nehemiah [as cited in B below] and R. Yohanan b. Beroqa [as cited in M. 7:9C] both said the same thing.

II:2:   We learned there

II:3:   It is taught [in regard to Lev. 6:17-23's rule of the sin offering]:

YERUSHALMI PESAHIM 7:10

I:2:   And let [one] strip the flesh from the bone and enjoy the bone? [Why then does the Mishnah require burning of the bone?]

I:3:   R. Immi [said] in the name of R. Eleazar, "Why did [they] say, 'The bones and the sinews and the leftover portions should be burned on the sixteenth ' [M. 7:10A?

YERUSHALMI PESAHIM 7:11

I:1:   Soft sinews that are not necessarily destined to harden] — R. Yohanan said, "[People] are registered on them [so that the sinews would comprise their portion in the Passover offering]." R. Simeon b. Laqish said, "[People] are not registered on them."

II:1:   And how much must one break [in a bone of the Passover offering so as to make oneself liable]?

III:1:   R. Abun in the name of R. Eleazar [said], "The teaching deals with a case in which [the offering] initially came in [a state of] uncleanness, but if it came in [a state of] cleanness and [then] became unclean [it is considered] like [one] that came in [a state of] cleanness and they impose lashes on breaking it[s bone]."

YERUSHALMI PESAHIM 7:12

I:1:   R. Simon, R. Joshua b. Levi in the name of bar Pedayah,"Sacrificial meat in the status of refuse and remnant of sacrificial meat join to impart uncleanness to hands, bringing about a punishment when they comprise an olive's amount."

I:2:   That part [of the offering that] projects out [from the holy precincts, thereby becoming invalid], what do you do with it? Does it impart uncleanness to hands or does it not impart uncleanness to hands?

II:1:   Ba in the name of R. Judah [said], "They did not sanctify below the door frame of Jerusalem [within the area of the door way]."

II:2:   Rab asked R. Hiyyah the Elder, "What is the law regarding the roofs of Jerusalem?"

YERUSHALMI PESAHIM 7:13

I:1:   It is written, "[It shall be eaten in one house;] you shall not take out from the house any of the flesh outside" (Exod. 12:46). I only know [from this verse regarding] outside the house; where [do I learn regarding] outside the association?

I:2:   If the members of the association] registered on the Passover offering —
[if] one [person] took out [flesh in the measure of] an olive, [that person
is] liable; [if] two or three [took out an olive's amount, they are] exempt
[from liability for punishment for violating a negative commandment],
because the members of the association are fit to extend themselves to
them [moving the site of the association to the place of the two or three
individuals

II:1:   A waiter who ate [flesh of a Passover offering in the amount of] an olive
and he was at the side of the oven [and not with the rest of the association
with which he is registered], if he is clever, he fills his stomach from it
[from the oven

II:2:   An individual [from a association, during the time of eating] roams around
the whole house and a association does not roam around the whole house.
And do we not learn

YERUSHALMI PESAHIM 8:1

I:1:   [Addressing (originally) the meal offering for a suspected adulteress,
which, according to Num. 5:15, her husband brings, and in response to
the question whether, if we assume the husband may set aside the meal
offering for her without her knowledge because he is a partner in it with
her, may another person do so as well?] Said R. Yohanan, "[In the case
of] four [types of individuals who are] lacking purification, they designate [an offering] for them without their knowledge. And these are they:
a one unclean with flux [Lev. 15] [a man with a flux] and a zabah [a
woman who bled for three days running, making her a severe hemor-
rhage (Lev. 15:25)], and one who gives birth, and a leper, "for similarly
a person designates [one of these offerings] for his infant child [lit., 'son']
when [even] he is in the crib."

I:2:   Said R. Yohanan, "They taught [that the woman eats with her father] in
regard to an 'anxious festival' *(regel redufin)."* [Because of that special
situation, the wife on the first festival eats with her father, but otherwise
she could or would eat with her husband — as M. 8:1B contemplates.]

I:3:   Said R. Eleazar, "The Passover offering of women is optional, but for it
they [nevertheless] override the Sabbath."

II:1:   The teaching treats a case of a minor orphan [whose preference is incon-
sequential because he is under the authority of the guardians], but in the
case of an adult orphan, should we consider [it] like one who registers
himself on two Passover offerings simultaneously?

III:1:   Yosé says, "His master has no right to tell him, 'You are not permitted to
be registered on the Passover offering.'

IV:1:   R. Hiyya in the name of R. Yohanan [said], "One who is half slave and
half-free [who] sanctified a woman [to be his wife] — they are not concerned regarding sanctification [lest the marriage took effect]."

YERUSHALMI PESAHIM 8:2

I:1:   Teaches R. Hiyya, "One who is registered on two Passover offerings simultaneously eats from whichever of them is slaughtered first, [for whatever is first will satisfy him since presumably he does not have a preference regarding from which offering he eats]" [T. 7:3].

II:1:   Eleazar and R. Yohanan, both of them say, "It [the author of the Mishnaic passage who in M. 8:2D does not require the preparation of the second Passover

YERUSHALMI PESAHIM 8:3

I:1:   Said R. Yohanan, "Do not [understand] here, 'Behold I will slaughter' [literally]. Rather [the text means], 'I will designate.' And why does it teach, 'Behold I will slaughter'? In order to prod [them to go to Jerusalem quickly]."

I:2:   R. Eleazar in the name of R. Hoshaia [said], "It is a stipulation imposed by the court that one designates his Passover offering and the other designates his coins [so as to obtain a portion in someone else's animal], [the former] assigns him [the latter] a portion from his [animal] and the coins [the former receives] become unconsecrated by themselves."I:3: On what basis in Scripture do we know that they register [on a Passover offering]?

YERUSHALMI PESAHIM 8:4

I:1:   The members of the association one of whose members had strong hands [that could quickly grab food] have the right to tell him, "Take your share and eat by yourself." [They may do this] not only [regarding the] Passover offering but even if [the members of the association] made a joint meal, they have the right to tell him, "take your share and eat by yourself" [T. 7:10].

I:2:   Huna said, "[If a person] designated his Passover offering and said, 'On condition that no one else will be registered with me' — no one else may be registered with him.

YERUSHALMI PESAHIM 8:5

I:1:   Teaches R. Hiyya: "A menstruant — [they] slaughter [a Passover offering] for her on the eighth [day

YERUSHALMI PESAHIM 8:6

I:1:   R. Yosé b. R. Bun, Abba b. Bar Hanah in the name of R. Yohanan, "The teaching [in the Mishnah] deals with a case in which Israelites imprisoned him [then the promise to free him may be relied on], but if gentiles captured him [their promise is unreliable as conveyed in the following verse speaking of foreigners:] 'Whose mouths speak lies and whose oaths are false' (Ps. 144:8).

I:2:   At times he is considered like them [the other categories in M. 8:6].At times they are considered like him

YERUSHALMI PESAHIM 8:7

I:1:   Said R. Yohanan, "R. Judah's [reasoning is based upon the following verse:] 'You are not permitted to slaughter the Passover offering in one of your settlements' (Deut. 16:5) [with the 'in one' taken to mean 'for one,' i.e., for one individual]."

I:2:   It is taught

YERUSHALMI PESAHIM 8:8

I:1:   Said R. Yosé b. R. Bun, "The teaching [the Mishnah in differentiating between the eating of the Passover offering and other Holy Things] speaks of a case in which

I:2:   It is taught

I:3:   It is taught

II:1:   What is the reason of the House of Shammai?

YERUSHALMI PESAHIM 9:1

I:1:   [Whoever was unclean (M. 9:1A)]: "Unclean by [contact with] the dead" (Num. 9:10):

I:2:   [If] it is possible for Israel to [re-]build the Temple [between the first Passover and second Passover], [then] an individual offers the second Passover, but the community does not offer the second Passover.

I:3:   If the community was [unclean], half of them *zabim* [afflicted with a flux, Lev. 15] and half of them unclean [because of contact with the dead]

YERUSHALMI PESAHIM 9:2

I:2:   Abbahu in the name of R. Yohanan: "Both of them [R. Aqiba and R. Eliezer in M. 9:2B-C] are interpreting the same scriptural passage[s as the basis for an argument based on the identity of words in two distinct passages.

YERUSHALMI PESAHIM 9:3

I:1:   It is written [regarding the second Passover offering], "And they shall not leave any of it over until morning" (Num. 9:12).

I:2:   There are [some] teachers who teach, "For [omission of] the second [Passover offering] one is punished by excision; for [omission of] the first [Passover] one is not punished by excision." There are [other] teachers who teach, "For [omission of] the first [Passover] one is punished by excision; for [omission of] the second [Passover] one is not punished by excision."

II:1:   Said R. Yohanan in the name of R. Simeon b. Yehosedeq, "It is written, 'For you, there shall be singing as on a night when a festival is hallowed' (Isa. 30:29 [taken to be referring to Passover night]). [The obligation to recite the Hallel psalms on] Passover evening comes to teach [that in a similar way the Hallel psalms are to be recited] upon the downfall of Sennacherib.

YERUSHALMI PESAHIM 9:4

I:1:   It was taught: R. Meir declares liable [those in M. 9:4A if they ate], but R. Simeon declares [them] exempt [in agreement with M. 9:4B].

II:1:   [Referring to M. 9:4C:] If one [who is prohibited from entering the Temple] entered at night [or] entered before the sixth hour [noon, when the obligation to slaughter the Passover offering has not yet come into effect, what is the law? Is such a person still exempt according to R. Eliezer? The question is left unanswered.]

II:2:   Said R. Yosé, "If R. Eleazar were to adopt the opinion of R. Simeon [hence M. 9:4B], what is the reason [for the two commands regarding a woman after childbirth during her period of uncleanness

YERUSHALMI PESAHIM 9:5

I:1:   There are [some] teachers who teach: "Cataracts and growths in the eye disqualify it [i.e., the Passover of Egypt]." There are [other] teachers who teach: "Cataracts and growths in the eye do not disqualify it." [According to] the one who says, "Cataracts and growths in the eye disqualify it," it is fine, for it is written, "Your [Passover] lamb shall be without blemish" (Exod. 12:5). [According to] the one who says, "Cataracts and growths in the eye do not disqualify it," how can he explain [the need for the command], "Your [Passover] lamb shall be without blemish" (Exod. 12:5)?

I:2:   Concerning where the blood was placed on the door frame and the meaning of Hebrew *saf*, usually translated "threshold":]

I:3:   It was taught: "Ben Bag Bag says, 'Your lamb shall be without blemish' (Exod. 12:5); [even] if there has been shearing [and the fleece has been removed, the animal still is considered [perfect and] without blemish." But lo, it has been taught: "'If his offering is from [among] the flock' (Lev. 1:10); to exclude the smooth [shorn] ones among them [from being offered as sacrifices, for shearing is tantamount to a blemish]?"

I:4:   Said R. Yosé, "Even R. Yosé the Galilean agrees with them [with the sages, M. 9:5] that the Passover of Egypt lasted for only one day].

YERUSHALMI PESAHIM 9:6

I:1:   R. Yudan asked, "The law is the same in the case of the substitute for a guilt offering. There is a case in which the substitute for a guilt offering is sacrificed, and there is a case in which the substitute for a guilt offering is not sacrificed. [So why was R. Joshua confused about the law in M. 9:6A?]"

I:2:   If he made a substitution for it on the thirteenth [of Nisan], R. Zeira says, "Its substitute is offered as a whole offering." R. Samuel b. R. Isaac says, "Its substitute is not offered as a whole offering."

I:3:   There [M. Tem. 4:1] we learned

I:4:   [If] he set aside his Passover offering and it was lost, and so he set aside another in its stead, but did not have a chance to offer the second before

the first was found, and both are available:There are [some] teachers
who teach, "It is required to offer the first" [T. 9:12].There are [other]
teachers who teach, "It is required to offer the second."

YERUSHALMI PESAHIM 9:7

I:1:   The teaching [of the Mishnah, 9:7A] [refers] to [a point] after atonement
         has been gained [by the tossing of the blood of a Passover offering].

I:2:   Did we not think to say the same [in reference to M. 9:7B]? Whatever
         [animal] was fit to be offered on the day of the Passover offering [the
         fourteenth of Nisan] itself is not offered as a whole offering. [Once the
         animal entered the fourteenth of Nisan while its owner was still alive, it
         can never be offered as a whole offering, but must instead be pastured
         until it becomes unfit for sacrifice.]

YERUSHALMI PESAHIM 9:8

I:1:   In reference to M. M.S. 3:2: It is forbidden to buy heave offering (which
         may only be eaten by priests) with the money of (second) tithe (which
         must be brought to Jerusalem and spent on food to be eaten there). be-
         cause one reduces (the opportunity for) eating it. But R. Simeon permits
         (it). Since heave offering has more strictures regarding its eating, being
         limited to priests and their families, exchanging the money of second
         tithe for heave offering may lead indirectly to the tithe's not being eaten
         as prescribed. R. Simeon believes that there is no prohibition on indi-
         rectly causing offerings to become disqualified and, hence, has no objec-
         tion to this exchange,] it was taught: "It is forbidden to purchase [pro-
         duce of] the Sabbatical year with money of the [second] tithe [since when
         the time for disposing of Sabbatical produce comes, it will be disquali-
         fied and will never be eaten]" [T. Shebi'it 7:1].R. Yosé says, "It is a
         dispute."

YERUSHALMI PESAHIM 9:9

I:1:   Said R. Yohanan, "This [M. 9:9B] is according to R. Nathan, for R. Nathan
         said: 'They fulfill their obligation [of offering the Passover] by the toss-
         ing [of the blood, even without eating]' [T. 7:5]."

I:2:   [If before leaving to search for the missing animal,] he said to them, "If I
         am late, [go out and] slaughter on my behalf," and so forth [T. 9:2].

YERUSHALMI PESAHIM 9:10

I:1:   Said R. Yohanan, "This [M. 9:10B] is according to R. Judah, for we have
         learned: 'We do not slaughter a Passover offering for an individual,' the
         words of R. Judah. But R. Yosé permits [it]' (M. 8:7)." [In accord with R.
         Judah, the Mishnah requires that there be more than one person regis-
         tered on the Passover offering.]

YERUSHALMI PESAHIM 10:1

I:1:   The teaching [the Mishnah] represents the position of R. Judah

I:2:   What is the law, is it permissible to eat dried fruit [which whets one's
         thirst]?

I:3:   Said R. Levi, "Because it is the custom of slaves to eat standing, here [on Passover night, the Mishnah requires people] to eat reclining to proclaim that they have gone out from slavery to freedom."

II:1:   Said R. Hiyya b. Adda, "Because it is not pleasant for a person to eat from the communal fund, here [he is required] 'even if [the funds come] from the charity plate.'"

II:2:   It is taught

II:3:   Whence [did they derive the requirement] for four cups?

II:4:   There [in M. Shab. 8:1] we learned, "One who takes wine out [on the Sabbath from a public domain to a private one or vice versa incurs a liability when the wine is] — sufficient to mix. a cup " [Since one part of raw wine is diluted with three parts of water to make a cup of drinkable wine, the Mishnah speaks of the minimum amount of wine that will prove useful.]

II:5:   What is the size of the cups? Is it permitted to drink the [four cups] in a single span [without interruption]? Is it permitted to drink them bit by bit

II:6:   It is taught

II:7:   Said R. Haninah, "The log-measure referred to in the Torah is the Sepphorian old tomanta [one-eighth of a qab] for brine."

II:8:   It is taught

YERUSHALMI PESAHIM 10:2

I:1:   What is the reason of the House of Shammai?

YERUSHALMI PESAHIM 10:3

I:1:   The Associates [said] in the name of R. Yohanan, "[A person] is required to dip the lettuce [bitter herbs] twice" [once before and once with the bread condiment — along with the other prescribed elements of the celebration, as indicated in M. 10:3A-B].

I:2:   Merchants of Jerusalem used to say, "Come and take the spices of the commandment" [T. Pes. 10:10]. [The language attributed to the venders indicates that people believed that the *haroset,* which contained spices, was prescribed by law, thus supporting Eleazar b. Sadoq's view in M. 10:2B.]

I:3:   It is taught: "And in the outer areas [outside the holy precincts where the Passover offering was eaten] [they bring] two cooked foods, one as a remembrance of the Passover offering and one as a remembrance of the festive offering."

YERUSHALMI PESAHIM 10:4

I:1:   R. Hiyya teaches: "The Torah [in explaining the Passover events] spoke corresponding to four [types of] children: a wise child; an evil child; a foolish child; and a child who does not know [or have intelligence] to ask."

I:2:   Rab said, "As [our ancients, i.e., Joshua, practiced] at the [very] beginning, 'In olden times, your ancestors [Terah, father of Abraham and fa-

ther of Nahor] lived [beyond the Euphrates]' ['and worshiped other gods'].
'But I took your father Abraham from beyond the Euphrates,' ['and led
him though the whole land of Canaan'] 'and multiplied' ['his offspring. I
gave him Isaac....'] (Josh. 24:2-3).75 [We therefore follow Joshua's model
in tracing our ignoble origins to the idolatrous background of our ancestors.]"

YERUSHALMI PESAHIM 10:5

I:2:   It was taught

I:3:   [Hallel, the Psalms praising and thanking God for redemption:] It is writ-
         ten, "In exacting retribution for Israel, when people offer willingly —
         Praise the Lord" (Jud. 5:2).

YERUSHALMI PESAHIM 10:6

I:1:   After [eating from] the Passover offering, they do not end [with] afiqomon
         [dainties; alt.: revelry] (M. 10:6F):Why [is it prohibited]? So that he should
         not become drunk.

I:2:   [Defining the term *afiqomon:*] R. Simon [said] in the name of R. Inanini
         bar R. Sisay, "Kinds of music [characteristically played at after-dinner
         revelries]." R. Yohanan said, "Kinds of sweet things [commonly eaten
         after the meal to whet one's thirst for further drinking]."

YERUSHALMI PESAHIM 10:7

I:1:   Why [if they all fall asleep, may they not eat again]? Is it because of
         being distracted from the thought [of the offering], or is it because mid-
         night passed?

I:2:   [Regarding the application of the laws of sacrificial meat in the status of
         refuse and remnant of sacrificial meat to prevent improper eating of an
         offering:] R. Simon in the name of R. Joshua b. Levi, "Sacrificial meat in
         the status of refuse and remnant of sacrificial meat join to impart un-
         cleanness to hands, bringing about a punishment when they comprise an
         olive's amount."

I:3:   That part [of the offering that] projects out [from the holy precincts,
         thereby becoming invalid as prescribed in Exod. 12:46], what do you do
         with it? Does it impart uncleanness to hands or does it not impart un-
         cleanness to hands?

I:4:   [As to a association all of whom fall asleep:] You may say that [it is a
         case in which] midnight passed. Is [the reason for proscribing such a
         association from further eating] not because of being distracted [for oth-
         erwise even a association of which less than all fell asleep would be
         prohibited from eating further]? Thus the reason that [the group all of
         whom fall asleep] may not [eat further] must be because of being dis-
         tracted [from concentration on the sacrifice].

II:1:   [Regarding the blessing over one sacrifice applying to the other sacri-
         fice:] Said R. Zeira, "Is it [not logical] that [if one] said the blessing over
         the Passover offering, one did not exempt that over the festive offering,

but [if one said] that of the festive offering one exempts that of the Passover offering, because the Passover offering is included under the category of a festive offering?"

VI. SUKKAH

YERUSHALMI SUKKAH 1:1

I:1:   [The following discussion serves M. 1:1A: A sukkah which is taller than twenty cubits is invalid. R. Judah declares it valid, and also M. Er. 1:1A: The entry to an alleyway which is taller than twenty cubits must be lowered.

I:2:   [What is the reason that sages declare a *sukkah* taller than twenty cubits to be invalid?]

I:3:   [As to the invalidity of a *sukkah* more than twenty cubits high,] R. Ba in the name of Rab: "That applies to a sukkah that will hold only the head and the greater part of the body of a person and also his table. But if it held more than that, it is valid [even at such a height]."

I:4:   Hoshaiah raised the following question: "[In the case of a *sukkah* twenty cubits tall,] if one brought a plank [suitable for serving as *sukkah roofing*] and placed it [at an angle] on the piece of a column [ten handbreadths high, set in the middle of the *sukkah*], it *is* obvious that if one should measure from the board [which extends at an angle upward to the roof of the *sukkah*], there is a distance of twenty cubits *[or more, as* the board projects beyond the *sukkah roofing*].

I:5:   If *a* sukkah was lower than ten handbreadths, and one hung up in it garlands [of produce, as decorations] which are suitable to serve as *sukkah roofing,* the garlands diminish the height of the *sukkah to* less than what is required [ten handbreadths], so that the *sukkah is* invalid.

I:6:   How do we know that air space ten handbreadths above the ground constitutes a different domain [from the ground]?

I:7:   It has been taught

I:8:   Hiyya in the name of R. Yohanan: "If two walls are four by four handbreadths and the third is even a handbreadth, the *sukkah* is valid."

I:9:   R. Simeon b. Laqish said in the name of R. Judah b. Haninah, "If one inserted four reeds into the four corners of a vineyard and tied a thread above [the reeds, from one to another], it affords protection as a braid, [that is, it forms a partition with regard to mixed seeds, and it is therefore permitted to sow seed near the vineyard, as if the vineyard were separated from the seed by a wall]. [This braided partition suffices for such a purpose.]"

I:10:   [With reference to M. Kil. 4:4

I:11:   The tips of lathes [used for the sukkah roofing] that protrude from the *sukkah* are treated as part of the *sukkah.* R. Hunah in the name of rabbis over there:

II:1:   One the light of which is greater than its shade is invalid [M. 1:1E-F]. Lo, if it is half and half, it is valid.

YERUSHALMI SUKKAH 1:2

I:1:   It has been taugh

I:2:   The same dispute pertains to unleavened bread [for use for Passover]. As to unleavened bread that is old, there is a dispute between the House of Shammai and the House of Hillel.

I:3:   [In T.'s version:] The sukkah made by shepherds, the sukkah made by field-workers in the summer, [or] a sukkah which is stolen — is invalid [T. Suk. 1:4A-B].

I:4:   He who makes a *sukkah* for himself — what blessing does he say?

YERUSHALMI SUKKAH 1:3

I:1:   In the case of two sukkah-roofs, one on top of the other, in which the upper roofing was such that the light was greater than the shade [and hence invalid], while the lower one was such that the light was not greater than the shade on its own, but, together with the other roof, the shade was greater than the light

II:1:   Is the law that there must actually be residents above [to invalidate the one beneath], or may it merely be suitable for residents [to invalidate the one beneath]?

YERUSHALMI SUKKAH 1:4

I:1:   It has been taught

II:1:   Said R. Yosé, "They have stated only, 'On account of droppings.' Lo, if one does so not on account of droppings, it is valid."

III:1:   R. Bibi in the name of R. Yohanan: "[This cover forms a kind of covered space, of which we do not take account,] just as one may have created an enclosed space by raising his two hands [within a covering]. [Doing so has no bearing on the validity of the *sukkah;* this does not constitute a roof within the roof.]"

YERUSHALMI SUKKAH 1:5

I:1:   [As to M. 1:5C,] R. Ba in the name of Rab: "[The trained vines are valid roofing when cut down, if to begin with] the man trained them for that purpose."

II:1:   [Illustrating M. 1:5F-G:] R. Ba, Hinena bar Shelamayya, R. Jeremiah in the name of Rab: "If one covered a sukkah with wedges, it is invalid."

II:2:   Said R. Yohanan: "It is written, 'You shall keep the feast of booths seven days, when you make your ingathering from your threshing floor and your wine press' (Deut. 16:13)." From the refuse of your threshing floor and your wine press you may make sukkah roofing for yourself."

YERUSHALMI SUKKAH 1:6

I:1:   [As to M. 1:6A-B,] R. Hiyya in the name of R. Yohanan: "It is because [the sukkah] will look like a storage-house."

I:2:   Hinena bar Shelemayya in the name of Rab: "If one cut sheaves for use
         for sukkah roofing, they are not regarded as having 'handles.'
I:3:   Yosé in the name of R. Hama bar Haninah: "'[And you shall put in it the
         ark of the testimony,] and you shall screen the ark with the veil' (Ex.
         40:3). "On the basis of the use of the root for *sukkah,* as 'screen,' we learn
         that the side [of the *sukkah* also] is called *sukkah* covering. "On the basis
         of this verse, further, we learn that they may make the sides of the *sukkah*
         with something that is susceptible to uncleanness [since the veil is sus-
         ceptible in that way]."

YERUSHALMI SUKKAH 1:7

I:1:   R. Jeremiah in the name of Rab: "The dispute applies when the board is
         four handbreadths broad." R. Yosé in the name of R. Yohanan: "The dis-
         pute applies to boards that have been planed for use in making utensils."
II:1:   [As to M. 1:7C-D, that it is not permitted to sleep under a board of that
         size] Samuel said "That which you have said ap plies to a board of the
         specified length. But as to one of that breadth it is permitted [to sleep
         under it].

YERUSHALMI SUKKAH 1:8

I:1:   [In the view of R. Meir], if one has loosened a board, he does not have to
         remove one out of every two.

YERUSHALMI SUKKAH 1:9

I:1:   It was taught
II:1:   [As to M. 1:9D-E,] R. Abbahu in the name of R. Yohanan: "The reason is
         that it appears like a storage-bin." R. Hiyya taught, "When Scripture says,
         '...you will make for yourself . . .' (Deut. 16:13)

YERUSHALMI SUKKAH 1:10

I:1:   Said R. Yohanan, "R. Yosé spoke only in regard to the matter of the sukkah
         [at M. 1:10G-H]. But as to the matter of [a partition to permit carrying in
         a courtyard] on the Sabbath

YERUSHALMI SUKKAH 1:11

I:1:   R. Hiyya taught, "If there is uncovered, hence invalid air space, it invali-
         dates at a measure of three handbreadths. If there is invalid sukkah roof-
         ing [as in the unroofed gap at M. 1:11B], it invalidates only at a measure
         of four cubits."
I:2:   What is the rule as to sleeping *underneath* it? [That is, if the owner of the
         sukkah slept under inadequately roofed-over space, hence the open air
         space, does he thereby carry out his obligation to dwell in the *sukkah?*]

YERUSHALMI SUKKAH 1:12

I:1:   R. Eliezer concedes [in regard to M. 1:12A-C] that if its roof is a hand-
         breadth in size, or if it was a handbreadth above the ground, it is valid [T.
         Suk. 1:10B-D].
II:1:   Abba bar Hana in the name of R. Yohanan: "The teaching [at M. 1:12E-
         G] concerns mats made in Usha."

YERUSHALMI SUKKAH 2:1

I:1:   There we have learned: But he spreads it over the frame of a two-poster bed [M. 1:4E], and here does the law say this [M. 2:1A]!

I:2:   The theories attributed to R. Judah are contradictory. There he has said that a concrete practice of the law takes precedence over a matter of study [at Y. Pes . 3:7], and here he has said this [that when they came to study, they would sleep under the bed, and the elders did not object]! [The supposition is that Judah claims the elders kept silent because they regarded the study as more important and were not interested in whether or not the disciples carried out their religious duties in the proper way.]

I:3:   The theories assigned to Rabban Gamaliel are contradictory. For it has been taught: Tabi, the slave of Rabban Gamaliel, would wear tefillin, and sages did not object to his doing so. Here, by contrast, they objected to his doing so [accounting for Gamaliel's need, M. 2:1D, to explain himself.

YERUSHALMI SUKKAH 2:2

I:1:   ["The reason for Judah's view,"] said R. Immi, "is that there is not a distance of ten handbreadths between the bed and the *sukkah roofing.* [The sukkah roofing rests on the ends of the bed. The roofing cannot stand on its own.]" Said R. Ba, "The reason is that they do not set up a sukkah on something that is susceptible to uncleanness."

YERUSHALMI SUKKAH 2:3

I:1:   Rab and Samuel: One said that the word for "loosely put together" is "thin" (DLL), and the other that it is "loosely put together" (DBLL).

II:1:   [With reference to M. 2:3E,] is that to say that [to begin with] the stars must be visible through the sukkah roofing? R. Levi in the name of R. Hama bar Haninah: "That teaching pertains to the possibility of seeing sun shafts through the sukkah roofing [and not stars by night]."

YERUSHALMI SUKKAH 2:4

I:1:   [With reference to M. 2:4, making a *sukkah* on a boat,] how shall we interpret the matter? If the boat is beached, then all parties concur that it is permitted to do so. If the boat is en route, there is a dispute between R. Eleazar b. Azariah and R. Aqiba.

I:2:   Simeon b. Karsena in the name of R. Aha: "R. Meir, R. Yosé, and R. Eleazar all expressed the same principle."

I:3:   Now here is the question: If the erub is valid, it should be permitted to carry it about, and if it is not permitted to carry it about, then it should not be a valid erub. [The prohibition against climbing a tree to get at the erub is merely by reason of the general laws on Sabbath rest, which include the one against making use of the tree on that day.] Indeed, it would be appropriate for him to violate the restrictions governing Sabbath rest [and to utilize the tree by climbing it, and so to] eat the erub. If that is the case, then even if the erub is higher than ten handbreadths, it should be valid in all regards.

YERUSHALMI SUKKAH 2:5

I:1:   [As to M. 1. 2:5B:] R. Hunah went to Ein Tab for the sanctification of the New Moon. [He thus was engaged in a religious duty.] As he was going along, he became thirsty while on the road, but he did not agree to taste a thing until he had entered the shade of the *sukkah* of R. Yohanan, the scribe of Gopta.

II:1:   [As to M. 2:5C,] said R. Mana, "It is not the end of the matter that those who are so sick as to be dying [and those who serve them] are exempt. But even those who are sick but in no danger are exempt [cf. T. 2:2B-C]. It has been taught

II:2:   It has been taught

II:3:   M'SH B: R. Ilai went to R. Eliezer in Lud. He said to him, "Now what's going on, Ilai? Are you not among those who observe the festival? Have they not said that it is not praiseworthy of a person to leave his home on a festival? For it is said, 'And you will rejoice on your festival'"(Deut. 16:14) [T. Suk. 2:1C].

III:1:   [As to M. 2:5D:] Said R. Eleazar, "There is such a thing as a random meal [that may be taken outside of a sukkah], but there is no such thing as random sleep. [All sleeping must be in the sukkah .]"

YERUSHALMI SUKKAH 2:6

I:1:   With reference to M. 2:6,] they theorized that he did not say a blessing after it [M. 2:6C] means that he did not say the three complete blessings, but lo, he did say an abbreviated version.

I:2:   It has been taught

I:3   In the case of any food after which they do not say three blessings

YERUSHALMI SUKKAH 2:7

I:1:   What is the Scriptural basis for the position of R. Eliezer?

II:1:   What is the Scriptural basis for the position of R. Eliezer

II:2:   The opinions assigned to R. Eliezer are contradictory. There he has said, "Fourteen meals is a person obligated to eat in the sukkah " [M. 2:7A], and here he has said this [that if one did not eat on the first night in the sukkah, he makes it up on the last night]. [But on the last night there is no sukkah any longer. It is no longer obligatory to eat there.]

YERUSHALMI SUKKAH 2:8

I:1:   It is not the end of the matter [from the viewpoint of the House Shammai] that the whole table be in the house. Even if only of it is there, [it is invalid].

I:2:   With reference to M. Ter. 5:4,Judah bar Pazzi and R. Aibu bar Nigri were in session, say 'We have learned: After they had agreed. "Who agreed with whom? Was it the House of Shammai with the view of the House of

Hillel, or the House of Hillel with the position of the House of Shammai?" They said, "Let us go out and learn [what others may know about the matter], and they heard R. Hezekiah, R. Aha in the name of R. Judah b. Levi [state], 'We have heard that the House of Shammai accepted the view of the House of Hillel only in regard to this matter alone.'"

I:3: Why did the House of Hillel have the merit that the law should be decided in accord with their views?

I:4: Said R. Zeirah, R. Hunah in the name of Rab: "The law accords with the position of the House of Shammai [at M. 2:8]."

YERUSHALMI SUKKAH 2:9

I:1: What is the definition of a minor [at M. 2:9B]?

YERUSHALMI SUKKAH 2:10

I:1: It is written, "You shall dwell in booths for seven days; all that are native in Israel shall dwell in booths" (Lev . 23::2). And there is no "dwelling" except in the sense of "living permanently."

II:1: If it began to rain, at what point t is it permitted to empty out the sukkah?

II:2: Rabban Gamaliel would go in and out all night long. R. Eliezer would go in and out all night long.

YERUSHALMI SUKKAH 3:1

I:1: [Explaining why a stolen palm branch is invalid,] R. Hiyya taught: "And you shall take for yourselves [on the first day the fruit of goodly trees. branches of palm trees, and boughs of leafy trees, and willows of the brook]" Lev. 23:4). The meaning is that they must be yours and not stolen."

II:1: [As to M. 3:1B, One deriving from an apostate town:] A ram's horn belonging to a Temple of idolatry, or one belonging to an apostate town — R. Eleazar said, "It is valid." R. Hiyya taught, "It is valid." R. Hoshaiah taught, "It is invalid." All concur in the case of a palm branch [deriving from such a source] that it is invalid. What is the difference between a ram's horn and a palm branch?

II:2: If one stole a palm branch from one source, myrtle from a second, and a willow from yet a third and then he bound the three together into a bunch, [what is the law]?

III:1: R. Abin in the name of R. Judah bar Pazzi: "A dried up one is invalid, in line with the following verse of Scripture: 'The dead do not praise the Lord, nor do any that go down into silence'"(Ps. 115:17).

III:2: They asked before R. Abina, "If the ends of the *lulab* dried up, what is the law?"

III:3: R. Malokh in the name of R. Joshua b. Levi: "If the central rib of a branch of palm leaves was divided, it is in the status of its leaves being spread apart [and valid, in line with M. 3:1D]."

III:4:   As to palm branches [Lev. 23:10] — R. Tarfon says, "They must be bunches of palms." R. Aqiba says, "Palm branches as their name implies." R. Judah says, "If it is separated, he should tie it together."

IV:1:   What are the thorn-palms of the Iron Mountain that are valid [M. 3:1F]?

IV:2:   It has been taught: If a palm branch is dried up, it is invalid. If it merely appears to be dried up, it is valid.

IV:3:   It has been taught: A myrtle and a willow are to be three handbreadths long, and a palm branch, four.

IV:4:   Jonah and R. Simeon b. Laqish in the name of R. Judah the Patriarch: "A palm branch is to be a handbreadth in length."

YERUSHALMI SUKKAH 3:2

I:1:   It is written, "[And you shall take on the first day the fruit of goodly trees, branches of palm trees, and] boughs of leafy trees, [and willows of the brook; and you shall rejoice before the Lord your God seven days]" (Lev. 23:40).

II:1:   Hiyya bar Ada in the name of R. Yohanan: "[As to M. 3:2D, If the berries were more numerous than the leaves, it is invalid,] this has been taught in the case of black ones." Why should it be invalid? Is it because they are not the same color as the wood [since the wood is green, the berries black]? Or is it because the fruit is ripe [and scripture wants the boughs, not the fruit, to be waved]?

YERUSHALMI SUKKAH 3:3

I:1:   It is written, "Willows of the brook" (Lev. 23:40). I know only that I may use willows that grow by a brook. How do I know that I may use willows that grow in a field that is watered by rain or a field in the mountains?

YERUSHALMI SUKKAH 3:4

I:1:   [With reference to Lev. 23:40: "And you shall take on the first day the fruit of goodly trees, branches of palm trees, boughs of leafy trees, and willows of the brook,"] R. Ishmael provided the following exegesis [in support of his position at M. 3:4A]

I:2:   Yosé: When he came here [to the Land of Israel] he saw people choosing the correct myrtle. He said to them, "Why are the people of the West selecting one sort of myrtle [as against some other sort]?"

I:3:   He who prepares a *lulab* for his own use says, "Blessed ...who has sanctified us by his commandments, and commanded us to make a *lulab.*" If he did so for someone else, he says,

I:4:   Hiyya son of Rab said a blessing for each time [one takes the *lulab*]. R. Hunah said a blessing only one time alone.

YERUSHALMI SUKKAH 3:5

I:1:   It is written, "The fruit of a goodly tree" (Lev. 23:40). This refers to a tree the fruit of which is good

I:2: Jacob, the Southerner, raised the question [concerning M. Er. 3:2]: "The Mishnah [at M. Er. 3:2] does not accord with the view of the House of Shammai.

YERUSHALMI SUKKAH 3:6

I:1: R. Isaac bar Nahman in the name of Samuel: "All those traits that invalidate do so only on the first day of the Festival alone."

I:2: There they say, "[Even if it is scarred] on the greater part of it only on one side [it is invalid]. [If] its nipple [was scarred, it is as if the greater part of it [was scarred]."

II:1: There they say, "Its rose."

III:1: But it did not perforate within [through the skin], it remains valid.

IV:1: A dark-colored citron is invalid [M. 3:6H]: That which comes from Ethiopia is valid [vis-a-vis M. 3:6H]. One which is green like a leek [M. 3:6/I]: R. Zeira asked before R. Immi, "Is it exactly as green as a leek, or is it merely similar to leek-green?" He said to him, "Exactly as green as a leek."

YERUSHALMI SUKKAH 3:7

I:1: An *etrog* that was half-ripe — R. Aqiba says, "It is not regarded as fruit." And sages say, "It is fruit."

II:1: [With regard to M. 3:7B, the size of a nut:] We have learned to repeat the formulation of the Mishnah, "Like a nut." There is a Tannaite authority who teaches, "Up to the size of a nut."

III:1: [With reference to M. 3:7D-F,] said R. Yosé, "If Scripture had said, 'And the tops of palm branches,' it would have been well [for Judah's view that one can hold two in one hand]. "But Scripture has said only, 'The tops of palm branches.' "That is, even if this one is in one hand, and that one is in the other hand."

YERUSHALMI SUKKAH 3:8

I:1: [With reference to M. 3:8E-H:] Lo, in "O give thanks to the Lord, for he is good" (Ps. 118:1), do they not [wave the lulab, in line with M. 3:8H]?

II:1: [With reference to M. 3:8/I-L] R. Hiyya bar Ashi in the name of Rab: "This one who gets up very early to go on a trip takes the *lulab* and shakes it, the ram's horn and sounds it [before he leaves home]. When, later in the day, the time for saying the *Shema* comes, lo, this one recites the *Shema* and says the Prayer."

II:2: It has been taught:

YERUSHALMI SUKKAH 3:9

I:1: It has been taught: But they have said, "A woman says a blessing for her husband, a slave for his master, a child for his father."

YERUSHALMI SUKKAH 3:10

I:1: Rab and Samuel: One said, "It is Halleluyah [in one word]," and the other said, "It is Hallelu Yah [in two words]."

I:2:   R. Zeira asked before R. Abbahu, "What do we answer after the one who recites the *Hallel* psalms?"

II:1:   [With reference to M. 3:10B-C,] they asked before R. Hiyya bar Ba, "How do we know that if one heard the *Hallel* psalms but did not respond, he nonetheless has carried out his obligation?"

II:2:   R. Hoshaiah taught, "A man answers, 'Amen,' [to others who say Grace], even though he did not eat. But he does not say, 'Blessed is He, of whose food we have eaten,' if he did not eat."

II:3:   It has been taught

II:4:   It has been taught: As to a pagan who said a blessing for the Name — they answer, "Amen," after him.

II:5:   [With reference to M. 3:10A-B,] Rabbi would repeat certain words in it. R. Eleazar b. Parta would augment certain words in it.

III:1:   [With reference to M. 3:10E-F,] said R. Eleazar, "This rule represents the view of the Elders of the Galilee.

YERUSHALMI SUKKAH 3:11

I:1:   It is written, "You shall rejoice before the Lord your God seven days" (Lev. 23:40). There is a Tannaite authority who teaches, "It is with regard to the rejoicing with the lulab that Scripture speaks." There is a Tannaite authority who teaches, "It is with regard to the rejoicing [brought on by eating the meat] of peace-offerings that the Scripture speaks."

II:1:   [As to the view that taking the *lulab* does not override the restrictions of the Sabbath except when the first day of the Festival coincides with the Sabbath, even in the Temple, which is implied at M. 3:11E and made explicit at M. 4:1] associates asked before R. Jonah, "Just as you say, 'Seven days you shall present offerings by fire to the Lord; on the eighth day you shall hold a holy convocation and present an offering by fire to the Lord; it is a solemn assembly; you shall do no laborious work' (Lev. 23:36)

III:1:   [With reference to M. 3:1 l/I-J:] Associates say, "The reason for the position of R. Yosé is that a positive commandment [to carry the lulab] overrides the negative commandment [of not carrying an object from private to public domain on the Sabbath]."

YERUSHALMI SUKKAH 3:12

I:1:   [If a minor] knows how to wave the *lulab,* he is liable to the requirement of waving the *lulab.* If he knows how to wrap himself up in a cloak, he is liable to put show-fringes on his garment.

YERUSHALMI SUKKAH 4:1

I:1:   Zeirah, R. Ila, R. Yosé in the name of R. Yohanan: "The willow-branch rite was revealed to Moses at Sinai [orally, not in writing]."

I:2:   [With reference to M. Sheb. 1:6, served by the foregoing, it is permitted to plough a field planted with saplings up to the New Year of the Seventh

Year, but forbidden to plough a field planted with old trees beginning in the spring prior to the Seventh Year. This is claimed to represent a law revealed to Moses at Sinai. At M. Sheb. 1:6 it is stated, If ten saplings are spread out over a seah's space, the whole space may be ploughed for their sake until the New Year.] R. Hiyya bar Ba asked before R. Yohanan, "Why at this time, then, do they plough among old trees?"

I:3:   R. Yohanan said to R. Hiyya bar Ba, "O Babylonian! Two matters came up in your possession [from the Exile], prostration on a fast day [by spreading out the hands and feet], and the willow rite on the seventh day [M. 4:1A, H-I]." Rabbis of Caesarea say, "Also the matter of blood-letting [indicating the times at which it is, or is not, beneficial]."

YERUSHALMI SUKKAH 4:2

I:1:   Jacob, the Southerner, raised the question: "The Mishnah passage [M. 4:2E] before us does not conform to the view of R. Dosa.

YERUSHALMI SUKKAH 4:3

I:1:   What is the meaning of the name, "Mosa"?

I:2:   [As to the willow branches,] Bar Qappara said, "They were eleven cubits tall."

II:1:   [As to walking around the altar,] it was taught: [Priests who are] maimed [participate in the procession].

II:1:   R. Abbahu in the name of R. Yohanan: "This is how the Mishnah is to be read:'Ani waho, save us we pray! Ani waho, save us we pray [two times]' [M. 4:3E].

III:2:   R. Ba Saronegayyah interpreted, "'And the Lord will give victory to the tents of Judah first, [that the glory of the house of David and the glory of the inhabitants of Jerusalem may not be exalted over that of Judah]' (Zech. 12:7). It is written, 'And ...give victory.'"

IV:1:   Said R. Aha, "This is a memorial to [the victory at] Jericho."

YERUSHALMI SUKKAH 4:4

I:1:   [M. 4:4E] has said only, "Children." Lo, adults do not do so. Did not R. Abina say in the name of Rab: "An *etrog* that was invalidated on the first day of a Festival — it is permitted to eat it"? [It is not set aside for a religious duty. In that case, why can adults not do so?]

YERUSHALMI SUKKAH 4:5

I:1:   It was taught

I:2:   Zeira, Ulla bar Ishmael in the name of R. Eleazar: "With [an animal designated as] peace-offerings for the festal offering, which one slaughtered on the eve of a festival [that is, prior to the festival day itself], one does not fulfill his obligation [to bring a festal offering] on the festival itself.

II:1:   [As to M. 4:5F,] R. Abba bar Kahana, R. Hiyya bar Ashi in the name of Rab: "A person has to invalidate his *sukkah* while it is still day [on the seventh day of the Festival, if he proposes to eat in it on the Eighth Day of

Solemn Assembly, so that he will not appear to be eating in the *sukkah* and so adding to the Festival itself].

YERUSHALMI SUKKAH 4:6

I:1:   [They sound the *shofar,* M. 4:6C,] said R. Yosé b. Haninah, "so as to publicize the matter."

I:2:   Yosé bar Asyan in the name of R. Simeon b. Laqish: "The bowls have to be stopped up at the time of the libation.

I:3:   It has been taught: R. Yosé says, "The cavity of the Pits was perforated down to the abyss. "What is the scriptural basis for this view? "'He dug it and cleared it of stones, and planted it with choice vines; he built a watch-tower in the midst of it, and hewed out a wine vat in it; and he looked for it to yield grapes, but it yielded wild grapes' (Is. 5:2). "'He built a watch-tower in the midst of it' — this refers to the Temple. "'He hewed out a wine vat in it' — this refers to the altar. "'And also a wine vat . . .' — this refers to the cavity" [T. Suk. 3:15C-F].

II:1:   [As to M. 4:6G-H:] They proposed to state, "The wide one was for water, the narrow one for wine."

II:2:   Simeon b. Laqish asked before R. Yohanan, "If one carried out the liba-tion-offering before the sacrifice [of the daily whole offering], what is the rule? "If one poured out the water libation by night, what is the rule? "If one did not pour out the water libation on one day, what is the law as to doing so on the next day?"

II:3:   With reference to M. 4:1C, the water libation is for seven days, and Judah says, "It is for eight days"; and M. 4:6L, "There was a water libation of a *log,*" while sages say, "Three logs," so M. 4:6B, we may then observe, in T.'s formulation:] You turn out to rule, He who wants more water dimin-ishes the number of days, and he who wants more days diminishes the volume of the water [T. Suk. 3:16K].

II:4:   There is he who proposes to state: "[The one who poured the water on his feet, M. 4:6N] is the same priest who misbehaved in connection with the burning of the red cow [at T. Par. 3:8, a Sadducee who rejected the con-ception of the law], and is also the same one who misbehaved in connec-tion with the rite of the Day of Atonement [at Y. Yoma 1:5, burning the incense outside and bringing it inside the Holy of Holies]. [All three inci-dents were the work of one Sadducean priest.]"

II:5:   [With reference to M. 4:6N-O,] The courtyard cried out, "Get out of here! Get out of here, sons of Eli! For you have contaminated the house of our God."

II:6:   [Reverting to the story of that the priest on the Day of Atonement had a footprint of a calf on his forehead, where could it have come from?"] they asked before R. Abbahu, "For lo, it is written, 'There shall be no man in the tent of meeting when he enters to make atonement in the holy place until he comes out' (Lev. 16:17).

YERUSHALMI SUKKAH 4:7

I:1:   What difference does it make to me that the gold jug [M. 4:7B] was not sanctified? Even if it had been sanctified, [it should be acceptable]. [The man may pour the water in with the intent that the water not be regarded as sanctified. The concern of M. 4:7B is that if the water should be sanctified by the jug, then it will be invalidated by being left overnight.] For did not R. Aha, R. Hinena in the name of R. Yosé say, "'You shall also anoint the altar of burnt offering and all its utensils, and consecrate the altar; and the altar shall be most holy' (Ex. 40:10)?]

I:2:   R. Pedat in the name of R. Hoshaiah: "Water used for the rite of the accused wife is invalidated if left standing overnight."

II:1:   [As to M. 4:7E, wine and water left uncovered may not be used for the altar,] they proposed to rule, "If one transgressed and brought [such wine or water], it is valid." R. Joshua, the Southerner, taught before R. Jonah, that water and wine left uncovered are invalid for use on the altar.

YERUSHALMI SUKKAH 5:1

I:1:   Lo, [the flute playing] that accompanies the offering overrides [the prohibitions of the Sabbath, but otherwise, it does not]. The Mishnah therefore has been formulated in accord with the view of R. Yosé b. R. Judah. For it has been taugh

I:2:   R. Jonah in the name of R. Ba bar Mamel: "'You shall have a song as in the night when a holy feast is kept; and gladness of heart, as when one sets out to the sound of the flute to go to the mountain of the Lord, to the Rock of Israel' (Is. 30:29). So long as the flute playing is practiced, the Hallel psalms are part of the custom as well."

I:3:   Said R. Joshua b. Levi, "Why is it called *bet hashshoebah* [place of drawing]?"

YERUSHALMI SUKKAH 5:1

I:5:   It has been taught

I:6:   Simeon b. Yohai taught, "The Israelites were warned at three points not to go back to the Land of Egypt.

YERUSHALMI SUKKAH 5:2

I:1:   Said R. Joshua b. Hananiah, "In all the days of celebrating Bet hashshoebah, we never saw a moment of sleep.

II:1:   What was this enactment that they made there?

III:1:   Bar Qappara said, "And they were a hundred cubits high."

IV:1:   What is the meaning of: With jars of oil ...[M. 5:2D]?

YERUSHALMI SUKKAH 5:3

I:1:   It has been taught

I:2:   Said R. Samuel bar R. Isaac, "It is written, '[And you shall command the people of Israel that they bring to you pure beaten olive oil for the light,] that a lamp may be set up to burn continually' (Ex. 27:20). They determined that you have nothing that produces a good flame except for a wick of linen."

I:3:   What is the meaning of the word for they made wicks [at M. 5:3A]?

II:1:   It was taught: There was not a courtyard in Jerusalem which was not lit up from the light of bet hashshoebah [M. 5:3C]. It was taught: A woman can sift wheat by the light of the fire [of the Temple pile].

II:2:   There were six sounds that they could hear from Jerich

YERUSHALMI SUKKAH 5:4

I:1:   The pious men and wonder-workers [M. 5:4A]: [In T.'s version:] What did they sing?

I:2:   Hillel the Elder: When he would see people acting arrogantly, would say to them, "If I am here, who is here?"

I:3:   [As to the dancing,] Ben Yehosedeq was praised because of his jumping about. M'SH B: Rabban Simeon b. Gamaliel danced with eight flaming torches, and not one of them fell to the ground. Now when he would prostrate himself, he would put his finger on the ground, bow low, kiss [the ground], and forthwith straighten up [T. Suk. 4:4].

I:4:   "And David returned to bless his household. But Michal the daughter of Saul came out to meet David, [and said, 'How the king of Israel honored himself today, uncovering himself today before the eyes of his servants' maids, as one of the vulgar fellows shamelessly uncovers himself!']" (2 Sam. 6:20). What is the meaning of "one of the vulgar fellows"?

YERUSHALMI SUKKAH 5:5

I:1:   [As to M. 5:5B, When the cock crowed,] Rab interpreted before the members of the house of R. Shiloh, "The cock crowed," as "The crier proclaimed."

II:1:   R. Jeremiah asked, "[With reference to the tenth step, M. 5:5C,] is this the tenth from the top, or the tenth from the bottom?"

II:2:   Said R. Hiyya bar Ba, "It is not written here [at Ezek. 8:16], 'They made an act of prostration' [one time], but rather, 'They made two acts of prostration' [twice]. For they prostrated themselves both to the sun and to the Temple."

YERUSHALMI SUKKAH 5:6

I:1:   It has been taught [as against M. 5:6A]:

II:1:   ["With respect to M. 5:6H, Three for the drawing of the water,"] said R. Zeirah, "that is to say that they sounded the horn only at the water-libation

III:1:   [As to M. 5:6D, nine for the Additional Offering:] Are these the only ones?

III:2:   Hiyya bar Ba said, "The lyre is the same as the lute, except that there are more strings in the one [lyre = *nebel*] than in the other." Said R. Hiyya b. Abba, "Why is it called a lyre

III:3: The pipe which was in the sanctuary was made of reed

III:4: [When the New Moon coincides with the Sabbath,] as to the Additional Offerings of the Sabbath and of the New Moon, which is offered first [and so takes precedence]? R. Jeremiah contemplated ruling, "When the Additional Offerings of the Sabbath and the Additional Offerings of the New Moon coincide, the Additional Offerings of the New Moon take precedence."

YERUSHALMI SUKKAH 5:7

I:1: It has been taught:

YERUSHALMI SUKKAH 5:8

I:1: [Proving that all the priestly watches share equally on the festivals,] it is written, "They shall have portion to portion to eat" (Deut. 18:8).

II:1: At Pentecost they would say to him, "Here you have unleavened bread, here is leavened bread for you " [M. 5:8B]: There is a Tannaite authority who reverses the order and repeats the tradition as follows: "Here is leavened bread for you, here is unleavened bread for you."

II:2: Said R. Levi, "[At the outset, before the division of the priestly emoluments,] all the watches are located in the south [of the altar, and then the officiating watch goes to the north, so as to distinguish it from the watch whose term of service has ended]."

III:1: Said R. Hananiah, son of R. Hillel, "[the ones coming in are given the place of honor, at the north of the altar] so as to pay respect to the ones who are corning on duty."

IV:1: [The priestly watch of] Bilgah always divided it in the south, and their ring was fixed, and their wall-niche was blocked up [M. 5:8]. [In T.'s version:] because of Miriam,

V:1: R. Ba in the name of R. Judah: "They made rings for themselves, broad at the top and narrow at the bottom."

VI:1: This was so that they would not use the space for their knives.

VII. BESAH

YERUSHALMI BESAH 1:1

I:1: What is the reason for the position of the House of Shammai [M. 1:1B]? The egg is deemed ready [in advance, for use on the festival day [by the fact that] its mother [was prepared in advance for eating]. What is the reason for the position of the House of Hillel [M. 1:1C]? The egg is treated as equivalent to fruit left out to dry,

I:2: All concur in the case of an egg, the greater part of which came forth on the eve of the festival, that it is eaten on the festival [as if the whole of it had been laid prior to the festival] [T. Y.T. 1:3A-B].

I:3: [An egg which is laid on the festival day (M. 1:1A)] — others said in the name of R. Eliezer, "Both it and its dam may be eaten" [T. Y.T. 1:1A-B]. What is the meaning of the statement."Both it and its dam may be eaten"?

I:4:   A calf which is born on the festival day may be slaughtered on the festival day, because it subjects itself to permission [to be slaughtered, and therefore to be eaten, on that same day] [T. Y.T. 1:1C-D].

I:5:   A bird which is born on the festival day may be [slaughtered on the festival day,] because it subjects itself to permission [to be slaughtered, and therefore to be eaten] [T. Y.T. 1:1E-F].

I:6:   Abbahu in the name of R. Yosé b. R. Haninah asked, "Any creature that has sexual relations by day gives birth by day, and any that has sexual relations by night gives birth by night."

I:7:   R. Zeira in the name of Giddul: "A calf that is born from a terefah-beast [that is, a beast that may die of itself, and therefore may not be eaten by Israelites] on a festival day is permitted [for Israelites to slaughter and eat on a festival day].

I:8:   There we have learned: "An egg from the carrion of a bud is permitted, if an egg of the same sort is sold in the market [that is, if it is fully fashioned. with a hard shell], and otherwise, it is forbidden." the words of the House of Shammai. And the House of Hillel forbids [M. Ed. 5:1]. What is the reason behind the position of the House of Shammai?

I:9:   "[If] it was born on the Sabbath, it may be eaten on the festival [immediately following]. [If it was born] on the festival day, it may be eaten on the Sabbath [immediately following]. R. Judah says in the name of R. Eliezer, "Still the dispute is in place" [T. Y.T. 1:3C-E]. '

I:10:   In the name of four elders they have ruled, "If a person's *erub is* eaten up on the first day [of a festival], lo, he is in the status of his fellow townsfolk on the second

I:11:   All parties [that is, the House of Shammai as well] concur in the case of produce that falls from the tree [on the festival] that it is forbidden.

I:12:   Jeremiah raised the question, "As to wreaths of nuts [and chains of berries] used to decorate a sukkah, what is the law governing them [May they be eaten on the eighth day of the Festival, that is, the Eighth Day of Solemn Assembly, which is not part of the Festival of Tabernacles but is adjacent to it?]"

YERUSHALMI BESAH 1:2

I:1:   R. Zeriqan in the name of R. Yosé b. Haninah, "They have taught [the dispute as to the minimum volume of leaven] only in respect to

YERUSHALMI BESAH 1:3

I:1:   R. Hiyya in the name of R. Yohanan: "He who cooks [meat in the status of] carrion on a festival day is not subjected to a flogging

II:1:   [Commenting on M. 1:3F, the ashes are deemed made ready for use in covering the blood, that is, a lenient ruling], R. Abun in the name of rabbis over there: "That is to say that

II:2:   It has been taught : R. Yosé says, "As to a koy, they to not slaughter it on the festival day, "because [precisely what it is] is subject to doubt. "But if they have slaughtered it, they do not cover up its blood" [T. Y. T. 1:5G-I].

II:3:   And they concur that if be actually did slaughter, he may dig with a mattock and cover up the blood and that the ashes of the oven arc deemed to have been made ready on the preceding day, and they too may be used for covering up the blood [M. I:3E-F]. That which you have said applies to

II:4:   Zeirah asked, "As to a dish that an ape formed [on a festival day], what is the law [about using it on the festival day]?

YERUSHALMI BESAH 1:4

II:1:   The opinions assigned to the House of Shammai are contradictory. For we have learned there

III:1:   The opinions assigned to the House of Hillel are contradictory. For we have learned there

III:2:   Said R. Yosé b. R. Bun, "Levi [merely] tops at his dovecot while it is still day and says, 'Let my dovecot effect acquisition for me for use [of the pigeons] on the morrow' [and that suffices, without even the designation indicated at M. 1:4E]."

YERUSHALMI BESAH 1:5

I:1:   The Mishnah passage represents the view of Rabbi. For it has been taught

I:2:   There we have learned: One who says to his son, "Coins in the status of second tithe are in this corner," but the son found coins in a different corner — lo, these coins are deemed unconsecrated. [If there was there in the corner specified by the father a maneh in the status of second tithe, but the son found two hundred zuz, the extra maneh 's worth of coins is deemed unconsecrated [M. M.S. 4:12A-F]. [As above,we proceed to show that Rabbi is the authority for this view.] R. Jacob bar Aha in the name of R. Yosé, "This represents the view of Rabbi.

II:1:   [With reference to M. 1:5F, If one designated pigeons in the nest and found them in front of the nest, they are prohibited.] R. Yudan said, "That which you have said [in prohibiting the birds] applies to a case in which

YERUSHALMI BESAH 1:6

I:1:   Samuel said, "He who inserts the shutters [of a shop] on a festival day is liable on the count of building."

II:1:   [With reference to M. 1:6B, the Hillelites permit taking up a pestle to hack meat on it:] if it is not to hack meat on it, then it is forbidden [to take up a pestle on a festival day].

III:1:   They concur that one may not scrape [the hide]. How shall we interpret the dispute [at M. 1:6C- F]? If the meat is affixed to the hide, it is tantamount to the body of the hide, [and it is self-evident that it is permitted to lift it up].

III:2:   And they concur that they to not salt hides on the festival day. But on it
          one puts salt on meat which is for roasting [T. Y.T. 1:11B-C].

YERUSHALMI BESAH 1:7

I:1:   [From the viewpoint of the House of Hillel,] lo, it is forbidden [to take]
          an adult [out into public domain]

I:2:   It has been taught:

YERUSHALMI BESAH 1:8

I:1:   It has been taught [in Tosefta's version]: Said R. Judah, "The House of
          Shammai and the House of Hillel concur that they bring [to the priest]
          gifts which were taken up to the day before the festival along with gifts
          which were taken on the festival [vs. M. 1:8A-C].

I:2:   Now there is the following question to be addressed to the position of the
          House of Hillel [who maintain that] one may not designate heave offer-
          ing on the festival day [M. 1:8G]

I:3:   There is the following, as it has been taught

YERUSHALMI BESAH 1:9

I:1:   And why should one not crush the spices on the preceding day [rather
          than on the festival day itself]?

I:2:   Isaac, R. Eleazar in the name of R. Immi father of R. Abodema of
          Sepphoris, "Where there is a dispute, [it has to do with

YERUSHALMI BESAH 1:10

I:1:   R. Jonah asked, "If one did so on the Sabbath, in the view of the House of
          Shammai what is the law as to his being liable?

I:3:   It was taught

I:4:   Zeira, R. Hiyya bar Ashi in the name of Rab: "He who strains wine [to
          remove the lees] is liable on the count of selection [winnowing]." Said R.
          Zeira, "It is surely more reasonable that it is on the count of sifting."

YERUSHALMI BESAH 1:11

I:1:   Now there is the following challenge to the position of the House of
          Shammai

I:2:   It has been taught

YERUSHALMI BESAH 1:12

I:1:   This is the meaning of the rule of the Mishnah [at M. 1:12F, requiring the
          craftsman]: It is because it requires a clod containing silicate of iron [for
          blacking the leather].

II:1:   The Mishnah [at M. 1:12D, regarding the unsown shoe as unfinished,]
          accords with the view of R. Eliezer

II:2:   What is the law as to curdling milk on a festival day?

II:3:   R. Halapta *b.* Saul taught, "It is forbidden to send ornaments."

II:4:   It has been taught

II:5:   Up to this point we have dealt with golden ornaments. But is the law the
          same for silver ones?

YERUSHALMI BESAH 2:1

I:1:   It is written, "He said to them, '[This is what the Lord has commanded: Tomorrow is a day of solemn rest, a holy Sabbath to the Lord;] bake what you will bake and boil what you will boil, and [all that is left over lay by to be kept until the morning]'" (Ex. 16:23). [On the basis of this proof-text,] R. Eliezer says, "They bake relying on what is already baked, and they boil relying on what is already boiled." R. Joshua says, "They bake or boil relying on what is already boiled."

I:2:   [Reverting to the issue of I:1, M. 2:1D, that one may prepare a dish on the eve of the festival and, relying on that, continue cooking on the festival itself food which then may be used for the Sabbath as well.] Now see here! Is there a matter which is forbidden by the law of the Torah, but rendered permissible by the preparation of a meal of commingling [that is, preparing food prior to the festival for use on the festival and on the Sabbath following]?

I:3:   [As to preparing a cooked dish on the festival day and leaving something over for use on the Sabbath, M. 2:1C:] R. Kahana b. R. Hiyya bar Ba said, "That is on condition that one not practice deception [by baking or cooking a great deal of food]."

I:4:   [With reference to M. Hal. 1:8: Dog's dough, if herdsmen can eat it, is liable to dough offering . . . and they make it on a festival day (since it is food for man),] the cited passage of the Mishnah accords with the view of R. Simeon b. Eleazar.

II:1:   [With reference to M. 2:1D,] R. Hiyya in the name of R. Yohanan: "One has to declare, 'It is for me and for anyone else who has not prepared a meal of commingling.'

II:2:   Hiyya the Elder came to his home. They said to him, "We forgot to prepare a meal of commingling." He said to them, "Are there any lentils prepared yesterday?" They said to him, "Yes." [Since he regarded that single dish as sufficient,] that indicates that even a single dish suffices [in line with M. 2:1F].

II:3:   It has been taught

II:4:   Rab said, "I say, '[A meal of commingling] may not be less than an olive's bulk in volume.'" Does this not stand at variance with the view of R. Yohanan

II:5:   [On a festival which coincided with the eve of the Sabbath [Friday] [M. 2:1A]: "they do not prepare an erub either for courtyards or for Sabbath boundaries"—the words of R. Meir. And sages say, "They prepare an erub for courtyards, but not for Sabbath boundaries" [T. Y. T. 2:1A].

YERUSHALMI BESAH 2:2

I:1:   [The Houses of Hillel and Shammai agree that people may not immerse vessels on the Sabbath in order to render them cultically clean. The Yerushalmi asks to what sort of vessels the Houses refer. At Mishnah 2:3, the Houses refer] to large vessels, [which are not used to draw water]. But in the case of small vessels, [which are used to draw water, the Houses agree that

I:2:   All those who are obligated to immerse [to remove uncleanness], immerse in the usual way on the ninth of Ab and on the Day of Atonement [although those days are fast days when bathing is prohibited].

II:1:   For a man immerses on the Sabbath on account of a seminal emission.

YERUSHALMI BESAH 2:3

I:1:   The rule of the Mishnah does not accord with the view of Rabbi.

II:1:   How so from use to another use?

YERUSHALMI BESAH 2:4

I:3:   [Said R. Yosé b. R. Bun, "R. Simeon b. Laqish came by the schoolhouse and heard the voice of the students reciting the following verse of Scripture, 'And they performed sacrifices to the Lord, and on the next day offered burnt offerings to the Lord, [a thousand bulls] a thousand rams. and a thousand lambs, with their drink offerings, and sacrifices in abundance for all Israel]'" (I Chron. 29:21). "He said, 'He who cuts this verse off, [citing only part of it], accords with the view [M- 2:4 A-B] of the House of Shammai.

YERUSHALMI BESAH 2:5

I:1:   One may supply two interpretations to the Mishnah]. In the view of the House of Shammai, he has to have drunk some of it. In the view of the House of Hillel [the rule is that one may heat such water] if it is merely suitable for drinking [moving the Hillelite position to a more stringent view, relative to the movement of the Shammaites.

II:1:   This represents *the* opinion of both parties. But it is on the condition that there is a pot [of water heating] by the fire.

II:3:   A philosopher asked Bar Qappara, Ablat asked Levi the eunuch, "Is it permitted to drink water, but forbidden to wash?"

YERUSHALMI BESAH 2:6

I:1:   [With reference to M. 2:6B,] Abba bar R. Huna said, "That which you have stated [about not covering up hot water on the festival for use on the Sabbath (M. 2:6B)]

II:1:   That which you have said applies to a collapsible candelabrum [that is made up of parts], but as to a candelabrum that may not be dismantled, it is not in such a case that the ruling pertains.

III:1:   If you make a person tired [by the process of making a lot of little loaves,] he will bake only what he needs for the festival.

III:2:   R. Aha derived from the following verse [the meaning of the word, HRY (M. 2:6G) "Thick bread"]

YERUSHALMI BESAH 2:7

I:1:   The members of the household of Rabban Gamaliel would sweep between the couches during the festival [cf. M. 2:7B; T. Shab. 9:13]. Said

R. Eleazar b. R. Sadoq, "Many times did we eat in the house of Rabban Gamaliel, and not once did I ever see them sweeping between the couches [after a meal].

II:1: What is a kid roasted whole [M. 2:7D]?

II:2: Said R. Yosé, "Todos of Rome taught the Romans the custom of buying lambs for the night of Passover and preparing them roasted whole."

YERUSHALMI BESAH 2:8

I:1: R. Ba, Rab, and Samuel — the two of them say, "In the view of sages, even [if the strap between the horns, M. 2:8B,] is to lead [the cow], it is forbidden [for the cow to go forth on the Sabbath with such a strap]." R. Ba in the name of Samuel: "If the cow's horns were pierced [so that the strap was integral to them], it is permitted."

I:2: Genibah said, "It is merely a theoretical law that Eleazar came to teach, [but it is not that he actually did so]." R. Jonah of Bosrah asked, "If it was merely a theoretical law, is this in line with that which we have learned: [R. Eleazar b. Azariah's cow used to go out with a strap between its horns.]

I:3: Not with the consent of the sages [M. Shab. 5:4]? [That is, they did not agree with him?]" [Differing from this view of the theoretical character of Eleazar's position,] R. Judah bar Pazzi of Bar Delayyan taught

II:1: What is currying? This refers to a comb with small teeth, which make a wound.

III:1: They do not curry the beast, so as not to cause a wound. They do not comb the beast, so as not to tear out hair.

III:2: The members of the household of Rabban Gamaliel would crush pepper in a pepper mill [on the festival day] [cf. M. 2:D]. Said R. Eleazar b. R. Sadoq, "One time father was reclining before [= eating with] Rabban Gamaliel,

YERUSHALMI BESAH 2:9

I:1: The part on the bottom is on the count of forming a receptacle. The part on the top because it is a metal utensil. The part in the middle because it forms a sieve.

YERUSHALMI BESAH 2:10

I:1: It has been taught

YERUSHALMI BESAH 3:1

I:1: [With reference to M. Shab. 13:5: R. Judah says, "He who hunts a bird into a tower-trap, or a deer into a house, is liable." And sages say, "(He who drives) a bird into a tower-trap, or a deer into a house, [Y: garden] into a courtyard, or into a vivarium." Rabban Simeon b. Gamaliel says, "Not all vivaria are the same. Thus is the governing principle: (If) it yet lacks further work of hunting, he (who pens it in on the Sabbath) is exempt. (If) it does not lack further work of hunting, he is liable."] Said R. Hinena, "The Mishnah [before us] does not accord with the view of R. Judah

I:2:   The opinions assigned to R. Judah are inconsistent

II:1:   Ulla said, "They asked before R. Aha, 'What is the meaning of the fol-
         lowing, that we have learned: Whatever lacks some phase of the process
         of hunting is prohibited to be caught, but whatever does not lack some
         phase of the process of hunting is permitted to be caught [M. Bes. 3:IF]?'

II:2:   They slaughter animals kept in enclosures, but not those kept in hunting-
         nets or gins [which may have been caught on the festival day itself] [T. Y.
         T. 3:1G].

YERUSHALMI BESAH 3:2

I:1:   [At issue here is M. Shab. 1:6 = Y. Shab. 1:7, as follows: The House of
         Shammai says, "They do not spread out nets for wild beasts, fowl, or fish,
         unless there is sufficient time for them to be caught while it is still day."
         And the House of Hillel permits. The question now must be asked how
         one knows when the beast got caught:] What lets [the owner] know
         [whether or not the beast was caught while it was still day]? If the trap
         was in disarray [while it was yet daylight], it is obvious that the beast was
         caught while it was still day. If it was not in disarray [in daylight], then it
         is obvious that nothing was trapped in it while it was still day. [No.] Even
         if the trap was in disarray, one takes account of the possibility that a beast
         was not trapped while it was yet daylight.

II:1:   [As to M. 3:2D, Gamaliel's view that fish caught by a gentile are permit-
         ted, but he would not accept them:] R. Zeira in the name of Rab: "They
         considered ruling that [when he said that they are permitted, he meant]
         that they are permitted on the next day [but may not be used on the festi-
         val" just as M. 3:2A-C maintain].] [Bl

YERUSHALMI BESAH 3:3

I:1:   R. Ba in the name of rabbis over there: "If one slaughtered [a beast out in
         the field] and then wolves ate its innards, it li.e., the beast] is regarded as
         acceptable, for the assumption concerning the innards is that they are
         acceptable [even though one can no longer inspect them]."

II:1:   It has been taught

YERUSHALMI BESAH 3:4

I:1:   The opinions assigned to R. Judah are at variance with one another, for
         we have learned there

II:1:   [With reference to M. 3:4C, A beast the blemish of which was not dis-
         cerned while it was still day before the festival is not in the category of
         that which is ready for festival use while it is still day before the festival,]
         R. Abbahu in the name of R. Yosé b. Haninah: "Any beast, the blemish of
         which indeed has been discerned on the eve of the festival, but which the
         expert declared permissible for slaughtering only on the festival day it-
         self

YERUSHALMI BESAH 3:5

I:1:   [Since the sages ruled in accord with the position of Judah, that we take account of whether or not the beast had been designated in advance of the festival day, rather than in accord with the view of Simeon, that we do not take that into account Samuel said, "The five elders who instructed R. Tarfon in Lud erred, [since in fact the law does not follow Judah]."

I:2:   They asked before Levi, "What is the law on examining signs that a beast is terefah in a dark house."

YERUSHALMI BESAH 3:6

I:1:   [With reference to M. 3 6, not taking shares to begin with:] And as to adding [others on the festival to take a share in the animal]. they may add to them [on the festival itself].

I:2:   Hiyya the Elder and R. Simeon the son of Rabbi: "They may weigh out *a maneh's* worth of meat against another *maneh's* worth in the case of a firstling. Under what circumstances?

I:3:   It has been taught

I:4:   It has been taught

I:5:   It has been taught

YERUSHALMI BESAH 3:7

I:1:   They do not whet a knife on the festival day, but one draws it over another [knife]. R. Hiyya said. That view is R. Judah's." But R. Judah said in the name of Samuel, lt represents the opinion of all parties. since one does so in order to remove the hilt from the knife.

YERUSHALMI BESAH 3:8

I:1:   R. Huna said, "[when the storekeeper fills the measure] it must be either too little or too much [so that the measure is not filled exactly]." R. Eleazar said to Zeirah bar Hama, "Fill this utensil for me [today], and tomorrow we'll measure it [after the festival]."

I:2:   It has been taught

YERUSHALMI BESAH 3:9

I:1:   It is taught on Tannaite authority: One may say to the other, "Give me a measure of spices," for that is in any case how a householder puts a measure of spice into his soup.

YERUSHALMI BESAH 4:1

I:1:   With reference to M. 4:1B, said R. Hanin bar Levi, "The Mishnah speaks of slender jars

II:1:   With reference to M. 4:1C R. Judah raised the following question

II:2:   Jacob bar Aha in the name of R. Yosé, "Fruit that had attained the condition of being fully dried [only on the festival day itself but was not ready for eating as dried fruit prior to the festival] may not be touched [on the festival]."

YERUSHALMI BESAH 4:2

I:1:   The do not take pieces of wood from the roof or walls of a sukkah, but they do from that wood which is near it [M. 1:2]. Samuel said, "[One may take pieces of wood from that which is near the sukkah] when [in putting wood on the sukkah] he did not have the intention of covering it more densely [that is, undoing bundles of wood and spreading the wood over the sukkah topping].

I:2:   Said R. Simeon b. Eleazer, "The House of Shammai did not differ [with the House of Hillel] concerning pieces of wood which were gathered together, which were in the outer area [M. 4:2B-E], "that one may bring it; "or concerning that which was scattered about in the field [M. 4:2C], that one should not bring it. "Concerning what did they differ?

II:1:   [With reference to M. 1:2E-F.] the views assigned to R. Judah are at variance.

YERUSHALMI BESAH 4:3

I:1:   They do not chop fire-wood either from beams or from a beam that broke on a festival day. That which you have said applies, then. to a beam which broke on the festival day itself. But as to a beam which broke on the eve of the festival. it is permitted [to chop wood from such a beam].

I:2:   It has been taught

I:3:   Rab said. 'They make a fire with [wooden] utensils. and they do not make I fire with the splinters. "That which you have said applies To utensils that broke on the festival. But as to utensils that broke on the eve of the festival. it is permitted [to use the splinters].

I:4:   R. Hiyya taught, "They make a fire with wood but not with husks or pits. [Tosefta's version follows:] Nuts and almonds which one ate on the eve of the festival day —

II:1:   Members of the household of R. Yannai say, "They may chop wood with an ax."

III:1:   There is a Tannaite authority who teaches, "They cut wood with a saw," and there is a Tannaite authority who teaches, "They do not cut wood with a saw."

IV:1:   Ba, R. Judah in the name of Samuel: "But that is on condition that one takes out produce by the door."

YERUSHALMI BESAH 4:4

I:1:   It has been taught

I:2:   Ba in the name of R. Judah: "As to a log [that is burning], one puts it near a wall so that it will not be consumed [and it will go out by, itself against the wall]."

I:3:   Three rules were stated with reference to a wick, three on the strict side, and three on the lenient side

YERUSHALMI BESAH 4:5

I:1:   That is to say. the sausage-maker is forbidden to work on a festival day because he cuts the sausage bags apart.

II:1:   on the count of building [it is prohibited].

II:2:   It has been taught: nor may a blind man go out with his staff, nor may a shepherd go out with his leather bag [T. Y. T. 3:17C-D]. R. Simeon permits doing so.

YERUSHALMI BESAH 4:6

I:1:   What is at issue between them [at M. 4:6C-D]? Whether or not it is permitted to sweep things up into piles is at issue between them. In the view of R. Eliezer it is permitted to sweep things into piles. and in the opinion of sages it is prohibited to do so.

YERUSHALMI BESAH 4:7

I:1:   And they do not heat tiles white hot to roast on them: There is a Tannaite authority who teaches: They do heat [tiles] white hot. There is a Tannaite authority w who teaches. They do not heat [tiles] white hot.

II:1:   The opinions assigned to R. Eliezer are contradictory.

III:1:   The opinions assigned to the sages are contradictory.

YERUSHALMI BESAH 5:1

I:1:   When the rule, M. 5:1A-B. permits letting down pieces of produce through a hatchway on a festival,] the .Mishnah speaks of [fruit from] the roof of that house in particular. But as to [fruit on] the roof of some other house

I:2:   Jeremiah in the name of Rab: "[On the Sabbath] they spread out mats on shavings which cover bricks."

I:3:   It has been taught

I:4:   It has been taught

YERUSHALMI BESAH 5:2

I:1:   [Some of the listed actions are liable on grounds of Sabbath rest. in which category come optional acts, [and some of the listed actions are liable] on grounds of optional acts, which fall into the category of acts of religious duty.

I:2:   It has been taught

II:1:   On what account have they said, They do not climb a tree [M. 5:2D]?

III:1:   R. Jacob bar Zabedi in the name of R. Abbahu: 'That is to say that it is forbidden to float something and lead it away from oneself. And along these same lines, it is forbidden to float something and lead it to oneself."

IV:1:   This refers to clapping , which a person himself does [in anger].

V:1:   This is slapping that expresses pleasure.

VI:1:   R. Jeremiah, R. Zeirah in the name of R. Hunah: "Jumping is when one picks up both feet at once. Stamping is when one picks up one foot and puts down the other."

VII:1:   R. Hezekiah, R. Aha in the name of R. Abbahu: "It is forbidden to undertake a trial for a property case on a Friday."

VIII:1:   R. Ba bar Kohen said before R. Yosé, R. Aha in the name of R. Jacob bar Idi: "It is forbidden to betroth a woman on Friday."

IX:1:   Jacob bar .Aha in the name of R. Immi: "R. Yohanan and R. Simeon b. Laqish differed.

X:1:   Is this the only, difference. Lo, there are others.

X:2:   The sole difference between the festival and the Sabbath is in the preparation of food: It was taught in the name of R. Judah: "Also they have permitted [on the festival] preparing those things that are required for the preparation of food as well." What is at issue between [the authority of M. Meg. 1:6A = M. Bes. 5:2J] and [Judah]?

X:3:   What is the law on kindling a lamp that serves no useful purpose [on the festival day]? Hezekiah said, "It is forbidden to do so."

YERUSHALMI BESAH 5:3

I:1:   The Mishnah speaks of a case in which

YERUSHALMI BESAH 5:4

I:1:   Said R. Ba, [with respect to M. 5:1C,] in matters affecting the Sabbath boundary, the sages have imposed the strict rule of the law as it affects property

II:1:   What is the practical difference between these two positions?

YERUSHALMI BESAH 5:6

II:1:   [Referring to M. 5:6C,] that is to say. he who takes a utensil out into the public way — lo, the utensil is in the status of the person who takes it out [just as at M. 5:6C with reference to the cistern's water enjoying the status of the person who draws it].

YERUSHALMI BESAH 5:8

I:1:   What are field animals [M. 5:7H]?

VIII. TAANIT

YERUSHALMI TAANIT 1:1

I:1:   The reason [for the position] of R. Eliezer is that

I:2:   [The prayer for rain is included in the paragraph of the Prayer dealing with the resurrection of the dead, because] just as the resurrection of the dead means life for the world, so the corning of rain means life for the world.

I:3:   Zeirah in the name of R. Haninah: "[If] someone arose [to repeat the prayer for the community] on the occasion of saying the Prayer for rain and instead said the prayer for dew, they do not make him go back.

I:4:   It has been taught

I:5:   [With regard to M. 1:2:] R. Ba in the name of R. Huna: "As to the two festival days observed in the exile, [in which we are not sure whether it is the Eighth Day of Solemn assembly, on which it is necessary to mention rain, or the seventh day of Tabernacles on which it is not, and so for Passover, in reverse],

I:6:   Said R. Hananiah, son of the brother of R. Joshua, "In the Exile they are not accustomed to do things in this way [as indicated at M. 1:3].

II:1:   Said R. Joshua, "Since rain is not a sign of a blessing when it comes on the Festival itself, why should one mention it?" Said to him R. Eliezer, "I too have said so only [for mentioning] restoring the wind and bringing down the rain," [that is,] in its due season [M. 1:1D-E].

II:2:   On account of five matters were the Israelites redeemed from Egypt: Because the end had come, because of oppression, because of their outcry, because of the merit of the fathers, and because of repentance.

YERUSHALMI TAANIT 1:2

I:1:   Said R. Yohanan, "The law is in accord with the opinion of R. Judah, which he expressed in the name of R. Judah b. Batera."

I:2:   It has been taught

YERUSHALMI TAANIT 1:3

I:1:   The Mishnah passage before us is framed in terms of the view of R. Meir.

I:2:   How much rain must descend for a person to be liable to say a blessing?

I:3:   R. Judah bar Ezekiel said, "This is how my father, Ezekiel, would say a blessing when it rained

I:4:   How much rain must fall to contain the first rainfall?

I:5:   Said R. Levi, "The upper water is male, and the lower water is female. "

I:6:   It has been taught

YERUSHALMI TAANIT 1:4

I:1:   What is the definition of the individual [of M. 1:4A]?

YERUSHALMI TAANIT 1:4

I:4:   It has been taught

YERUSHALMI TAANIT 1:5

I:1:   Said R. Yohanan, "In the case of any fast that a court decrees, which is of the kind of fast that may be interrupted [e.g., should it rain, people may then eat and drink on such a day,] pregnant and nursing mothers do not fast at all."

YERUSHALMI TAANIT 1:6

I:1:   R. Zeirah in the name of R. Jeremiah: "He who performs an act of labor on a community fast is as if he did an act of labor on the Day of Atonement.

I:2:   Women who are accustomed not to work on the night following the Sabbath — that is no custom.

II:1:   They are forbidden] to bathe [M. 1:6C]: Zeirah bar Hama, Yosé b. R. Joshua b. Levi in the name of R. Joshua b. Levi: "On the occasion of a public fast, one may wash his hands, his face, and feet in the usual way.

III:1:   It has been taught as a Tannaite rule: [As to putting on a sandal:] A mourner and one who had been excommunicated who were going from one town to another on the road are permitted to put on a sandal. When they come to a town, they must take them off. The same rule applies to the ninth of Ab and to a public fast.

IV:1:   As to anointing, that is in line with the following, which has been taught:

IV:2:   As to putting on a sandal, it has been taught

V:1:   Sexual relations: Now look here! If someone is forbidden to bathe, is it not an argument a fortiori that it is forbidden to have sexual relations? [Why does the framer of the Mishnah find it necessary to specify this item?]

V:2:   Judah bar Pazzi, R. Hanin in the name of R. Samuel bar R. Isaac: "When Noah entered the ark, he was forbidden to have sexual relations." What is the scriptural basis for that statement?

YERUSHALMI TAANIT 1:7

I:1:   R. Yudan son of R. Hama of Kepar Tahamin: "[The thirteen fasts, each involving three days] are equivalent to the forty days that Moses spent on the Mountain. The reason they did not decree more fasts than these,"] said R. Yosé, "is so that they do not place too great a burden on the community."

II:1:   One opens one [door], closes [another], [in a shop with two entries].

III:1:   What is the meaning? Is it that one opens one door and closes the other?

YERUSHALMI TAANIT 1:8

I:1:   [As regards cutting down on building,] said R. Joshua b. Levi, "That which you have said applies to building for purposes of pleasure [e.g., a house for one's son, who is getting married], but if one's wall was infirm, one may tear it down and rebuild it."

I:2:   R. Ba bar Kohen said before R. Yosé, R. Aha in the name of R. Jacob bar Idi: "It is forbidden to betroth a woman on Friday." That which you have said indicates that one should not make the banquet in celebration of the betrothal. But lo, as to the actual betrothal, it is permitted.

I:3:   Since M. 1:8A says they cut down on greeting one another, in fact there should be no greeting at all.] For has it not been taught as follows: There is to be no greeting of one's close associates on the ninth of Ab. And as to ordinary folk, one [answers their greeting] in a low voice [T. Ta. 3:12].

II:1:   Once Nisan has ended, if it then rains, it is a sign of a curse [M. 1:8D]. Said R. Yosé b. R. Bun, "That refers specifically to the season of Nisan [thirty days after the vernal equinox, hence, April 21]."

YERUSHALMI TAANIT 2:1

I:1:   Said R. Hiyya bar Ba "And why do they go out into the street of the town? "

II:1:   And they put wood ashes on the ark [M. 2:1B]: It is in line with this verse: "[When he calls to Me, I will answer him]; I will be with him in trouble, [I will rescue him and honor him]" (Ps.91:15).

II:2: R. Yudan b. R. Manasseh and R. Samuel bar Nahman: One said, "[They put on ashes] in order to call to mind the merit of Abraham." The other said, "[They do so] in order to call to mind the merit of Isaac [at the binding of Isaac]."

II:3: When R. Judah bar Pazzi would go forth to a fast, he would say before them, "O our brethren! To whomever the beadle [of the synagogue] has not come, let him take dust and put it on his head."

III:1: And on the head of the patriarch [M. 2:1B]: Said R. Tahalipa of Caesarea, "It is so as to make the matter known. One who degrades himself is not the same as one who is de graded by others."

III:2: It is written, "Let the bridegroom leave his room, and the bride her chamber" (Joel 2:16). "The bridegroom leave his room"— this refers to the ark. "And the bride her chamber"— this refers to the Torah.

III:3: One verse of Scripture says [with regard to the bullock of the congregation], "[And the priest shall dip his finger in the blood and sprinkle it seven times before the Lord] in front of the veil" (Lev. 4:17). And another verse of Scripture [with regard to the bullock of the anointed priest] says, "[And the priest shall dip his finger in the blood and sprinkle part of the blood seven times before the Lord] in front of the veil of the sanctuary" (Lev. 4:6). [Why then does the latter specify the sanctuary and the former not?]

YERUSHALMI TAANIT 2:2

I:1: [As to the experienced elder,] it has been taught

I:2: And why are there eighteen [benedictions said every day]?

I:3: What is the origin of the seven blessings to be said in the Prayer on the Sabbath?

I:4: What is the origin of the nine blessings that are to be said in the Prayer on the New Year?

I:5: What is the origin of the twenty-four blessings that are to be said in the Prayer on a fast day?

I:6: Zeira in the name of R. Jeremiah, "An individual [praying by himself, prior to the reader's repetition] at the time of a public fast has to make mention of the incident [which has caused the fast] .

I:7: What is the prayer of seven sticks that serves to summarize the eighteen blessings [of the Prayer]?

YERUSHALMI TAANIT 2:3

I:1: [Clarifying M. 2:3D, concluding with an appropriate ending:] Each blessing must accord with its appropriate ending.

YERUSHALMI TAANIT 2:4

I:1: And was not Isaac [also] redeemed on Mount Moriah]? Since Isaac was redeemed, it was as if all Israel was redeemed

YERUSHALMI TAANIT 2:5

I:1:   At the sea our fathers were divided into four parties.

YERUSHALMI TAANIT 2:7

I:1:   It is written, "So they gathered at Mispeh, and drew water and poured it out before the Lord [and fasted on that day]" (1 Sam. 7:6).

YERUSHALMI TAANIT 2:8

I:1:   It is written, "And at the time of the offering of the oblation [at evening], Elijah the prophet came near and said, 'O Lord, God of Abraham, Isaac, and Israel, let it be known [this day that thou art God in Israel]'" (1 Kings 18:36).

YERUSHALMI TAANIT 2:9

I:1:   It is written, "I called to the Lord, out of my distress, and he answered me" (Jonah 2:2).

I:2:   Was it not appropriate to list David and Solomon, and only afterward, Elijah and Jonah [who came after their time]?

I:3:   For the seventh — Sumkhos says, "... he who humbles the proud" [T. Ta. 1:10A-B].

I:4:   There is no problem as to Solomon [who said a prayer concerning Jerusalem], for it is written, "I have built thee an exalted house, a place for thee to dwell in forever" (I Kings 8:13). But why David?

YERUSHALMI TAANIT 2:10

I:1:   It has been taught

YERUSHALMI TAANIT 2:11

I:1:   On what account are men of a given priestly watch permitted to drink wine by night but not by day [M. 2:11 G]?

I:2:   There we have learned: These are the ones who may get a haircut on the intermediate days of a festival: He who comes home from overseas or from captivity, and he who goes forth from prison, and he who had been excommunicated but at that time had been released from the ban by sages [M. M. Q. 3:1J. Lo. all other persons [apart from those listed at M. 3:1] are forbidden to get haircuts. Said R. Simon, "They made such a decree for them so that they should not enter the festal season in an unkempt appearance."

I:3:   It has been taught

YERUSHALMI TAANIT 2:12

I:1:   The Mishnah represents the view of R. Meir.

I:2:   [With reference to M. Meg. 1:4F-G: Even though they have said they push it up and they do not postpone the reading of the Scroll of Esther, on the days on which they read the Scroll of Esther they are permitted to hold a lamentation for the dead, to call fasts, and to give gifts to the poor:] [When the Mishnah states that it is permitted to mourn and to fast, this passage of] the Mishnah speaks either of the eleventh of Adar, in accord with the view of R. Yosé, or of the twelfth of Adar, in accord with the view of R. Meir.

I:3:   But as to Sabbaths and festival days, one may fast both on the day before them and on the day after them. Why do you impose a lenient rule on these [Sabbaths and festivals] and a strict rule on those [the days listed in the fasting scroll]?

YERUSHALMI TAANIT 2:13

I:1:   Simeon bar Ba said, "A case came before R. Yohanan, and he decided it in accord with the view of R. Yosé."

YERUSHALMI TAANIT 2:14

I:1:   [As to M. 2:14B, If they had begun . . . ,] how many fasts constitute a beginning [in line with the view of Gamaliel]? R. Ba said, "One." R. Yosé said, "Two."

I:2:   And what do they read [on a fast that coincides with the New Moon] ?

I:3:   It has been taught

YERUSHALMI TAANIT 3:1

I:1:   What is the definition of "forthwith" applying to their [proclamation of fasts]?

I:2:   It has been taught

YERUSHALMI TAANIT 3:2

I:1:   If the rain fell sufficient for crops but not for trees: Little by little.

I:2:   Berekhiah, R. Helbo, Pappa in the name of R. Eleazar: "There are times that rain comes on account of the merit of a single man, a single vegetation, a single field. "

YERUSHALMI TAANIT 3:3]

I:1:   Said R. Simeon, "It is written, 'And I caused it to rain upon one city, and caused it not to rain upon another city, one piece was rained upon, and the piece on which it rained not did wither' (Amos 4:7):the merit associated with a particular field is what did it."

YERUSHALMI TAANIT 3:3]

II:1:   And all its neighbors fast but do not sound the shofar [M. 3:3D]: For so we find that on the Day of Atonement, they fast but do not sound the shofar. R. Aqiba says." They sound the shofar but do not fast" [M. 3:3E]: For so we find that on the New Year they sound the shofar but do not fast.

YERUSHALMI TAANIT 3:4

I:2:   Zeirah in the name of R. Haninah: "What will the truly great men of the generation do?

II:1:   And all its neighbors fast but do not sound the shofar [M. 3:4C]: For so we find that on the Day of Atonement they fast but do not sound the *shofar.* R. Aqiba says." They sound the shofar but do not fast" [M. 3:4D]. For so we find that on the New Year they sound the *shofar* but do not fast.

YERUSHALMI TAANIT 3:5

I:1:   Said R. Levi, "It is written, 'The Lord will make the pestilence cleave to
         you [until he has consumed you off the land which you are entering to
         take possession of it]' (Deut. 28:21). "

I:2:   [As to the reference at M. 3:4A to the collapse of houses:] The houses of
         which they have spoken must to begin with be solid ones. But we do not
         take account of the collapse of dilapidated ones.

I:3:   It has been taught

YERUSHALMI TAANIT 3:6

I:1:   Hama bar Uqba in the name of R. Yosé b. Haninah: "They sound the
         shofar when the flax in the field is threatened with ruin through sprout-
         ing. "What is the scriptural verse pertinent to this matter?

II:1:   [With reference to the catalogue of M. 3:5B:] Locusts are not the end of
         the matter. But even [if one finds] a wing [of a locust].

YERUSHALMI TAANIT 3:7

I:1:   That which you have said applies to a case in which [blight], M. 3:7A]
         appeared in a concentrated area.

I:2:   Said R. .Mana, "The wolves [M. 3:7C] appeared running after people."

YERUSHALMI TAANIT 3:8

I:1:   ["The prayer for raising an alarm on the Sabbath"] said Rab, "Thus please
         answer me, O Lord. answer me' [= a supplication]." The .Mishnah s state-
         ment differs from the view of Rab: R. Yosé says."They sound the shofar
         on the Sabbath] for help, not for supplication." But lo. the earlier Tannaite
         authority [in the same passage concurs with the view of Rab and holds
         that one may] express even supplications.

YERUSHALMI TAANIT 3:9

I:1:   R. Jonah, Simeon bar Ba in the name of R. Yohanan [with reference to
         Mal. 3:10: "Bring the whole tithe into the storehouse . . . And try Me now
         herewith, says the Lord of hosts, if I will not open for you the windows of
         heaven, and pour out for you a blessing that there shall be more than
         sufficiency," on the meaning of the final words of the verse,] "A matter
         for which it is impossible for you m say, 'Enough,'— that is a blessing.
         [If, however, you can say, 'Enough,' that is no real blessing.]"

II:1:   That is to say, it was the eve of Passover. But that is stated explicitly by
         the Tannaite rule: on the twentieth day [of Adar] the people fasted for rain
         and it rained for them.

III:1:   [Why did the rain not come properly?] Said R. Yosé b. R. Bun, "Because
         he did not come before God with humility."

IV:1:   They said to him, This rain has come only to release you from your vow
         [M. 3:9G]."

V:1:   Samuel taught, "[It poured out] as if from a wineskin."

VI:1:   He said, "This is not what I wanted, but rain of good will, blessing, and
         graciousness" [M. 3:9K]. Now it rained the right way, until the Israelites

had to flee from Jerusalem up to the Temple Mount because of the rain [M. 3:9L]. That implies that the Temple Mount was roofed over. And so has it been taught: There was a colonnade within the Temple portico.

VII:1: What purpose did this stone of the lost serve?

VII:2: He said, "Just as it is not possible for this stone to be blotted out of the world, so it is not possible to pray that rain will go away. "

VII:3: They asked R. Eleazar, "When do they pray that rain should go away " He said to them, "If a man is standing on Qeren Ofel [a high rock] and splashes his foot in the Qidron brook. [Then] we shall pray that the rain will stop."

YERUSHALMI TAANIT 3:10

I:1: [Spelling out M. 3:10A, "In demanding rain as you did, you improperly importuned.] For if a punitive decree had been issued, as was the case in the time of Elijah, would you not have turned out to cause a public profanation of the Name?

II:1: R. Berekhiah, R. .Abba bar Kahana, R. Zeirah in the name of R. Judah; and there are those who state the matter in the name of R. Hisda; and there are those who state the matter in the name of R. .Mattenah:" You will decide on a matter and it will be established tor you' (Job 22:2). What is the meaning of, 'For you'?

III:1: Why does Scripture refer [after speaking of the mother] to "her that bore you"? R. Mana said, "Your nation." R. Yosé b. R. Bun said, "Your time [that is. the hour at which you were born]." Rabbis say, "Just as [an evil son] brings a double curse on [the mother]. so he brings troubled rejoicing to her [when he does good]."

YERUSHALMI TAANIT 3:11

I:1: If they were fasting and it rained for them before sunrise. they should not complete the fast. This is indicated in the following statement of Scripture:

YERUSHALMI TAANIT 3:11

I:3: R. Aha, R. Abbahu in the name of R. Yosé b. Haninah: "It is forbidden to a person to fast on the Sabbath beyond six hours [noon]."

II:1: What is the great Hallel [M. 3:11D]?

YERUSHALMI TAANIT 4:1

I:1: On the basis of the statement of the Mishnah], you may infer three points.

I:2: And why should a priest not raise his hands [in a priestly benediction] not on an occasion of prayer [as against M. 4:1B's specification of the priestly benediction for times of prayer alone]?

I:3: It has been taught

I:4: Zeirah, R. Hiyya, R. Joshua b. Levi in the name of Bar Pedaiah: "On what account did the Scripture link the pericope of the Nazirite [Num. 6:1-21] to that of the raising of hands [in the priestly benediction, Num. 6:22-27]?

I:5:   What is the scriptural basis for the raising of hands [the priestly benedic-
          tion]?

I:6:   And what is the scriptural basis for [saying an additional] prayer [on the
          Day of Atonement, that is, the prayer] of the closing of the gates [M.
          4:1B]?

I:7:   To what does "the closing of the gates" [correspond that is, why is this the
          name of the service] [M. 4:1B]?

I:8:   As to the prayer of the closing of the gates, what is the law on its releasing
          [one from the obligation of saying] the prayer of the evening? Said R. Ba
          to R. Hunah, "[But if one does not say the evening prayer,] at what point
          would one make mention of the prayer marking the separation [of the
          holy day that has passed from the ordinary day that has begun which is
          said during the evening Prayer]?"

I:9:   Isaac bar Nahman in the name of R. Joshua b. Levi: "On the Day of
          Atonement which coincides with the Sabbath, even though there is no
          service of the closing of the gates on the Sabbath, one makes mention of
          the Sabbath in the service of the closing of the gates."

I:10:   [On the occasion of the New Moon that coincides with a fast day,] what
          [passage of the Torah] do they read

I:11:   Jeremiah, the scribe, asked R. Jeremiah, 'On the occasion of a New Moon
          that coincided with the Sabbath, what passage do they read?"

I:12:   Rab instructed Abedan, his spokesman, "Announce before them: 'He who
          wants to say the evening prayer may do so while it is still day.'"

I:13:   Said R. Jacob bar Aha, "It has been taught there

YERUSHALMI TAANIT 4:2

I:1:   Would it not have been more appropriate to express the Mishnah by say-
          ing, What is the delegation?...

I:2:   Said R. Jonah, "The daily whole offering represents the offering of all
          Israelites.

II:1:   Rather, the early prophets made the rule of twenty-four watches, and for
          each watch there was a delegation in Jerusalem made up of priests, Levites,
          and Israelites [M. 4:2D]. It has been taught

II:2:   The priests go to participate in the Temple labor, and the Levites to the
          platform [on which they] would sing Psalms], and the Israelites take upon
          themselves to serve as the messengers of all Israel.

II:3:   It has been taught

II:4:   R. Jacob bar Aha, R. Hiyya in the name of R. Yohanan [in the Tosefta's
          version]: "Eight priestly watches did Moses set up for the priesthood, and
          eight for the Levites

II:5:   Four priestly watches came up from the Exile: Jediah, Harim, Pashhur,
          and Immer [Ezra 2:36 - 39].

II:8:   Three scrolls did they find in the Temple courtyard.

II:9:   Said R. Levi, "A scroll listing genealogies they found in Jerusalem

II:10:   It has been taught

II:11:   Jacob bar Aha in the name of R. Yosé: "Under no circumstances does the world endure, except on the basis of the offerings."

YERUSHALMI TAANIT 4:3

I:1:   Huna said, "The three who are called up to the Torah should not read less than ten verses of Scripture."

I:2:   It has been taught

II:1:   The .Mishnah accords with the view of R. .Meir

III:1:   [As to the view of M. 1:3R, that there is no delegation rite at the closing of the gates on the occasion of a wood offering,] R. Simon said, "Is it too much trouble to carry the burden of a little wood? [Why cancel the delegation?]"

YERUSHALMI TAANIT 4:4

I:1:   Why did they set aside [special times for] the wood offering of priests and people [M. Ta. 4:4]?

I:2:   What was the matter having to do with the families of the pestle smugglers and the fig pressers [M. 4:4H]?

YERUSHALMI TAANIT 4:5

I:1:   It is written, "The glory of the Lord settled on Mount Sinai, *and* the cloud covered it six *days; and* on the seventh *day* he called to Moses out of the midst of the cloud" (Ex. 2:16). [And it also says] "and Moses went up...(Ex. 2:15)." This was the seventh day after the declaration of the Ten Commandments, and the beginning of the forty [days that Moses spent on the mountain].

II:1:   Simon in the name of R. Joshua b. Levi: "In the days of the Greek empire [when Jerusalem was besieged], they would let down two baskets containing gold

III:1:   It is written, "[In the eleventh year of Zedekiah, in the fourth month, on the ninth day of the month], a breach was made in the city" (Jer. 39:2). And yet you say this?

III:2:   Simeon b. Yohai taught, "R. Aqiba. my master, interpreted as follows

IV:1:   Where did he burn it?

V:1:   There is a Tannaite authority who teaches, "An idol was set up." He who said, "An idol was set up" refers to a statue of Manasseh. He who said, "He set up an idol" refers to a statue of Apostemos [which he himself set up].

V:2:   [As to the seventeenth of Tammuz ,] who did they not designate it as a fast day

VI:1:   [As to the decree against the forefathers about not entering the land [M. 4:5C]: that is in line with the following verses of Scripture

VI:2:   It has been taught

VII:1:   Rabbi would derive by exegesis twenty-four [tragic] events from the verse

VII:2:   It has been taught
VIII:1:   Rufus — may his bones be crushed!— ploughed the Temple building.

YERUSHALMI TAANIT 4:6

I:1:   [As regards cutting down on building (M. 1:8),] said R. Joshua b. Levi,
          "That which you have said applies to building for purposes of pleasure
          [e.g., a house for one's son, who is getting married], but if one's wall was
          infirm, one may tear it down and rebuild it."

I:2:   R. Ba bar Kohen said before R. Yosé, R. Aha in the name of R. Jacob bar
          Idi: "It is forbidden to betroth a woman on Friday."

I:3:   Said R. Jonah, "That which you have said [that it is prohibited to wash
          clothing] applies to laundering in order to wear the garment immediately].
          But it is permitted to launder in order to repair it [for use after the ninth of
          Ab]."

II:1:   [As to the rule of M. 4:6B,] R. Ba bar Kohen said before R. Yosé, R. Aha
          in the name of R. Abbahu: "In the case of the ninth of Ab which coincides
          with the Sabbath, both weeks [before and after] are released [from the
          restrictions of M. 4:6B].

II:2:   R. Jeremiah in the name of R. Hiyya bar Ba: "According to strict law they
          should fast on the tenth of that month [of Ab], on which day the Temple
          was burned. And why is it that the fast is on the ninth? For it was on that
          day that the punishment [of Israel] got underway."

III:1:   What is the meaning of [M. 4:6F: Rabban Simeon b. Gamaliel says,] "He
          should make some change from ordinary procedures"? He should revise
          [the way he does things]. If he was accustomed to eat a litra of meat. Let
          him eat a half. It he was accustomed to drink a xestes of wine let him
          drink half that volume.

IV1:   [As to M. 4:6G-H:] R. Judah ruled quite properly.

YERUSHALMI TAANIT 4:7

I:1:   There is no difficulty understanding the joy of the Day of Atonement, for
          it serves as atonement for Israel. But why the fifteenth of Ab?

II:1:   R. Yannai b. R. Ishmael said, "Even those that are placed in a chest [must
          be immersed]."

III:1:   And what did they say? "Fellow, look around and see — choose what you
          want! Don't look for beauty. Look for family [M. 4:7E-G]: The daughter
          of the king would borrow from the daughter of the high priest.

III

Disputes

Disputes are catalogued only when that form defines the basic pattern of a given composition. Disputes may take several forms:

1. Statement of the issue
   Two parties dispute
   X said or: one said
   And Y said and the other said
2. X + statement
   Y + contrary statement
3. Statement of the issue
   X said
   And Y said

In the context of the Yerushalmi, most disputes contribute to the work of Mishnah-commentary. But some define the form of a well-crafted composition. I see no important formal differences between the dispute-form in this document and its counterpart in Genesis Rabbah and related writings.

I. BERAKHOT

I. YERUSHALMI BERAKHOT 1:1

I:8: One who stands and prays must keep his feet even. Two Amoraim [disputed the interpretation of A]: R. Levi and R. Simon. One said, And one said, "Like the priests."

YERUSHALMI BERAKHOT 4:4

I:3: One who was praying and he remembered that he had already prayed — Rab said, "He should break off [from praying]." And Samuel said, "He should not break off." [He may complete the second recitation of the Prayer.]

I:4: One who was praying on the Sabbath and he forgot [to say] the Sabbath Prayer, but [instead] he said the weekday Prayer — R. Huna says, "[Concerning this case] there is a dispute between R. Nahman bar Jacob and R. Sheshet. One said, '[When he remembers] he must break off from reciting [even in the middle of] a blessing.' And the other said, 'He should

191

finish [saying] the blessing [he is reciting when he remembers it is the Sabbath].'

YERUSHALMI BERAKHOT 4:5-6

I:2: "[Then Solomon began to build the house of the Lord in Jerusalem on] Mount Moriah" [II Chron. 3:1]. R. Hiyya the Elder and R. Yannai [disputed over the reason it was called mwryh, Moriah]. One said it was because from that place instruction [hwryh] goes forth to the world. The other said it was because from that place fear [yr'h] goes forth to the world.

YERUSHALMI BERAKHOT 6:1

I:8: Jacob bar Aha said, "R. Nahman disputed with the sages [over the correct formula for the blessing recited over bread]." R. Nahman said, "Who brings forth [hmwsy'] bread from the earth," [indicating past and continuous action]. And sages said, "Brings forth [mwsy'] bread from the earth," [indicating continuous and future action].

II. SHABBAT

YERUSHALMI SHABBAT 3:3

IV:1: As to hot water heated on the festival, and so too, hot water heated on the eve of the Sabbath for use on the Sabbath, Rab and Samuel — One of them said, "One may with such water wash one's face, hands, and feet." The other said, "One may with such water wash his entire body, limb by limb."

YERUSHALMI SHABBAT 7:1

III:3: An adult who was taken captive among gentiles [and he loses track of the calendar] — Rab and Samuel: One said, "He counts six days and then observes the Sabbath." The other said, "He observes the Sabbath and then counts six days." R. Isaac bar Eleazar in the name of R. Nahman bar Jacob: "He counts six days and observes the Sabbath, five and observes the Sabbath, four and observes the Sabbath, three and observes the Sabbath, two and observes the Sabbath, one and observes the Sabbath. [If he was taken on a Sunday, he counts six days, on a Monday, five, and so on down. He would remember that he was observing the Sabbath, hence we do not make provision for that possibility.]"

YERUSHALMI SHABBAT 7:2

VI:3: If one selected one kind of food from some other kinds of food — Hezekiah said, "He is liable." R. Yohanan said, "He is exempt."

YERUSHALMI SHABBAT 8:7

I:1: A potsherd of any size — R. Yohanan said, "They consecrate [the water for the red heifer process of purification] with it." R. Simeon b. Laqish says, "They do not do so."

III. ERUBIN

YERUSHALMI ERUBIN 1:1

I:3:   The Mishnah [at M. 1:1A] states only, higher than twenty cubits. Lo, up
        to twenty cubits [in height], [the symbolic gateway formed by the
        crossbeam] remains valid. The formulation of the Mishnah accords with
        the view of Rab, for Rab said, "The purpose of specifying exact measure-
        ments is to impose a lenient ruling. [In cases of measurements, one is
        lenient.] [As at A, one may go right up to the full extent of the specified
        measurement.]"
            R. Yohanan said, "The purpose of specifying exact measurement is to
        impose a strict ruling."
            R. Hiyya in the name of R. Yohanan: "In the case of a crossbeam above
        an alleyway which is located above twenty cubits [from the ground], one
        sets a crossbeam within the space twenty cubits from the ground, and so
        diminishes the distance to within twenty cubits of the ground
                    [In this regard] R. Yosé said, "And that is the case if the
                    entire construction providing the crossbeam lies within twenty
                    cubits of the ground [and not only part of it]. [The beam has to
                    be level with the ground, not at an angle, for this corrective pro-
                    cedure to be valid.]"

YERUSHALMI ERUBIN 1:1

II:4:   An alleyway which is bent and open at both ends [so that there is an L-
        shaped alleyway, open to the street at each end of the L] —
            R. Yohanan said, "One puts a side bar and a crossbeam at one end [thus
        forming a valid gateway at one open end of the alleyway], and prepares
        something like the shape of a doorway at the other end as well [so that
        each stick of the L is served by a gateway]. [This has the effect of treating
        each stick of the L as a separate domain.]"
            R. Simeon b. Laqish said, "One sets up either a side post or a crossbeam
        [so forming a gateway}, and that serves to permit [carrying on the Sab-
        bath throughout the alleyway]." [At the corner of the L, however, no ar-
        rangement is required.]

YERUSHALMI ERUBIN 1:1

II:10:   There we have learned [M. 6:8:] If one of the occupants of an alley forgot
        to share in the meal of commingling for the alley, the occupants are unre-
        stricted, since the alley is to the courtyards as the courtyard is to the houses.
        How many courtyards are there in an alleyway?
            Both Rab and Samuel say, "There may be no fewer than two courtyards
        to constitute an alleyway."
            R. Jacob bar Aha in the name of R. Yohanan: "Even if there is one court-
        yard on one side and one courtyard on the other."
            R. Aha, R. Hinena in the name of R. Yohanan said, "Even if there is one

courtyard on one side, a house on another side, a house on yet another side, and a store on the fourth side, [that adds up to an alleyway]."

R. Nahman bar Jacob in the name of R. Yohanan: "An alleyway is made up of no fewer than two courtyards, a courtyard is made up of no fewer than two houses."

YERUSHALMI ERUBIN 1:1

III:2:　Hananiah, son of the brother of R. Joshua, says, "[With reference to alleyways opening out onto public domain,]

the House of Shammai say, 'One has to put up a door on one side and a door on the other, and, when the people go in or come out, they have actually to close the door.'

The House of Hillel say, 'One must put up a door on one side, and the shape of a door on the other.'"

YERUSHALMI ERUBIN 5:3

I:2:　If from the surveyor to a ravine was a distance of seventy-five cubits — two Amoraim deal with this matter.

One said, "He measures with a rope fifty cubits long; then he doubles it up to a length of twenty-five."

The other said, "He measures with a rope of fifty cubits, and as to the remaining distance, he measures with a rope four cubits long." If a ravine was narrow at the top and broad at the bottom, up to a depth of fifty cubits, you regard the ravine as if it were filled with dirt and pebbles [and ignore the greater span at the bottom of the ravine], but if not, you regard it as if one would climb up and climb down [the ravine].

YERUSHALMI ERUBIN 5:7

I:5:　A city which was destroyed [in which one put his *erub*] —

R. Eleazar says, "He may traverse the entire area and two thousand cubits beyond." Samuel said, "He has only two thousand cubits from the location of his *erub.*"

R. Ba bar Kahana, R. Hiyya bar Assi in the name of Rab: "He who puts his *erub* in a stall or in an enclosed field may traverse the entire area and two thousand cubits beyond."

YERUSHALMI ERUBIN 7:8

I:1:　Rab said, "The definition of 'numerous' is seventeen, and the definition of 'few' is sixteen."

R. Yohanan said, "Wherever [the food for two meals], if divided among them, would not be sufficient to allow for each a volume of food as much as the *size* of a dried fig, the residents are held to be many,' and a quantity of food for two meals suffices; otherwise they are regarded as 'few.'"

The foregoing does not conform to the requirement of the form, which includes an effort to balance or somehow interrelate the two (or more) positions that are set forth.

YERUSHALMI ERUBIN 8:2

I:1:   R. Meir says, "On an ordinary day, for he does not have much to eat, so
         he eats only a small quantity of bread. On the Sabbath, when he has much
         to eat, he also eats a great deal of bread."
         R. Judah says, "On an ordinary day, on which he does not have much to
         eat, he eats a great deal of bread. On the Sabbath, on which he has much
         to eat, he eats only a little bread."

IV. YOMA

YERUSHALMI YOMA 2:1

I:2:   A non-priest who raised up [the ashes of the altar] — R. Yohanan said,
         "He is liable." R. Simeon b. Laqish said, "He is exempt."

YERUSHALMI YOMA 2:1

I:12:   Said R. Yohanan, "Taking up the ashes from the altar is the beginning of
         service of the next day. One has, therefore, to wash his hands and feet
         from the laver, which is filled with water [throughout the night]. [The
         water is not spoiled by being left overnight.]"
         R. Hiyya bar Joseph said, "Once one has handed over the day to the night,
         that suffices. [That is, the laver did not have to be filled with water all
         night. The concern is that the water not be left standing all night; if it is,
         when the morning star appears, the water is invalidated. A solution to the
         problem will now be presented.]"
         Associates in the name of R. Yohanan: "Once the priest had raised up
         [water, and then washed his hands and feet in it prior to taking up the
         ashes], he puts it back [into the laver, prior to the appearance of the morn-
         ing star, marking the passage from night to day and imparting unclean-
         ness to the water on the count of having been left all night]. [Accordingly,
         the issue of using invalid water is not a problem in the case of the wash-
         ing prior to taking the ashes off the altar, since this is done before the rise
         of the morning star.]"

YERUSHALMI YOMA 4:1

II:7:   The two goats required for the Day of Atonement which one slaughtered
         outside of the Temple court —
         there is a Tannaite authority who teaches that he is liable.
                  And there is a Tannaite authority who teaches that he is exempt.
                  [There is no conflict between these opinions,]" said R. Hisda.
                  "He who maintains that one is liable deals with a case in which
                  the goat which is not to be prepared inside is the one which he
                  has offered up. "The one who maintains that he is exempt speaks
                  of a case in which the man offered up the goat which was to be
                  prepared inside the Temple court."

YERUSHALMI YOMA 4:3

I:4:   If the high priest slaughtered the bullock and then died — what is the law
         as to someone else's bringing the blood in?

R. Simeon b. Laqish said, "'[But thus shall Aaron come into the holy place: with] a young bull' (Lev. 16:3). But not with blood. [The new high priest has to kill his own bullock and bring in its blood.] "

Both R. Haninah and R. Jonathan say, "Even with the blood [of the bullock killed by the recently deceased high priest]."

YERUSHALMI YOMA 4:6

I:4:   Joshua b. Levi said, "The show bread was not invalidated when the tribes made their journeys [in the desert and so dismantled the tabernacle]."

R. Yohanan said, "The show bread was invalidated when the tribes made their journeys."

R. Hiyya in the name of R. Joshua b. Levi: "'As they encamp, so they shall journey' (Num. 2:17). Just as, when they are in camp, it is not invalidated, so, when they are journeying, it is not invalidated." R. Ammi in the name of R. Joshua b. Levi: "'Then the tent of meeting shall set out, with the camp of the Levites in the midst of the camps' (Num. 2:17). It is as if it is in the midst of the camps [and valid]."

The foregoing does not meet the requirements of the form.

V. PESAHIM

YERUSHALMI PESAHIM 1:4

I:1:   Meir says, "From the sixth hour onwards [until the festival itself, the presence of leaven is prohibited] by reason of their words [on the basis of rabbinic injunction]."

Judah says, "From the sixth hour onwards [leaven is prohibited] by reason of the authority of the Torah."

YERUSHALMI PESAHIM 1:4

I:2:   Lo, R. Meir says, "From the sixth hour onwards [leaven is prohibited] by reason of their words. [That is, the time is added by decree of scribes, not by the rule of the Torah.] The seventh [hour, i.e., the latter half of the day, it] is prohibited because of a fence [as a precautionary period preceding the day's final hour when leaven becomes biblically prohibited]. The sixth [hour, just prior to noon], why [is it prohibited]? Because of a fence? And is there a fence for a fence? [But precautionary measures generally are not instituted to prevent the violation of a precautionary measure.] Rather [the sixth hour is prohibited not as a fence but because] the sixth hour gets confused with the seventh." [Hence it is directly prohibited as part of the prohibition of the seventh hour.]

Lo, R. Judah says, "From the fifth hour onwards [eating leaven is prohibited] by reason of the authority of the Torah,' the sixth [hour] is prohibited because of a fence [lest the sixth become confused with the seventh hour]. The fifth why? Because of a fence? And is there a fence for a fence? Rather [the fifth is prohibited] because the fifth gets confused with the seventh" [and thus the fifth and sixth hours form part of the same fence].

I:3: Rab said, "According to R. Meir, one who sanctifies [a marriage, betrothing a woman,] with leaven from the sixth hour onwards [when leaven, then becoming prohibited, loses its value] has not accomplished anything [for a marriage must be performed with an object having some value."

YERUSHALMI PESAHIM 1:6

I:1: Bar Qappara says, "The Father of Uncleanness [imparts uncleanness] by reason of the authority of the Torah. The Offspring of Uncleanness [imparts uncleanness] by reason of their words [on the basis of rabbinic injunction]."

R. Yohanan says, "Both the former and the latter [impart uncleanness] by reason of the authority of the Torah."

Bar Qappara's position causes no problems. [In his understanding, the force of the Mishnah's ruling is understandable, since two things of very different nature — something biblically unclean with something only rabbinically unclean — would be mixed.] According, however, to R. Yohanan [who claims that all the meat is made unclean by the Torah], the Father of Uncleanness [which the Mishnah mentions] makes [something] a first [generation], [and] an Offspring of Uncleanness [which the Mishnah mentions and which at this point is assumed to be a first generation] makes [something] a second [generation]. [But] a second [generation] that touches a first [generation], lo it remains in its place as a second generation! [A second that touches a first remains a second generation because objects (here the first generation) generally make something unclean at one remove from their own uncleanness. Here the object already is at the second generation so that its degree of uncleanness is merely repeated.]

YERUSHALMI PESAHIM 1:7

I:1: According to the position of R. Yohanan [who explains that the Offspring of Uncleanness is unclean on rabbinic authority], there [in M. 1:6] they burn something unclean by reason of the Torah with something unclean by reason of the Torah [Hananiah's ruling] and [Aqiba in M. 1:7] comes to add [that they may burn] something invalid by reason of the Torah [a third generation re moved of uncleanness, something unclean but unable to impart uncleanness] with something unclean by reason of the Torah.

According to the position of Bar Qappara [who explains that the Offspring of Uncleanness is unclean biblically, however], there [M. 1:6] they burn something unclean by reason of their words with something unclean by reason of the Torah, and here [R. Aqiba would add that they may burn] something invalid by reason of the Torah with something unclean by reason of the Torah — [this being the case he] comes only to subtract [that is,

narrow the application of the principle and not to extend it, for while M.
1:6 treats two injunctions of disparate origins, one biblical and one rabbinic, M. 1:7 would treat two injunctions both biblical in origin]!

YERUSHALMI PESAHIM 3:3

II:5:   It [an animal] and its young that fell into a pit [on a festival] —
        R. Eliezer says, "[One] should raise up the first with the plan to slaughter
        it and should slaughter it, and the second, [they] feed it] so that it not
        die."
        R. Joshua says, "[They] should raise up the first one with the plan to
        slaughter [it] but [need] not slaughter [it] and practicing shrewdness,
        should raise up the second. Even though [one] intends not to slaughter
        either one of them — it is permitted." [T. Y.T. 3:2, which augments M.
        Bes. 2:4]. [Noting that R. Eliezer in M. Pes. 3:3 and T. Y.T. 3:2 appare

YERUSHALMI PESAHIM 5:4

I:4:   Simeon b. Laqish said, "[The Mishnah's rule applies] so long as the
        slaughterer is one of the members of the association."
        R. Yohanan said, "[The rule applies if the leaven] belongs to the slaughterer
        even though he is not a member of the association."
        R. Jacob b. Aha [said in the name of] R. Yohanan, "[The rule applies if
        the leaven] belongs to the slaughterer even though he is not a member of
        the association [or if it] belongs to one of the members of the association
        even though he is not the slaughterer."
                R. Yohanan said, "Even [if the leaven] was placed with him in
                Jerusalem."
                R. Simeon b. Laqish said, "So long as [it] is placed with him in
                the [Temple] courtyard."

YERUSHALMI PESAHIM 7:10

I:1:   A bone on which there is no flesh —
        R. Yohanan said, "It is prohibited to break it."
        R. Simeon b. Laqish said, "It is permitted to break it."

YERUSHALMI PESAHIM 7:11

I:1:   Soft sinews that are not necessarily destined to harden] —
        R. Yohanan said, "[People] are registered on them [so that the sinews
        would comprise their portion in the Passover offering]."
        R. Simeon b. Laqish said, "[People] are not registered on them."

YERUSHALMI PESAHIM 8:8

II:2:   A Nazir who became unclean through a condition of doubt [occurring in]
        a private domain —
        R. Hoshaya the Elder said, "The Nazir shaves [at the end of the seven-
        day period of purification that he had to undertake because he is consid-
        ered to have become definitively unclean (Num. 6:9)] ."
        R. Yohanan said, "The Nazir does not shave [for as he is not considered

to have become definitely unclean, he does not undergo the process of purification], for we learn there: Every uncleanness from a corpse because of which a Nazir shaves [in that it aborts his period of Naziriteship] makes one liable on its account for entering the Temple. And every uncleanness from a corpse because of which a Nazir does not shave does not make one liable on its account for entering the Temple [M. Naz. 7:4]. [On the basis of the above principles, because one who experienced a condition of doubt in a private domain is not considered unclean as far as entering the Temple is concerned, that person does not have to shave.]"

YERUSHALMI PESAHIM 9:2

I:1: R. Simon said, "R. Hiyya the Elder and Bar Qappara are in dispute: one says, '[To be liable for not offering the first Passover, one has to be close enough] in order that he should come and eat.'

The other says, 'in order that he should come and toss [the blood]." [The latter opinion implies a lesser distance, since he must arrive earlier at the Temple to be present for the tossing of the blood which took place before the meat was eaten.]

And even according to the one who says, "[one has to be close enough] in order that he should come and eat," this applies in a case where he is within two thousand cubits [ca. 3000 feet] of the [Sabbath] boundary [of Jerusalem] by nightfall. [If he is further away, he is exempt.]

YERUSHALMI PESAHIM 10:5

I:1: Said the House of Shammai to them, "And have the Israelites gone forth from Egypt that he mentions the Exodus from Egypt?" [Since the communal meal over the Passover lamb in recreating the Egyptian event precedes the actual Exodus, it is inappropriate at night to give thanks for the Exodus.]

Said the House of Hillel to them, "If he waits until the cock crows [to mention the redemption, e.g., in the morning service, it is still inappropriate, for] they still did not reach halfway to redemption. [Therefore] how do they mention "redemption" [later or in the morning service] while [the Israelites] have not yet been redeemed? "And lo, they only went forth at midday, as it is said, 'And it was in the middle of that day the Lord took the Israelites out,' ['from the land of Egypt'] (Exod. 12:51) [T. Pes. 10:9].

VI. SUKKAH

In this tractate find nothing that fits into this category.

VII. BESAH

YERUSHALMI BESAH 1:10

I:2: If one selected one kind of food from some other kinds of food —
R. Hezekiah said, "He is liable."

R. Yohanan said, "He is exempt."

> The following Tannaitic teaching differs from the view of Hezekiah, [for it has been said]: "One makes his selection of food and eats it right away or makes his selection of food and leaves it on the table." [This then indicates that selecting food from among a selection of foods is not the sort of selection that is prohibited on the Sabbath. Leaving it on the table is the key, then, since it clearly is not selection merely in order to eat right away what has been selected.] R. Bun bar Hiyya in the name of R. Samuel bar R. Isaac: "Interpret the rule to apply to a case in which there were guests who were eating, one by one. [This is not selection for some later purpose; the guests will eat the food as they come along.]"

YERUSHALMI BESAH 2:4

I:1:   The House of Shammai says, "Laying on of hands not in the ordinary way has been permitted."

The House of Hillel says, "Laying on of hands not in the ordinary way has not been permitted."

> What is laying on of hands not in the ordinary way? It is doing so on the previous day [so that the laying on of hands is not done on the festival but on the day before the festival]. Said R. Zeira, "All parties concur in the case of the guilt offering of a *mesora,* on which the sacrifier laid hands the previous day, that he has not carried out his obligation by doing so. "As to peace offerings brought as a thank offering on which one laid hands on the previous day, one has carried out his obligation. "Concerning what do they differ? Concerning peace offerings [brought in fulfillment of the requirement to bring] a festal offering. "The House of Shammai treats them as equivalent to peace offerings brought as a thank offering. The House of Hillel treats them as equivalent to the guilt offering of a *mesora.* "

Now we have a debate along with the dispute, articulated with considerable formal precision:

> I:2:   Said the House of Hillel, "Now if at a time at which you are not permitted to prepare [food] for an ordinary person, you are permitted to prepare [foot] for the Most High [for on the Sabbath, one is not permitted to prepare foot for himself, but one is permitted to offer up daily burnt offerings ant additional offerings], "at a time at which you are permitted to prepare [foot] for an ordinary person [for on the festival day one is permitted to prepare food], should you not be permitted to pre-

pare [food] for an ordinary person, but you are not permitted to prepare [these, as offerings on a festival day]
for the Most High."

The House of Hillel said to them, "No. you have stated
the rule concerning sacrifices brought in fulfillment of
vows and as thank offerings, which are not subject to a
fixed time [for their offerings], will you state the same
rule concerning the festal offering, the time of which is
fixed?"

The House of Shammai said to them, "Also in the case
of the festal [appearance] offering, there are occasions
at which its time is not fixed. "For he who did not
bring a festal offering on the first day of the festival
may bring a festal offering on any other day of the
festival including [according to your theory] the last
day of the festival" [T. Hag. 2:10E-I].

The House of Hillel said to them, "The festal offering
is subject to a fixed time. For if one did not present the
festal offering on the festival itself, he does not have
the power to do so after the festival."

The House of Shammai said to them, "And has it not
been written, '[On the first day you shall hold a holy
assembly; and on the seventh day a holy assembly; no
work shall be done on those days;] but what every one
must eat, that only may be prepared by you'" (Ex.
12:16).

The House of Hillel said to them, "Is there any proof
from that passage? For you it will not be prepared, but
it will be prepared for the Most High."

> Abba Saul would say the tradition in an other
> language in the name of the House of Hillel,
> "Now if at the time at which your oven is
> closet [on the Sabbath], the oven of your
> Master is open; at a time at which your oven
> is open [on a festival], should not the oven of
> your Master be open? "Another matter: Your
> table should not be full while your Master's
> table lies barren" [T. Hag. 2:10/I-K].

YERUSHALMI BESAH 2:5

II:2:   As to water that was heated on a festival, and so too, water that was heated on the eve of the Sabbath for the Sabbath —

Rab and Samuel —

one of them said, "One may wash one's face, hands, and feet in such water" [T. Y. T. 2:10C].

The other said, "One may wash in such water his entire body, limb by limb." But we do not know who said this rule and who said that one.

YERUSHALMI BESAH 3:2

II:2:   R. Hiyya the Elder and R. Simeon b. Rabbi —

one said, "What comes from a gentile requires preparation [that is, designation for use on the festival day in advance of the festival day just as is the case with an Israelite]."

The other said, "What comes from a gentile does not require preparation [in advance of the festival day, that is, designation for use on the festival day]."

YERUSHALMI BESAH 3:4

II:2:   "A dam and its offspring" (Lev. 22:28) which fell into a pit —

R. Eliezer says, "One raises up the first with the plan of slaughtering it and does slaughter it and for the second one provides food while it is in its present location, so that it not die."

R. Joshua says, "One raises up the first one with the plan of slaughtering it but does not slaughter it, and practicing deception, one then raises up the second. "[If] he wanted to slaughter neither one of them, he has the right [to refrain]" [T. Y. T. 3:2].

YERUSHALMI BESAH 4:5

I:3:   Rab said, "They save food from burning on the oven by putting it on the stove [to let it simmer], but they do not take food from the stove and put it into the oven [for that same purpose]."

R. Abba bar Hannah said."They save food from burning on the oven by putting it on the stove. and the- also save food from burning on the stove by putting it into the oven, but the- do not do so in the even for the purposes of [eating the food] in the morning ."

R. Abun in the name of Rab: "They save food from burning on the oven by putting it on the stove; the- also save food from burning on the stove by putting it into the oven; and they do so in the evening for use in the morning. But they do not do so on the festival day for use on an ordinary day."

YERUSHALMI BESAH 5:6

I:1:   A spring between the Sabbath limits of two [communities] —

R. Yohanan said, "They make a partition of iron for it [to keep the water serving one side from intermingling with that serving the other side]."

R. Yosé b. Haninah said, "Even a partition of reeds [will do], so long as the water [up above] does not flow in both directions."

YERUSHALMI BESAH 5:7

I:1:   Rab and Samuel:

One of them said, "[In the case of someone who left a bailment of produce with someone else,] the produce is in the status of the one who left the bailment."

The other said, "It is in the status of the one with whom the bailment was left."

> The Mishnah differs from the view of him who said that the produce is in the status of the one with whom the produce was left, for we have learned: He whose pieces of fruit were located in another town, and the residents of that town prepared an erub so as to bring him some of his produce — they should not bring it to him [M. 5:7A-C]. Now if you say that the produce is in the status of the person with whom it was left, then the residents of the other town should be able to bring the produce to him.

VIII. TAANIT

YERUSHALMI TAANIT 2:12

I:4:   Both R. Haninah and R. Jonathan say, "The rules of the fasting scroll have been annulled."

Both R. Ba and R. Simon say, "The rules of the fasting scroll have been annulled."

R. Joshua b. Levi said, "The rules of the fasting scroll have been annulled."

> Said R. Yohanan, "Last night I was repeating the following: "There was a case in which they decreed a fast on Hanukkah in Lud, and they said concerning R. Eliezer that on that day he got a haircut [which is not to be done on a fast day]. "And concerning R. Joshua that he took a bath [also prohibited on a fast day]. [Thus Eliezer and Joshua maintain that it is forbidden to fast on Hanukkah, just as the fasting scroll says, and so the laws remain valid.] "Said to them R. Joshua, 'Go and carry out a fast, because you fasted on this day [Hanukkah, when it is forbidden]'" [T. Ta. 2:5]. "Now can you really say, therefore, that the laws of the fasting scroll have been annulled?" Said R. Ba, "And even if you maintain that the laws of the fasting scroll have been annulled, you cannot possibly say that the observance of Hanukkah and Purim has been annulled!"

IV

Propositional Form

Here we catalogue compositions that set forth free-standing propositions, not in relationship to the Mishnah. The form sustains two separate tasks: [1] collect and organize information in such a way as to convey a proposition; [2] set forth a proposition and demonstrate its validity through cases and arguments. The form requires a declarative sentence and sustains, also, probative complements thereto, ordinarily also in simple declarative sentences (or citations of verses of Scripture or passages of the Mishnah). I underline the proposition that I identify in each case.

I. BERAKHOT

I:12:   Rabbi says, "There are four watches [ashmorot] in the day and four watches in the night." The 'onah is one twenty-fourth of an hour. The 'et is one twenty-fourth of an 'onah. The rega' is one twenty-fourth of an 'et. [Tosefta 1:1H-J]. R. Nathan says, "There are three watches in the night. As it says, "At the beginning of the middle watch" [Judges 7:19]." [T.1:1.]

YERUSHALMI BERAKHOT 1:6

I:5   Bar Qappara said, "One who calls Abraham, Abram violates a positive commandment." R. Levi said, "[He violates both] a positive and a negative commandment." "And you shall not be called by your name Abram" [Gen. 17:5] [is the source of] the negative commandment. "And your name shall be Abraham" [ibid.] [is the source of] the positive commandment.

   a.   I:6: The same theme extended.

The next item does not set forth a proposition but invites one, that is, it sets forth choices one of which one may affirm. Here the form sustains a secondary argument, in place of the probative evidence for or against a given proposition.

YERUSHALMI BERAKHOT 6:1

I:10:   R. Zeriqin said, "R. Zeira posed this question: One who took lupine to eat and recited the blessing over it, and dropped it, [before eating it, when he goes to take another piece to eat] what does he do? Must he recite the blessing a second time before eating it [since it is a different piece]? How does this case differ from the case of one who drinks from a [flowing] channel of water [where the water over which he recites the blessing flows by and he then drinks other water]? [But these are different situations.] We may say there [in the case of one who drinks from a channel], he had in mind when he recited the blessing [that it should apply to the water which will flow down the stream]. But here [in the case of one who dropped the lupine over which he recited a blessing], he initially did not have in mind to eat another piece. [Accordingly he should recite the blessing again.]"

YERUSHALMI BERAKHOT 8:6

I:3:   Five things were said about [the glow of] a glowing coal, and five things about [the flame of] a torch. [In the following cases, the principle is that the flame of a torch is considered to be pure fire, without any material substance.] It is a sacrilege to use [the light of] a glowing coal belonging to the Temple, but it is neither [a matter of] any [forbidden] benefit nor a sacrilege to use the light of a torch of the Temple. (2) It is forbidden to use [the light of] a glowing coal used for idolatry. But it is permissible [to use the light of] a torch [used for idolatry]. (3) One who vows not to benefit from his associate, may not use [the light of] his glowing coals, but is permitted to use [the light of] his torch. (4) One who takes a glowing coal out to the public thoroughfare [on the Sabbath] is liable [for punishment]. But one who takes a torch out is free [from any liability]. (5) They may recite the blessing [for the light after the Sabbath] over a torch. But they may not recite the blessing over a glowing coal.

YERUSHALMI BERAKHOT 9:1

I:6-7:   The heretics asked R. Simlai, "How many gods created the world?" He said to them, "Why are you asking me? Go and ask Adam himself [i.e. look in the verse]. As it says, 'For ask now of the days that are past, [which were before you since the day that God created man upon the earth' [Deut. 4:32]. It is not written in the plural form,] 'That gods created man upon the earth,' but [in the singular form,] 'That God created man upon the earth'." They said to him, "Is it not written, 'In the beginning God ['lhym] created' [Gen. 1:1] [using what appears to be a plural noun — 'Gods']?" He said to them, "It is not written [plural] 'gods created,' but [singular] 'God created.'" Said R. Simlai, "In every instance that the heretics have raised a question [out of Scripture] the answer [to their question] is right beside it [in Scripture]." [The heretics] returned and asked him, "What is this which is written, 'Let us make man in our image, after our likeness' [Gen. 1:26]?" He said to them, "It does not say, 'The gods created [plural] man in their own images' [Gen. 1:27]. But it says, 'So God created [singular] man in his own image.'" His [Simlai's] students said to him, "You have deflected their question with a straw [i.e. a weak argument]. What will you answer us? [How will you explain this verse to us?]"

YERUSHALMI BERAKHOT 9:2

I:3:   Elijah [the prophet] of blessed memory asked R. Nehorai, "Why do earth-quakes occur?" He said to him, "On account of the sins of [those who do not separate] heave-offerings and tithes [from their produce]." One verse says, "[God protects the Land of Israel], the eyes of the Lord your God are always upon it" [Deut. 11:12]. And a second verse says, "[God] who looks upon the earth and it trembles, who touches the mountains and they smoke" [Ps. 104:32]. How can one reconcile these two verses? When Israel obeys God's will and properly separates tithes then, "The eyes of the Lord your God are always upon it, from the beginning of the year to the end of the year" [Deut. 11:12], and the Land cannot be damaged. But when Israel does not obey God's will, and does not properly separate tithes [from the produce of the earth], then he, "Looks upon the earth and it trembles" [Ps. 104:32]." [Elijah] said to him [Nehorai], "My son, on your life, what you say [about earthquakes] does make sense. But this is the main [reason that there are earthquakes]. When the Holy One, blessed be He, looks down on the theaters and circuses that sit secure, serene and peaceful [in Israel], and [he looks down] on the ruins of the Temple, he shakes the world to destroy it [and the earth trembles]. In this regard [the verse says], 'The Lord will roar from on high, and from his holy habitation utter his voice' [Jer. 25:30]. [It means he will roar] on account of [the destruction of] his Temple."

I:4:   Elijah of blessed memory asked R. Nehorai, "Why did God create insects and creeping things in his world?" He said to him, "They were created to serve a need. When God's creatures sin, he looks upon them and says, 'Lo, I sustain those creatures that serve no [useful] purpose, all the more must I sustain those creatures that serve some [useful] purpose [even though they sin].'" He [Elijah] said to him, "They serve other useful purposes: flies [may be crushed and used as ointment] for a wasp's sting; bed bugs [may be prepared in a potion to remove] a leech; lizards [may be made into an ointment] for sores; snails [may be used to treat] skin eruptions; spiders [may be used in an ointment to treat] a scorpion's bite."

YERUSHALMI BERAKHOT 9:5

I:2:   Let love motivate your actions and let fear motivate your actions. [How so?] Let love motivate your actions. And if you begin to despise [the commandments or Torah], recall that you love [God]. And one who loves [God] cannot despise [His commandments]. Let fear [also] motivate your actions. And if you begin to rebel [against God's commandments or To-rah], recall that you fear him. And one who fears does not rebel. There are seven kinds of pietists: The showy [pietist], the haughty [pietist], the bookkeeper [pietist], the parsimonious [pietist], the repaying [pietist], the fearing [pietist], the loving [pietist]. The "showy [pietist]" carries his good deeds on his shoulder [to show them off]. The "haughty [pietist]" says, "Wait for me. I am [busy using my time] to fulfill the commandments! [I have no time for you.]" The "bookkeeper [pietist]" pays off each debt [i.e. sin] by performing a commandment [good deed]. The "parsimonious [pietist]" says, "From the little I have, what can I set aside for performing commandments?" The "repaying [pietist]" says, "Tell me what sin I have committed and I will perform a commandment to offset it." [These five types are negative, pompous, ostentatious models.] The "fearing" [pietist emulates] Job. The "loving" [pietist emulates] Abraham. And none is more beloved of God than the "loving" [pietist who emulates] Abraham.

YERUSHALMI BERAKHOT 9:5

V:1:   Said R. Joshua of the South, "In three instances a decree was issued by an earthly court and the heavenly court confirmed it. And they are (1) [the decree concerning] the ban on using the property of Jericho [that it either go to the treasury of the Lord, or be destroyed, cf. Joshua 6:18-19]; (2) [the decree concerning the obligation to read on Purim] the scroll of Esther; (3) [the decree to] greet one's fellow with God's name. The ban on using the property of Jericho [was confirmed by God and the Heavenly court, as the verse says,] "Israel has sinned" (Joshua 9:11). [They took from the property which God forbade them.] Was it not Joshua who issued the decree? The verse teaches that the heavenly court confirmed their decree. The [obligation to read] the scroll of Esther [was confirmed by God and the Heavenly court as its says,] "The Jews ordained and they accepted" (Esther 9:27).

II. SHABBAT

Here is a great example of a proposition set forth and then systematically expanded, following a clear formal program. I include further developments of the same construction, indented, to show the care with which the whole is expressed.

III:2:   There are four domains so far as the Sabbath is concerned: private domain, public domain, neutral domain, and closed alleyways [a place of non-liability]. What is private domain? A ditch ten [handbreadths] deep and four wide, and so too: a mound ten handbreadths high and four wide — this constitutes absolutely private domain. What is [PT: "absolutely"] public domain? A high road or a [large] public square, [PT: "and a desert"] and open alleyways [which open out at both ends] — [Tosefta:] this constitutes absolutely public domain. They do not transport an object from private domain into public domain, and they do not transport an object from public domain into private domain. And if one transported an object out, or brought an object in, advertently, he is liable for a sin offering. [If he did so] deliberately, he is subject to the punishment of extirpation, or he is stoned. The same rules apply to the one who takes out and the one who brings in, the one who stretches [something] out, and the one who throws [something] in — [Tosefta: in all such cases,] he is liable. But the sea, a valley, a colonnade, and a threshold (karmelit) ground are neither private domain nor public domain.[On the Sabbath] they do not carry out of, or put [things] into, such places. But if one carried out or put [something] into [such a place], he is exempt [from punishment] [T. Shab. 1:1-4C].

III:3: As to the meaning of the word for neutral domain, karmelit, R. Hiyya taught, "It follows the meaning of barley [karmel] which is tender (RK) and fully ripened (ML'). It is not green or dried up but middling. Here too, it is not public domain nor private domain but neutral domain (karmelit)."

III:4: What is the definition of neutral domain [in the present context]? R. Yosé in the name of R. Yohanan: "It would be, for example, typified by the store of Bar Yustini" [which apparently was fully within the colonnade and not separated off by partitions].

III:5: [In the case of] a courtyard belonging to public domain, with blind alleyways [which do not open out], [if] they prepared an erub, they are permitted [to carry across the boundaries from one domain to the other]. [If] they did not prepare an erub, they are prohibited [from doing so] [T. Shab. 1:5].

III:6: And said R. Yosé, "The threshold of which they spoke [in the earlier passages] is one which is four handbreadths broad and is not ten high." If you say it is ten high and four broad, it constitutes a domain unto itself. If you say it is ten high but not four broad, then you deal with that of which R. Hisda spoke in the name of Assi: "A reed stuck into the ground in public domain, ten handbreadths high — it is permitted [to take objects out of that reed and utilize them in public domain, or vice versa, since it is not a domain unto itself but part of public domain]. But that is on condition that one not exchange positions [by standing in an exempt area and take something from private domain and hand it on to public domain, by reason of his standing in a neutral

area]." [So what case can be at hand at A?]
Rather, the threshold with which we deal is
one which is not four handbreadths broad or
ten high [so as not to go over the ground of
A].

III. ERUBIN

YERUSHALMI ERUBIN 1:8

I:2:   [With reference to M. Kil. 4:4: If the three handbreadths, which would
suffice for a kid to enter, it is deemed a valid partition. If a fence was
breached for a space of ten cubits, such may be deemed an entrance (= M.
1:8E). If it is wider than this, it is forbidden to sow opposite the breach. If
many breaches were made in the fence, yet what is yet standing is greater
than the area that is broken down, it is permitted to sow opposite the
breach; if the broken-down part is broader than the standing part, it is
forbidden:] You turn out to rule as follows: As to mixed seeds in a vineyard [in which a fence must be erected to keep distinct the patches of a
field sown in different seeds], if there is a breach less than three handbreadths, it is as if it were closed up. If the breach were from three to four
handbreadths, if the standing part of the fence is greater than the broken-
down part of the fence, it is permitted [to sow seeds by the breach, as if it
were a fully valid fence], and if the breaches were greater than the standing part of the fence, it is forbidden. If the breaches were from four to ten
handbreadths, if the standing part of the fence was greater than the broken-down part, it is permitted [to sow opposite the breaches]. If the broken-down part is greater than the standing part, then opposite the standing part of the fence it is permitted to sow [seeds of a different sort from
what is on the other side of the fence], and in the area opposite the breach,
it is forbidden. If it is greater than ten handbreadths, even though the
standing part of the fence is greater than the broken-down part of the
fence, while it is permitted to sow opposite the standing part of the fence,
it is forbidden to sow opposite the broken-down part of the fence.

IV. YOMA

I find nothing pertinent.

V. PESAHIM

YERUSHALMI PESAHIM 5:5

I:1:   Jacob bar Aha [said] in the name of R. Yosé, "Power was given to Moses'
voice, "and his voice traveled throughout the land of Egypt, the distance
of a forty-days journey. "And what did [it] say? 'From place x to place y
[makes up] one group. And from place y to place [makes up] one group.'
"And do not be surprised [that Moses' voice could travel so far]. For if
[concerning] dust, the nature of which is not to travel, you [Scripture]
said, 'and it shall become a fine dust all over the land of Egypt' (Exod.

9:9), a voice, the nature of which is to travel, is it not [the case] all the more so?" Said R. Levi, "Just as power was given to Moses' voice, so [it] was given to Pharaoh's voice, "and his voice traveled throughout the land of Egypt the distance of a forty-days journey. "And what did [it] say, "'Up, depart from among my people you and the Israelites with you! Go worship the Lord" (Exod. 12:31). [n the past you were the servants of Pharaoh; from now on you are the servants of the Lord." "At that very moment [the Israelites in response] said, "'Hallelujah. Give praise, O servants of the Lord" (Ps. 113) and not the servants of Pharaoh.'"

VI. SUKKAH

In this tractate find nothing that fits into this category.

VII. BESAH

YERUSHALMI BESAH 5:5

I:1:   Five rules did they state concerning a burning coal and five concerning a flame: A burning coal belonging to the sanctuary is subject to the laws of sacrilege. But a flame is neither available for common use nor subject to the laws of sacrilege [if it is subjected to common use] [M. 5:5C-D]. A burning coal belonging to an idol [worshipper] is prohibited, but a flame is permitted. He who takes out a burning coal to the public domain [on the Sabbath] is liable, [but if he takes out] a flame, he is exempt [M. S:5E-F]. He who is prohibited by vow from deriving benefit from his fellow is prohibited from using his burning coal, but permitted to make use of a flame belonging to him. And they say a blessing over a flame [on Saturday night in the Habdalah], but they do not say a blessing over a burning coal [T. Y. T. 4:7].

VIII. TAANIT

The classification of the following collection of stories executed through dialogue is not self-evident, since the group is assembled to make a point, and the stories serve to demonstrate a proposition that is not fully spelled out, which is that the merit of self-sacrifice — love that cannot be coerced but that compels a response — takes priority over merit attained in any other way, even through Torah-study. On that basis, I classify the set of stories, told through dialogue but authentic in the tensions and resolutions that they work out, as a propositional composite.

YERUSHALMI TAANIT 1:4

I:2:   A certain man came before one of the relatives of R. Yannai. He said to him, "Rabbi, attain merit through me [by giving me charity]." He said to him, "And didn't your father leave you money?" He said to him, "No." He said to him, "Go and collect what your father left in deposit with others." He said to him, "I have heard concerning property my father deposited with others that it was gained unlawfully [so I don't want it]." He said to him, "You are worthy of praying and having your prayers answered." A certain ass-driver appeared before the rabbis [in a dream] and prayed, and rain came. The rabbis sent and brought him and said to him, "What is your trade?" He said to them, "I am an ass-driver." They said to him, "What good deed have you done?" He said to them, "One time I rented my ass to a certain woman, and she was weeping on the way, and I said to her, 'What troubles you?' She said to me, 'The husband of that woman [me] is in prison [for debt], and I wanted to see what I can do to free him.' So I sold my ass and I gave her the proceeds, and I said to her, 'Here is your money, free your husband, but do not sin [by becoming a prostitute to raise the necessary funds].'" They said to him, "You are worthy of praying and having your prayers answered."

I:3:   In a dream that appeared to R. Abbahu Mr. Pentakaka ["Five sins"] prayed that rain would come, and it rained. R. Abbahu summoned him. He said to him, "What is your trade?" He said to him, "Five sins does that man [I] do every day, hiring whores, cleaning up the theater, bringing home their garments for washing, dancing, and banging cymbals before them." He said to him, "And what good deed have you done?" He said to him, "One day that man [I] was cleaning the theater, and a woman came and stood behind a pillar and cried. I said to her, 'What troubles you?' And she said to me, 'That woman's [my] husband is in prison, and I wanted to see what I can do to free him,' so I sold my bed and cover, and I gave the proceeds to her. I said to her, 'Here is your money, free your husband, but do not sin.'" He said to him, "You are worthy of praying and having your prayers answered."

YERUSHALMI TAANIT 3:3]

I:2:   It is for four reasons that rain comes from above [rather than depending on water rising up from the nethermost water, or having people rely upon irrigation from wells]: It is because of high-handed men [who would divert the current of irrigation ditches and invade others' riparian rights]. It is because of noxious mist. It is so that the one above will drink water as does the one below. And it is so that all will look to heaven. I:3: It is because of the merit of three parties that rain falls: It is because of the merit of the land, the merit of steadfast loyalty, and the merit of suffering. And all three derive from a single verse of Scripture: "Whether for correction, or for his land, or for love ['kindness'], he causes it to happen" (Job 37:13). I:4: On account of four sorts of sin are rains withheld: Because of the sins of idolatry, fornication, and murder, and because of people who pledge charity in public but do not hand over the money. How do we know that it is because of the sin of idolatry? "Take heed lest your heart be deceived, and you turn aside and serve other gods and worship them" (Deut. 11:16). What is written thereafter? "And the anger of the Lord be kindled against you, and he shut up the heavens, so that there be no rain, [and the land yield no fruit, and you perish quickly off the good land which the Lord gives you]" (Deut. 11:17). How do we know that it is because of the sin of fornication? '[Lift up your eyes to the bare heights, and see! Where have you not been lain with? By the waysides you have sat awaiting lovers like an Arab in the wilderness.] You have polluted the land with your vile harlotry" (Jer. 3:2).

I:5:   Mist is called by five names: thick, destruction, meek, prince, and storm. Whence do we know that it is called "mist?" "But a mist went up from the earth and watered the whole face of the ground" (Gen. 2:6). "Thick"— because it thickens [and darkens the sky:] "[And the Lord said to Moses], 'Lo, I am coming to you in a thick cloud, [that the people may hear when I speak with you and may also believe you forever.' Then Moses told the words of the people to the Lord]" (Ex. 19:9). "Meek"— because it makes people meek toward one another [when they fast]. "Prince"— because it makes householders into princes: "He it is who makes the clouds [the Hebrew word for clouds can also mean 'princes'] rise at the end of the earth, who makes lightnings for the rain and brings forth the wind from his store houses" (Ps. 135:7). "Storm" — because it turns the firmament into storm clouds: "[Ask rain from the Lord in the season of the spring rain], from the Lord who makes the storm clouds, [who gives men showers of rain, to every one the vegetation in the field]" (Zech. 10:1).

V

Topical Composites

A topical composite collects miscellaneous compositions on a given theme; no clear proposition is demonstrated through the collection, and I discern no form that dictates the way in which the writing is carried out. I list these items simply to allow for a systematic account of the Yerushalmi's program of writing, not all components of which utilize patterned prose.

I. BERAKHOT

YERUSHALMI BERAKHOT 2:2

FREE-STANDING COMPOSITE ON THE WEARING OF TEFILLIN

II:1:   R. Hiyya in the name of R. Yohanan, "Why did they say, 'A person should put on tefillin, then recite the Shema', then pray'? So that he may accept the yoke of the kingdom of heaven completely [i.e. he recites the Shema' while wearing the tefillin which contain the verses of the Shema' on a parchment.]" Rab said, "One recites the Shema', and then puts on his tefillin, and then prays [reciting the eighteen blessings]."

II:2:   Said R. Yannai, "[One who wears] tefillin must have a clean body." Why did they not make a presumption concerning them [that one may trust any person who wears tefillin that he keeps the commandments, such as the laws of cleanness]? Because of the impostors. [Some people put on tefillin as a ruse to deceive their fellows as in the following story:] One time a person entrusted an article to his fellow [to watch for him]. And later he denied [having received it]. He said to him, "It was not you that I trusted [when I gave you the article]. I trusted the [tefillin] upon your head." [I thought that it was a sign that you were trustworthy. I was misled.]

II:3:   In what way does one recite the blessings over them [the tefillin]?

II:4:   We learned there, Women and slaves [and minors] are exempt from [the obligations of] the recitation of the Shema' and [wearing] tefillin [M. 3:3 A]. Whence [do we learn the exemption for] women? "And you shall teach them to your sons" [Deut. 11:19] and not to your daughters. Whoever is obligated [to perform the commandment] to study Torah is obli-

---

215

gated [to perform the commandment] to wear tefillin. Women who are not obligated to study Torah, are not obligated to wear tefillin.

II:5:   We learned: One who enters a bath house, [when he stands] in a place where people stand dressed, he may recite the Shema' or Prayer (Y. has the reading 'wear tefillin') there, and it goes without saying that he may extend a greeting there. He may put on his tefillin and it goes without saying that he need not remove them [if he enters wearing them]. [When he stands] in a place where most people stand naked, one may not extend a greeting, and it goes without saying that he may not recite the Shema' or Prayer there. And he must remove his tefillin, and it goes without saying that he may not put them on. [When he stands] in a place where some stand naked and some stand dressed, one may extend a greeting and one may not recite the Shema' or Prayer. And one need not remove his tefillin, but he may not put them on. [T. 2:20.]

II:6:   R. Jeremiah posed a question before R. Zeira, "If a bath house is used for bathing in the summer months but not in the winter months [does it have the status of a bath house in the winter with respect to the recitation of the Shema' and the Prayer and wearing the tefillin?]"

II:7:   R. Zeira in the name of R. Abba bar Jeremiah, "[While wearing tefillin] one may eat a snack but not a regular meal, and one may take a nap but not a regular sleep."

II:8:   R. Zeira in the name of R. Abba bar Jeremiah, "A person should not enter a cemetery and relieve himself there. But concerning one who did so Scripture says, 'He who mocks the poor [i.e. the dead] insults his Maker' [Prov. 17:5]."

II:9:   [The unit first cites three traditions of R. Idi, then deals with the subject of prayer.] [A scribe] who connected two letters together [in a scroll] — there is one opinion that it is valid, and there is another opinion that it is invalid. R. Idi in the name of R. Simeon in the name of R. Yohanan [says there is no dispute]. The ruling which says it is valid [refers to a case of one who connected them together] at the bottom. And the ruling which says it is not valid [refers to a case of one who connected them together] at the top. For example: two words [whose last two letters are connected together at the bottom, we would say that it is valid. And if they were connected at the top it should be judged invalid.] But in the case of two words [whose last two letters were connected at the center, in such a case] we have a doubt [whether or not the scroll is valid]. R. Idi b. R. Simeon in the name of R. Yohanan [L: Yosa], "A person should not stand on a high place and pray." What is the Scriptural basis for this? Said R. Abba b. R. Papi, "Out of the depths I cry to thee, O Lord [Ps. 130:1]." Said R. Idi b. R. Simeon in the name of R. Yohanan, "A person should not stand up to pray if he needs to relieve himself." What is the Scriptural basis for this? "Prepare to meet your God, O Israel [Amos 4:12]."

YERUSHALMI BERAKHOT 3:1
TOPICAL COMPOSITE ON THE PRIEST AND UNCLEANNESS RULES

6. I:6: May a priest render himself unclean [by coming into proximity or contact with a corpse, by participating in his teacher's funeral] out of honor to his master? May a priest render himself unclean in order to honor [i.e. study] the Torah?

7. I:7: It was taught: A priest is permitted to go out of the Land of Israel, and thereby render himself unclean, for monetary judgments, for capital judgments, for sanctifying the new moon, for intercalating the year, and to save a field from seizure by a gentile. And he may go out even with a claim to contest [the seizure]. [The principle is that all lands outside of Israel are unclean with a form of uncleanness decreed by the rabbis.] [And a priest may leave Israel] to study Torah and to get married. R. Judah says, "If he has somewhere to study [in Israel] he may not render himself unclean [by leaving the Land]." R. Yosé says, "Even if he [the priest] has somewhere to study [in Israel], he may render himself unclean [and leave Israel to study]. For one may not be worthy enough to learn from all persons. [He may need a different teacher.]" They said concerning Joseph the priest that he used to go out and defile himself [by leaving the Land of Israel] to follow his teacher to Sidon. But they said: a priest should not leave the Land of Israel [to get married on the chance that he may find a wife. He may leave] only if he was promised a bride [in a place outside of the Land of Israel] [T. A.Z. 1:8-9].

8. I:8: May a priest render himself unclean in order to recite the priestly blessing [in a synagogue in which there is uncleanness]? May a priest render himself unclean in honor of a patriarch [by attending his funeral]? May a priest render himself unclean in order to honor his father or mother [in their lifetime, e.g. to visit them outside the Land of Israel]? May a priest render himself unclean for the public honor?

II. SHABBAT
I find no examples of topical composites.

III. ERUBIN
This tractate presents no examples of topical composites.

IV. YOMA
I find nothing that pertains.

V. PESAHIM
I find nothing relevant.

VI. SUKKAH
In this tractate find nothing that fits into this category.

VII. BESAH

VIII. TAANIT

YERUSHALMI TAANIT 1:1

COMPOSITE ON THE EVILS OF GOSSIP

II:3:   A certain man would sin with his tongue [as a rumor monger]. He came
         before R. Yohanan, who sent him to R. Haninah. He said to him, "Go,
         repent, and study the learning of Torah, for it is written, 'A gentle tongue
         is a tree of life [but perverseness in it breaks the spirit]'" (Prov. 15:4).

II:4:   Said R. Haninah son of R. Abbahu, "In the book of R. Meir they found
         that it was written, 'The oracle concerning Dumah, [that is,] the oracle
         concerning Rome. One is calling to me from Seir [Watchman, what of the
         night? Watchman, what of the night?]'" (Is. 21:11). Said R. Yohanan,
         "One is calling to me because of Seir." Said R. Simeon b. Laqish, "'To
         me.' From whence will there be a match for me? 'From Seir.'" Said R.
         Joshua b. Levi, "If someone should say to you, 'Where is your God,' say
         to him, 'He is in a great city in Edom [V.: in Rome].' What is the scrip-
         tural basis for this view? 'One is calling to me from Seir'" (Is. 21:11).

II:5:   It has been taught by R. Simeon b. Yohai, "To every place to which the
         Israelites went into exile, the presence of God went with them into exile.
         "They were sent into exile to Egypt, and the presence of God went into
         exile with them. What is the scriptural basis for this claim? '[And there
         came a man of God to Eli, and said to him, Thus the Lord has said], I
         revealed myself to the house of your father when they were in Egypt
         subject to the house of Pharaoh' (I Sam. 2:27). "They were sent into exile
         to Babylonia, and the presence of God went into exile with them. What is
         the scriptural basis for this claim? '[Thus says the Lord, your Redeemer,
         the Holy One of Israel]: For your sake I will send to Babylon [and break
         down all the bars, and the shouting of the Chaldeans will be turned to
         lamentations]' (Is. 43:14). "They were sent into exile into Media, and the
         presence of God went into exile with them. What is the scriptural basis
         for this claim? 'And I will set my throne in Elam [and destroy their king
         and princes, says the Lord]' (Jer. 49:38). And Elam means only Media, as
         it is said, '[And I saw in the vision; and when I saw], I was in Susa the
         capital, which is in the province of Elam; [and I saw in the vision, and I
         was at the river Ulai]' (Dan. 8:2). "They went into exile to Greece, and
         the presence of God went into exile with them. What is the scriptural
         basis for this claim? '[For I have bent Judah as my bow; I have made
         Ephraim its arrow]. I will brandish your sons, O Zion, over your sons, O
         Greece, [and wield you like a warrior's sword]' (Zech. 9:13). "They went
         into exile to Rome, and the presence of God went into exile with them.
         What is the scriptural basis for this claim? '[The oracle concerning
         Dumah]. One is calling to me from Seir, "Watchman, what of the night?
         Watchman, what of the night?" Is. 21:11).'"

YERUSHALMI TAANIT 2:1

COMPOSITE ON PRAYER, CHARITY, AND TRUE REPENTANCE

III:5: Said R. Eleazar, "Three acts nullify the harsh decree, and these are they: prayer, charity, and repentance." And all three of them are to be derived from a single verse of Scripture: "If my people who are called by my name humble themselves, [pray and seek my face, and turn from their wicked ways, then I will hear from heaven and will forgive their sin and heal their land]" (2 Chron. 7:14). "Pray"— this refers to prayer. "And seek my face"— this refers to charity, as you say, "As for me, I shall behold thy face in righteousness; when I awake, I shall be satisfied with beholding thy form"] (Ps. 17:15). "And turn from their wicked ways"— this refers to repentance.

III:6: Said R. Eleazar, "'Is such the fast that I choose, a day for a man to humble himself? [Is it to bow down his head like a rush, and to spread sackcloth and ashes under him? Will you call this a fast and a day acceptable to the Lord?]' (Is. 58:5). This is not the [kind of] fast that I desire.'" What kind of fast do I desire? "'Is not this the fast that I choose: to loose the bonds of wickedness, to undo the thongs of the yoke, to let the oppressed go free, and to break every yoke? Is it not to share your bread with the hungry and bring the homeless poor into your house; [when you see the naked, to cover him, and not to hide yourself from your own flesh (Is. 58:6- 7)]?' 'What is written thereafter? "'That when you call, the Lord will answer; when you cry, He will say: Here I am . . . (Is. 58:8).'"

III:7: It is written, "Rend your hearts and not your garments. Return to the Lord, your God, for he is gracious and merciful, [slow to anger and abounding in steadfast love, and repents of evil" (Joel 2:13). Said R. Joshua b. Levi, "If you tear your hearts in repentance, you will not tear your garments as a sign of mourning either for your sons or for your daughters." But: "[Return] to the Lord your God." Why? "For he is gracious and merciful, slow to anger ['long in acts of patience'] and abounding in steadfast love, and repents of evil" (Joel 2:13).

III:8: It has been taught in the name of R. Meir: "'For behold, the Lord is coming forth out of his place [to punish the inhabitants of the earth for their iniquity, and the earth will disclose the blood shed upon her and will no more cover her slain]' (Is. 26:21). "He goes forth from one attribute to another. He leaves the attribute of justice for the attribute of having mercy for Israel." It is written, "God is not man, that he should lie, [or a son of man, that he should repent. Has he said, and will he not do it? Or has he spoken and will he not fulfil it?]" (Num. 23:19). Samuel bar Nahman and rabbis: R. Samuel bar Nahman said, "When the Holy One, blessed be He, plans to do good, 'God is not man, that he should lie.' "If he plans to do evil, in that case Scripture has said, 'Has He said, and will he not do it? Or has He spoken, and will He not fulfil it?'" Rabbis say, "'He is not man,' that he should treat the words of God as if they were not." "O Lord, why does thy wrath burn hot against thy people" (Ex. 32:11). "Or a son of man, that he should repent" (Num. 23:19).

YERUSHALMI TAANIT 4:5
COMPOSITE ON THE SUFFERING IN THE WAR AGAINST ROME

VII:3:   There were two brothers in Kefar Haroba. The Romans at tacked [the village] and killed the people. They said, "To end the matter, let us bring a crown for their heads." They said, "Let us try one more time." They went forth [to attack the Romans again]. An old man met them and said to them, "May your Creator be your help!" [One of the brothers] said to him, "May he not help nor support us: 'Has thou not rejected us, O God! [Thou dost not go forth, O God, with our armies]'" (Ps. 60:10).

VII:4:   There were two cedars on the .Mount of Olives. Under one of them there were four stalls, selling food preserved in a condition of cultic cleanness [to be eaten in Jerusalem]. And from one they would produce forty *seahs'* weight of pigeons a month, and from these they would provide bird offerings for all of Israel. [From] Simeon's Gate they would put forth 300 barrels of thin cakes among the poor every Sabbath eve. Then why was it destroyed? There is he who says, "It was because of fornication." There is he who says, "It was because they would play ball [waste their time, instead of studying Torah]."

VII:5:   Said R. Yohanan, "Eighty thousand apprentice priests were killed because of the shedding of the blood of Zechariah." R. Yudan asked R. Aha, "Where did they kill Zechariah, in the Women's Court or in the Israelites' Court?" He said to him, "It was neither in the Women's Court nor in the Israelites' Court, but in the courtyard reserved for the priests." And they did not treat his blood either as one does with the blood of a ram or as one does with the blood of a deer. There it is written, "[Any man also of the people of Israel, or of the strangers that sojourn among them, who takes in hunting any beast or bird that may be eaten] shall pour out its blood and cover it with dust" (Lev. 17:13). But here it is written, "For the blood she has shed is still in the midst of her; she put it on the bare rock, [she did not pour it upon the ground to cover it with dust]" (Ezek. 24:7). And why? "To rouse my wrath, to take vengeance, I have set on the bare rock the blood she has shed, that it may not be covered" (Ezek. 24:8). Seven sins did the Israelites commit on that day. They killed priest, prophet, and judge. They spilled innocent blood. They contaminated the courtyard. And it was a Sabbath that coincided with the Day of Atonement as well. Now when Nebuzaradan came here, he saw the blood bubbling up. He said to them, "What is this?" They said to him, "It is the blood of the bullocks, sheep, And rams that we offer on the altar." Forthwith he brought bullocks, rams, and sheep and slaughtered them on it, and still the blood was bubbling up. Since they did not confess to him. he [ordered them] suspended on the gallows [for torture]. They said, "It appears that the Holy One, blessed be he, wants to escape from our hand vengeance for his blood." They said to him." It is the blood of a priest, prophet, and judge, who prophesied against us concerning everything that you are now doing to us, and we rose up against him and killed him." Forthwith he brought 80,000 appearance priests and slaughtered them on it, and still the blood bubbled up. At that moment he grew angry [at the blood], saying to it, "What to you want? Should we destroy your entire nation on your account?"

VII:6: Said R. Yohanan, "Eighty thousand apprentice priests fled to the stoves of the Temple, and they were burned up. "And of them all there survived only Joshua b. Yehosedeq, the high priest. ' This is in line with that which is said. '[And the Lord said to Satan, "The Lord rebuke you, O Satan! The Lord who has chosen Jerusalem rebuke you! ' Is not this a brand plucked from the fire?'" (Zech. 3:2). Said R. Yohanan, "Eighty thousand apprentice priests fled to the army of Nebuchadnezzar and they [went] to the Ishmaelites. "They said to them. Give us something to drink, because we are thirsty. ' "They brought them salty things and skins that were blown up with air. "They said to them, 'Eat and drink.' "When one of them opened a skin and put it to his mouth, the air that was in it burst forth and choked him, "That is in line with what is written, 'The oracle concerning Arabia. In the thickets in Arabia you will lodge, O caravans of Dedanites. To the thirsty bring water, meet the fugitive with bread, O inhabitants of the land of Tema'" (Is. 21:13-14). "The oracle concerning Arabia — 'A great burden is on Arabia.' "In the thickets of Lebanon"— those who were located in the "forest of Lebanon" [the Temple] now are in 'the thickets of Arabia.'" "Caravans of Dedanites"— is this the way for cousins to act? For when Ishmael was thirsty was, 'To the thirsty bring water' not the case? [For so it says]: "Then God opened her eyes, and she saw a well of water; [and she went, and filled the skin with water, and gave the lad a drink]" (Gen. 21:19). It was not because of your goodness that they came to you." For they have fled from the swords (Is. 21:15)." "From the drawn sword" (Is. 21:15) — since they did not want to keep the years of release.

VII:7: Said R. Yohanan, "Between Gabbath and Antipatris there were sixty myriads of townships. The smallest among them was Beth Shemesh. As it is written: 'And he slew some of the men of Bethshemesh, because they looked into the ark of the Lord; [he slow seventy men of them, and the people mourned because the Lord had made a great slaughter among the people]' (I Sam. 6:19). And these were in only one direction. And now if you tried to stick sixty myriads of reeds there, it would not hold them."

VII:8:   Said R. Zeirah, "Come and take note of how the land of Israel is impudent, that it continues to produce crops [even though so much of the land has been destroyed through fire and brimstone]."

VII:9:   It was taught: R. Yosé says, "For fifty-two years no bird appeared in flight in the land of Israel."

VII:10: Said R. Hanina, "Forty years before the Israelites went into exile to Babylonia, they planted date palms in Babylonia, since they wanted to have something sweet, for that prepares the tongue to study Torah. [B] Said R. Hanina, son of R. Abbahu, "Seven hundred species of clean fish, eight hundred species of clean locusts, and fowl without number, all went into exile with the Israelites to Babylonia. "And when they came back, all of them came back with them, except for the fish called, 'Shibuta.'"

VI

Narratives

Narratives exhibit no patterning of language that I can discern, but do sustain classification; when grouped, each set shows certain traits in common. The groups tend, also, to divide by the function carried out within the larger construction by a given sort of narrative. In general three main groups emerge: narratives about sages, which bear a moral or, more commonly, illustrate a law; parables; and authentic stories, with a beginning, middle, and end, a point of conflict and resolution. A large proportion of the Yerushalmi's narratives is devoted to exemplary precedents in the law and exemplary incidents in the lives of sages. I find surprising the rather modest proportion of the whole contributed by parables, which play a much more critical part in the narratives of the Aggadic sector than they do here.

I. BERAKHOT

The following group illustrates virtue as embodied in sages' words and deeds:

YERUSHALMI BERAKHOT 2:8

I:3:   [The young] Kahana was a prodigy [in rabbinic learning]. [According to legend R. Yohanan caused Kahana to die. Yohanan then prayed and he was resurrected.] When he arrived here [in the Land of Israel], a scoffer saw him and said to him, "What did you hear up in heaven?" He said to him, "Your fate is sealed." And so it was. He died. Another [scoffer] met him and said, "What did you hear up in heaven?" He said to him, "Your fate is sealed." And so it was. He [Kahana] said, "What is this? I came here to [gain] merit [and study Torah]. And now I have sinned. Did I come here to kill the inhabitants of the Land of Israel? I must go back to whence I came."

YERUSHALMI BERAKHOT 4:1

I:3:   R. Abba bar Zabedi used to pray [reciting the Eighteen Blessings] in a loud voice.

YERUSHALMI BERAKHOT 4:1

II:2:   R. Yosé b. Haninah used to recite [the Afternoon] Prayer at sunset, so that he would be in fear of heaven all the day long. Said R. Yosé b. Haninah, "May my lot be cast with those who recite their prayers at sunset." What is the Scriptural basis [for this practice]? "Therefore, let everyone who is worthy offer prayers to thee; at a time they are pressed" [Ps. 32:6]. What is a time they are pressed [msw']? A time in the day [when people] are pressed [i.e. at the end of the day — mswyw sl ywm, lit. the squeezing of the day — a word play]. [We follow S.H. here. P.M. interprets differently.]

The distinction between the foregoing narratives and an authentic story, with a beginning, middle, and end, provoked by tension and concluded with a resolution thereof is illustrated by the following exceptionally-well-crafted story.

YERUSHALMI BERAKHOT 4:1

II:8:   Once a student came and asked R. Joshua, "What is the rule concerning the Evening Prayer?" He said to him, "It is optional." He came and asked Rabban Gamaliel, "What is the rule concerning the Evening Prayer?" He said to him, "It is compulsory." He said to him, "But behold, R. Joshua told me that it is optional." He said to him, "Tomorrow, when I enter the meeting house, stand and ask me concerning this law." The next day this student stood up and asked Rabban Gamaliel, "What is the rule concerning the Evening Prayer?" He said to him, "It is compulsory." He said to him, "But lo, R. Joshua told me it is optional." Said Rabban Gamaliel to R. Joshua, "Are you the one who said it is optional?" He said to him, "No." He said to him, "Stand on your feet and they will testify [that you said it]." And Rabban Gamaliel sat and expounded, and R. Joshua stood [in disgrace] until the people cried out. And they said to R. Huspit the Meturgaman, "Dismiss the people." And they said to R. Zenon the Hazzan, "Begin saying." He began to say. The people began. And they stood up and they said to him [Gamaliel], "For upon whom has not come your unceasing evil [Nahum 3:19]?" They [deposed Gamaliel and] appointed R. Eleazar ben Azariah to [head] the Academy. He was sixteen years old and all his hair had turned grey. And R. Aqiba sat, troubled [that he had not been selected]. And he said [concerning Eleazar], "It is not that he is more learned in Torah than I. Rather he is of greater parentage than I. Happy is the person who has ancestral merit! Happy is the person who has a 'peg' to hang upon!" Rabban Gamaliel immediately went to each one's house to appease him. He went to Joshua. *He found him sitting and making needles. He said to him, "Is this how you make a living?" He said to him, "Are you finally finding out [how hard it is for us to make a living]?* Woe to the generation of which you are the steward." He [Gamaliel] said, "I submit to you." And they sent a fuller to R. Eleazar b.

Azariah [to inform him of the reconciliation]. *And some say it was R. Aqiba.* He said to him [Eleazar], "He who is [a priest authorized] to sprinkle [the water of purification], the son of one who sprinkles, let him sprinkle. He who is neither [a priest authorized] to sprinkle, nor the son of a sprinkler, shall he [have the authority] to say to one who sprinkles, who is the son of one who sprinkles, '[You are unfit for your duties.] Your water is water from a cave, and your ashes are from wood'?" [Shall you, Eleazar, have the authority to replace Gamaliel, the legitimate heir to the patriarchate?] He [Eleazar] said to him, "You have appeased me. Let us go to Rabban Gamaliel's door [and inform him]." Even so they did not depose him [Eleazar] from his high position. Rather they appointed him Chief Judge.

Here, by contrast, narrative simply supplies a setting for a teaching.

YERUSHALMI BERAKHOT 5:1

I:7:   The ancient saints used to tarry for a while, pray a while, and tarry a while after their Prayer. When did they [have time to] study Torah? When did they [have time to] do their work? Said R. Isaac b. R. Eleazar, "Because they were saints, their Torah-study was blessed, and their work was blessed, [and they were able to complete them expeditiously]."

YERUSHALMI BERAKHOT 5:1

II:2:   R. Haninah and R. Joshua b. Levi went before the proconsul of Caesarea. When he saw them he stood up. They [his courtiers] said to him, "Why do you stand up for these Jews?" He said to them, "I saw in them the faces of angels."

Miracle-stories do not undertake ambitious accounts but are stripped down to the bare minimum of detail.

YERUSHALMI BERAKHOT 5:5

I:2:   Once Rabban Gamaliel's son fell ill and he sent two students to R. Haninah b. Dosa in his town [to find out from him what his son's fate would be]. He [Haninah] said to them [the students], "Wait for me while I go up to the attic [to pray]." He went up to the attic, came down, and said to them, "I am certain that Rabban Gamaliel's son has recovered from his illness." [The students] made note [of the time of day that this happened]. [Later they confirmed that] at that very moment [back in Gamaliel's town, his son recovered] and asked for food.

Here narrative provides a setting for a legal-analytical discussion.

YERUSHALMI BERAKHOT 6:2

I:3:   Judah in the name of Abba bar bar Hannah, "Bar Qappara and two of his students once stayed over with a certain householder at an inn in the village of Birkata. He brought before them chicken, and plums, and leeks [porret]. "They said 'If we recite the blessing over the leeks, we will exempt [ourselves from the obligation to recite the blessing over] the plums [since one can fulfill his obligation for both with the blessing for vegetables, 'Creator of the produce of the ground']. But we shall not exempt [ourselves from the obligation to recite the blessing over] the chicken. [It requires a different blessing, 'For all.'] "And if we recite the blessing over the plums ['Creator of the fruit of the tree'] we shall exempt [ourselves from the obligation to recite the blessing for] neither one [i.e. the leeks] nor the other [i.e. the chicken].'"One student jumped in and recited over the chicken the blessing, 'For all came into being by his word.' His associate laughed at him. "Bar Qappara said to them, 'He [who jumped to bless] should not have been so gluttonous, but you [who laughed] should not have mocked him. What he did, was out of gluttony. Why did you mocked him? [His choice of blessing was acceptable.]' "And he said to that [student who jumped in to bless], 'Is there not a sage present? Is there not an elder present? [You should have waited to see what I would do.]'"

The same use of narrative to set the stage for an exchange of views of the law appears in the following two items:

YERUSHALMI BERAKHOT 8:2

I:4:   Samuel went to stay with Rab. He saw him eating with his hands covered [by a napkin]. He said to him, "What are you doing? [Did you not wash your hands?]" Samuel answered, "I am sensitive [and even though I washed my hands, I need to act according to my own habits]." When R. Zeira came here [to the Land of Israel] he saw priests eating [heave-offering] with their hands covered [by napkins without first washing!]. He said to them, "This [nevertheless] accords with the story told of Rab and Samuel [because the priests are more careful, so they need not wash before eating]."

I:5:   Zeira went to R. Abbahu in Caesarea. He found [Abbahu] and he said, "Let us go and eat." He [Abbahu] gave him a round loaf of bread for slicing and he said, "Sit and recite the blessing." He [Zeira] said to him, "The host should know the value of his loaf. [You should recite the blessing.]" [D] When they had eaten, Abbahu said, "Sit and recite the blessing." [Zeira] said to him, "My master surely knows that R. Huna was a great man and he used to say, 'The one who opens [the meal by reciting the blessing], should also close [the meal and recite the blessing at the end of the meal].'" The teaching disputes R. Huna. For it was taught: This is the order for washing hands. For [a group of] up to five people — they start [washing] with the highest in rank. For more than this — they start [washing] with the lowest in rank [so the important people do not have to wait for long between washing and the meal]. [This is the order for mixing the cup.] In the middle of the meal they start [to mix the cup] from the highest [in rank]. At the end of the meal, they start from the one who recites the blessing [T. 5:6].

Here is the sole parable of the present tractate, with the moral or application of the parable underlined:

YERUSHALMI BERAKHOT 9:1

I:8:   [Regarding this [relationship between God and his people,] R. Yudan in the name of R. Isaac gave four discourses [in the form of parables]: A person had a human patron. [One day] they came and told him [the patron], "A member of your household has been arrested." He said to them, "Let me take his place." They said to him, "Lo, he is already going out to trial." He said to them, "Let me take his place." They said to him, "Lo, he is going to be hanged." Now where is he and where is his patron [when ultimately he needs him]? But the Holy One, blessed be He, [will save his subjects, just as he] saved Moses from [execution by] the sword of Pharaoh. This is in accord with what is written, 'He delivered me from the sword of Pharaoh' [Ex. 18:4].

I:9:   Pinhas said [concerning this] two [parables], one in the name of R. Zeira, one in the name of R. Tanhum bar Hanilai. R. Pinhas in the name of R. Zeira said, "A person has a human patron. If he bothers his patron, the patron will say, 'Did you ever see a fellow who can bother you so much?' "But the Holy One, blessed be He, is not like this. Rather he accepts whatever you burden him with. "In this regard it says, 'Cast your burden on the Lord and he will sustain you' [Ps. 55:22]." R. Pinhas in the name of R. Tanhum bar Hanilai, "A person has a human patron. If his enemies come and seize him at the gate of his patron's courtyard, before he can cry out, before anyone can come forth [to save him], the enemies' sword will sever his neck and kill him. "But God saved Jehoshaphat from the sword of the Syrians. As it is written, 'And Jehoshaphat cried out and the Lord helped him. God drew them away from him' [II Chron. 18:31]. The verse teaches us that just as they were about to decapitate him, 'God drew them away from him.'"

Stories of sages' deaths, including how some were martyred, form a distinct category; in the following case, the story serves as a powerful, dramatic setting for what amounts to a teaching, pure and simple.

YERUSHALMI BERAKHOT 9:5

3. I:3: Aqiba was being tortured [lit.: being judged] by the evil Tinneius Rufus. When [he was close to death,] the time to recite the Shema' approached. He began to recite the Shema' and he smiled. He [Tinneius] said to him, "Elder, either you are a sorcerer [who does not feel pain] or you mock the torture [which I inflict upon you]. He [Aqiba] said to him, "Woe unto you. I am neither a sorcerer, nor a mocker. But [I now was thinking,] all my life when I recited this verse, I was troubled and wondered when I would be able to fulfill all three aspects [of this verse]: 'And you shall love the Lord your God with all you heart, and with all your

soul, and with all you might' (Deut. 6:5). I have loved Him with all my
heart. And I have loved him with all my wealth. But I did not know how
I would [fulfill the verse and] love him with all my soul. "And now the
time has come [for me to love him] with all my soul, and the time has
come to recite the Shema'. It is now clear to me [how I shall serve Him
with all my soul]. For this reason I now am reciting and smiling." And
just as he said this his soul passed from him. Nehemiah Emsoni served
R. Aqiba for twenty-two years [as his disciple]. And [Aqiba] taught him
[what one could include in the interpretation of a verse based on the presence of the particles in the Torah] 't and gm [and what one could exclude
in the interpretation of a verse based on each particle] 'k and rq. He said
to him, "What about that which is written, You shall fear ['t] the Lord
your God' (Deut. 6:13)?" He said to him," [The presence in the verse of
the particle 't teaches: You shall fear] Him and His Torah."

II. SHABBAT

Here again, narrative encapsulates a teaching.

III:2:   [In T.'s version:] Said R. Ishmael, "One time I read by the light of a lamp
and I wanted to tilt it. [L: "'I shall read and not tilt,' and he was just about
to tilt [the lamp and remembered] and said,"] "I said, 'How great are the
words of sages, who rule (They do not read on Sabbath nights by the light
of a lamp' [M. 1:3D] (L. reads: lest one forget and tilt it)." R. Nathan
says, "He [Ishmael] most certainly did tilt it. "And written on his note-
book is the following: 'Ishmael b. Elisha tilted a lamp on the Sabbath.
"'When the sanctuary will be rebuilt, he will bring a sin offering'" [T.
Shab. 1:13A-E].

Nothing much happens in the following tale, which provides a dramatic
setting for what is little more than rabbinical colloquies.

YERUSHALMI SHABBAT 16:1

4. II:4: There was the incident in which Rabbi, R. Hiyya the Elder, and R.
Ishmael b. R. Yosé were in session and reviewing the scroll of Lamentations on the eve of the ninth of Ab which coincided with the Sabbath,
doing so from the time of the afternoon offering and onward. They omitted one alphabetical chapter, saying, "Tomorrow we will go and complete it." Now when [Rabbi] was leaving for his house, he fell and injured
his finger, and he recited in his own regard the following verse: "Many
are the sufferings of the wicked" (Ps. 32:10). Said to him R. Hiyya, "These
things happened to you on our account, for so it is written, 'The breath of
our nostrils, the anointed of the Lord, was caught for their corrupt deeds'
(Lam. 4:20)." Said to him R. Ishmael b. R. Yosé, "Even if we had not
been studying this very passage, it would have been appropriate for us to
say so. How much the more so is it appropriate since we have been studying this passage!" [Rabbi] went home and put on his finger a dry sponge,

and he wrapped reed grass around it, on the outside of the sponge. Said R. Ishmael b. R. Yosé, "From this matter we have learned three rules: (1) A sponge does not bring healing, but only protects the sore; (2) reed grass is regarded as made ready in advance for its purpose; (3) it is permitted to read in the sacred writings only from the afternoon offering onward."

III. ERUBIN

The narrative sets the stage for the ruling, with its accompanying explanation.

I:2: Rab came to a certain place. He saw an alleyway, which was rendered permitted [for carrying] merely by means of a single crossbeam [that was very thin]. He gave it a knock with his staff and knocked it down. Said to him R. Huna, "There is a palm tree yet standing [which can serve as the crossbeam]." He said to him, "Does R. Huna have eyes to see, and Rab not have eyes to see [that tree]? But lo, I shall prohibit them from carrying in the alleyway relying on that crossbeam on the present Sabbath, and for the next Sabbath [when in advance they may form the proper intention] I shall permit them to carry on the count of the palm tree, and in this way they will know that if the palm tree should be cut down, it will be forbidden to carry in the alleyway."

IV. YOMA

The narratives that follow in the next two entries set the stage for the homilies:

YERUSHALMI YOMA 2:1

V:1: There was the case of two who got there at the same time, running up the ramp. One shoved the other [M. 2:1H-I], within four cubits [of the altar]. The other then took out a knife and stabbed him in the heart. R. Sadoq came and stood on the steps of the porch and said, "Hear me, O brethren of the House of Israel! Lo, Scripture says, 'If in the land which the Lord your God gives you to possess, anyone is found slain, lying in the open country, and it is not known who killed him, then your elders and your judges shall come forth, and they shall measure the distance to the cities which are around him that is slain' [Deut. 21:1-2]. "Come and let us measure to find out for what area it is appropriate to bring the calf — for the Sanctuary, or for the courts!" All of them moaned after his speech. And afterward the father of the youngster came to them, saying, "O brethren of ours! I am your atonement. His [my] son is still writhing, so the knife has not yet been made unclean." This teaches you that the uncleanness of a knife is more grievous to Israelites than murder [T. Yoma 1:12A-G].

YERUSHALMI YOMA 3:2

3. I:3: One time R. Hiyya the Elder and R. Simeon b. Halapta were walking in the valley of Arabel at daybreak. They saw that the light of the morning star was breaking forth. Said R. Hiyya the Elder to R. Simeon b. Halapta,

"Son of my master, this is what the redemption of Israel is like — at first, little by little, but in the end it will go along and burst into light. "What is the scriptural basis for this view? 'Rejoice not over me, O my enemy; when I fall, I shall rise; when I sit in darkness, the Lord will be a light to me' (Mic. 7:8). "So, in the beginning, 'When the virgins were gathered together the second time, Mordecai was sitting at the king's gate' (Esther 2:19). "But afterward: 'So Haman took the robes and the horse, and he arrayed Mordecai and made him ride through the open square of the city, proclaiming, Thus shall it be done to the man whom the king delights to honor' (Esther 6:11). "And in the end: 'Then Mordecai went out from the presence of the king in royal robes of blue and white, with a great golden crown and a mantle of fine linen and purple, while the city of Susa shouted and rejoiced' [Esther 8:15]. "And finally: 'The Jews had light and gladness and joy and honor' (Esther 8:16)."

The miracle-story is told in the briefest possible form, with no development or secondary amplification, little drama (apart from the miracle itself), and no effort at sustaining the tale.

YERUSHALMI YOMA 3:8

IV:1:   It has been taught: They say: When Nicanor was bringing them from Alexandria, in Egypt, a gale rose in the sea and threatened to drown them. They took one of them and tossed it into the sea, and they wanted to throw in the other, but Nicanor would not let them. He said to them, "If you throw in the second one, throw me in with it." He was distressed all the way to the wharf at Jaffa. Once they reached the wharf at Jaffa, the other door popped up from underneath the boat. And there are those who say one of the beasts of the sea swallowed it, and when Nicanor came to the wharf at Jaffa, it brought it up and tossed it onto dry land [T. Yoma 2:4F-G]

The following narrative is simply an exchange of statements, he said to me… I said to him….

YERUSHALMI YOMA 3:9

3.II:3: Said R. Aqiba, Simeon b. Luga told me, "A certain child of the sons of their sons and I were gathering grass in the field. Then I saw him laugh and cry. I said to him, 'Why did you cry?' He said to me, 'Because of the glory of father's house, which has gone into exile.' I said to him, 'Then why did you laugh?' He said, 'At the end of it all, in time to come, the Holy One, blessed be he, is going to make his descendants rejoice.' I said to him, 'What did you see [to make you think of this]?' He said to me, 'A smoke-raiser in front of me made me laugh].' I said to him, 'Show it to me.' He said to me, 'We are subject to an oath not to show it to anyone at all.'"

Said R. Yohanan b. Nuri, "One time I was going along the way, and an old man came across me and said to me, 'I am a member of the house of Abtinas. At the beginning, when the house of father was discrete, they would give to one another their scrolls [containing the prescriptions for frankincense]. Now take it, but be careful about it, since it is a scroll containing a recipe for spices.' "And when I came and reported the matter before R. Aqiba, he said to me, 'From now on it is forbidden to speak ill of these people again'"[T. Yoma 2:7A-C].

Here again, narrative is stripped down to dialogue, with an implicit story — someone did so and so and people asked him and had an exchange of views.

YERUSHALMI YOMA 5:2

III:1:   There was the case of one high priest who prolonged his prayer, so they decided to go in after him. They say it was Simeon the Righteous. They said to him, "Why did you take so long?" He said to them, "I was praying for the sanctuary of your God, so that it should not be destroyed." They said to him, "Even so, you should not have prolonged your prayer." For forty years Simeon the Righteous served as high priest. In the final year, he said to them, "This year I am going to die." They said to him, "How do you know?" He said to them, "Every year when I entered the house of the Holy of Holies, an old man dressed in white and cloaked in white went in with me and came out with me. This year he went in with me but he did not come out with me."

In the following set, the narrative preserves miracles or noteworthy events but tells no story that I can discern.

YERUSHALMI YOMA 6:3

I:3:   So long as Simeon the Righteous was alive, the goat did not get halfway down the mountain before it had been torn limb from limb. Once Simeon the Righteous died, the goat would flee to the wilderness, and the Saracens would capture and eat it. All the time that Simeon the Righteous was alive, the lot bearing the Divine Name would come up in the right hand. When Simeon the Righteous died, sometimes it would come up in the right hand, sometimes in the left. All the time that Simeon the Righteous was alive, the western lamp would burn well. When Simeon the Righteous died, sometimes it would flicker out, and sometimes it would burn. All the time that Simeon the Righteous was alive, the strap of crimson would turn white. When Simeon the Righteous died, sometimes it would turn white, sometimes red. All the time that Simeon the Righteous was alive, the flame of the wood-offering would burn strongly. When they had placed two logs of wood in the morning, they would not then put on more all day long. When Simeon the Righteous died, the strength of the wood-offering diminished, so they did not hesitate to put wood on the fire all day long. All the time that Simeon the Righteous was alive, a blessing was set upon the two loaves of bread and the show bread. The result was that each priest would get about an olive's bulk of bread, and some of them ate and had enough, while others ate and left bread over. When Simeon the Righteous died, this blessing was taken away from the two loaves of bread and the show bread, so that each priest got bread the size of a bean. So the modest priests kept their hands off the bread, while the gluttons divided it up among themselves [T. Sot. 13:7].

I:4:   It has been taught: Forty years before the destruction of the Temple the western light went out, the crimson thread remained crimson, and the lot for the Lord always came up in the left hand. They would close the gates of the Temple by night and get up in the morning and find them wide open. Said [to the Temple] Rabban Yohanan ben Zakkai, "O Temple, why do you frighten us? We know that you will end up destroyed. "For it has been said, 'Open your doors, O Lebanon, that the fire may devour your cedars!'"(Zech. 11:1).

I:5:   Forty years did Simeon the Righteous serve Israel as high priest. In the final year he said to them, "This year I am going to die." They said to him, "Whom shall we appoint as your successor?" He said to them, "Lo, there is my son, Nehunion, before you." They went and appointed Nehunion. Simeon, his brother, was jealous of him, and he went and put on a gown and a girdle. He said to them, "See what he has vowed to his beloved [wife], saying, "On the day on which I take office as high priest, I shall put on your gown and gird myself with your girdle." They looked into the matter, and they did not find that it was so. They said: He fled from there to the Royal Mountain, and from there he fled to Alexandria, and he went and built an altar there, and in that regard he recited the following verse: "In that day there will be an altar to the Lord in the midst of the land of Egypt, and a pillar to the Lord at its border" (Isa. 19:19).

v. Pesahim

Here the narrative consists of setting the stage for an exchange of views.

Yerushalmi Pesahim 5:3

I:3:   Simlai came before R. Jonathan [and] said to him, "Teach me aggadah." [He] said to him, "I have a tradition from my ancestors not to teach aggadah to Babylonians or to Southerners, for they are haughty and light-weight in Torah, and you are a Nehardean [by origin] and reside in the South and moreover a minor I [who is likely to misunderstand]." He said to him, "[At least] tell me one [Lg: "this," i.e., halakhic,] thing, What is the difference between [a Passover offering which was slaughtered] under its designation and [at some point in the activity] not under its designation [M. 5:2, where the offering is invalid] and [one both] for those who can eat it and for those who cannot eat it [M. 5:3A.2, where the offering is fit]?" He said to him, "Under *its* designation and [at some point in the activity] not under its designation — its disqualification [derives] from [the animal] itself; for those who can eat it and for those who cannot eat it — its disqualification [derives] from other people. Under its designation and [at some point in the activity] not under its designation — you are not able to clarify [or "separate"] its invalid portion from amidst its fit portion; for those who can eat it and for those who cannot eat it — you are able to clarify [or "separate"] its invalid portion from amidst its fit portion. Under its designation and [at some point in the activity] not under its designation — applies to all sacrifices; for those who can eat it and for those who cannot eat it — applies only to the Passover offering."

Here the narrative sets the stage for the debate between Hillel and the Elders on a law in the Temple. The vehicle for the narrative is simply *they said to him...he said to them...*, with some secondary action tacked on.

YERUSHALMI PESAHIM 6:1

I:1:   These matters regarding the Passover sacrifice, [M. 6:1]. This law [of M. 6:1A-B] was forgotten by the Elders of Beterah. Once the fourteenth [of Nisan] fell on the Sabbath and they did not know if the Passover sacrifice overrides the Sabbath or not. [They] said, "There is here a certain Babylonian, and Hillel is his name, who served Shemaiah and Abtalion. [Perhaps he] knows whether a Passover sacrifice overrides the Sabbath or not. Possibly something good [can come] from him." [They] sent and called him. They said to him, "Have you ever heard when the fourteenth [of Nisan] falls on the Sabbath, whether [it] overrides the Sabbath or not?" He said to them, "Do we have only one Passover offering alone that overrides the Sabbath in the whole year? And are there not many Passover offerings that would override the Sabbath in the whole year?" They said to him, "We have already said that 'something good [can come] from you." He started to expound for them from an [analogy], and from a an argument a fortiori and from a inference by analogy] based on identity of words. "From an analogy: since a Daily Whole Offering offering is a community sacrifice and a Passover offering is a community sacrifice [being brought in a group joined with others, just as a Daily Whole Offering offering, a community sacrifice, overrides the Sabbath, so a Passover offering, a community sacrifice, overrides the Sabbath. "From an argument a fortiori: If a Daily Whole Offering offering, for [improperly or not] offering which one does not become liable to extirpation, overrides the Sabbath, a Passover offering, for [improperly] offering which one becomes liable to extirpation, all the more so should override the Sabbath. "From an inference by analogy based on identity of words: it is said regarding a Daily Whole Offering offering 'in its time' (Num. 28:2) and it is said regarding the Passover offering 'in its time' (Num. 9:2) just as the Daily Whole Offering offering regarding which it says 'in its time' overrides the Sabbath, so a Passover offering regarding which it says 'in its time' [surely] overrides the Sabbath." [They] said to him, "We have already said, 'Is there something good [that can come] from the Babylonian?' "The analogy that you stated has an answer: No — [for] if you hold regarding a Daily Whole Offering offering which has a limit [two only each Sabbath], would you say regarding a Passover offering that has no limit [since it depends on the number of Israelites, that it too overrides the Sabbath]? "The argument a fortiori that you stated has an answer: No — [for] if you hold thus regarding a Daily Whole Offering offering which is [of] the most holy sacrifices [, being a burnt offering completely burned on the altar, and hence superseding the Sabbath], would you say [thus] regarding a Passover offering which is of the lesser sacrifices? "The argument by analogy based on the appearance of the same words in two passages, that you stated [has an answer:] for a person does not deduce a such an argument n his own." [On the notion of not deducing an analogy based on the appearance of the same word in two contexts, on one's own authority:] And even though [Hillel] sat and expounded to them all day, [they] did not accept [the teaching] from him until he told them [using the language of an oath], "May [evil] befall me [if I lie]. Thus I have heard from Shemaiah and Abtalion." As soon as they heard this from him, they stood up and appointed him patriarch over them. As soon as [they had appointed him patriarch over them,"] he began to castigate them with words, saying, "What caused you to need this Babylonian? Is it not because you failed to serve the two great men of the world, Shemaiah and Abtalion, who were sitting with you?" As soon as [Hillel] castigated them with words, a law escaped his memory, specifically: [They] said to him, "What should [we] do for the people, for [before the Sabbath] they did not bring their knives [to slaughter the animal, which you have now demonstrated is permitted] ?" He said to them, "This law I have heard but I have forgotten. Rather, [then,] leave Israel [alone]. If they are not prophets, they are the children of prophets [and will know by themselves what to do]." Immediately whoever had Passover offering was a lamb would stick the knife in its wool; [if it was a kid, he would tie it between his horns. As a result, the beasts they had designated for use as their Passover offerings brought their knives with them [T. 4:13-14].

I:2:   For [clarifying] three matters Hillel went up from Babylonia [to the land of Israel]: [Regarding Lev. 13:37's ruling:] "[The scall is healed;] he is clean" [said in reference to a person afflicted on his head or beard who has gone through a second set of seven days of isolation and whose "scall has remained unchanged in color, and black hair has grown in it" (Lev. 13:37)]. Is it possible [that] he is exempt and can just go [at that point]? The teaching [therefore] says, "The priest shall pronounce him clean" (the conclusion of v. 37). If [the verse stated only], "The priest shall pronounce him clean," is it possible that if the priest stated regarding one unclean [that he is] clean, perhaps he will be clean? [Obviously not.] The teaching [therefore] states [both], "He is clean" and "The priest shall pronounce him clean." For this [clarification of the two clauses] Hillel went up from Babylonia. One verse says, "You shall slaughter the Passover offering for the Lord your God, from the flock and the herd" (Deut. 16:2). And another verse says, "From the sheep or from the goats you may take it" (Exod. 12:5) [and not from the herd]! How is this possible: The flock for the Passover offering g and the herd for the festive offering [that accompanied the Passover sacrifice]. One verse says, "Six days you shall eat unleavened bread" (Deut. 16:8). And another verse says, "Seven days you shall eat unleavened bread" (Exod. 12:15). How is this possible? Six [days you shall eat] from the new grain [which is permitted after bringing the first sheaf of new grain on the second day] and seven you shall eat from the old grain [which may be consumed also on the first day of the festival, when the new grain is still prohibited]. And he expounded [thus on his own] and [fortuitously] taught [it] in agreement [with the correct position, as he was to learn later] and he went up [to Israel] and received [it as a] halakhah [as an accepted tradition, e.g., from Shemaiah and Abtalion].

vi. Sukkah

The narrative here sets the stage for the speeches.

Yerushalmi Sukkah 5:1

I:4:   There is the following story: R. Levi and Judah bar Nahman were collecting two *selas* [a week] to gather together a congregation before R. Yohanan. R. Levi entered and preached, "Jonah the son of Amittai came from the tribe of Asher, for it is written, 'Asher did not drive out the inhabitants of Akko nor the inhabitants of Sidon' (Judges 1:3 1). "And it is written, 'Arise, go to Zarephath, which belongs to Sidon, and dwell there. Behold, I have commanded a widow there to feed you'"(I Kings 17:9). R. Yohanan went up and preached, "Jonah b. Amittai came from the tribe of Zebulun, for it is written, 'The third lot came up for the tribe of Zebulun, according to its families. And the territory of its inheritance reached as far as Sarid' (Josh. 19:10). "And it is written, 'Thence it goes to Daberath, then up to Japhia; from there it passes along on the east toward the sunrise to Gath-hepher, to Eth-kazin, and going on to Rimmon it bends toward Neah' (Josh. 19:13). "And it is written, 'He restored the border of Israel from the entrance of Hamath as far as the Sea of the Arabah, according to the word of the Lord, the God of Israel, which he spoke by his servant Jonah the son of Amittai, the prophet, who was from Gath-hepher'"(2 Kings 14:25). On another Sabbath, said R. Levi to Judah bar Nahman, "Take these two *selas* and go, gather the congregation before R. Yohanan." He went in and said before them, "Correctly did R. Yohanan teach us. His mother came from Asher, while his father came from Zebulun. 'Zebulun shall dwell at the shore of the sea; he shall become a haven for ships, and his border shall be at Sidon' (Gen. 49:13). "An offshoot that went forth from him was from Sidon. "And it is written, 'He went down to Joppa'"(Jonah 1:3). Was it not necessary to say, "He went down to Akko"? Said R. Jonah, "Jonah b. Amittai was one of those who came up for the festivals [to Jerusalem], and he came in for the rejoicing of *bet hashshoebah,* and the Holy Spirit rested on him. "This serves to teach you that the Holy Spirit rests only on someone whose heart is happy.

Here is an authentic story, told with great brevity but considerable effect.

YERUSHALMI SUKKAH 5:1

I:7:   In the time of Tronianus, the evil one, a son was born to him on the ninth of Ab, and [the Israelites] were fasting. His daughter died on Hanukkah, and [the Israelites] lit candles. His wife sent a message to him, saying, "Instead of going out to conquer the barbarians, come and conquer the Jews, who have rebelled against you." He thought that the trip would take ten days, but he came in five. He came and found the Israelites occupied in study of the Light [Torah], with the following verse: "The Lord will bring a nation against you from afar, from the end of the earth, as swift as the eagle flies, a nation whose language you do not understand" (Deut. 28:49). He said to them, "With what are you occupied?" They said to him, "With thus-and-so." He said to them, "That man [I] thought that it would take ten days to make the trip, and I arrived in five days." His legions surrounded them and killed them. He said to the women, "Obey my legions, and I shall not kill you." They said to him, "What you did to the ones who have fallen do also to us who are yet standing." He mingled their blood with the blood of their men, until the blood flowed into the ocean as far as Cyprus. At that moment the horn of Israel was cut off, and it is not destined to return to its place until the son of David will come.

VII. BESAH

Here is another story that sets the stage for an exchange of views.

YERUSHALMI BESAH 1:4

I:1:   Judah bar Hiyya went on a circuit [to the outlying villages]. They asked him, "As to a ladder serving an upper room, what is the law [of moving it about on the festival day]?" He said to them, "It is permitted." When he came back to his father, [Hiyya] asked him, "What case came into your jurisdiction?" He said to him, "I permitted them on the festival day to move about a ladder serving an upper room." [The father] called on a Tannaite authority to appear before him, and the Tannaite authority repeated the following: "Under what circumstances [toes the House of Hillel permit moving a ladder]? In the case of a ladder serving a dovecot. But in the case of a ladder serving an upper room, it is prohibited to move it about [Tosefta adds: even in the upper room itself] [T. Y.T. 1:8 G-H] ."

Like the story cited above, what we have here is simply a narrative pretext for setting forth an exchange of views.

YERUSHALMI BESAH 2:4

I:4: M'SH B: Hillel the Elder laid on hands on a burnt offering in the courtyard [cf. M. Hag. 2:3B], ant the disciples of Shammai ganged up on him. He said to them, "Go and see it, for it is a female, and I have to prepare it as sacrifices of pace offerings." He put them off with a bunch of words, and they went their way. But the power of the House of Shammai forthwith became strong, and they wanted to decide the law permanently in accord with their opinion. Now there was present Baba b. Buta who was one of the disciples of the House of Shammai, but who acknowledged that the law is in accord with the opinions of the House of Hillel in every last detail. One time he came to the courtyard and found it desolate. He said, "May the houses of those who desolated the house of our God be made desolate." What did he do? He went and brought the whole Qedar-flock and set them up right in the courtyard and announced, "Whoever is required to bring whole offerings and peace offerings — let him come and take a beast and lay on hands" [= M. Hag. 2: 3B]. So [everybody] came along and took a beast and offered up whole offerings, having laid on hands. On that very day the law was confirmed in accord with the opinion of the House of Hillel, and not a single person griped about it. SWB M'SH B: Another disciple of the disciples of the House of Hillel laid hands on a burnt offering. One of the disciples of Shammai found him out. He said to him, "What's this laying on of bands?!" He said to him, "What's this shutting up?!" And he shut him with a rebuke [T. Hag. 2:10E-2:12E].

Here the narrative conveys a precedent.

YERUSHALMI BESAH 4:5

I:2: The daughter of R. Hiyya the Elder came to do baking in the oven [on the festival day]. She found stone in it. She came and asked her father. He said to her, "Go and sweep it out." She said to him, "I cannot do so." [In fact, it is prohibited to sweep out the oven. in line with M. 4:5C.] He said to her."Go and level it down [= M. :4:5D]." In fact she knew the answer but she wanted to hear it from her father.

VIII. TAANIT

The narrative sets the stage for the homily.

YERUSHALMI TAANIT 2:1

III:4:   There is the following story. R. Ba bar Zabeda and R. Tanhum bar Ilai and R. Josiah went out to a fast. R. Ba bar Zabeda preached as follows: "'Let us lift up our hearts and hands to God in heaven' (Lam. 3:41). "Now is it possible for a mortal to take his heart and put it into his hands? But what is the meaning of 'let us lift up'? Let us exalt our hearts, making them [as clean as] the palms of our hands. And then, turn to God in heaven."' Now if there was a dead creeping thing in someone's hand, even if he immersed himself in Siloam [a fountain] or in all of the waters of creation, he will never, ever be clean. [But if] he tossed the dead creeping thing from his hand, then he gains the benefit of immersion in [only] forty seahs of water [T. Ta. 1:8H].

The narrative once more allows the sermon to be given.

YERUSHALMI TAANIT 3:4

I:1:   There was a pestilence in Sepphoris, but it did not come into the neighborhood in which R. Haninah was living. And the Sepphoreans said, "How is it possible that that elder lives among you, he and his entire neighborhood, in peace, while the town goes to ruin?" [Haninah] went in and said before them, "There was only a single Zimri in his generation, but on his account, 24,000 people died. And in our time, how many Zimris are there in our generation? And yet you are raising a clamor!" One time they had to call a fast, but it did not rain. R. Joshua carried out a fast in the South, and it rained. The Sepphoreans said, "R. Joshua b. Levi brings down rain for the people in the South, but R. Haninah holds back rain for us in Sepphoris." They found it necessary to declare a second time of fasting and sent and summoned R. Joshua b. Levi. [Haninah] said to him, "Let my lord go forth with us to fast." The two of them went out to fast, but it did not rain. He went in and preached to them as follows: "It was not R. Joshua b. Levi who brought down rain for the people of the south, nor was it R. Haninah who held back rain from the people of Sepphoris. But as to the southerners, their hearts are open, and when they listen to a teaching of Torah they submit [to accept it], while as to the Sepphoreans, their hearts are hard, and when they hear a teaching of Torah, they do not submit [or accept it]." When he went in, he looked up and saw that the [cloudless] air was pure. He said, "Is this how it still is? [Is there no change in the weather?]" Forthwith, it rained. He took a vow for himself that he would never do the same thing again. He said, "How shall I say to the creditor [God] not to collect what is owing to him."

Narratives about fasting set the stage for homilies. In the following, we find resort to a parable, but the parable itself provides little more than a narrative formulation of a metaphor.

YERUSHALMI TAANIT 3:4

I:4:   Eleazar called a fast, but it did not rain. R. Aqiba called a fast, and it rained. [Aqiba] went in and preached before them: "I shall give you a simile. To what may the matter be likened? To the case of a king who had two daughters, one of them haughty, the other proper. When the haughty one wanted something, she went before him, and he said, 'Let them give her whatever she wants and send her away.' "Whenever the proper daughter [wanted something], she would come before him, and he would spend time with her and enjoy hearing her requests."

The colloquy that follows requires the narrative to make its point, as with Haninah's sermon above and Levi's below.

YERUSHALMI TAANIT 3:4

I:5:   Aha carried out thirteen fasts, and it did not rain. When he went out, a Samaritan met him. [The Samaritan] said to him [to make fun of him], "Rabbi, take off your cloak, because it is going to rain." He said to him, "By the life of that man [you]! Heaven will do a miracle, and this year will prosper, but that man will not live [to see it]." Heaven did a miracle, and the year prospered, and that Samaritan died. And everybody said, "Come and see the fruit [of the] sun."

YERUSHALMI TAANIT 3:8

II:1:   As to Levi ben Sisi: troops came to his town. He took a scroll of the Torah and went up to the roof and said, "Lord of the ages! If I have neglected a single word of this scroll of the Torah, let them come up against us, and if not. Let them go their way." Forthwith people went looking tor the troops but did not find them, [because they had gone their way]. A disciple of his did the same thing, and his hand withered, but the troops went their way. "A disciple of his disciple did the same thing. His hand did not whither. but they also did not go their way.

Here is an authentic story, not just a setting for a saying of some sort.

YERUSHALMI TAANIT 3:9

III:2:   Said R. Yudan Giria, "This is Honi the circle drawer [of M. 3:9], the grandson of Honi the circle drawer. Near the time of the destruction of the Temple, he went out to a mountain to his workers. Before he got there, it rained. He went into a cave. Once he sat down there, he became tired and fell asleep. "He remained sound asleep for seventy years, until the Temple was destroyed and it was rebuilt a second time. At the end of the seventy years he awoke from his sleep. He went out of the cave, and he saw a world completely changed. An area that had been planted with vineyards now produced olives, and an area planted in olives now produced grain. "He asked the people of the district, 'What do you hear in the world?' "They said to him, 'And don't you know what the news is?' "He said to them, 'No.' "They said to him, 'Who are you?' "He said to them, 'Honi, the circle drawer.' "They said to him, 'We heard that when he would go into the Temple courtyard, it would be illuminated.' "He went in and illuminated the place and recited concerning himself the following verse of Scripture: 'When the Lord restored the fortune of Zion, we were like those who dream'" (Ps. 126:1).

The following narrative supplies a precedent and example of how the law works.

YERUSHALMI TAANIT 3:11

I:2: In the time of R. Yudan they decreed a fast. and rain tell in the evening. R. Mana went up to see him. He said to him, "Since I am now thirsty, what is the law on my being permitted to drink?" He said to him, "Wait, for the people may decide to complete the fast [through the coming day and an individual must then observe it too]."

The stories about the saints here are not articulated.

YERUSHALMI TAANIT 3:11

I:4: Rabban Yohanan b. Zakkai: when he wanted it to rain, he would say to his barber, "Get up and go to the Temple, [and say,] 'Now my master wants to get a haircut, and he does not have the power to accept suffering [through a fast].'" Forthwith it would rain.

R. Adda bar Ahvah: When he wanted it to rain, he would merely take off his sandal [as a mark of the fast, and it would rain]. If he took off both of them. the world would overflow. There was a house that was about to collapse over there, and Rab set one of his disciples to work in the house until he had cleared out everything from the house. When the disciple left the house, the house collapsed. And there are those who say that it was R. Adda bar Ahvah.

We have already examined the following authentic story above, at Y. Berakhot.

YERUSHALMI TAANIT 4:1

I:14: WM'SH B: A certain student came and asked R. Joshua, "What is the law about the evening prayer?" He said to him, "Optional."

Here we have not a story but a fragment, told through dialoguje.

YERUSHALMI TAANIT 4:2

II:6: Rabbi would make two appointments [to his administration, at one time]. If they proved worthy, they were confirmed. If not, they were removed. When he was dying he instructed his son [Gamaliel], "Don't do it that way. Rather, appoint them all at one time. "And appoint R. Hami bar Haninah at the head [of the group]. And why had Rabbi not appointed him? Said R. Derosa, 'It was because the people of Sepphoris cried out against him in Sepphoris." And merely because people raise a cry do they do things they want? Said R. Eleazar b. R. Yosé, "It was because [Haninah] publicly answered [what Rabbi had said]."

II:7: Samuel and members of the household of Shila would greet the patriarch every day. The members of the house of Shila went in first and sat down first. They paid honor to Samuel and sat him down in front. Then Rab came there, and Samuel paid him honor and sat him down before [himself]. The members of the house of Shila said, "We have always been second." Samuel agreed to be seated third in line.

The Tosefta's narrative deals not with a specific event but with a general situation, what people would do, an historical account.

YERUSHALMI TAANIT 4:4

I:2: What was the matter having to do with the families of the pestle smugglers and the fig pressers [M. 4:4H]? Now when the Greek kings set up border presidios on the roads, so that people should not go up to Jerusalem, just as Jeroboam the son of Nebat did, then, whoever was a suitable person and sin-fearing of that generation — what did he do? [V. lacks 'Now when...Jerusalem' and begins: 'When Jeroboam the son of Nebat set up border presidios.'] He would take up his first fruits and make a kind of basket and cover them with dried figs, and take the basket with the first fruits and cover them with a kind of dried figs, and he would put them in a basket and take the basket and a pestle on his shoulder and go up. [Y. has: Whoever was suitable and sin-fearing of that generation would bring his first fruits and put them in a basket and cover them with dried figs, and take the pestle and put the basket on his shoulder and the pestle m his hand.] Now when he would come to that guard, [the guard] would say to him, "Where are you going?" He said to him, "To make these two rings of dried figs into cakes of pressed figs, in that press over there, with this pestle which is on my shoulder [Y.: in my hand]." Once he got by that guard, he would prepare a wreath from them and bring them up to Jerusalem [T. Ta. 3:7]. What is the matter having to do with the family of Salmai the Netophathites [cf. I Chron. 2:54: "The sons of Salma: Bethlehem, the Netophathites . .."]? Now when the Greek kings set up guards on the road so that the people should not go up to Jerusalem, just as Jeroboam the son of Nebat did. [Y. lacks reference to 'Greek kings' at B and reads: Whoever contributed wood and logs for the pile on the altar would bring wood and make steps of a sort and make a kind of ladder...], then whoever was a suitable and sin-fearing person of that generation would take two pieces of wood and make them into a kind of ladder and put it on his shoulder and go up. When he came to that guard, [the guard] said to him, "Where are you going?" "To fetch two pigeons from that dovecot over there, with this ladder which is on my shoulder." Once he got by that guard, he would dismantle [the pieces of wood of the ladder] and bring them up to Jerusalem. Now because they were prepared to give up their lives for the Torah and for the commandments, therefore they found for themselves a good name and a good memorial forever. And concerning them Scripture says, The memory of a righteous person is for a blessing" (Prov. 10:7). [Y. lacks:] But concerning Jeroboam son of Nebat and his allies, Scripture says, "But the name of the wicked will rot" (Prov. 10:7) [T. Ta. 3:8].

South Florida Studies in the History of Judaism

240167	The Documentary Form-History of Rabbinic Literature, I. The Documentary Forms of Mishnah	Neusner
240168	Louis Finkelstein and the Conservative Movement	Greenbaum
240169	Invitation to the Talmud: A Teaching Book	Neusner
240170	Invitation to Midrash: The Workings of Rabbinic Bible Interpretation, A Teaching Book	Neusner
240171	The Documentary Form-History of Rabbinic Literature, II. The Aggadic Sector:Tractate Abot, Abot deRabbi Natan, Sifra, Sifré to Numbers and Sifré to Deuteronomy	Neusner
240172	The Documentary Form-History of Rabbinic Literature, III. The Aggadic Sector: Mekhilta Attributed to R. Ishmael and Genesis Rabbah	Neusner
240173	The Documentary Form-History of Rabbinic Literature, IV. The Aggadic Sector: Leviticus Rabbah and Pesiqta deRab Kahana	Neusner
240174	The Documentary Form-History of Rabbinic Literature, V. The Aggadic Sector: Song of Songs Rabbah, Ruth Rabbah, Lamentations Rabbati, and Esther Rabbah I	Neusner
240175	The Documentary Form-History of Rabbinic Literature, VI. The Halakhic Sector: The Talmud of the Land of Israel A. Tractates Berakhot and Shabbat through Taanit	Neusner
240176	The Documentary Form-History of Rabbinic Literature, VI. The Halakhic Sector: The Talmud of the Land of Israel B. Tractates Megillah through Qiddushin	Neusner
240177	The Documentary Form-History of Rabbinic Literature, VI. The Halakhic Sector: The Talmud of the Land of Israel C. Tractates Sotah through Horayot and Niddah	Neusner
240178	The Documentary Form-History of Rabbinic Literature, VII. The Halakhic Sector: The Talmud of the Land of Israel A. Tractates Berakhot and Shabbat through Pesahim	Neusner

South Florida Academic Commentary Series

243001	The Talmud of Babylonia, An Academic Commentary, Volume XI, Bavli Tractate Moed Qatan	Neusner
243002	The Talmud of Babylonia, An Academic Commentary, Volume XXXIV, Bavli Tractate Keritot	Neusner
243003	The Talmud of Babylonia, An Academic Commentary, Volume XVII, Bavli Tractate Sotah	Neusner
243004	The Talmud of Babylonia, An Academic Commentary, Volume XXIV, Bavli Tractate Makkot	Neusner
243005	The Talmud of Babylonia, An Academic Commentary, Volume XXXII, Bavli Tractate Arakhin	Neusner
243006	The Talmud of Babylonia, An Academic Commentary, Volume VI, Bavli Tractate Sukkah	Neusner
243007	The Talmud of Babylonia, An Academic Commentary, Volume XII, Bavli Tractate Hagigah	Neusner
243008	The Talmud of Babylonia, An Academic Commentary, Volume XXVI, Bavli Tractate Horayot	Neusner

243048	The Talmud of the Land of Israel, A Complete Outline of the Second, Third and Fourth Divisions, Part I, The Division of Appointed Times, A. Berakhot, Shabbat	Neusner
243049	The Talmud of the Land of Israel, A Complete Outline of the Second, Third and Fourth Divisions, Part I, The Division of Appointed Times, B. Erubin, Yoma and Besah	Neusner
243050	The Talmud of the Land of Israel, A Complete Outline of the Second, Third and Fourth Divisions, Part I, The Division of Appointed Times, D. Taanit, Megillah, Rosh Hashannah, Hagigah and Moed Qatan	Neusner
243051	The Talmud of the Land of Israel, A Complete Outline of the Second, Third and Fourth Divisions, Part III, The Division of Damages, A. Baba Qamma, Baba Mesia, Baba Batra, Horayot and Niddah	Neusner
243052	The Talmud of the Land of Israel, A Complete Outline of the Second, Third and Fourth Divisions, Part III, The Division of Damages, B. Sanhedrin, Makkot, Shebuot and Abldah Zarah	Neusner
243053	The Two Talmuds Compared, II. The Division of Women in the Talmud of the Land of Israel and the Talmud of Babylonia, Volume A, Tractates Yebamot and Ketubot	Neusner
243054	The Two Talmuds Compared, II. The Division of Women in the Talmud of the Land of Israel and the Talmud of Babylonia, Volume B, Tractates Nedarim, Nazir and Sotah	Neusner
243055	The Two Talmuds Compared, II. The Division of Women in the Talmud of the Land of Israel and the Talmud of Babylonia, Volume C, Tractates Qiddushin and Gittin	Neusner
243056	The Two Talmuds Compared, III. The Division of Damages in the Talmud of the Land of Israel and the Talmud of Babylonia, Volume A, Tractates Baba Qamma and Baba Mesia	Neusner
243057	The Two Talmuds Compared, III. The Division of Damages in the Talmud of the Land of Israel and the Talmud of Babylonia, Volume B, Tractates Baba Batra and Niddah	Neusner
243058	The Two Talmuds Compared, III. The Division of Damages in the Talmud of the Land of Israel and the Talmud of Babylonia, Volume C, Tractates Sanhedrin and Makkot	Neusner
243059	The Two Talmuds Compared, I. Tractate Berakhot and the Division of Appointed Times in the Talmud of the Land of Israel and the Talmud of Babylonia, Volume B, Tractate Shabbat	Neusner
243060	The Two Talmuds Compared, I. Tractate Berakhot and the Division of Appointed Times in the Talmud of the Land of Israel and the Talmud of Babylonia, Volume A, Tractate Berakhot	Neusner
243061	The Two Talmuds Compared, III. The Division of Damages in the Talmud of the Land of Israel and the Talmud of Babylonia, Volume D, Tractates Shebuot, Abodah Zarah and Horayot	Neusner
243062	The Two Talmuds Compared, I. Tractate Berakhot and the Division of Appointed Times in the Talmud of the Land of Israel and the Talmud of Babylonia, Volume C, Tractate Erubin	Neusner
243063	The Two Talmuds Compared, I. Tractate Berakhot and the Division of Appointed Times in the Talmud of the Land of Israel and the Talmud of Babylonia, Volume D, Tractates Yoma and Sukkah	Neusner

South Florida-Rochester-Saint Louis
Studies on Religion and the Social Order

South Florida International Studies in Formative Christianity and Judaism

DATE DUE

Printed
in USA